Effective Cybersecurity Operations for Enterprise-Wide Systems

Festus Fatai Adedoyin
Bournemouth University, UK

Bryan Christiansen
CYGERA, LLC, USA

IGI Global
PUBLISHER of TIMELY KNOWLEDGE

A volume in the Advances in Information Security, Privacy, and Ethics (AISPE) Book Series

Published in the United States of America by
IGI Global
Information Science Reference (an imprint of IGI Global)
701 E. Chocolate Avenue
Hershey PA, USA 17033
Tel: 717-533-8845
Fax: 717-533-8661
E-mail: cust@igi-global.com
Web site: http://www.igi-global.com

Library of Congress Cataloging-in-Publication Data

Names: Adedoyin, Festus, 1989- editor. | Christiansen, Bryan, 1960- editor.

Title: Effective cybersecurity operations for enterprise-wide systems / edited by Festus Adedoyin, Bryan Christiansen.
Description: Hershey, PA : Information Science Reference, [2023] | Includes bibliographical references and index. | Summary: "This publication examines current risks involved in the cybersecurity of various systems today from an enterprise-wide perspective. While there are multiple sources available on cybersecurity, many such publications do not include an enterprise-wide perspective of the research. The proposed publication will enhance the field by providing such a perspective from multiple sources that include investigation into critical business systems such as supply chain management, logistics, ERP, CRM, knowledge management, and others"-- Provided by publisher.
Identifiers: LCCN 2023009974 (print) | LCCN 2023009975 (ebook) | ISBN 9781668490181 (h/c) | ISBN 9781668490198 (s/c) | ISBN 9781668490204 (eISBN)
Subjects: LCSH: Business enterprises--Computer networks--Security measures. | Computer networks--Security measures. | Computer security.
Classification: LCC HD30.38 .E35 2023 (print) | LCC HD30.38 (ebook) | DDC 658.4/78--dc23/eng/20230421
LC record available at https://lccn.loc.gov/2023009974
LC ebook record available at https://lccn.loc.gov/2023009975

This book is published in the IGI Global book series Advances in Information Security, Privacy, and Ethics (AISPE) (ISSN: 1948-9730; eISSN: 1948-9749)

British Cataloguing in Publication Data
A Cataloguing in Publication record for this book is available from the British Library.

For electronic access to this publication, please contact: eresources@igi-global.com.

Advances in Information Security, Privacy, and Ethics (AISPE) Book Series

Manish Gupta
State University of New York, USA

ISSN:1948-9730
EISSN:1948-9749

Mission

As digital technologies become more pervasive in everyday life and the Internet is utilized in ever increasing ways by both private and public entities, concern over digital threats becomes more prevalent.

The **Advances in Information Security, Privacy, & Ethics (AISPE) Book Series** provides cutting-edge research on the protection and misuse of information and technology across various industries and settings. Comprised of scholarly research on topics such as identity management, cryptography, system security, authentication, and data protection, this book series is ideal for reference by IT professionals, academicians, and upper-level students.

Coverage

- Telecommunications Regulations
- Computer ethics
- Electronic Mail Security
- Privacy-Enhancing Technologies
- Risk Management
- Cookies
- Privacy Issues of Social Networking
- Network Security Services
- CIA Triad of Information Security
- Device Fingerprinting

IGI Global is currently accepting manuscripts for publication within this series. To submit a proposal for a volume in this series, please contact our Acquisition Editors at Acquisitions@igi-global.com or visit: http://www.igi-global.com/publish/.

The Advances in Information Security, Privacy, and Ethics (AISPE) Book Series (ISSN 1948-9730) is published by IGI Global, 701 E. Chocolate Avenue, Hershey, PA 17033-1240, USA, www.igi-global.com. This series is composed of titles available for purchase individually; each title is edited to be contextually exclusive from any other title within the series. For pricing and ordering information please visit http://www.igi-global.com/book-series/advances-information-security-privacy-ethics/37157. Postmaster: Send all address changes to above address.

Titles in this Series

For a list of additional titles in this series, please visit: http://www.igi-global.com/book-series/advances-information-security-privacy-ethics/37157

AI Tools for Protecting and Preventing Sophisticated Cyber Attacks
Eduard Babulak (National Science Foundation, USA)
Information Science Reference • © 2023 • 300pp • H/C (ISBN: 9781668471104) • US $250.00

Protecting User Privacy in Web Search Utilization
Rafi Ullah Khan (The University of Agriculture, Peshawar, Pakistan)
Information Science Reference • © 2023 • 336pp • H/C (ISBN: 9781668469149) • US $240.00

Information Security and Privacy in Smart Devices Tools, Methods, and Applications
Carlos Rabadão (Computer Science and Communication Research Centre, Polytechnic of Leiria, Portugal) Leonel Santos (Computer Science and Communication Research Centre, Polytechnic of Leiria, Portugal) and Rogério Luís de Carvalho Costa (Computer Science and Communication Research Centre, Polytechnic of Leiria, Portugal)
Information Science Reference • © 2023 • 328pp • H/C (ISBN: 9781668459911) • US $250.00

Applications of Encryption and Watermarking for Information Security
Boussif Mohamed (University of Tunis El Manar, Tunisia)
Information Science Reference • © 2023 • 245pp • H/C (ISBN: 9781668449455) • US $240.00

Handbook of Research on Cybersecurity Risk in Contemporary Business Systems
Festus Fatai Adedoyin (Bournemouth University, UK) and Bryan Christiansen (Southern New Hampshire University, USA)
Information Science Reference • © 2023 • 446pp • H/C (ISBN: 9781668472071) • US $295.00

Fraud Prevention, Confidentiality, and Data Security for Modern Businesses
Arshi Naim (King Kalid University, Saudi Arabia) Praveen Kumar Malik (Lovely Professional University, India) and Firasat Ali Zaidi (Tawuniya Insurance, Saudi Arabia)
Business Science Reference • © 2023 • 347pp • H/C (ISBN: 9781668465813) • US $250.00

Handbook of Research on Cybersecurity Issues and Challenges for Business and FinTech Applications
Saqib Saeed (Department of Computer Information Systems, College of Computer Science and Information Technology, Imam Abdulrahman Bin Faisal University, Dammam, Saudi Arabia) Abdullah M. Almuhaideb (Department of Networks and Communications, College of Computer Science and Information Technology, Imam Abdulrahman Bin Faisal University, Dammam, Saudi Arabia) Neeraj Kumar (Thapar Institute of Engineering and Technology, India) Noor Zaman (Taylor's University, Malaysia) and Yousaf Bin Zikria (Yeungnam University, South Korea)
Business Science Reference • © 2023 • 552pp • H/C (ISBN: 9781668452844) • US $315.00

IGI Global
PUBLISHER of TIMELY KNOWLEDGE

701 East Chocolate Avenue, Hershey, PA 17033, USA
Tel: 717-533-8845 x100 • Fax: 717-533-8661
E-Mail: cust@igi-global.com • www.igi-global.com

Table of Contents

Detailed Table of Contents

Privacy and security have common elements but are different. Digital privacy choices are made based on the beliefs and perceptions of what can be shared and what should be kept discreet during communication. There has been a proliferation in the use of social networking sites. As a result, many individuals, firms, and communities view a loss in privacy as the result of a cybersecurity incident. However, not all cybersecurity incidents result in a privacy loss and not all privacy loss is the result of a cybersecurity incident. Privacy regulations provide the building blocks to ensure that sufficient data privacy standards are abided and that there are consequences for non-compliance, which in most cases are fines and levies to the defaulting organization. These regulations should provide guardrails to protect individuals and organizations by requiring data owners to be better stewards of that data. The problem is that technology changes at a faster pace than regulations can be created, so there is always a lag in the implementation.

In this technology-driven era, software development and maintenance are rapidly growing domains and are predestined to thrive over the coming decade. But the growing demand for software solutions also brings its own implications, and software vulnerabilities are the most crucial of these. Software vulnerabilities can be referred to as weaknesses or shortcomings of software solutions, which increase the risks of exploitation of resources and information. In the past few years, the number of exploits has been increasing rapidly, reaching an all-time high in 2021, affecting more than 100 million people worldwide. Even with the presence of existing vulnerability management models and highly secure tools and frameworks, software vulnerabilities are harder to identify and resolve as they may not be independent, and resolving them may cause other vulnerabilities. Moreover, a majority of the exploits are caused by known vulnerabilities and zero-day vulnerabilities.

Sometimes security and technology professionals confuse their state of compliance with their security posture. While an organization can meet the requirements to any regulatory standard (HIPAA, SOC, etc.), doing so should not be construed as meeting the requirements to defend a potential cyberattack, provide data protection during business processing, or maintain a highly secure development environment. In this chapter, the authors discuss how security and compliance can co-exist. They associate each one of these with controls that are either derived from formal frameworks or meet custom operational or other requirements of an organization. They explore how each control needs to be implemented with a risk perspective in mind, and finally, they suggest methods on how to manage such a control catalog.

The COVID-19 pandemic has led to the implementation of digital health surveillance systems worldwide, including Turkey's Hayat Eve Sığar (HES) platform. While effective in monitoring and tracing the virus, these systems also raise concerns about data privacy and cybersecurity risks. This chapter examines potential risks such as data breaches, malware attacks, unauthorized access, misuse of personal health information, and inadequate security protocols. To mitigate these risks, healthcare organizations must implement strong security measures and adopt a culture of security with a focus on continuous improvement and proactive risk management. The HES in Turkey provides a valuable case study for understanding these risks and measures to mitigate them. The chapter highlights the growing trend of digital health services invading individuals' private spaces and regulating their lives, emphasizing the importance of data privacy and security in safeguarding personal health information.

As the relevance of the digital economy increases, the need for secured cyberspace increases. Cyber threats are inescapable in digital progress. In the growth of cyber dominance, cybersecurity is necessary and very essential. Risk analysis is the process of assessing the likelihood of an adverse event occurring within the corporate, government, or environmental sectors. This chapter, therefore, explores the imperatives of risk analysis and asset management on cyber security in a technology-driven economy from the existing body of knowledge in the field. The chapter is divided into five sections, where the first section has to do with the introduction. The remaining four sections deal with the concepts of risk and risk analysis, asset management, factors determining attainment of continuous improvement of an asset performance management (APM) solution, cyber-crime and cyber-security, and conclusion and recommendations.

This chapter emphasizes the importance of cybersecurity for a corporation as today's organizations are more vulnerable than ever and their enemies are in the form of viruses and malware. The work provides evidence that cybersecurity can have an impact on brand value, market value, and overall corporate reputation. It focuses on depicting the global scenario with reference to cybersecurity disclosures by corporations and how it is important in today's digitized era where data is the most valuable and vulnerable asset. With rapid digitalization, cybersecurity has become a major concern for all businesses, especially when there is financial and reputational damage to cybersecurity breaches and incidents. Even in the absence of clear cybersecurity laws and regulations, corporations are opting for voluntary disclosure.

Preface

It should come as a surprise to nobody that cybersecurity remains a critical element in the computer and information technology industry on a global scale, especially with regards to enterprise-wide systems that operate in Fortune 500 firms and smaller. Cybersecurity is critical because it helps to protect organizations and individuals from cyberattacks as well as to prevent data breaches, identity theft, and other types of cybercrime. Therefore, organizations must have strong cybersecurity measures to protect their data and customers. There is abundant news over the past decade regarding major data breaches that have affected millions of consumers, and the problem is exacerbated by the continued shortfall of competent cybersecurity professionals worldwide.

The purpose of this publication is to examine various perspectives on present-day cybersecurity issues ranging from data privacy to research on the industry. Chapter 1 examines the influence of demographic conditions on those psychosocial conditions resulting from the pandemic to predict cyber security behaviors. Multiple Linear and Logistical Regression Models showed that addicted users who barely worked from home before the pandemic are more likely to exhibit risky cyber security behaviors, which is also similar for lonely users who barely worked from home to predict internet addiction. One interesting finding is that addicted female users were found to be more susceptible to cyberattacks. The implications and recommendations focused on therapeutic interventions, social change, awareness campaigns, and so forth. The limitation of this study is also covered, and possible future research areas are recommended.

Chapter 2 covers how education, technology, national and international regulations contribute to a comprehensive cybersecurity framework for present and future global IT companies. IT-driven enterprises may utilize the following security recommendations. Businesses who seek to examine their external and internal security with security upload and establish settings for success regardless of location must solve these issues. To produce more effective legislation, education efforts, and technologies that are resistant to cyberattacks. This work explores fundamental research gaps in cybersecurity and demonstrates how cybersecurity may be divided into these three fundamental categories and integrated to tackle problems such as the creation of training environments for authentic cybersecurity situations. It will explain links between technology and certification and discuss legislative standards and instructional frameworks for merging criteria for system accreditation and cybersecurity. The study finishes with wireless network security recommendations.

Chapter 3 states that Privacy and Security have common elements but are different. Digital privacy choices are made based on the beliefs and perceptions of what can be shared and what should be kept discreet during communication. There has been a proliferation in the use of social networking sites. As a result, many individuals, firms, and communities view a loss in privacy as the result of a cybersecurity incident. However, not all cybersecurity incidents result in a privacy loss and not all privacy loss is the result of a cybersecurity incident. Privacy regulations provide the building blocks to ensure that sufficient data privacy standards are abided-by and that there are consequences for non-compliance, which in most cases are fines and levies to the defaulting organization. These regulations should provide guardrails to protect individuals and organizations by requiring data owners to be better stewards of that data. The problem is that technology changes at a faster pace than regulations can be created, so there is always a lag in the implementation.

Chapter 5 suggests that sometimes security and technology professionals confuse their state of compliance with their security posture. While an organization can meet the requirements to any regulatory standard (HIPAA, SOC, etc.), doing so should not be construed as meeting the requirements to defend a potential cyberattack, provide data protection during business processing or maintain a highly secure development environment. In this chapter the authors will discuss how security and compliance can co-exist. They will associate each one of these with controls that are either derived from formal frameworks or meet custom operational or other requirements of an organization. The chapter also will explore how each control needs to be implemented with a risk perspective in mind, and finally the authors will suggest methods on how to manage such a control catalog.

Chapter 6 explores how the COVID-19 pandemic has led to the implementation of digital health surveillance systems worldwide, including Turkey's Hayat Eve Sığar (HES) platform. While effective in monitoring and tracing the virus, these systems also raise concerns about data privacy and cybersecurity risks. This chapter examines potential risks such as data breaches, malware attacks, unauthorized access, misuse of personal health information, and inadequate security protocols. To mitigate these risks, healthcare organizations must implement strong security measures and adopt a culture of security with a focus on continuous improvement and proactive risk management. The HES in Turkey provides a valuable case study for understanding these risks and measures to mitigate them. The chapter highlights the growing trend of digital health services invading individuals' private spaces and regulating their lives, emphasizing the importance of data privacy and security in safeguarding personal health information.

Chapter 7 investigates the imperatives of Risk Analysis and Asset Management on Cybersecurity in a Technology-Driven Economy from the existing body of knowledge in the field. The chapter is divided into five sections, where the first section has to do with the introduction. The remaining four (4) sections deal with the concepts of Risk and Risk Analysis, Asset Management, Factors determining attainment of continuous improvement of an Asset Performance Management (APM) solution, Cyber-Crime and Cyber-Security, Conclusion and Recommendations.

Chapter 8 emphasizes the importance of cybersecurity for a corporation as today's organizations are more vulnerable than ever and their enemies are in the form of viruses and malware. The chapter provides evidence that cybersecurity can have an impact on brand value, market value, and overall corporate reputation. It focuses on depicting the global scenario with reference to cybersecurity disclosures by corporations and how it is important in today's digitized era where data is the most valuable and vulnerable asset. With rapid digitalization, cybersecurity has become a major concern for all businesses, especially when there is financial and reputational damage to cybersecurity breaches and incidents. Even in the absence of clear cybersecurity laws and regulations, corporations are opting for voluntary disclosure. Existing literature explains this as an attempt to mitigate any potential risk or occurred risk through increased transparency which will build the trust of all stakeholders.

Chapter 9 postulates that cybersecurity is inherently uncertain due to the evolving threat vectors. Indeed, the constant battle between attackers and defenders in cyberspace is compounded by the multiplicity of causes, environments, threat vectors, motives, and attack outcomes. The role of improvisation and equifinality are investigated in understanding cyber incidents as incident bundles that may include both the presence and/or absence of factors that can contribute to a single outcome. Equifinality in cybersecurity operations is discussed along five dimensions: stakeholders, cyber operation bundles, end users, networks, and the threat environment for future research. For each of these dimensions, a set of themes and an associated portfolio of examples of cybersecurity activities at three levels – individual, firm, and community is provided. Qualitative case analysis (QCA) can be employed to understand incident bundles better to understand that incidents vulnerabilities and solutions use equifinality in their paths to a given outcome.

Chapter 10 asserts that critical infrastructure is reliant on automation to efficiently deliver services. Supervisory Control and Data Acquisition (SCADA) systems monitor and control the operational network and these devices can be compromised with a cyberattack. This chapter evaluates the significance of such threats, the economic impact, reviews foreign ownership of critical infrastructure and the current legislation as it relates to the water industry. The chapter concludes with potential recommendations the United Kingdom might consider protecting this vital service.

Chapter 11 acknowledges that interference in the election process from both abroad and within the United States has produced chaos and confusion in business markets, communities, and among voters. Elections have become less reliable as a result of misleading statements. Election deniers are actively working to undermine confidence in US elections and suppress turnout, particularly among voters of color and other communities that have historically been marginalized. The false information spread, which includes lies about the voting process and election workers, has the potential to have significant repercussions for people's abilities to vote and their faith in our elections. Election misinformation poses a threat to democratic processes in the United States. Sixty-four percent of election officials reported in 2022 that spreading false information had made their jobs more dangerous. This chapter uses emerging content from the extant literature to discuss cyberpsychology and the complex dynamics of these issues with a primary focus on finding solutions to these problems.

Chapter 12 affirms the escalating number of cyberattacks on universities worldwide resulted in universities losing valuable information assets leading to disruption of operations and loss of reputation. The research sought to explore a framework for human-factor vulnerabilities related to cybersecurity knowledge and skills, which enabled cybercriminals to manipulate human elements into inadvertently conveying access to critical information assets through social engineering attacks. Descriptive and Inferential statistics were used to test the data and Pearson's correlation statistics were used to measure the statistical relationships and association of variables. The results revealed that students and staff are vulnerable to social engineering attacks and their ability to protect themselves and other information assets is limited mainly due to poor cybersecurity knowledge and skills resulting from poor cybersecurity awareness and education.

We trust this volume will prompt additional research that can be applied effectively to the cybersecurity field in an era of growing global cyberattacks.

Festus Fatai Adedoyin
Bournemouth University, UK

Bryan Christiansen
CYGERA, LLC, USA

Chapter 1
Predicting Cyber Security Behaviors Through Psychosocial and Demographic Conditions During COVID-19

Mololuwa Oluseyi Arogbodo
Bournemouth University, UK

Vasilis Katos
Bournemouth University, UK

ABSTRACT

This research examines the influence of demographic conditions on those psychosocial conditions resulting from the pandemic to predict cyber security behaviors. Multiple linear and logistical regression models showed that addicted users who barely worked from home before the pandemic are more likely to exhibit risky cyber security behaviors, which is also similar for lonely users who barely worked from home to predict internet addiction. One interesting finding is that addicted female users were found to be more susceptible to cyberattacks. The implications and recommendations focused on therapeutic interventions, social change, awareness campaigns, and so forth. The limitation of this study is also covered, and possible future research areas are recommended.

INTRODUCTION

The United Kingdom (UK) formally declared its first lockdown on the 23rd of March 2020 due to the rapid spread of Covid-19. The outbreak of coronavirus and the enormous lockdown measures have significantly changed people's way of living. When people were told to remain at home and maintain physical distancing, the lives of all citizens were affected. Humans are naturally social creatures, meaning that we all rely on social interactions to survive (Young, 2008). For months, people were neither able to go to work/school nor hang out with friends occasionally. What was unexpected was that the UK had over

DOI: 10.4018/978-1-6684-9018-1.ch001

3 lockdowns due to the pandemic, each with varying levels of restrictions (Zhou & Kan, 2020). Two years on, people's lives are not the way they used to be pre-pandemic, and the pandemic is still not over.

Due to the nature of humans, the observed lockdown regulations resulted to a mental and psychological breakdown of citizens. During this period, there has been an enormous increase in cyber-crime with criminals taking advantage of people's fears, resulting in Covid-19 being classed as the biggest threat to cyber security at the time (Panda Security, 2020). The rapid growth of the pandemic had severe impacts on living including mental and financial consequences. In a report by IBM (2020), the shift to work from home (WFH) model was found to have increased the average cost of a data breach by $137,000. Within the UK alone, reports claim that over £1.3 billion was lost to cybercrime activities between 1st of January and 31st of July 2021 (Scroxton, 2021).

More recently, Meyer (2022) states that British taxpayers could lose at least £4 billion of Covid-19 support funds to fraudsters and mistakes. These financial impacts and damage to victims highlights the relevance of psychosocial factors contributing to cyber security during the current crisis. The pandemic has undoubtedly changed the way people use technology, and there is evidence of people increasing their use of digital devices during the lockdown. While the adoption of new technology signifies growth among the population (Feldmann et al., 2020; Király et al., 2020), a major concern is the increased rate of problematic internet use (PIU) and internet addiction (Cellini et al., 2020; Garfinn, 2020).

Similarly, the pandemic along with its stay-at-home restrictions has cause people to feel depressed and lonely, the inability to participate in social gatherings caused people to get their social satisfaction online. Research conducted by Deutrom et al. (2021) highlighted the relationship between these two social factors. It also added Life satisfaction and how all three can be used to predict security behaviour during the pandemic. This current research follows on by examining the effect of demographic conditions in the existing predictions to give a more detailed insight on the cause of these behaviors. Considering that the effects of the pandemic are long-term and the increased demand for remote work, the findings of the research could be used to provide guidance for the new post-pandemic norm, or even similar future crises.

Aims

The primary aim of this research is to identify the demographic characteristics that affect psycho-social behaviors in predicting cyber security behaviors.

Research Objectives

- To review the existing literature on the overview of Covid-19, the lockdowns, and its effects particularly within the UK.
- To examine the status of cybersecurity before and during the pandemic. This gives room for comparisons, and effective analysis of the pandemic on cybersecurity sector in UK.
- To highlight the psychosocial impacts of the pandemic and its effect on cyber security industry in the UK.
- To analyze the already existing data acquired during the pandemic and create effective combinations and find statistically significant data of psychosocial and demographic factors.
- To create multiple regression models and determine its relevance to the stated hypothesis.
- To interpret the current findings and provided recommendations for businesses and government on how to minimise the effect of similar current/future events.

Chapter Structure

Section 1 contains the introduction of the paper, its aims, and objectives. The relevant literature was then examined in section 2 which creates the hypothesis of the paper. Section 3 explains the methodology used to validate/reject the hypothesis of this research. The result of the applied methodology is shown is section 4 and its implications is discussed in Section 5. Section 5 also contains the recommendations, limitations, and direction for future research in this field. Section 6 contains all references highlighted within the paper and the last section contains the approved ethics from conducted in line with all BU guidelines for this study.

LITERATURE REVIEW

Emergence of COVID-19 Pandemic and Lockdowns

The world witnessed the birth of Corona Virus in December 2019. The first case was reported in Wuhan China (Ciotti et al., 2020), and it has since spread across multiple countries around the globe. The Covid-19 mortality rate was estimated to be approximately 3.4% globally (Worldometer 2022), with a higher risk observed in older adults and those with pre-existing health conditions. At the time of this writing, over 45 million cases have been recorded along with over 6.1 million deaths (Worldometer, 2022). The virus was officially declared as a pandemic in March 2020 by the World Health Organisation (WHO, 2020).

The pandemic has resulted to a global change to society in various sectors, particularly in health, education, businesses, and economy. The UK is one of the countries with the most recorded cases with over 19 million cases and approximately 162 thousand deaths, falling behind only USA, India, Brazil, and France (Worldometer, 2022). Despite multiple attempts to control the spread of the virus, the UK Prime Minister announced the first lockdown which limited people to only essential contact and travel. Although the rate of infection reduced at the time, there was further restriction weeks later with an announcement of all movement suspended on the 23rd of March 2020 (UK GOV, 2022). The major concern at the time was the fear that the amount of health care workers would be significantly lower than the projected victims if normal interactions had continued.

Affected entities include fast food restaurants, skin care shops, hairdressers and barbers, religious worship centres, academic institutions, and so forth. Formal businesses were specifically advised to carry out their activities from home where possible, and only those who could not work from home had to report to their place of work. This mostly consisted of health care workers, large scale shopping stores, delivery personnel, etc. The lockdown was somewhat effective in reducing the infection rate of the virus in the UK as there was a significant drop in May 2021. As the cases dropped and virus was contained, the UK has eased its lockdown restrictions steadily, starting by allowing children/students to return to face-to-face education in schools and colleges. Further reduction in infection cases eased the restriction on non-essential services, and total ease of lockdown restriction was underway on the 21st June 2021.

Cyber Security Pre-Pandemic, Peak-Pandemic

The Cybersecurity sector was among the most impacted industries by the globalization of the pandemic, seeing a large increase of cyber-attacks and targeted cyber-crime. Since the outbreak, there have been reports of cybercrime related activities particularly targeted at impersonating health care organisations (such as WHO) to spread false information about the pandemic at the time (Bryan 2020). The scams were directed to the general public, as well as millions of citizens who were working from home due to existing restrictions (Lallie et al., 2021). Cyber attackers have used this opportunity to expand on their Tactics, Techniques and Procedures (TTPs), using traditional trickery which also preys on the heightened stress, anxiety and worry facing individuals (Nurse, 2018). In addition, the shift to WFH and remote working was unplanned for, and this was particularly evident in software vendors, as far as the security of their products was concerned (Lallie et al., 2021). Due to the rapid growth of cyberattacks during this period, the UK National Cyber Security Centre (NCSC) published a report on how cyber-criminal and advanced persistent threat (APT) groups were exploiting the pandemic and ongoing restrictions (NCSC 2020).

Prior to the emergence of Covid-19, there were concerns about the status of cyber security across most industries. Most companies did not prioritize safe cyber security practices and policies. Data privacy was a secondary concern to these companies, the frequency of cybersecurity incidents was on a rise and threat response were not keeping up with the unabated risks. The most common forms of cyber threat faced at the time were: Phishing (56%), Insider threats (51%), and ransomware/malware (48%) (CyberArk, 2018). The nature of common threats has remained the same in recent years and despite this, many organisations have not proactively adopted cyber defence mechanisms that would help them stay ahead of attackers and protect their private data (CyberArk, 2018). The CyberArk study also identifies negative cyber security behaviors in its study stating that over 45% rarely changed their security strategy after cyberattacks and known risks.

Considering the state of cybersecurity before Covid-19, the emergence of the pandemic and its associated restrictions to online activities meant that the existing risk/vulnerabilities were amplified. There are reports that support this claim. One report predicted cyber-crime to cost the world $10.5 trillion in losses by 2025 (Morgan, 2020), a significant increase compared to $3 trillion in 2015, and others stressed that the frequency of cyber-attacks would match traditional criminal activities in number and cost (Anderson et al., 2019). Borlovich and Skovira (2020) explains how the compulsory shift to WFH structure created security challenges for business. While cyber attackers have improved their TTPs and have become more sophisticated and targeted to specific victims depending on attacker's motivation, opportunistic untargeted attacks are also quite common. Opportunistic attacks refer to attacks without pre-chosen victims, instead the victims are selected based on the likelihood of being attacked (Lallie et al., 2021).

Opportunistic attackers exploit victims that have specific vulnerabilities or use social engineering to create needed vulnerabilities (Lallie et al., 2021). It is inevitable to recognize the importance of human factors to curbing cybersecurity risks. The human factor in all organization is mostly ignored, unmanaged and untrained, yet it is fundamental in building a strong cyber defence. One report suggests that there are 87% of workers who work remotely from pre-pandemic period (Apollo, 2021), and this shift to remote working puts data security at greater risk as staffs are more likely to send confidential information to personal e-mail accounts. This is backed up quantitatively by Proband in a report stating that over 60% of U.S. and U.K. employees have forwarded customer emails to their personal email accounts and 84% of them did not realise they were exhibiting risky cyber security behaviors (Papadatou, 2018).

In another survey conducted by Pham (2020), it discovers that 20% of participants said they had not received any updated company policy for data security while working remotely. Worryingly, 41% of workers claim they still use personal applications to transmit confidential files on at least a weekly basis (Pham, 2020). In addition to human vulnerabilities during the pandemic, the lack of appropriate security controls necessary to implement WFH model effectively contributed to the increased cyber-attacks during this period. The sudden change of working conditions has meant that companies had to improvise new working mechanisms, which potentially left its assets less protected to accommodate normal company procedures (Lallie et al., 2021).

The World Economic Forum (WEF) reported that Covid-19 led to a 50.1% increase in cyber-attacks and amongst that, 30,000 incidents where specifically related to the pandemic between December 31st, 2019 and April 14th, 2020 (World Economic Forum, 2020). Similarly, another report highlights a 30,000% increase in the number of cyber threats specifically as a result of the pandemic (Zscaler, 2020). To compounds this argument, Google reportedly identified and blocked 18 million malware and phishing emails related to the virus on a daily basis (Kumaran & Lugani, 2020).

Post-Pandemic and Vaccine Generation

The race for the conception of vaccine has been ongoing ever since the emergence of the virus. Public and Private Medical Institutions have dedicated time and resources towards the discovery of a vaccine for the virus. That said, the traditional vaccine development cycle, which takes an average of 10 years from its conception to its licensing (Thanh et al., 2020), was unrealistic in this situation due to its mortality and urgency.

The efforts of medical experts all over the world has yielded positive results; particularly, Pfizer and Bio-N Tech announced the development of a vaccine, which was authorised by UK in December 2020. The introduction of the vaccine contributed to the curbing of the pandemic, and early ease of lockdown restriction within the UK. However, due to limited supply of vaccine at the time, the restrictions lasted longer than expected as guidelines were constantly fluctuating. Despite the return of activities to its pre-pandemic state, the impacts of the pandemic and its associated lockdown restrictions remained. Organisations and adjusted their mode of operation to the WFH model and some were willing to continue this model despite the ease of restrictions.

Impacts of Pandemic and Lockdowns

Recent evidence shows that the Covid-19 pandemic and its associated restrictions have had differential impacts on various social groups (Zhou & Kan, 2021). For example, women and parents were found to have experienced a huge reduction in subjective well-being (Davillas and Jones 2020) (Pierce et al., 2021). Similarly, people that fall among the Black, Asian, and Minority Ethnicity (BAME) were predicted more likely to experience economic hardship in the event of multiple lockdowns (Witteveen, 2020). These findings identified the presence of immediate differential impacts for various social groups. That said, longer-term impact of the pandemic has varied at various stages of restrictions. The pandemic has lasted for two years, and the UK has experienced over three lockdowns with different levels of restrictions. It is worth noting that the impacts of the pandemic are more significant to certain social groups compared to others, however, a degree of each impact is present in all groups.

Work From Home/WFH Model

Over the years, digital technologies have come up with innovations within organisations that facilitate distance work, including telework, remote work and WFH model (Anderson et al. 2014). Work-from-home (acronym as WFH) refers to a concept where employees of a firm carry out their duties/roles from home using company approved assets, policies and tools. This model is a relatively modern work approach that is enabled through improved technology, internet and mobility where employees can carry out their duties without being within the company premises. The emergence of the pandemic caused a spike in the number of workers who were made to work from home. In the UK, reports suggests that 37% of workers work from home in 2020 (ONS, 2021), a significantly high number compared to years before the pandemic (i.e., 27% in 2019 and less than 20% in 2018).

The report also notes the ease of restrictions meant that employees were able to offer a hybrid approach of both on-site activities and WFH model. This was particularly evident in 2021 as 67% of working adults reported traveling to work at least two times in a week (ONS, 2021). The WFH model presented multiple convenient advantages given the restrictions at the time. For one, it creates a stable work life balance as the environment in homes were a lot more friendly, and enabled workers concentrate on getting their job done.

In a survey carried out to analyze WFH during lockdown and how it changes preferences to the future of work, a total of 81% of parents identified that spending more time with their children is a positive outcome of being able to work from home (Chung et al., 2020). The number is not so high for the effect of mental and physical health, as 30% of respondents said the WFH model improves their mental health. While the work-from-home model presents numerous benefits, its disadvantages are equally significant. One report highlights isolation as the most significant disadvantage of WFH (Ipsen et al., 2021). A major result from the shift to WFH model is the reduced social interactions leading to isolation and deterioration of mental health amongst people. Other drawbacks of this model include cyber security, technical cost of implementation, and proper monitoring of network.

Problematic Internet Use

Over the years, there has been a constant rise in the amount of internet users across the globe. Within the UK alone, precisely 92% of the population use the internet for one reason or the other in 2020 (ONS, 2021). While this figure signifies modern growth within the mass population, there is a growing concern about problematic internet use (PIU), alternatively known as Internet Addiction (Brenner, 1997), pathological Internet use (Davis 2001), and internet dependence (Spada, 2014). There has been a failure to reach general consensus / an official paradigm in the definition of problematic internet use (PIU) across multiple literatures. Researchers studying the concept of PIU still need to differentiate between dependence "on" the internet and dependence "to" the internet (Griffiths, 2000). Griffiths (2000) further argues that most individuals presenting with PIU are only using it as an opportunity to promote other addictive behaviors. The report goes on to explain that certain behaviors are only exhibited on the internet because of the anonymity advantage the internet presents.

In another publication, PIU is referenced as a syndrome that manifests in multiple dimensions (Caplan et al., 2009), these dimensions include cognitive, emotional, and behavioural symptoms that results in difficulties with managing one's offline life. In later research, the author explains that PIU includes using the internet as a form of maladaptive mood regulation, compulsive use of internet leading to negative outcomes (Caplan, 2003). While analysing media psychology and behaviors, Larose et al. (2003) describes PIU as the use of the internet to distract from negative moods such as loneliness, depression, or anxiety.

The common theme across these definitions is the psychological relevance with human behaviors and cognitive reasoning. For the purpose of this research, Problematic Internet Use (PIU) is described as a psychological disorder arising from an addictive use of internet in a bid to outgrow negative moods present is one's offline life.

PIU and the Big Five

Given the relevance of psychology to the concept of PIU, researchers have studied how personality traits can be used to predict PIU. A theory has been developed that narrow down each individual within five basic personality traits which are Openness, Conscientiousness, Extraversion, Agreeableness, Neuroticism (Fiske, 1949; Goldberg, 1992). Conscientiousness refers to the level of one's organization, meeting deadlines, and dutifulness (Przepiorka et al., 2019).

Blachnio et al. (2016) conducted a study to discover the role of personality traits in Facebook and internet addictions, the study highlights a negative relationship between conscientiousness and PIU. This means that the diligent individuals at work are less likely to experience problematic internet use. Similarly, there is a consistent negative relationship between PIU and Neuroticism as well as Agreeableness (Andreassen et al., 2013; Durak & Senol-Durak, 2014). These personality traits hinder the development of addictive internet use. In contrast to the above discovery, some studies have shown that Neuroticism has a positive relationship to internet addiction, along with Extraversion and Neuroticism (Zhou et al., 2017). Kuss et al. (2013) confirmed this in a report stating that a combination of online gaming and Openness to Experience fosters the risk of Internet addiction.

There are other studies that disagree with these findings. Other researchers highlight that Extraversion, Openness to Experience, and Intellect are inversely proportional to PIU (Blachnio et al., 2016; Przepiorka et al., 2019; Servidio, 2014). The inconsistencies in results from various researchers are a reflection of various independent various impacting the research. Przeipiorka et al. (2019) explains that age is responsible for the divergence of patterns in past studies of the topic area.

PIU in the Age of COVID-19

The multiple lockdowns experienced during the covid-19 outbreak has brought about a concern for the mental health of citizens within the country (Brooks et al., 2020). Bonenberger (2020) explains that Pandemic-related social, financial health, and other stressors may affect people's motivations to exhibit potentially addictive behaviors, including on the internet. Relevant research has focussed on the mental health of people during Covid-19 by examining the effects of fear of infection, isolation and economic insecurity on their well-being, particularly anxiety, depression and stress. Mental health advisors anticipated that technology could play a significant role in mitigating isolation and mental health related issues, through social media and online communication (Mucci et al., 2020).

This expectation was validated by research that discovered that internet usage was a predictor for social support level, and loneliness in older adults under social isolation. The report claims that higher internet use results in high social support and reduced loneliness which in turn results in health mental status (Girdhar et al., 2020). Despite the recognised importance of internet in aiding people with declining mental health during the lockdown, Mucci et al (2020) raised concerns of possible consequences of its excessive use, leading to PIU. Past research has showed that internet addiction and PIU are related with conditions such as loneliness, social withdrawal, emotional instability, depression, low-self-esteem, and other addictive behaviors (Aybar et al., 2000; Yen et al., 2007).

Social isolation brought about by the lockdown has also been proven to increase PIU. One observed addictive behavior that spiked over the lockdown period is pornography (Mestre-Bach et al., 2020). Similarly, King et al. (2020) explains that some individuals develop, increase or relapse into unhealthy patterns of gaming to relieve pandemic-related stress. The research also acknowledges that online game addiction could pose significant risks for vulnerable individuals including minors.

Cyberpsychology

One of the most affected aspects of life by the pandemic in on the mental health of citizens across the globe. Psychologists and mental health professionals explained that the pandemic affected the mental health of people globally with a rise in cases of depression, suicide, and self-harm (Li et al., 2020; Moukaddam, 2020). World Health Organization also explains that the induced lockdowns leading to self-isolation and quarantine, have affected usual activities, routines and livelihoods of people, and this in turn caused an increase in loneliness, anxiety, depression, insomnia, harmful alcohol, drug use, etc. (WHO, 2020). These observed psychological effects are significant predictors of cyber security behaviors and online decision making. This part of the review explores the previous literatures that have used the observed psychological effects to predict cybersecurity behaviors.

Social Isolation and Loneliness

The migration of natural activities to online/virtual environments has inevitably led to more socially isolated environments for a lot of people (ONS 2020). Isolation, which is characterised by loneliness, has been found to negatively affect decision making (Rakshasa and Tong 2020). Although, this finding was made by experimenting with mice, its conclusion can be accepted and relevant to human conditions within the context of mental health and human cognition (Cryan & Holmes, 2005).

In an experiment to show relationship between cyberbullying victimisation and Loneliness, the results indicated that cyberbullying victims all suffer from general loneliness (Olenik-Shemesh et al., 2012). It is important to note that this study was from a defined age group of adolescence and its result are significant considering social status and peer relations have great importance amongst this age group (Steinberg & Morris, 2001). Loneliness has also been found to be a significant predictor of Problematic internet usage. While trying to figure out behaviors that cause pathological internet use among college students, Martin and Schumacher explained that lonely and depressed individuals exhibit low self-esteem traits and this makes them have high online interaction, since they perceive that online communication might be the "Prozac of social communication" (Martin & Schumacher, 2000).

The anonymity and reduced risk in online environment contribute to increased time spent online by lonely individuals. This however, results in a compulsive use of internet as they devote more time and attention to their online social interaction, finding it hard to regulate internet time (Kim et al., 2009). Loneliness has also been found to trigger PIU indirectly through attribution bias. In a study to design a cognitive-behavioural model of pathological internet use, it is found that lonely people often attribute their failure in offline interactions to their lack of social skills, which causes them to turn to uncontrolled online interactions (Davis, 2001).

Other researchers have approached the relationship between loneliness and Problematic internet use from a different perspective. There have been multiple studies into viewing loneliness as an effect of PIU rather than its cause. Individuals with preference for online interaction are more likely to have isolating behaviors offline since they value their online interactions and pay minimal attention to real-world interactions (Taylor & Turner, 2002; Wittenberg & Reis, 1986). That said, there are more literatures that support loneliness as a cause of problematic internet use rather than an effect. Lonely individuals are drawn to certain distinct features of synchronous online social interaction that are not available in traditional offline relationships. Mckenna et al (2002), emphasizes on the advantage of anonymity and control of self-presentation that online interaction encourages.

Cyber Security and Its Psychological Predictors

The growing use of internet and online communication has caused an increased importance of cybersecurity in the current day. Cyber security essentially refers to the process or state where Information and communication systems and its data are protected against damage, unauthorised access or modification. The goal of cyber security is confined within the horizon of three variables acronym as CIA, meaning Confidentiality, Integrity, and Availability. Majority of research has focused on improved cyber security through technology advances, software development and updated system patches (Sadkhan, 2019; Mcalaney & Benson, 2020). There are few studies that recognises the importance of cognitive capabilities and situational awareness of system analysts. There are cyber-attacks that exploit vulnerabilities in psychological weaknesses of victims. Dawson and Thomson (2018) support this claim, as they explained that individual differences in cognitive abilities can play a significant role in securing computer and information systems.

Impulsivity has been regarded as relevant predictor for internet behaviour. Haddlington (2017) found that internet addiction and impulsivity predict risky cyber behaviors. Similarly, another study found that individual differences in cognitive control recognised in impulsive behaviors, is related to a violation of information security policies (Hu et al., 2015). To further support these claims, Wiederhold (2014) found that victims of cyber-attacks are usually in pursuit of immediate gratification. This is a common theme among people prone to impulsive behaviour as they tend to act without concern for future consequences.

Another individual trait related to cyber security is risk-taking behaviors. Multiple literature has found that internet users who are high in risk taking are more likely to fall victim to cyber-crime (Henshel et al., 2015) (King et al., 2020). A major factor that enhances risky behaviors is media multitasking. Within the UK, an average household is said to have nine (9) connected devices (Laricchia, 2022). While trying to manage and use all devices adequately, humans are known to have poor attention load balancing (Lavie et al., 2014). The process of trying to multitask the use of all media devices is often related with risky cybersecurity behaviors and increased cognitive errors (Hadlington & Murphy, 2018). Optimism bias also contributes to risk-based decision making. West (2008) explains that people are inclined to assume that the best will happen to them and do not often recognise the risks that may be involved before making certain decisions. This is synonymous to confirmation bias where humans consciously search for/interpret information in a way that confirms their preconceptions (Kassin et al., 2013).

Additionally, the pandemic brought about an increase in distress levels and lower work performance among members of the public (Kumar et al., 2021). This led to a reduced life satisfaction score during the lockdown period. To further support this argument, another analysis indicated that the level of lockdown restriction was a significant predictor of life satisfaction levels (Trzebinski et al., 2020). This means that the higher the level of restriction, the lower the life satisfaction rating. The increased distress levels are also linked to high level of anxiety among people. Among other psychological effects, anxiety levels spiked up during the pandemic as there was uncertainty and misinformation about the virus, fear of infection, moral distress, and grief (Cullen et al., 2020).

Although there were increased mental health services to support people during this time, the sudden nature of the pandemic meant that the victims outnumbered the services available at the time. There are some literatures that discovered a relationship between social anxiety and PIU. For most of the existing research, anxiety is known as a risk factor of PIU (Erwin et al., 2004) (McKenna & Bargh, 1999). Caplan (2002) explains that social anxiety in individuals stems from a lack of self-confidence in their social identity. This then leads to social isolation and a dependence on internet for social interaction. The inability to regulate their internet use results in an impulsive behaviour embodied by PIU.

Human Cyber Security Behaviors/Errors

There are multiple reports that have regarded humans as the greatest vulnerability to cyber security (Furnell & Clarke, 2012; Schneier, 2015). According to a 2018 report, 95% of cyber and network attacks are due to human errors (Nobles, 2018). Basic security errors exhibited by humans include sharing passwords, weak passwords, oversharing information on social media, accessing suspicious links/websites, using unauthorised external storage media, password reuses, not updating software (Boyce et al., 2011) (Calic et al., 2016). Given these behaviors existed at a high rate before the pandemic, it is assumed that the pandemic lockdowns, self-isolation, and migration of activities to online environments, all magnified the already existing human vulnerabilities.

Sharing passwords with friends/family is a prevalent example of human cyber security errors. A study explains that older adults who have high perseverance and self-monitoring traits are more likely to share passwords with a threat actor (Whitty et al., 2015). The perception of security varies across different age groups. Older adults are more likely to conform to the demands of social environment, which means they are very trusting of others and strangers especially on the internet (Whitty et al., 2015).

This is quite different among younger adults, instead, they view security as an obstacle they had to work around (Smith 2003). This is because they are usually required to get the adequate security measures in place before they can have access to desired website/stream links. The act of sharing passwords is generally problematic as most people often use the same passwords for multiple websites, which is not good security practice (Moustafa et al., 2021).

PIU and Human Cyber Security Behaviors

PIU has been described as a form of internet addiction where internet use is unregulated. It can be operationalised to include multiple constructs such as obsession, neglect, control disorder, salience, withdrawal, mood modification and conflict (Demetrovics et al., 2016; Meerkerk et al., 2009). Additionally, human cybersecurity behaviors have been explained to involve factors such as passwords management, software patch updates and device securements (Egelman and Peer 2015). To draw a relationship between both concepts, it can be argued that PIU is characterised by impulsive urges which lead to risky cyber security behaviors. This means that concepts involved in PIU vary negatively to Cyber Security Behaviors (CSB).

While some literature restricts PIU to work place environments (Griffiths, 2010) (Greenfield & Davis, 2002), recent research found that PIU is a significant predictor of CSB (Hadlington & Parsons, 2017) (fzpour 2019). This research is limited as there are currently no frameworks to adequately explain the relationship between PIU and CSB, there are however theories that explains problem-behaviour relationships. An example of such theory is Jessor's Problem-Behaviour theory which suggests that engaging in one problem behaviour, such as drunk driving, increases the likelihood of involvement in another problem behaviour (rebellious attitude) (Jessor, 1987).

In the context of PIU-CSB relationship, it can be explained that the people who exhibit problematic internet use are more likely to engage in risky cyber security behaviors. This argument can be supported by the fact that PIU is characterised by Impulsive behaviors, which undoubtedly encourages risky behaviors online. Deutrom et al. (2021), also highlight this theory while trying to explain the PIU-CSB relationship, their research explains that "if an individual engages in problematic behaviors such as neglecting their basic needs in favour of internet use, then they may also be likely to engage in behaviors such as leaving their computer unlocked when they leave it unattended".

Literature Review Summary and Hypotheses for Current Study

Most of the literature concerned with the pandemic seem to be centred around people's experiences during the lockdown period, and due to the uncertainty and lack of clarity regarding the pandemic, there are a lot of articles and reports that contain misinformation and personal comments about the pandemic gotten from qualitative study. The findings are majorly based on Qualitative literature regarding the impact of the pandemic on cyber security behaviors. This current study therefore aims to perform an adequate quantitative analysis to explore the psycho-social impact of the pandemic and its induced restrictions. It will also explore the impact of other factors such as environment, age, gender, etc and its relationship with cyber security behaviour.

The examined literature emphasizes PIU as a significant predictor of CSB and is characterised by online impulsivity and risky behaviors. While there are few literatures that explores the relationship between PIU and CSB within Workplace environments, the current research aims to discover the relationship by stating which group of problematic internet users are more susceptible to cyber-attacks. Problematic Internet Use has been evaluated and shown to be a significant predictor of cyber security behaviour (Deutrom et al., 2021). Although the relationship between Gender and PIU was discussed in a follow-up study (Deutrom et al., 2022), the impact of gender on PIU in predicting CSB has not yet been evaluated. Therefore, the current study aims to evaluate whether Additive male genders are more susceptible to cyber-attacks compared to their female counterparts.

The relationship between Loneliness and PIU seems to be inconsistent across existing literature. While some suggest that Loneliness is a predictor of Problematic Internet use (Morahan-Martin & Schumacher, 2000), others believe that PIU is the parent psycho-social factor that predicts loneliness level (Taylor & Turner, 2002; Wittenberg & Reis, 1986). A common theme among these literatures is that they are based on theoretical/qualitative evidence. Therefore, another part of this current study is to use statistical analysis to confirm which factor is a more significant predictor of the other, as well as the impact of external influences, Gender, and Work-From-Home, on loneliness in predicting Internet Addiction.

Specific hypotheses are described as follows and presented visually in Figure 1:

H 1: Addictive users who had not worked from home before the pandemic exhibited risky cyber security behaviors.

H 2: Lonely people who had barely worked from home before the pandemic are more addicted to internet and may display impulsive internet usage.

H 3a: Addicted Male/Female users are lonelier than Unaddicted Male/Female users.

H 3b: Addicted Male users tend to be lonelier compared to addicted Female users.
H 3c: Addicted Male users exhibit riskier security behaviour compared to Addicted Females.

Figure 1. Research operational model and hypotheses

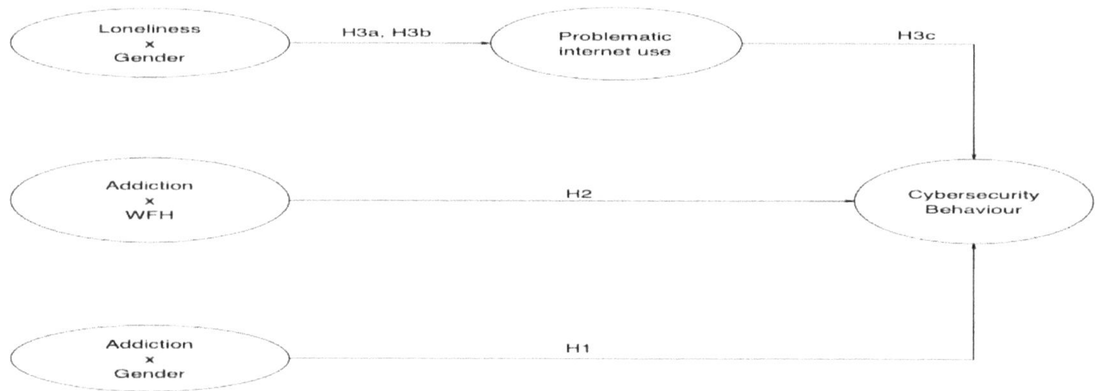

METHODOLOGY

Participants

This research is a continuous analysis from the study carried out during the pandemic by Deutrom et al (2021) and uses the same data set to draw out its findings. The data was gathered through an online survey where random voluntary participants were recruited through Prolific. Prolific is an online crowdsourcing platform with participant pool that willingly signed up to take part in the research. Ideally, a total of 300 participants registered to take part in the survey, however, one of the participants records was removed due to incomplete data which meant that a sample of 299 individuals was used to make findings relevant to the research. Participants of all abilities were recruited from all regions within the UK with each of them receiving £1.50 (One Pound, Fifty Pence) from prolific, as an incentive for their participation.

The participants ages ranged from 18 – 69 years with an average of 33.00, and Standard Deviation (SD) of .48. Amongst the 299 participants, 61.20% were female while 36.80% were male, this amounts to 183 females and 116 males respectively. To achieve accurate results, this study used pre-screening filters to ensure that the advertisement of the study was limited to individuals currently within the UK and have been working from home every day during the lockdown and only did so rarely (i.e., < 1 day a week) or sometimes (1 day a week or more) before.

This meant that people who were still travelling to work during the lockdown and those who regularly worked from home before the lockdown were excluded from participating in the survey. Data were collected in July 2020 while the UK was still in lockdown with many people still working remotely at the time, although restrictions had begun to ease. The experiment was of low risk and approved by Bournemouth University ethics committee.

Materials and Design

The survey used were presented almost precisely as from its original sources, with the initial statements changed to instruct participants to answer them solely based on their experiences during the pandemic and lockdown period. The scales were selected because they were adopted in similar relevant studies that have been stated in the literature review section and for comparisons.

Life Satisfaction

To measure life satisfaction of participants, the Satisfaction with Life Scale (SWLS) was used. The Life Satisfaction scale is made up of 5 items such as "*The conditions of my life are excellent*" measured on a 5-point Likert scale ranging from 1 (Strongly disagree) to 7 (Strongly agree). The advantage of this scale is its brevity as well as its well-established reality (α =0.87). The lowest possible range of scores is 5 and the maximum is 35, while a score of 20 represents a neutral point on the scale. Scores lower than 10 indicates an extremely dissatisfied life, while a score higher than 31 shows that the participant is extremely satisfied with life.

Loneliness

The loneliness first-order construct consists of three items, based on the UCLA-3 Item Loneliness Scale (UCLA-3) (Hughes et al. 2004). Similar to the SWLS, this scale was chosen because it has been rigorously tested and found to be robust (α=0.72), as well as its conciseness. The scale consists of three items including "*How often do you feel like you lack companionship*". Similar to the Life Satisfaction scale, the scores are measured on a 3-point Likert scale ranging from 1to 3 with 1 being "hardly ever" and 3 being "often". The possible score ranges from 3 to 9 and the score varies directly of the loneliness level of individuals, meaning that the higher the score, the higher the loneliness level of the participants. Scores above 6 are categorised as "lonely". A different scale considered to measure loneliness is the De Jong Gierveld Loneliness Scale (Gierveld & Tilburg, 2006). However, it was not applied to this study because it involves face-to-face interviews which would have been unable to fulfil due to time constraints.

Problematic Internet Use

To measure participants internet's additivity, this current study adopted the Problematic Internet Use Questionnaire Short-Form (PIUQ-SF-6) (Demetrovics et al. 2016). This questionnaire is a second-order construct that consists of six (6) items, allocated between three subscales namely: Obsession, Neglect and Control disorder. This PIUQ-SF-6 is a shortened version of its original 20-item scale (Thatcher and Goolam 2005) and has been verified (α=0.77). Example of items within this scale is "*How often do you try to conceal the amount of time spent online?*" and the inputs are measured on a 5-point Likert scale ranging from 1 (Never) to 5 (Always). Possible scores range from 6 to 30 and varies directly to participant's internet addiction. This means that the higher the score, the higher the addiction of participants. Scores above 15 generally indicate addiction.

Cyber Security Behaviors

To assess Cyber Security Behaviors, the participants were made to complete Security Behaviour Intentions Scale (SeBIS) as recommended by Egelman et al. (2016). This scale was selected due to its targeted demographic of end-users which was suitable for the current sample of participants working from home. The Risky Cybersecurity Behaviors Scale used in a previous relevant study (Hadlington, 2017) (Hadlington & Parsons, 2017) was considered as an alternative to the SeBIS, however, some of the items on that scale are un-applicable to this study given the distinctive conditions of working from home. An advantage of the SeBIS scale is that it provides a multidimensional measure predicting four final scores which are aligned to different aspects of cyber security namely: device securement, password generation, proactive awareness and updating behaviors.

The items on the SeBIS scale specifically target these 4 subscales, examples of the items include: “I manually lock my computer screen when I step away from it” which targets securement, “I do not change my passwords, unless I have to” which targets password generation, “when someone sends me a link, I open it first without checking where it goes” which targets awareness, “I try to make sure that the programs I use are up-to-date” which targets updating. The SeBIS has shown to have high psychometric characteristics and internal reliability (α=0.80 for whole scale and α=0.73, 0.76, 0.67, 0.72 for respective subscales). Overall, the SeBIS scale consist of 16 items and the scores are imputed using a 5-point Likert scale ranging from 1(Never) to 5 (Always), and like other scales, they vary directly to the security behaviour. This means that higher scores signify good security behaviors.

Other

Although the major questions were centred around the cognitive behaviors of participants, other questions relating to working environments were included. Questions were both open-ended and close-ended, examples of such questions include: “what device have you been carrying to work? Please tick all that apply” (close-ended), “How has the COVID-19 lockdown affected your work activities? Please write a short description)” (open-ended). Other statistical details of participants were gotten from prolific while still ensuring compliance with GDPR regulations. The details of participants include employment status, student status, country or residence, days WFH, and so forth.

Design

Previous research using this data adopted Structural Equational Modelling (SEM) as the main analysis to explore the variables and validate the existing hypothesis in their research (Deutrom et al., 2021). For the current research and hypothesis, this study utilized a similarly quantitative method by carrying multiple Linear and Logistical Regression in JASP. The analysis explored the impact of other factors on some of the latent variables to predict the other. For example, in the previous research, it was concluded that PIU has a negative relationship with CSB. This current research uses multiple linear regression to show the impact of WFH variables on PIU to predict CSB.

Procedure

Before the fulfilment of survey, participants were informed of the details of the study and were required to confirm their consent Participants who did not give consent were redirected to the end of the survey. To ensure correct completion, all questions in the survey were coded to require a forced-choice response. Most participants were able to complete the survey within eight minutes. Once consent was given, participants answered the first set of questions which focussed on demographic information, device use and working environments. This was followed by the SWLS, UCLA-3, PIUQ-SF-6 and SeBIS block of questions, respectively. In the concluding part of the survey, participants completed the qualitative/open-ended question. This question required a minimum of 150-characters to be entered and would only allow participants to progress to the next stage when that condition is fulfilled.

Once this is completed, participants were informed about the successful completion and redirected back to the Prolific website to confirm their completion and receive payment.

Once the Data was collated on excel, the sum of each block of questions was created in excel to assess the scores of each cognitive factor. New data sets were also created for each cognitive behaviour sum, they consisted of dummy variables that signified the two extremes of the spectrum. This means that for the PIU category for example, one dummy variable represents low additive behaviour (<15) while the other represents high addictive behaviour (>=15). This principle was applied across SWLS, UCLA WFH variables. A similar approach was done with age ranges as well but consisted of 7 categories of varying age groups.

Furthermore, to get the impact of two variables to predict another one, two dummy variables were multiplied. In the context of this study to determine the impact of WFH variable on PIU to predict Cyber security behaviour, two data sets were created consisting of dummy variables. The initial data sets include "WFH only" and "Not WFH only" (Note that these two sets are dummy variables of opposing sequences). Once this is achieved, both data sets are multiplied independently by the PIU categorised dummy data set. This results in two new data sets representing the PIUQ category of participants that work from home and the PIUQ category of participants that didn't work from home. These two data sets are then used to run a linear regression to predict security behaviour, and the results are recorded. This procedure is repeated across multiple variables relevant to the hypothesis of the current study.

RESULTS

Descriptive Statistics

Demographic and Other Relevant Statistical Data About Participants

A moderately heterogenous example of individuals was obtained based on latent variables like sex and age. As mentioned in the previous section, the survey was completed by 299 individuals, comprising of 183 women and 116 men. Table 1 gives a statistical overview of the demography of participants respective to their gender.

Table 1. Demographic overview of participants

Gender	Frequency	Percentage
Female	183	61.2%
Male	116	38.8%
Total	299	100%

Table 2. Age distribution for male and female participants

	Age Distribution Among Both Genders		
	Female	Male	Overall
Mean	32.404	33.931	32.997
Standard Deviation	7.256	9.858	8.379
Minimum	19	18	18.000
Maximum	58	69	69.000
Shapiro-Wilk	0.960	0.964	0.965

The ages of participants were further categorised into multiple age groups, as explained in Table 3 below.

Table 3. Age grouping category of participants

Age Years	Category	Frequency	Percentage
18-24	1	38	12.7
25-29	2	78	26.1
30-34	3	65	21.7
35-39	4	59	19.7
40-44	5	29	9.7
45-49	6	19	6.4
50+	7	11	3.7

The participants also recorded their level of academic education during the survey. This ranged from individuals with no formal education to some with Doctorate qualifications, there was also an option of "prefer not to say" for participants who did not want to reveal such information. Details of the academical qualifications of participants is shown in Table 4.

Table 4. Academic experience of participants

Education	Frequency	Percent
No formal Education	2	0.7
GCSEs or equivalent	14	4.7
A-Levels or equivalent	58	19.4
Bachelor's Degree	142	47.5
Master's Degree	61	20.4
PhD	17	5.7
Vocational Programme	4	1.3
Prefer not to say	1	0.3

As shown in Table 4, the majority of the participants had a bachelor's degree qualification (47.5%), followed by Master's degree and A-Levels qualification at 20.4% and 19.4% respectively. The WFH data was also recorded by participants during the survey, and there is a significant difference between those who barely worked from home before the pandemic and those who already used to work from home. The statistical overview of the WFH data is illustrated in Table 5.

Table 5. WFH conditions of participants

WFH Status Before Pandemic	Frequency	Percent
Rarely (<once a day per week)	205	68.6
Sometimes (>= once a day per week)	94	31.4

The WFH data was further categorised among multiple age groups to describe the ages of participants who worked from home previously and the ages of those who did not. The Age group for not working from home and working from home participants is shown in Figure 2 and 3, respectively.

Figure 2. Distribution of participant's age groups for non-WFH conditions

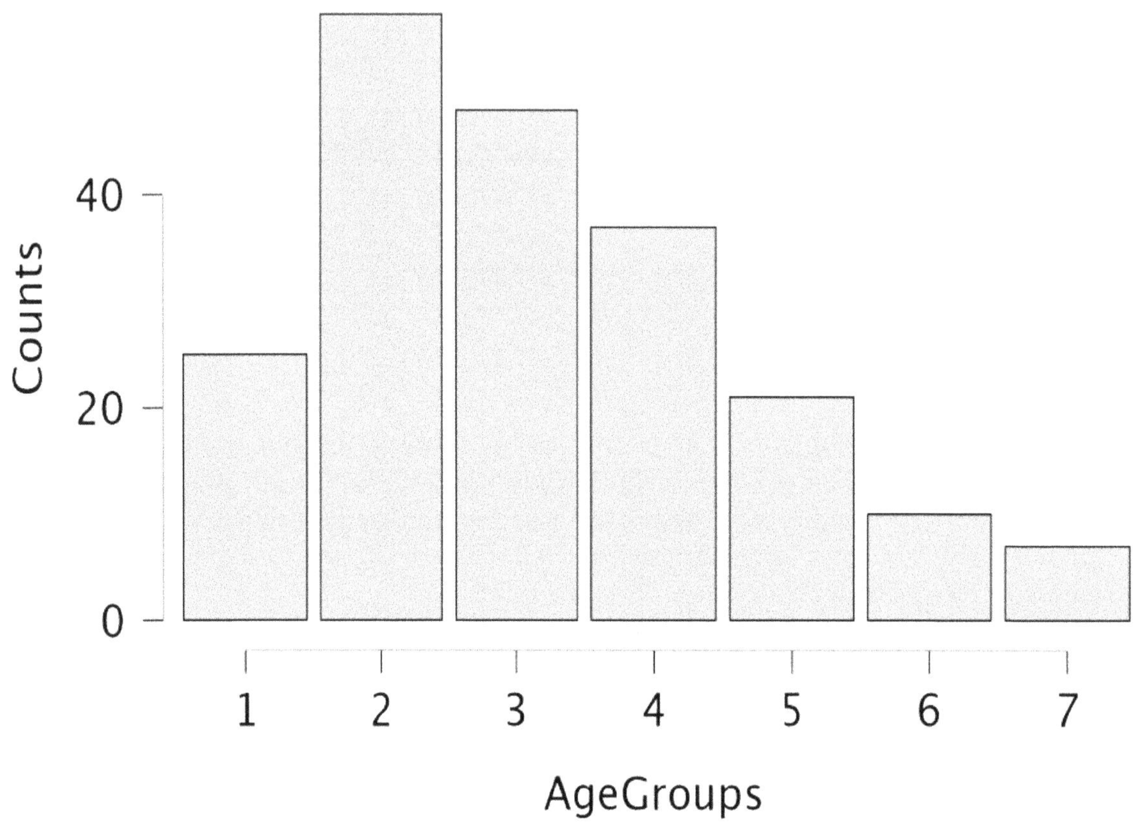

The data description shows majority of participants who barely worked from home during the pandemic fall within the age group of 25-29 followed by 30-34 and 35-39, respectively. While most age groups observed similar difference with both conditions (WFH and not WFH), there is a significant difference among participants above 45. The frequency among 45-49 age groups for both conditions are similar while more people aged 50+ already worked from home before the pandemic.

Figure 3. Distribution of participant's age groups for WFH condition

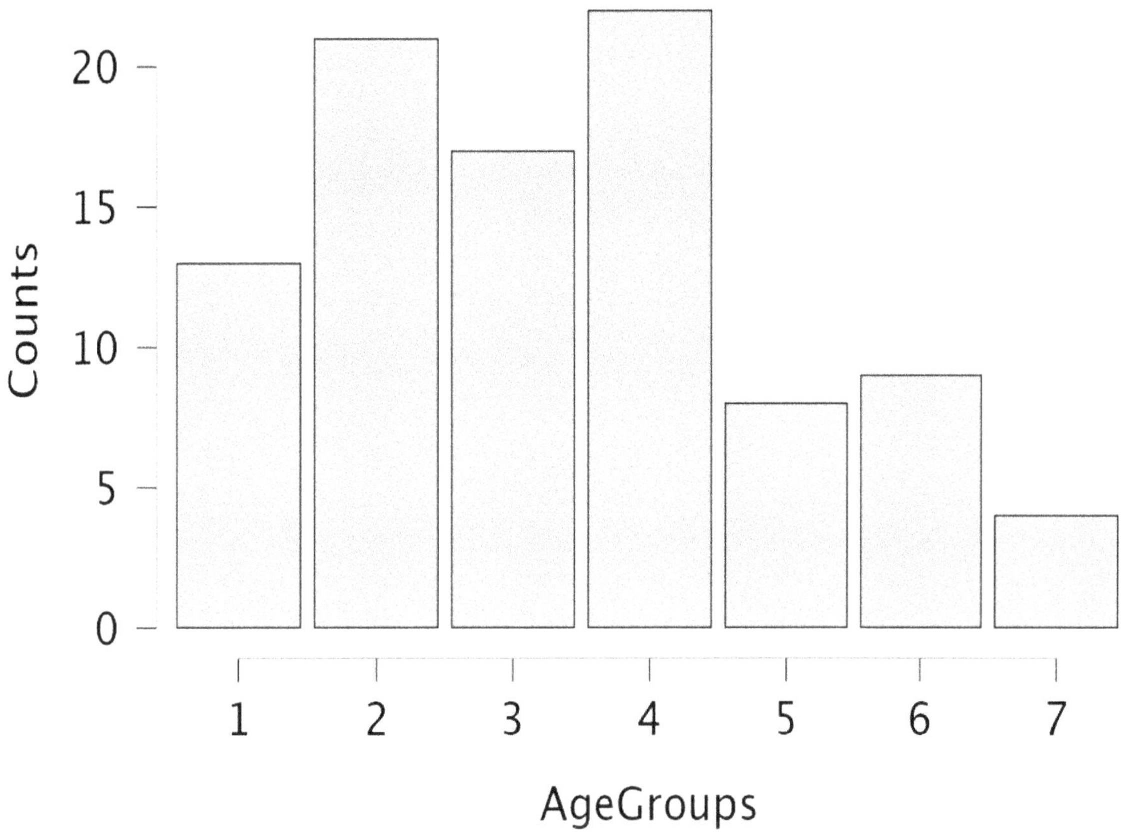

The WFH conditions was also categorised based on gender, this is particularly relevant to establish the impact of gender while validating the hypothesis of the current study. Figure 4 shows the Gender statistics of WFH conditions, respectively.

Figure 4. Gender category for non-WFH and WFH conditions respectively

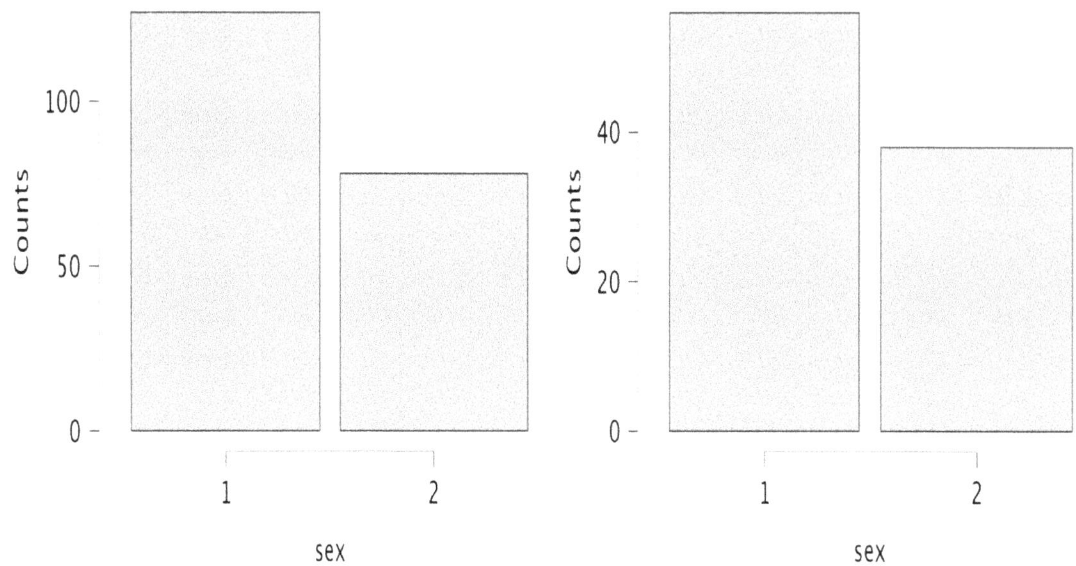

From the two charts shown, it is observed that the ratio of Female to Male across both WFH and not work from home conditions are similar. While both genders barely worked from home before the pandemic, there are significantly more females that barely worked from home than males. As part of the questionnaire demography, participants were made to record their devices usage, specifically whether or not they share the devices they use to carry out official duties. Only 23 participants reported that they share their devices with work, and about 233 participants reported using their devices for both personal use and work. The overview of the statistics is shown in Tables 6, 7, and 8.

Table 6. Grouping participants by the device sharing conditions

Device Shared	Frequency	Percentage
Yes	23	7.7
No	276	92.3
Total	299	100

Table 7. How participants use their devices

Device Use	Frequency	Percent
Work Only	66	22.1
Work and Personal	233	77.9
Total	299	100.0

Table 8. Grouping participants by the number of devices they use

Nos of Devices Used	Frequency	Percent
1	189	63.2
2	77	25.8
3	25	8.4
4	28	2.7
Total	299	100.0

Psychological and Cognitive Behavioural Measures

As mentioned in earlier sections, the survey included questions that focussed on the cognitive behaviour of participants during the pandemic. The statistics reported by participants include Life Satisfaction (SWLS), Loneliness Scale (UCLA), Problematic Internet Use (PIUQ) and Security Behaviour (SeBIS). The mean value of for the loneliness and Life satisfaction scale is 5.425 out a possible 9 and 21.107 out of a possible 35 respectively, indicating that most participants were lonely and significantly unsatisfied with life during the pandemic period. For the Problematic Internet Use Scale, it has a mean of 13.699 out of 30, indicating that most participants have a moderate level of internet addiction. For the corresponding sub-scales, the mean scores were 4.09 out of 10 for obsession, 4.89 for neglect and 4.71 for control disorder. The SeBIS scores had been analysed in the parent research (Deutrom et al., 2021), and the subscales (securement, passwords, awareness and updating) are shown in Table 9.

Table 9. Descriptive summary of psychosocial statistics of participants

Scale	Mean	S.D	Shapiro-Wilk	Minimum	Maximum
Life Satisfaction	21.10	6.37	0.972	5.00	34.00
Loneliness	5.42	1.88	0.912	3.0	9.00
Problematic Internet Use	13.70	4.46	0.979	6.0	27.00

To make detailed findings, the cognitive behaviour measures were further categorised based on other demographic factors including gender, work from home conditions and age groups.

Loneliness x Demographic Factors (Gender, WFH, and Age Groups)

Tables 10, 11, and 12 show the detailed statistics of loneliness combined with these factors.

Table 10. Descriptive overview of loneliness across both genders

	Frequency	Mean	Standard Deviation
Female (1)	183	5.481	1.892
Male (2)	116	5.336	1.865

The graphical representation of loneliness scale for female and male is shown in Figure 5 below

Figure 5. Loneliness score distribution of male and female participants

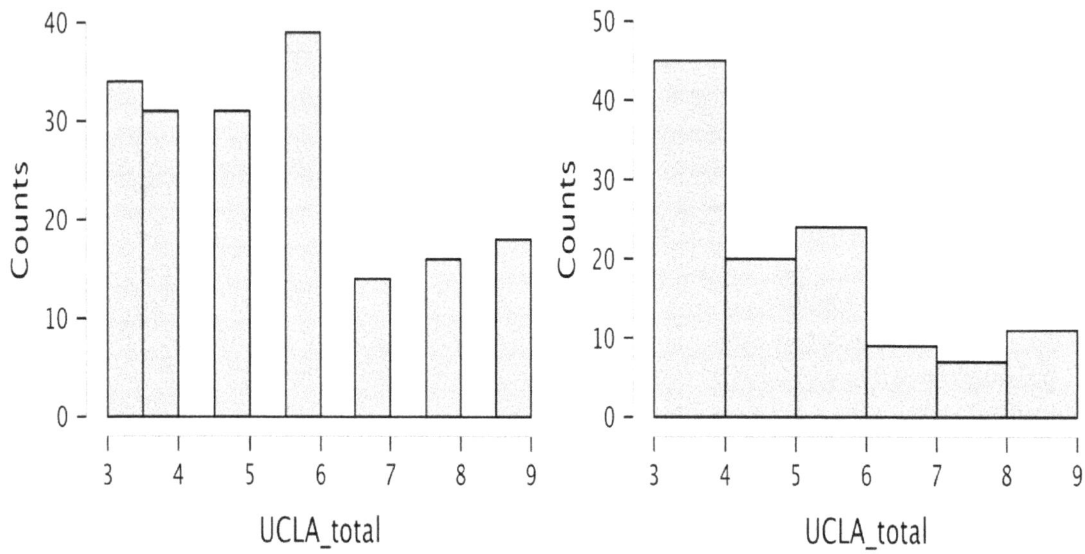

While the average values seem to be similar due to its scale, the difference is quite significant. The graph shows that female participants loneliness scale is evenly across all spectrums. The case for Males is quite different, the graph illustrates that more males fell below the mean, meaning that they were less lonely compared to their female counterpart during the pandemic.

Table 11. Descriptive overview of loneliness for WFH conditions

	Frequency	Mean	Standard Deviation
Rarely Worked From home (<once a day per week)	205	5.468	1.939
Work from home sometimes (>= once a day per week)	94	5.330	1.750

Similar with the gender variables, the means for the WFH conditions in terms of loneliness are homogenous. That said, the difference is significant ($p<.001$). Figure 6 shows the distribution of values among those who barely worked from home before the pandemic and those who already worked from home before the pandemic respectively. The scores for individuals who barely worked from home is slightly evenly distributed, while for those who work from home, most of their scores fell below the mean. In other words, most participants who used to work from home before the pandemic were less lonely.

Figure 6. Loneliness distribution across participants categorised by WFH conditions

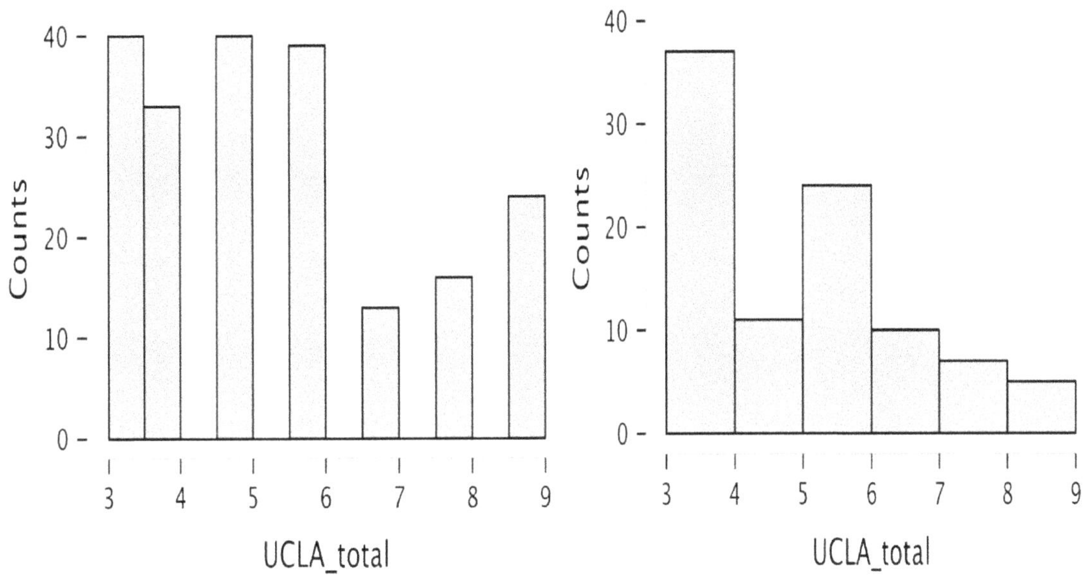

The relationship between loneliness levels and age groups is also interesting. The young adults (18-24) have the highest overall mean (6.132), followed by the mid-age individuals (25-29, 30-34, 35-39) mostly averaging approximately 5.4 scores. The lowest mean (4.789) is among individuals aged between 45-49, with elderly participants (50+) slightly higher with mean 4.909.

Table 12. Loneliness scores of participants categorised by age groups

	Frequency	**Mean**	**Standard Deviation**
1 (18-24)	38	6.132	2.042
2 (25-29)	78	5.487	1.829
3 (30-34)	65	5.092	1.774
4 (35-39)	59	5.542	1.822
5 (40-44)	29	5.448	1.975
6 (45-49)	19	4.789	1.751
7 (50+)	11	4.909	2.119

The distribution of loneliness scores across each age group is illustrated below.

Figure 7. Loneliness description for age: Groups 1 and 2

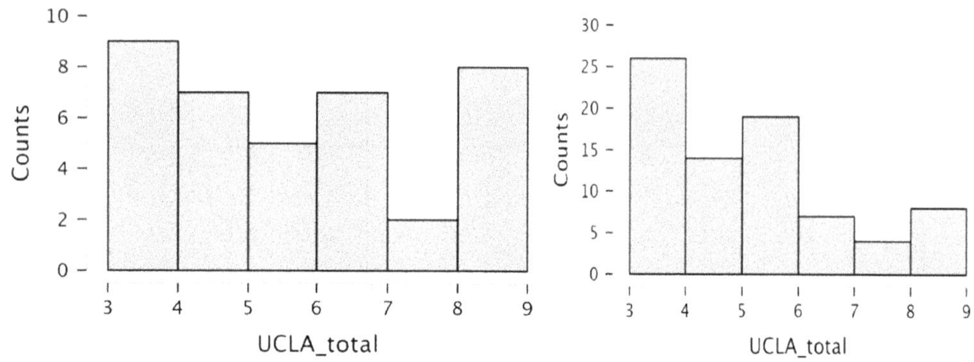

Figure 8. Loneliness distribution for age: Groups 3 and 4

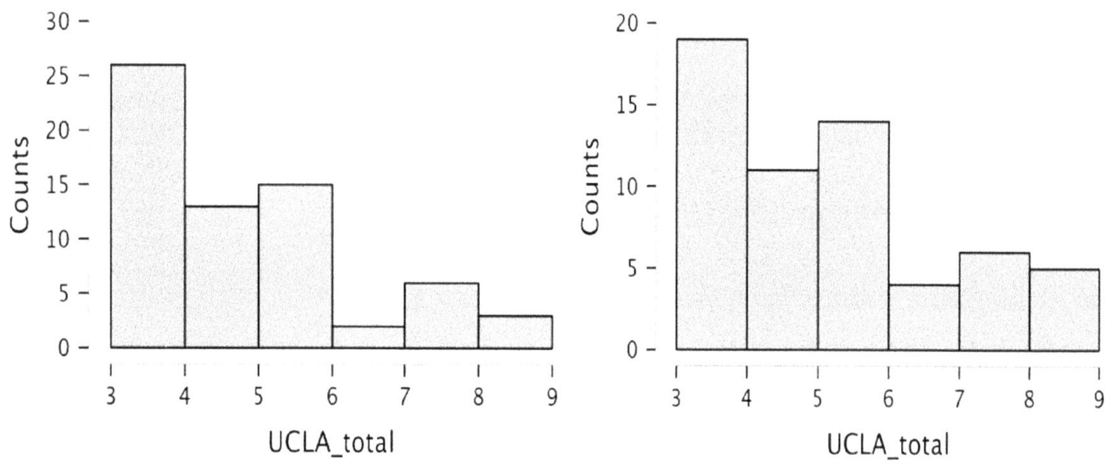

Figure 9. Loneliness distribution of age: Groups 5 and 6

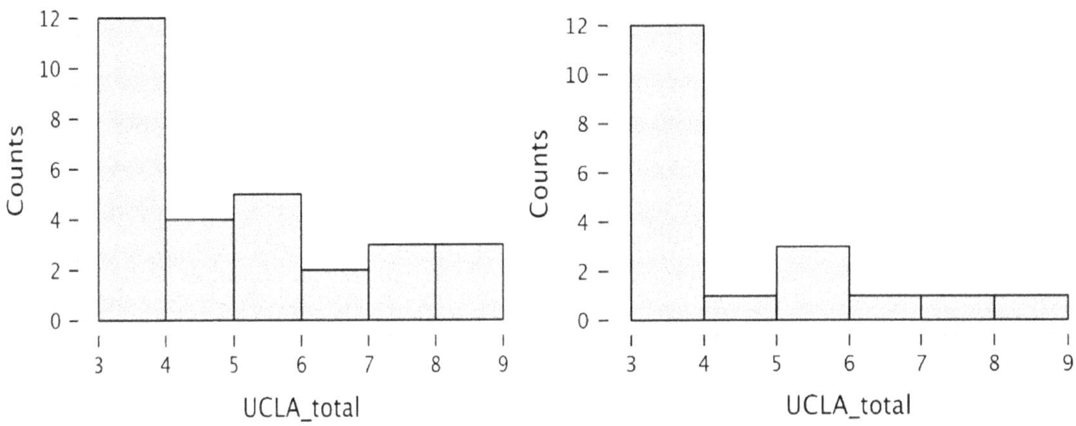

Figure 10. Loneliness distribution of age: Group 7

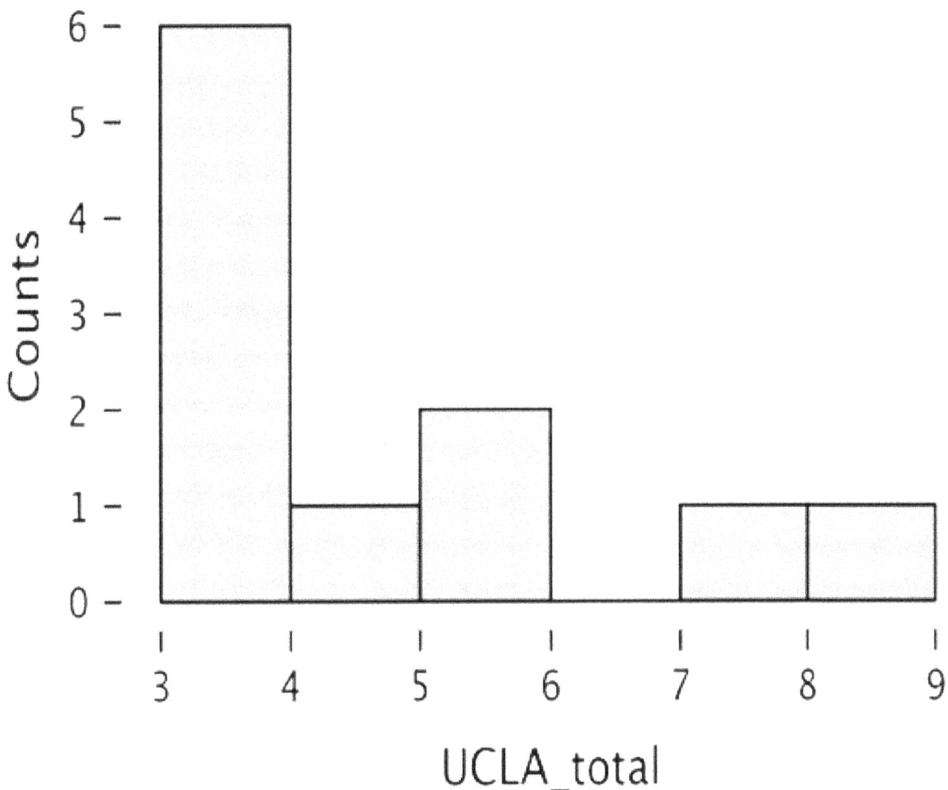

From the illustrations above, most participant across all age groups reported low levels of loneliness (with majority scoring 3/4). That said, the distribution among young adults is quite different. Unlike others, the scores among individuals aged between 18 and 24 are evenly distributed across all spectrums of loneliness levels. About 9 people have very low loneliness scores on the scale and under 8 participants have extremely high loneliness scores, all other participants in this age groups are evenly spread across other scales.

The mid aged participants have similar spread of distribution with majority of them scoring very low on loneliness. Among the older adults and elders (i.e., 45-49 and 50+ groups), there is a significant difference between the number of participants with very high and very low scores. While about 12 and 6 participants had very low scores for age 45-49 and 50+ respectively, a total of 3 individuals had high loneliness scores from the two age groups combined.

It is worth noting that although the mean loneliness scores of all age groups are quite close, the little differences are very significant. The similarity in means can be attributed to the score scale of the UCLA questionnaire which has a minimum possible value of 3 and maximum possible value of 9.

Problematic Internet Use X Demographic Factors

The recorded scores of participants who completed the PIUQ-SF-6 questionnaire is analysed against Gender, WFH conditions and Age groups. The findings give insight on what gender suffered more internet addiction, if work conditions affected problematic internet use, as well as the internet addiction across age groups during the pandemic.

The statistical overview describing the relationship between PIU scores and Gender, WFH conditions and Age groups is shown Tables 13, 14, and 15.

Table 13. Descriptive overview of PIU scores for both genders

	Frequency	Mean	Standard Deviation	Shapiro-Wilk	P-Value of Shapiro-Wilk
Female	183	13.699	4.392	0.976	0.975
Male	116	13.698	4.588	0.003	0.028

The PIU average scores for male and female are similar, indicating that gender is irrelevant in predicting PIU. Also, the scores for both genders are evenly distributed and the test for normality is rejected. The score distribution is illustrated in Figure 14 and 15.

Figure 11. PIU score distribution categorised by genders

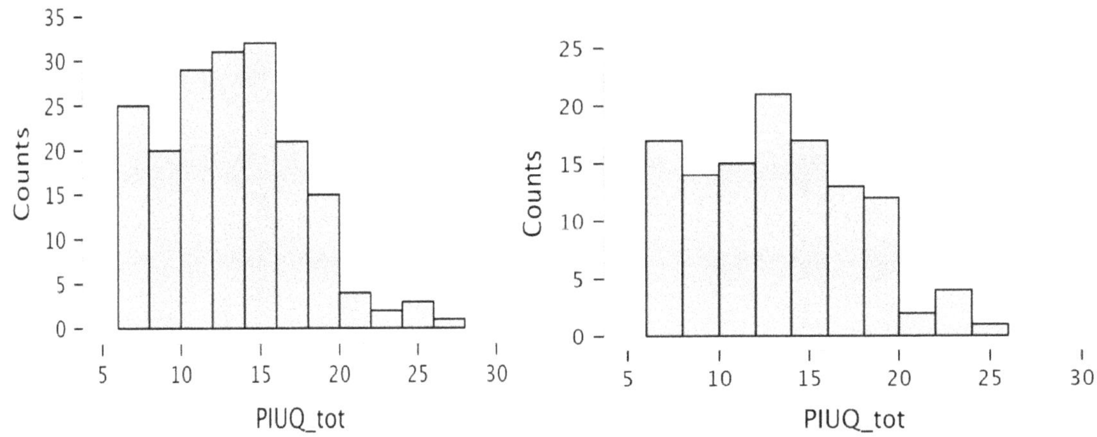

Similar to the sex results, the findings from the combination of PIU scores with WFH conditions is irrelevant. The means of both conditions are approximately the same, indicating that it is an insignificant predictor of Internet addiction. The distribution of PIU scores is shown in Figure 16 and 17. It is quite noticeable that there are higher scores among participant that work from home sometimes compared to those who barely did before the pandemic,

Table 14. PIU statistical overview grouped by WFH conditions

	Frequency	Mean	Standard Deviation
Rarely Worked From home (<once a day per week)	205	13.849	4.365
Work from home sometimes (>= once a day per week)	94	13.372	4.672

Figure 12. PIU distribution for both WFH conditions

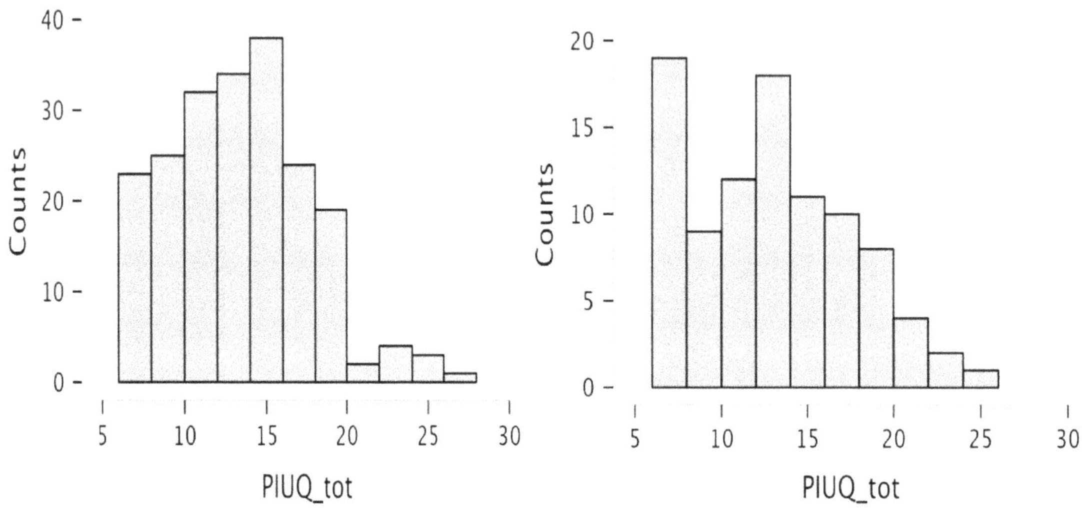

Inferential Statistics and Hypothesis Testing

JASP version 0.16.1 was used to investigate and discover patterns relevant to the data set. JASP, short for Jefferey's Amazing Statistics Program, is an open-source software that is majorly used for statistical and quantitative analysis. In the parent research for this study, AMOS-SPSS was used to make quantitative analysis on the data. However, SPSS is not compatible with the MacOS devices and this caused a limitation for the author of the current research. Unlike SPSS, JASP is free tool, that performs similar functions to AMOS-SPSS. Shapiro-wilk test is first conducted and its p-value is recorded to check whether or not any of the distributions are normal.

The Shapiro-Wilk test refers to a statistical test used to check if a continuous variable follows a normal distribution. The null hypothesis H_0 states that the distribution is normal and the alternative hypotheses (H_1) states that the distribution is not normal. The p-value of the Shapiro wilk test indicates the hypothesis that is valid and accepted. In the context of the current study, the sample size of 299 participants meant that the distribution of the variable needs to be determined so as to choose the appropriate statistical method. The two major hypothesis testing methods are Parametric and Non-Parametric testing. The parametric testing is most applicable to normal distributions while the non-parametric tests are independent of the normality status. The results of Shapiro wilk test and its corresponding p-values for relevant variables in the hypothesis is illustrated in the table below:

Table 15. Statistical tests results of psychosocial metrics

	Shapiro-Wilk (W)	P-Value of Shapiro-Wilk
PIUQ	0.979	<.001
SWLS	0.972	<.001
UCLA	0.912	<.001

The Shapiro-Wilk test showed that the distributions (PIUQ, SWLS, UCLA) departed significantly from normality (W= .979,.972 and .912, and p-value <.001). Based on this outcome, a non-parametric test was used. To test the relationship between variables relevant in the hypothesis, this study adopts the use of regression analysis to make findings. A combination of multiple linear regression and logistical regression was used to show relationships and determine the factors that are significant predictors of the observed psycho-social variables. For each relationship variable relationship investigated, the overall model summary is reported along with its Anova description and its individual regression results.

Model 1: Multiple Regression Predicting Security Behaviour Using Internet Addiction Levels and WFH Variable

Based on evidence identified in previous literature, internet addiction is known to be a significant predictor of an individual's online security behaviour (Hadlington & Parsons, 2017). This is confirmed in the current study using a linear regression ($p=.002$, $R^2=0.032$), the results signify there is a 3.2% variance in security behavior when addicted users and non-addicted users are compared. Although this value is quite small, the p-value shows that it is a significant difference. This model aims to investigate the impact of WFH conditions mixed with internet addiction levels, as a predictor for cyber security behaviors. The descriptive overview of the combined variable is shown below:

Table 16. Overview of PIUQ and WFH categories together

		PIUQ Level		
		1 (Unaddicted)	**2(Addicted)**	**Total**
WFH Conditions	1 (Barely)	114	91	205
	2 (Often)	58	36	94
	Total	172	127	299

Overall, there are more participants who barely worked from home, as well as participants who exhibit little internet addiction traits. Due to the significant difference in group density, the results can be interpreted in different ways. One way of interpreting this statistical overview is 38% of participants barely worked from home and were not addicted to the internet, a total of 91 participants barely worked from home and suffered problematic internet use, also, there are more participants who often worked from home and are non-addicts (19.4%) compared to those who often worked from home and had no internet regulation (12%). A more detailed way to interpret the statistical overview is addressing each variable with reference to the other variable. That said, the table shows that 62% of individuals who often worked from home are regulated internet users, while 44.3% of those who often work from home are addicted to the internet.

The results of the linear regression of this model are shown below:

Table 17. Model 1 summary

Model	R	R^2	Adjusted R^2	RMSE
H_0	0.000	0.000	0.000	8.388
H_1	0.196	0.038	0.032	8.253

The summary model shows the result of all variables taken together, and how these variables combined together predict the security behaviour. The R^2 value shows the proportion of variance in Security Behaviour that is impacted by the variables put together. In this case, the R^2 is 0.038, a considerably small value that indicates that there is a 3.8% in variance in security behaviour by both internet addiction and WFH conditions put together. RMSE, short "Root Mean Square Error", is a measure of how far from the regression line the data points are located. RMSE value for this regression model is 8.253.

Table 18. Model 1 anova summary

Model		Sum of Squares	df	Mean Squares	F	p
H_1	Regression	805.648	2	402.824	5.914	0.003
	Residual	20163.168	296	68.119		
	Total	20968.816	298			

The Anova table is a more detailed description of the overall model, it consists the F-statistics, the degree of freedom of the model and its p-value. The F-statistic is gotten from a regression analysis to find out the if the means of the predicting variables are significantly different. The degree of freedom in statistics indicates the number independent variables that can vary in the model without destabilising any constraints. The p-value is the most important feature of the model as its indicated whether the model is statistically significant or not. For the current model, the p-value ($<.0.001$) passes the significancy test ($p<=0.05$), which means that the R^2 value of 3.8% is significant. The low variance is a reflection of the number of sample size (299), it also means that there are other factors that are predictors of security behaviour along with Internet use and WFH conditions.

Overall, this model predicted approximately 4% of variance in security behaviour, $R^2 =.38$, $F(2,296) =5.914$, $p=.003$. The individual regression co-efficient of the individual variables is shows in the co-efficient table below. The results from the regression co-efficient results in two forms of co-efficient, unstandardized co-efficient (along with its standard error), and Standardized co-efficient. The table also consists of the t statistic, that is used in derived its corresponding p-value.

Table 19. Model 1 co-efficient description

							Confidence Level	
Model		**Unstandardized**	**Standard Error**	**Standardized**	**t**	**p**	**Lower**	**Upper**
H_0	(INTERCEPT)	56.856	0.485		117.202	<.001	55.902	57.811
H_1	WFH x PIUQ_CAT	-2.229	1.104	-0.186	-2.020	0.044	-4.401	-0.057
	NON_WFH x PIUQ_CAT	-3.240	0.979	-0.304	-3.311	0.001	-5.166	-1.314

All variables are significant in predicting security behaviour (both p values <0.05), however, the most significant predictor is determined by either the combination of unstandardised and standard error, or the use of the standardized value. The variable with the highest standard value irrespective of the sign (+ or -) before the value represent the most significant predictors of the security behavior. In this model, it is shown that overall, individuals who barely worked from home before the pandemic are better predictors (β=-0.304 95%CI= -5.166 to -1.314) of security behaviour than those who worked from home often (β=-0.186, 95%CI= -4.401 to -0.057). The 95% confidence interval is the measure of precision of the estimates, meaning that there is a 95% probability that the model is accurate.

The collinearity analysis is also reported along with the results and it indicates whether or not there is a correlation between predictor variables, such that they express a linear relationship in the model. It is recommended that the VIF collinearity statistics (Variance Inflation) is less than 3, as a value greater than 3 indicates multicollinearity between the predictor variables.

Model 2: Linear Regression Predicting PIU Through Loneliness and WFH Conditions

Reviewed literatures have stated that loneliness is a significant predictor of Problematic Internet Use (Kim et al., 2009; Davis, 2001). The current model confirms this finding, and also investigates the impact of WFH conditions on Loneliness in predicting PIU. Firstly, this model confirms the parent research as the results indicate that loneliness is a significant predictor of PIU ($p<.001$ $R^2=0.065$). To further investigate the impact of loneliness in predicting PIU, the current model combines Loneliness with WFH conditions to determine the relationship. The overall statistical details of the combines variable are shown in Table 20.

Table 20. Overview of loneliness and WFH conditions together

		Loneliness Level		
		1 (Not Lonely)	**2 (Lonely)**	**Total**
WFH Conditions	1(Barely)	92	113	205
	2 (Often)	46	48	94
	Total	138	161	299

The illustration shown can be described from two perspectives. In an overall view, it is observed that there are more lonely people among the sample size, and the ratio of lonely individuals to not lonely is 7:6. Among the 299 participants, 37.7% of them barely worked from home before the pandemic and were lonely, while 92 people were not lonely and barely worked from home during the period. There is little difference among those who often worked from home during the pandemic in terms of their loneliness. The percentage for both conditions (Lonely and Not lonely) is evenly split at 15% each. In a more detailed description of the illustration, it is observed that over 70% of those who were lonely barely worked from home while 48% of those who often worked from home were not lonely.

Similar to the first model, a linear regression is executed to test the model hypothesis. The results of the linear regression are shown in Table 21.

Table 21. Model 2 summary

Model	R	R^2	Adjusted R^2	RMSE
H_0	0.000	0.000	0.000	4.461
H_1	0.261	0.068	0.062	4.322

The model summary shows the result of the all the variables taken together. The RMSE value is considerably lower than the first model at 4.322, which indicates that this regression model fits the data set. It is important to note that the lower an RMSE value, the better a given model is able to fit a dataset. The R^2=0.068 explains that the predictor variables are responsible for a 6.8% of variance in the security behaviour of participants.

Table 22. Model 2 anova summary

Model		Sum of Squares	df	Mean Squares	F	p
H_1	Regression	805.648	2	201.480	10.788	<.001
	Residual	20163.168	296	18.676		
	Total	20968.816	298			

The Anova summary presents a more detailed description of the impact of the predictor variables (Loneliness and WFH) on security behaviour. The p value (<.001) indicates that the variables selected are significant predictors of the dependent variable. This means that despite the little variance in PIU scores (shown in the model summary), the variables combined together have a significant impact in determining the PIU category of an individual. Ultimately, the overall model predicted approximately 6.8% in variance in PIUQ scores, R^2 =.058, F (2,296) = 10.688, p<. 001. The co-efficient regression model that shows the how the predictor variables affect problematic internet use scores is summarised in Table 23.

Table 23. Model 2 co-efficient results

							Confidence Level	
Model		**Unstandardized**	**Standard Error**	**Standardized**	**t**	**p**	**Lower**	**Upper**
H_0	(INTERCEPT)	13.699	0.258		53.097	<.001	13.191	14.207
H_1	WFH x Loneliness CAT	-2.199	0.509	-0.410	-4.321	<.001	-3.201	-1.198
	NON_WFH x Loneliness CAT	-2.512	0.559	-0.426	-4.492	<.001	-3.612	-1.411

The conditions of the variables individually are significant predictors of problematic internet use, however, the difference in the predicting power of both conditions is quite similar. Both variables have p-values <.001 but the standardized values for WFH individuals and those who didn't are -0.41 and -0.426 respectively. Although the difference is small, the illustration shows that those who barely worked from home before the pandemic are better predictors of problematic internet use (β =0.426, 95%CI=-3.612 to -1.411), compared to those who worked from home often (β =-0.410, 95%CI =-3.201 to -1.198), irrespective of their loneliness level. The collinearity statistics is also presented with the results, the tolerance and VIF of both variables are 0.35 and 2.855 respectfully. The variance inflation is considered to be good (<3) as it shows there is no multicollinearity of both variables.

Model 3 (Part I): Logistical Regression predicting Loneliness Using PIUQ Levels and Female Gender

While reviewing literature in previous sections, some argue that loneliness is a predictor/cause of PIU, and this claim was backed up by most researchers and statistical studies (Deutrom, 2021). That said, there are other literatures that suggest that loneliness is an effect of PIU (Taylor & Turner, 2002), meaning that PIU is a predictor of loneliness among individuals. This current model aims to test this finding and investigate how age combined with internet addiction can affect loneliness levels. Firstly, the loneliness scores are categorised into two conditions (Lonely and Not lonely), this is done by categorising those above the mean score as lonely and those below as not lonely. This is done because the model uses logistical regression to analyse its hypotheses. Logistical regression is used to handle a classification problem, i.e., use variables to predict a categorical dependent variable. This model concentrates specifically for female gender, and how their PIUQ scores can predict their loneliness levels. The model summary is shown below:

Table 24. Model 3 summary

Model	Deviance	AIC	df	X^2	p	Tjur R^2
H_0	412.731	414.731	298			
H_1	406.726	412.726	296	6.005	0.050	0.020

The model summary consists of various characteristics including the deviance, Akaike Information Criterion (AIC), degrees of freedom (df), Chi square value, p value and Tjur R^2. Deviance and AIC are both measures of how fit the regression model is, and the value for variance range from zero to infinity. The chi-square value shows the difference between the observed and expected frequencies of the outcome variables, for this model, $X^2 = 6.005$, indicating that the combination of loneliness is not solely dependent on PIU for females. The p-value explains the significance of the predictor variables as a determinant of loneliness amongst individuals. In the current model, p=0.050, indicating a level of significance. It also means that although loneliness is not solely dependent on PIU for females, the impact of PIU among ladies is significant. The individual categories of PIU for females are also explained in Table 25.

Table 25. Model 3 co-efficient results

					Wald Test		
	Estimate	**Standard Error**	**Odds Ratio**	**z**	**Wald Statistic**	**df**	**P**
(Intercept)	0.243	0.187	1.275	1.297	1.681	1	0.195
Category 1 (Unaddicted	0.163	0.273	1.177	0.596	0.355	1	0.551
Category 2 (Addicted)	-0.553	0.296	0.575	-1.868	3.491	1	0.062

The Co-efficient table explains specifically how the categories of the PIU predict loneliness specifically for females. The relevant information is the Odds Ratio, it plays an important role of converting the model from probability based to likelihood based. The intercept represents the reference class (i.e., value zero (0)) of the continuous various and first factor level for the categorical variables. For this model, the intercept represents the male gender irrespective of its PIUQ category, as such, it is not relevant in this part of the model (Another logistical regression will be used to show the relationship between PIUQ and Loneliness specifically for Males). Category 1 represents unaddicted female individuals while category 2 represents addicted individuals, and the odds ratio for both are 1.177 and 0.575, respectively.

The p-value shows the significance of both categories. For addicted users, the p-value is reported as 0.062 meaning that internet addiction among females can significantly predict loneliness level. The case for Unaddicted female users is quite different, the p-value (0.551) indicates that there is not much being an unaddicted female does not significantly predict loneliness.

A major advantage of JASP is the ability to assess the performance of a model performance. It indicates how accurately the model can predict the outcome. One of the tools for assessing model performance in JASP is the confusion matrix. The results of the Performance Diagnostics are illustrated in Table 26.

Table 26. Model 3 confusion matrix

		Predicted		
	Observed	1	2	%Correct
1		45	93	32.609
2		33	128	79.503
Overall %Correct				57.860

The confusion matrix explains the percentage of correct predictions (1,1 and 2,2), the other diagonal represents the percentage of the model that has been incorrectly predicted (1,2 and 2,1). Following up from the confusion matrix, the performance metrics are calculated namely sensitivity and specificity. The results are shown below:

Table 27. Model 3 sensitivity and specificity

	Value
Sensitivity	0.795
Specificity	0.326

Sensitivity describes the portion of true positives, i.e., the correct prediction of those who are lonely depending on the predictor variables. Conversely, specificity is the proportion of the model that predicts true negative, i.e., the chances that the female individual is not lonely. The sensitivity and specificity of the current model is 79.5% and 32.6%, respectively.

Model 3 (Part II): Logistical Regression Predicting Loneliness Using PIUQ Levels and Male Gender

Using similar steps to the logistical regression in the female gender, this part of the model analysis the impact of PIUQ in predicting Loneliness for Male individuals. The summary of the model result for male is shown in Table 28.

Table 28. Model 3 (ii) summary

Model	Deviance	AIC	df	X^2	p	Tjur R^2
H_0	412.731	414.731	298			
H_1	406.338	410.338	296	8.393	0.015	0.028

Although the value of the chi-square in the same model for males is slightly higher than for females, it still means that the loneliness of male individuals is not solely dependent on their internet addiction levels. The p-value of 0.015 indicates that PIUQ is a significant predictor or loneliness among male individuals. The individual categories of PIU for males are also explained in Table 29.

Table 29. Model 3 (ii) co-efficient results

					Wald Test		
	Estimate	**Standard Error**	**Odds Ratio**	z	**Wald Statistic**	**df**	**P**
(Intercept)	0.098	0.148	1.103	0.665	0.442	1	0.506
Category 1 (Unaddicted	0.617	0.299	1.854	2.062	4.252	1	0.039
Category 2 (Addicted)	-0.470	0.326	0.625	-.1.441	2.076	1	0.150

The co-efficient table explains specifically how the categories of PIU predict loneliness specifically for male individuals. For this part of the model, the intercept represents the female gender irrespective of its PIUQ category and is not relevant for the part II of this model. Similar to the first part of this model, Category 1 represents male unaddicted users and its observed odds ratio is 1.854, while addicted male users have an odd ratio of 0.625. The p-value stands at 0.039 and 0.150 for unaddicted and addicted users respectively, indicating that only significant predictor of loneliness is unaddicted male users.

The performance diagnostic of this part of the model is summarised in Table 30.

Table 30. Confusion matrix model 3 (ii)

		Predicted		
	Observed	**1**	**2**	**% Correct**
1		29	109	21.014
2		20	141	87.578
Overall %Correct				56.856

Table 31. Model 3 (ii) sensitivity and specificity

	Value
Sensitivity	0.876
Specificity	0.210

Model 4: Linear Regression Predicting Cyber Security Behavior by Internet Addiction for Both Genders

As discussed earlier, Internet addiction has shown to be a significant predictor of a person's online security behaviour. The current model aims to show the impact of Gender on Internet addiction to predict cyber security behaviour. The descriptive overview of the predictor overview is shown below:

Table 32. PIU and gender overview grouped together

	PIUQ Level			
Gender		**1 (Unaddicted)**	**2 (Addicted)**	**Total**
	1(Female)	105	78	183
	2 (Male)	67	49	116
	Total	172	127	299

The illustration above shows that there are more unaddicted users for both female and male (105 and 67 respectively) compared to their addicted counterparts. That said, 61% of all unaddicted users are female while 38.5% of addicted users are male individuals. To see how the variables combine together to predict security behaviour, a linear regression is performed and its results is shown in Table 33.

Table 33. Model 4 summary

Model	R	R^2	Adjusted R^2	RMSE
H_0	0.000	0.000	0.000	8.388
H_1	0.186	0.035	0.028	8.270

This model summary shows the results of all variables taken together (i.e., how PIU and gender can predict security behavior). The R^2 of 0.035 shows there is only 3.5% difference in variance of security behaviour score that is impacted by both variables.

Table 34. Model 4 anova summary

Model		Sum of Squares	df	Mean Squares	F	p
H_1	Regression	725.030	2	362.515	5.301	0.005
	Residual	20243.786	296	68.391		
	Total	20968.816	298			

As shown in the Anova summary, the p-value (0.005) shows that the 3.5% variance shown in the model summary is significant, this means that the predictor variables significantly affect the security behaviour of individuals. Ultimately, the overall model predicted approximately 3.5% in variance of SeBis scores, R^2 =.035, F (2,296) = 5.301, p=.005. The co-efficient summary explains the how the individual predictor variables affect cyber security behaviors as shown in Table 35.

Table 35. Model 4 co-efficient results

							Confidence Level	
Model		**Unstandardized**	**Standard Error**	**Standardized**	**t**	**p**	**Lower**	**Upper**
H_0	(INTERCEPT)	56.856	0.485		117.202	<.001	55.902	57.811
H_1	Female x PIUQ_CAT	-3.249	0.999	-0.309	-3.252	0.001	-5.215	-1.283
	Male x PIUQ_CAT	-2.618	1.048	-0.237	-2.499	0.013	-4.680	-0.556

The conditions of the variables individually are significant predictors of security behaviour. The standardized values show that Female users are stronger predictors of security behaviour (β=-0.309) compared to the male users (β=-0.237). That said, both genders irrespective of their PIU_CAT significantly impact security behaviors with p-values of 0.001 and 0.013 for females and males respectively. The 95%CI ranges from -5.215 to -1.283 for female individuals and -4.680 to -0.556 for male participants.

Summary of Results

This section has successfully shown the results of the quantitative analysis carried out on JASP and has constructed 4 models to validate/reject the hypotheses of the current study. Model 1 focused on the predicting security behaviour by using the PIU scores of those who barely worked from home during the pandemic and those who often did, this model is relevant to H_1. Model 2 showed how loneliness and WFH conditions predict the internet addiction of users during the pandemic, this is particularly relevant because a common theme during the pandemic was isolation. This model is related to H_2.

Model 3 is a reverse of model 2 as it has been argued across multiple literature that loneliness is an effect of internet addiction and not the other way round. Hence, model 3 uses logistical regression to predict loneliness of an individual using their internet addiction and gender. This model is divided into two parts, one for Females and the other for Males, and its findings are relevant to H3a and H3b. The final model is done to predict security behaviour using the internet addiction levels of both genders, and it is used to analyse H3c. The hypotheses findings are discussed in the next sessions as well as comparisons with previous literature relevant to the current study.

DISCUSSION

Although the pandemic has significantly reduced particularly within the UK, its effects are still present, and it is hard to say whether life would ever return to its pre-pandemic status. Major organisations have made decisions to WFH more often than they used to, and some have abandoned the traditional on-site operations where online execution is possible. It is therefore important to analyse the psychological and behavioural impact of the pandemic and how these factors predict online security behaviour. As a follow up from the parent research (Deutrom et al., 2021), the current study aimed to analyse the relationships within the psycho-social factors resulting from the pandemic and to highlight the impact of other demographic factors while showing these relationships. This study utilized the same data as the parent research to make its findings. However, this study used linear and logistical regression to predict multiple behaviors.

Overview of Present Research Findings

The first model is relevant in analysing the first hypotheses (h1), which the current study argues that WFH conditions significantly impacts Internet addiction to predict online security behaviour. This means that addicted users who barely worked from home before the pandemic exhibit behaviors that are more susceptible to cyber-attacks, as opposed to those who had worked from home often before the pandemic. The result of this model shows that both conditions combined with internet use are significant predictors of online security behaviour ($p=0.044$ and 0.001. Specifically, people who had barely worked from home are stronger predictors $\beta=-0.304$), compared to people who often did ($\beta=-0.186$).

The negative coefficient of standardized values in regression suggests that the independent variables is inversely proportional to the dependent variable. In the context of this model, the negative coefficient indicates that for both categories of WFH conditions, addicted internet users have lower security behaviour scores compared to un-addicted users. The stronger coefficient means that individuals who barely worked from home are more susceptible to cyber-attacks. Overall, this model shows that addicted internet users who barely worked from home before the pandemic are the most vulnerable group of people and are more likely to exhibit risky behaviors online.

Given this result, the first hypotheses (H1) is accepted. This finding is consistent with existing reports that have explained the importance of workplace environment to promote security of devices and data. In traditional settings, work environments are governed by defined policy, and behaviors that must be strictly adhered to or risk getting a penalty. The sudden shift to WFH structure meant that employees who had felt previously burdened by the strict security policy, became complacent. One psychology behaviour common here is reactance, it is the reaction of people who are being forced/told to do something they would not willingly do. Usually, people do not like being told what to do or conform to a behaviour they do not believe in (Zhang et al. 2017), they instead deviate from the recommended behaviour to assure themselves of their freedom.

As such, employees who always saw security practices as a chore rather than their responsibility are more likely to exhibit reactance behaviour due to their misunderstanding of the importance of adhering to cyber security policies. The WFH structure encourages their reactive behaviour as there is no strict supervision as with the traditional office settings. Deutrom et al (2021) already established that impulsive internet users are likely to exhibit risky online behaviour. For people who had barely worked from home, it means that this risk is amplified. For people who had already worked from home often, one explanation is that they are already experienced in the model and are aware of the risk that come with WFH. As such, they know the importance of good online behaviors and are less susceptible to cyber attackers.

It is also interesting that most people who already worked from home often are within the IT and Academia industry, who are more conscious of security practices compared to those with non-IT professions (Bick et al., 2021). Analysis of Loneliness during the pandemic combined with WFH conditions proved to be significant predictors of problematic internet use among individuals. Similar to the first model, model 2 argues that lonely people who barely worked from home before the pandemic suffer the most problematic internet use and are more likely to display impulsive internet usage. For this model, both categories of WFH conditions combined with loneliness proved to be significant predictors of PIU ($p<0.001$ for both categories).

The results show similar standardized co-efficient ($\beta=-0.410$ and -0.426) for both categories. Similar to the previous model, the co-efficient are negative, meaning that they are inversely proportional to the independent variable, which is PIU in this case. Ultimately, this means that for those who feel lonely are more likely to exhibit impulsive internet behaviour and specifically those who had barely worked from home. This means that the second hypotheses (H2) is validated and accepted. The security policies present in office settings not only ensures good online security behaviour, but also regulates internet use for its employees. Most companies restrict their internet access to allow only work-related activities, which also ensures that employees internet use is well regulated. WFH model does not offer this safe practice for employees, as most users used their personal WIFI in their homes. The risk is heightened for people who feel lonely, as the lockdown undoubtedly increased loneliness amongst users.

For some who often looked to physical work environments to distract their loneliness, the WFH structure amplified their loneliness. The combined loneliness level as well as the sudden shift to work from home model, people are likely to look unto the internet to reduce their loneliness, which sometimes lead to an impulsive use of the internet.

Model 3 was broken down into 2 parts to predict loneliness through impulsive behaviour among both genders. Each part of the results focussed on each gender. This study argues that addicted female internet users are lonelier compared to their male counterpart. The result of the first part of the logistical regression found no significance for unaddicted female users in predicting loneliness ($p=0.551$), however, addicted female users prove to be significant predictors of loneliness. The result of the logistical regression shows that the likelihood of addicted female users to be lonely is 57.7% (Odds Ratio = 0.575). That said, the hypotheses, h3a, is not confirmed by this analysis.

The model for male individuals yielded different results. The result indicate that addicted internet users proved to be insignificant predictors of loneliness among male gender ($p=0.150$), while unaddicted male users significantly impacted loneliness. This finding is quite confusing as the odds ratio for unaddicted male users is 1.184. a logistical regression with an odds ratio of 1 means that the predictor and predicting variable are independent of each other. Although there is a significant relationship between unaddicted male users and problematic internet use, its odds ratio (1.854) indicates that both variables are independent of each other. Conversely, male users who experienced problematic internet use are 62.5% likely to experience loneliness symptoms (albeit insignificant).

Comparing the two parts of the model together, addicted users irrespective of their gender are more likely to experience lonely behaviors. Also, addicted male users have the highest likelihood of being lonely (62.5%) compared to addicted female users (57.7%). This confirms hypothesis 3a and 3b showing that addicted users are lonelier, particularly if the individual is of male gender. The validation of this hypotheses is consistent with reports that explains why addiction often leads to isolations and loneliness (Su et al. 2020). Online gaming and social media contribute the most to the impulsive internet use among both genders. Boys mostly spend hours gaming due to its addiction and worldwide interactions. Both male and female are addicted to social media, and this is particularly prevalent in adolescent and young adults, where their social identity is of utmost importance to them. The addiction to these internet services results in reduced sensations and a disconnection from real world engagements.

The final hypotheses of the current study focusses on predicting online security behaviour through internet addiction for male and female. Linear Regression was used to make this assessment. Both Genders combined with their PIU category proved to be significant predictors of security behaviour (p=0.001. p=0.013). Analysing the result, the standardized coefficient show that female users are strong predictors (Odds Ratio = -0.309, compared to the male ratios (Odds ratio = -0.237). The negative co-efficient shows that the relationship between PIU, for genders and, SeBis is negatively proportional. Addicted female users are the most likely to execute risky cybersecurity behaviors, as shown by the negative coefficient standardized values. This finding is quite interesting considering that addicted males are more likely to be lonely compared to females.

The result of this model is also contradictory with previous literatures that have explained that women are less likely to be exploited online compared to men (Rawlings 2020). The research identifies that woman generally exhibit safe password practices compared to male. That said, the result of this model can be as a result of the difference in sample size of both male and female participants.

Recommendations

This current research has made detailed findings regarding different groups categorised by psychosocial and demographic combinations. The findings have showed that certain groups of individuals are more susceptible to PIU, loneliness and risky cyber security behaviour. The following are recommendations that will improve online security behaviour as well as impulsive internet use among all the identified groups.

Cybersecurity Awareness Campaigns

While security policies are prioritized in most organisation, security awareness is an often-overlooked factor within these companies. Security awareness campaigns refer to a public awareness effort aimed at increasing the understanding of cyber threats and empowering people to be safer and more secure online (CISA, 2021). Considering the sudden change of work conditions, security policies is not as effective when people are made to work from home. Especially for employees who never understood the importance of security and only regard the policies as a burden. When an organisation's employees are cyber security aware, it means that they understand what cyber threats are, its possible impacts, and the steps required to minimise risk (Aloul, 2012). This encourages them to practice safe online security behaviors irrespective of the WFH conditions.

Awareness campaigns are to be carried out strategically to achieve effective result and change behaviors online. There are frameworks for changing online behaviors and raising awareness. Among others, MINDSPACE framework is one of the most effective methods of carrying out awareness programs (Dolan et al 2012). It focuses on nine forces that drive behaviour across a variety of contexts. The nine forces are: Messenger, Incentives, Norms, Defaults, Salience, Priming, Affect, Commitments, Ego. It is worth nothing that this framework is not an alternative to the current policy making methods, instead, it complements them to integrate behavioural science into the process (Dolan et al., 2012). Other frameworks for raising awareness and changing security behaviour include Fogg's Model (Fogg, 2009) and Cialdini's six principles of persuasion (Cialdini, 2007).

Figure 13. Fogg's model
Source: Fogg (2009)

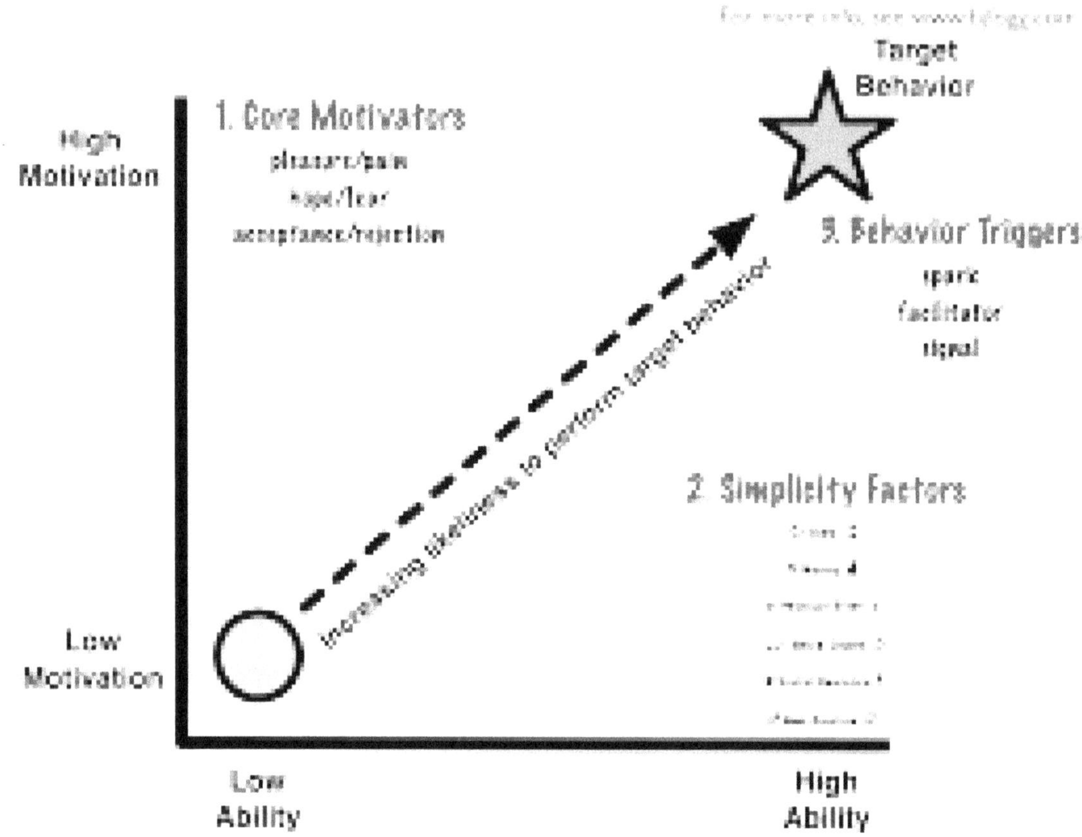

LIMITATIONS

Although awareness campaign is the best method of influencing people towards changing online behaviour, effective influencing requires more than just informing people about what they should and shouldn't do. Among others, a common limitation with awareness campaign is fear invocations (Ahluwalia, 2000). Users may find the message funny and approach the information with a nonchalant attitude, rather than understanding its importance. Cultural differences in risk perceptions can also influence the inability to change behaviour. People from different parts of the world have different mentality towards their online behaviour which is a reflection of their experiences. As such, it is usually difficult to people to adopt new behaviors even if they are willing to do so. This is backed up by other literature that explains that even when people are willing to change their behaviour, the process of learning a new behaviour needs to be supported (Higgins, 1998). Therefore, cultural differences should be considered when planning a cyber security awareness campaign.

Periodic Measurement of Psychosocial Behaviors

Multiple literature has stated that the biggest impact of the pandemic exists in the mental/psychological well-being of people (Davillas & Jones, 2020; Pierce et al., 2021). Companies need to pay attention to the mental status of its employees take adequate measures to achieving a positive mental state for all its staff. This research along with its parent research has highlighted the impact of loneliness and how it affects PIU. Loneliness along with other psychosocial behaviour should be measured periodically in workplaces, to create a healthy psychosocial space within work environment. After measuring loneliness in among employees, it is important to consider people who are lonely while enforcing WFH conditions. One idea is to give room for lonely people to visit the office at least once in a week. This ensures that there is always something for them to look forward to, as well as a form of accountability to distract them from being lonely while working from home.

Limitations:

Humans often have mental shortcuts when making judgements, particularly when it has to do with a self-report. These shortcuts are called Heuristics. Heuristics can be manifesting in different ways, for example, availability heuristics occurs when people use the information that comes to mind quickly to make decisions about the future (Keller et al., 2006). In the context of this recommendation, people are likely to think they are not lonely and general false reports of low loneliness level in the psychometrics.

Redefining Social Norms

There are multiple factors that significantly affect PIU across both genders including internet availability and psychological well-being. A major contributor to the differences in gender addiction is in social norms. According to WHO (2010), Gender-related norms and values may influence male and female exposure to environmental and online risks in different ways, including through the types of behaviour they adopt. Depending on the age group, there are various social norms for both genders that defines their use of the internet. Their online behaviour is usually defined by their social identity, which often results in a need to conform to social norms.

Goffman (1956) explains the concept of impression formulation stating that "humans display a series of masks to others, enacting roles, controlling and staging how they appear and come across so they set themselves in the best light". In a bid to control and match social identity online, people are made to conform to social norms such as sharing excess information online, which leads to PIU. Such social norms should be redefined by relevant organisations and bodies, to promote safer security practices online. It is important to note that this recommendation follows with awareness campaigns as the redefinition of social norms can also be publicised.

Limitations of Methodology

The current study was mainly limited by the measurement of PIU and CSB as a whole scale rather than its subscales. Although the current study highlighted various forms of PIU such as online gaming, social media addiction, etc. It does not reference this defined behaviour in its measurement of PIU. Other literatures relevant to this study highlighted certain behaviors that defined risky cyber security behaviour (Dufour et al., 2016; Su et al., 2020). For example, Su et al. (2019) specifically highlighted those men are more prone to internet gaming and women to social media. Unlike these studies, the current research used the PIUQ-SF-6 standard to measure problematic internet use as a whole rather than its nuanced manifestations.

It also means that participant only responded to the questionnaire based on what they perceived to be problematic internet use. For example, some participants who believe spending excess amount of time does not make them PIU may decide to dilute their actions due to their beliefs, whereas in actual fact, they do suffer from PIU. That said, this does not nullify the validity of the current findings, as regardless of the differences in internet usage, self-reported data still faces insight of perceived PIU which is just as impactful as actual PIU.

In addition, the current research is majorly checking the relationships of the psycho-social factors and demographic factors to predict behaviors, particularly during the pandemic. Although the questions in the survey explicitly told the participants to record their answers only based on their experiences during the pandemic, an overview of the status of these people before the pandemic would help make a detailed findings and decisions. But due to the nature of the pandemic, this data could not be achieved and was instead replaced by existing literatures to make its comparisons.

This study used regression technique to perform its analysis and make its predictions. A major limitation with regressions analysis is that it is not resistant to outliers. Outliers basically refer to an observation for which the residual is large compared to other observations in the data set. That said, JASP provides a way to check the effect of outliers in the data set. The results showed that the outliers did not significantly affect the result of the analysis.

As with all research literatures that involves self-report from participants, the results are usually affected by biases by participant. Self-serving bias occurs when people attribute positive events to their character and blame negative results to external factors unrelated to our character (Forsyth 2008). This makes participants to respond in a way that makes them appear favourable (Donaldson and Grant-Vallone 2002). That said, the effect of this bias is assumed to be minimised since the survey was conducted virtually and anonymity was ensured.

Furthermore, this study was limited by the difference in density of gender of participants with a divide of over 60% female and less than 40% male. The research council of Norway (2020) explains the importance of gender balance to help enhance the scientific quality and social relevance of the research. The ideal gender ratio for quality research should be between 60% and 40%, and the closer the better. While the gender ratio of our research does not fall between the recommended margin, the large sample size ensured that the findings remained significant. Also, the gender imbalance was not statistically significant and the findings relating to gender were combined with other psycho-social factors which reduced the risk.

DIRECTIONS FOR FUTURE RESEARCH

The pandemic is slowly going away, and life is edging closer to its pre-pandemic status. Future works can collect new data and compare its result with the current research and its parent research (Deutrom et al. 2021) and see whether the findings have been heightened or reduced. Also, future research can focus on more specific problematic behaviors and its corresponding risky behaviour. For example, findings can be that people who are addicted to social media are more likely to leave their work computers unattended.

CONCLUSION

The current study aimed to follow up on the previous research by combining psycho-social factors and the demography of participants to predict behaviors that are relevant to cyber security, particularly during the Covid-19 pandemic. The findings from the current study contributes to the existing literature focussing on psychosocial behaviors, particularly PIU, Loneliness and CSB, during the lockdown. A combination of WFH conditions and Internet addiction identified that addicted users who had barely worked from home prior to the pandemic, are the most susceptible group of individuals. The WFH conditions was also combined with loneliness status of individuals. The results showed that although the difference was little, lonely people who are new to WFH structure due to the pandemic would exhibit impulsive internet behaviors. Finally, this study identified that male users who suffer from internet addiction are more likely to experience feelings of loneliness compared to the females. What is more interesting about this study is that it highlights addicted female users as the most likely people to suffer cyber-attack.

Recommendations were made relevant to the findings that were discussed, the recommendations include strategic awareness campaigns and a change to the social norms for both genders. This study was limited by a number of factors ranging from self-serving bias of participants to the imbalance of gender ratio of the participants, however, the findings from the results were proving to be valid regardless of the highlighted limitations. Suggestions for future research focused on conducting a new survey where the specific PIU behaviors are identified, and it is used to predicts a corresponding security behaviour. Considering the long-term impact of the pandemic and the adoption of WFH conditions as a norm, the findings of this study may still be relevant in the future.

REFERENCES

Aivazpour, Z. (2019). *Impulsivity and Risky Cybersecurity Behaviors: A Replication Impulsivity View project*. Academic Press.

Aloul, F. A. (2012). The Need for Effective Information Security Awareness. *Journal of Advances in Information Technology*, *3*(3). Advance online publication. doi:10.4304/jait.3.3.176-183

Anderson, A. J., Kaplan, S. A., & Vega, R. P. (2014). The impact of telework on emotional experience: When, and for whom, does telework improve daily affective well-being? *European Journal of Work and Organizational Psychology*, *24*(6), 882–897. doi:10.1080/1359432X.2014.966086

Anderson, R., Barton, C., Böhme, R., Clayton, R., Gañán, C., Grasso, T., Levi, M., Moore, T., & Vasek, M. (2019). *Measuring the Changing Cost of Cyber-crime*. Available from: https://www.paccsresearch.org.uk/wp content/uploads/2019/06/WEIS_2019_paper_25.pdf

Andreassen, C. S., Griffiths, M. D., Gjertsen, S. R., Krossbakken, E., Kvam, S., & Pallesen, S. (2013). The relationships between behavioral addictions and the five-factor model of personality. *Journal of Behavioral Addictions*, *2*(2), 90–99. doi:10.1556/JBA.2.2013.003 PMID:26165928

Apollo Technical. (2021). *Statistics On Remote Workers That Will Surprise You (2021).* Apollo Technical LLC. Available from: https://www.apollotechnical.com/statistics-on-remote-workers /

Aybar, C. A. M., Speranza, M., Armstrong, L., Ames, J., Phillips, G., & Saling, L. (2000). Potential determinants of heavier internet usage Related papers Psychological predictors of problem mobile phone use margigretel An Investigation of Goodman's Addictive Disorder Criteria in Eating Disorders Potential determinants of heavier internet usage. *International Journal of Human-Computer Studies*, *53*, 537–550.

Bellekens, X. (2021). Cyber security in the age of COVID-19: A timeline and analysis of cyber-crime and cyber-attacks during the pandemic. *Computers & Security*, *105*, 102248. doi:10.1016/j.cose.2021.102248 PMID:36540648

Bick, A., Blandin, A., & Mertens, K. (2021). *Work from Home Before and After the COVID-19 Outbreak*. Federal Reserve Bank of Dallas, Working Papers.

Błachnio, A., Przepiorka, A., Senol-Durak, E., Durak, M., & Sherstyuk, L. (2017). The role of personality traits in Facebook and Internet addictions: A study on Polish, Turkish, and Ukrainian samples. *Computers in Human Behavior*, *68*, 269–275. doi:10.1016/j.chb.2016.11.037

Bonenberger, A. (2020). *Falling Through the Cracks in Quarantine*. Available from: https://medicine.yale.edu/news-article/falling-through-the-cracks-in-quarantine/

Borlovich, D., & Skovira, R. (2020). Working from home: Cybersecurity in the age of COVID-19. *Issues In Information Systems*.

Boyce, M. W., Duma, K. M., Hettinger, L. J., Malone, T. B., Wilson, D. P., & Lockett-Reynolds, J. (2011). Human Performance in Cybersecurity: A Research Agenda. *Proceedings of the Human Factors and Ergonomics Society Annual Meeting*, *55*(1), 1115–1119. doi:10.1177/1071181311551233

Brenner, V. (1997). Psychology of Computer Use: XLVII. Parameters of Internet Use, Abuse and Addiction: The First 90 Days of the Internet Usage Survey. *Psychological Reports*, *80*(3), 879–882. doi:10.2466/pr0.1997.80.3.879 PMID:9198388

Brooks, S. K., Webster, R. K., Smith, L. E., Woodland, L., Wessely, S., Greenberg, N., & Rubin, G. J. (2020). The psychological impact of quarantine and how to reduce it: Rapid review of the evidence. [online]. *Lancet*, *395*(10227), 912–920. doi:10.1016/S0140-6736(20)30460-8 PMID:32112714

Bryan, K. (2020). *Fraudsters impersonate airlines and Tesco in coronavirus scams*. https://www.thetimes.co.uk/article/fraudsters-impersonate-airlines-and-tesco-in-coronavirus-scams-5wdwhxq7p

Calic, D., Pattinson, M., Parsons, K., Butavicius, M., & Mccormac, A. (2016). *Naïve and Accidental Behaviors that Compromise Information Security: What the Experts Think*. Academic Press.

Caplan, S., Williams, D., & Yee, N. (2009). Problematic Internet use and psychosocial well-being among MMO players. *Computers in Human Behavior*, *25*(6), 1312–1319. doi:10.1016/j.chb.2009.06.006

Caplan, S. E. (2002). Problematic Internet use and psychosocial well-being: Development of a theory-based cognitive–behavioral measurement instrument. *Computers in Human Behavior*, *18*(5), 553–575. doi:10.1016/S0747-5632(02)00004-3

Caplan, S. E. (2003). Preference for Online Social Interaction. *Communication Research*, *30*(6), 625–648. doi:10.1177/0093650203257842

Cellini, N., Canale, N., Mioni, G., & Costa, S. (2020). Changes in sleep pattern, sense of time and digital media use during COVID-19 lockdown in Italy. *Journal of Sleep Research*, *29*(4). Advance online publication. doi:10.1111/jsr.13074 PMID:32410272

Chung, H., Seo, H., Forbes, S., & Birkett, H. (2020). *Working from home during the COVID-19 lockdown: changing preferences and the future of work.* Available from: https://kar.kent.ac.uk/83896/

Ciotti, M., Ciccozzi, M., Terrinoni, A., Jiang, W.-C., Wang, C.-B., & Bernardini, S. (2020). The COVID-19 Pandemic. *Critical Reviews in Clinical Laboratory Sciences*, *57*(6), 365–388. doi:10.1080/10408363.2020.1783198 PMID:32645276

CISA. (2021). *CISA Cybersecurity Awareness Program.* Available from: https://www.cisa.gov/cisa-cybersecurity-awareness-program

Cryan, J. F., & Holmes, A. (2005). The ascent of mouse: Advances in modelling human depression and anxiety. *Nature Reviews. Drug Discovery*, *4*(9), 775–790. doi:10.1038/nrd1825 PMID:16138108

Cullen, W., Gulati, G., & Kelly, B. D. (2020). Mental health in the Covid-19 pandemic. *QJM: An International Journal of Medicine*, *113*(5). Available from: https://academic.oup.com/qjmed/article/113/5/311/5813733?login=true

CyberArk. (2018). *Survey: 46 Percent of Organizations Fail to Change Security Strategy After a Cyber Attack.* CyberArk. Retrieved on May 6, 2022, from: https://www.cyberark.com/press/global-advanced-threat-landscape-report-2018/

Davillas, A., & Jones, A. M. (2020). *The COVID-19 Pandemic and its Impact on Inequality of Opportunity in Psychological Distress in the UK.* Available from: https://papers.ssrn.com/sol3/papers.cfm?abstract_id=3614940

Davis, R. A. (2001). A cognitive-behavioral model of pathological Internet use. *Computers in Human Behavior*, *17*(2), 187–195. doi:10.1016/S0747-5632(00)00041-8

Dawson, J., & Thomson, R. (2018). The Future Cybersecurity Workforce: Going Beyond Technical Skills for Successful Cyber Performance. *Frontiers in Psychology*, *9*, 9. doi:10.3389/fpsyg.2018.00744 PMID:29946276

Demetrovics, Z., Király, O., Koronczai, B., Griffiths, M. D., Nagygyörgy, K., Elekes, Z., Tamás, D., Kun, B., Kökönyei, G., & Urbán, R. (2016). Psychometric Properties of the Problematic Internet Use Questionnaire Short-Form (PIUQ-SF-6) in a Nationally Representative Sample of Adolescents. *PLoS One*, *11*(8), e0159409. doi:10.1371/journal.pone.0159409 PMID:27504915

Deutrom, J., Katos, V., Al-Mourad, M. B., & Ali, R. (2022). The Relationships between Gender, Life Satisfaction, Loneliness and Problematic Internet Use during COVID-19: Does the Lockdown Matter? *International Journal of Environmental Research and Public Health*, *19*(3), 1325. doi:10.3390/ijerph19031325 PMID:35162348

Deutrom, J., Katos, V., & Ali, R. (2021). Loneliness, life satisfaction, problematic internet use and security behaviors: Re-examining the relationships when working from home during COVID-19. *Behaviour & Information Technology*, 1–15.

Dolan, P., Hallsworth, M., Halpern, D., King, D., Metcalfe, R., & Vlaev, I. (2012). Influencing behaviour: The mindspace way. *Journal of Economic Psychology*, *33*(1), 264–277. doi:10.1016/j.joep.2011.10.009

Donaldson, S. I., & Grant-Vallone, E. J. (2002). Understanding Self-Report Bias in Organizational Behavior Research. *Journal of Business and Psychology*, *17*(2), 245–260. doi:10.1023/A:1019637632584

Dufour, M., Brunelle, N., Tremblay, J., Leclerc, D., Cousineau, M.-M., Khazaal, Y., Légaré, A.-A., Rousseau, M., & Berbiche, D. (2016). Gender Difference in Internet Use and Internet Problems among Quebec High School Students. *Canadian Journal of Psychiatry*, *61*(10), 663–668. doi:10.1177/0706743716640755 PMID:27310231

Durak, M., & Senol-Durak, E. (2014). Which personality traits are associated with cognitions related to problematic Internet use? *Asian Journal of Social Psychology*, *17*(3), 206–218. doi:10.1111/ajsp.12056

Egelman, S., Harbach, M., & Peer, E. (2016). Behavior Ever Follows Intention? *Proceedings of the 2016 CHI Conference on Human Factors in Computing Systems*. 10.1145/2858036.2858265

Egelman, S., & Peer, E. (2015). Predicting privacy and security attitudes. *Computers & Society*, *45*(1), 22–28. doi:10.1145/2738210.2738215

Erwin, B. A., Turk, C. L., Heimberg, R. G., Fresco, D. M., & Hantula, D. A. (2004). The Internet: Home to a severe population of individuals with social anxiety disorder? *Journal of Anxiety Disorders*, *18*(5), 629–646. doi:10.1016/j.janxdis.2003.08.002 PMID:15275943

Feldmann, A., Gasser, O., Lichtblau, F., Poese, I., Christoph, B., De-Cix, D., Wagner, D., De-Cix, M., Tapiador, J., Vallina-Rodriguez, N., Hohlfeld, O., Smaragdakis, G., & Berlin, T. (2020). The Lockdown Effect: Implications of the COVID-19 Pandemic on Internet Traffic. *Enric Pujol BENOCS, 20.*

Fiske, D. W. (1949). Consistency of the factorial structures of personality ratings from different sources. *Journal of Abnormal and Social Psychology*, *44*(3), 329–344. doi:10.1037/h0057198 PMID:18146776

Fogg, B. (2009). *A Behavior Model for Persuasive Design*. Academic Press.

Forsyth, D. R. (2008). *International Encyclopedia of the Social Sciences*. Available from: https://scholarship.richmond.edu/cgi/viewcontent.cgi?article=1164&context=jepson-faculty-publications

Furnell, S., & Clarke, N. (2012). Power to the people? The evolving recognition of human aspects of security. *Computers & Security*, *31*(8), 983–988. doi:10.1016/j.cose.2012.08.004

Garfin, D. R. (2020). Technology as a Coping Tool during the COVID-19 Pandemic: Implications and Recommendations. *Stress and Health*, *36*(4). PMID:32762116

Gierveld, J. D. J., & Tilburg, T. V. (2006). A 6-Item Scale for Overall, Emotional, and Social Loneliness. *Research on Aging*, *28*(5), 582–598. doi:10.1177/0164027506289723

Girdhar, R., Srivastava, V., & Sethi, S. (2020). Managing mental health issues among elderly during COVID-19 pandemic. *Journal of Geriatric Care and Research*, *7*(1). http://pu.edu.pk/MHH-COVID-19/Articles/Article22.pdf

Goffman, E. (1956). *The Presentation of Self in Everyday Life*. Available from: https://monoskop.org/images/1/19/Goffman_Erving_The_Presentation_of_Self_in_Everyday_Life.pdf

Goldberg, L. R. (1992). The development of markers for the Big-Five factor structure. *Psychological Assessment*, *4*(1), 26–42. doi:10.1037/1040-3590.4.1.26

Greenfield, D. N., & Davis, R. A. (2002). Lost in Cyberspace: The Web @ Work. *Cyberpsychology & Behavior*, *5*(4), 347–353. doi:10.1089/109493102760275590 PMID:12216699

Griffiths, M. (2010). Internet abuse and internet addiction in the workplace. *Journal of Workplace Learning*, *22*(7), 463–472. doi:10.1108/13665621011071127

Hadlington, L. (2017). Human factors in cybersecurity; examining the link between Internet addiction, impulsivity, attitudes towards cybersecurity, and risky cybersecurity behaviors. *Heliyon*, *3*(7), e00346. doi:10.1016/j.heliyon.2017.e00346 PMID:28725870

Hadlington, L., & Murphy, K. (2018). Is Media Multitasking Good for Cybersecurity? Exploring the Relationship Between Media Multitasking and Everyday Cognitive Failures on Self-Reported Risky Cybersecurity Behaviors. *Cyberpsychology, Behavior, and Social Networking*, *21*(3), 168–172. doi:10.1089/cyber.2017.0524 PMID:29638157

Hadlington, L., & Parsons, K. (2017). Can Cyberloafing and Internet Addiction Affect Organizational Information Security? *Cyberpsychology, Behavior, and Social Networking*, *20*(9), 567–571. doi:10.1089/cyber.2017.0239 PMID:28872364

Henshel, D., Cains, M. G., Hoffman, B., & Kelley, T. (2015). Trust as a Human Factor in Holistic Cyber Security Risk Assessment. *Procedia Manufacturing*, *3*, 1117–1124. doi:10.1016/j.promfg.2015.07.186

Higgins, E. T. (1998). Promotion and Prevention: Regulatory Focus as A Motivational Principle. *Advances in Experimental Social Psychology*, *30*, 1–46. Available from: https://www.sciencedirect.com/science/article/pii/S0065260108603810

Hu, Q., West, R., & Smarandescu, L. (2015). The Role of Self-Control in Information Security Violations: Insights from a Cognitive Neuroscience Perspective. *Journal of Management Information Systems*, *31*(4), 6–48. doi:10.1080/07421222.2014.1001255

Hughes, M. E., Waite, L. J., Hawkley, L. C., & Cacioppo, J. T. (2004). A Short Scale for Measuring Loneliness in Large Surveys. *Research on Aging*, *26*(6), 655–672. doi:10.1177/0164027504268574 PMID:18504506

IBM. (2020). *Cost of a Data Breach Report 2020 2 Contents*. Available from: https://www.capita.com/sites/g/files/nginej291/files/2020-08/Ponemon-Global-Cost-of-Data-Breach-Study-2020.pdf

Institute for Government. (2021). *Timeline of UK Government Coronavirus Lockdowns*. Available from: https://www.instituteforgovernment.org.uk/charts/uk-government-coronavirus-lockdowns

Ipsen, C., van Veldhoven, M., Kirchner, K., & Hansen, J. P. (2021). Six Key Advantages and Disadvantages of Working from Home in Europe during COVID-19. *International Journal of Environmental Research and Public Health*, *18*(4), 1–17. doi:10.3390/ijerph18041826 PMID:33668505

Jessor, R. (1987). Problem-Behavior Theory, Psychosocial Development, and Adolescent Problem Drinking. *Addiction*, *82*(4), 331–342. Retrieved on June 2, 2021 from: https://onlinelibrary.wiley.com/doi/abs/10.1111/j.1360-0443.1987.tb01490.x

Kassin, S. M., Dror, I. E., & Kukucka, J. (2013). The forensic confirmation bias: Problems, perspectives, and proposed solutions. *Journal of Applied Research in Memory and Cognition*, *2*(1), 42–52. doi:10.1016/j.jarmac.2013.01.001

Keller, C., Siegrist, M., & Gutscher, H. (2006). The Role of the Affect and Availability Heuristics in Risk Communication. *Risk Analysis*, *26*(3), 631–639. doi:10.1111/j.1539-6924.2006.00773.x PMID:16834623

Kim, J., LaRose, R., & Peng, W. (2009). Loneliness as the Cause and the Effect of Problematic Internet Use: The Relationship between Internet Use and Psychological Well-Being. *Cyberpsychology & Behavior*, *12*(4), 451–455. doi:10.1089/cpb.2008.0327 PMID:19514821

King P, D., Delfabbro, P., Billieux, J., & Potenza, M. (2020). *Problematic online gaming and the COVID-19 pandemic*. Academic Press.

Király, O., Potenza, M. N., Stein, D. J., King, D. L., Hodgins, D. C., Saunders, J. B., Griffiths, M. D., Gjoneska, B., Billieux, J., Brand, M., Abbott, M. W., Chamberlain, S. R., Corazza, O., Burkauskas, J., Sales, C. M. D., Montag, C., Lochner, C., Grünblatt, E., Wegmann, E., ... Demetrovics, Z. (2020). Preventing problematic internet use during the COVID-19 pandemic: Consensus guidance. *Comprehensive Psychiatry*, *100*, 152180. doi:10.1016/j.comppsych.2020.152180 PMID:32422427

Kumar, P., Kumar, N., Aggarwal, P., & Yeap, J. A. L. (2021). Working in lockdown: The relationship between COVID-19 induced work stressors, job performance, distress, and life satisfaction. *Current Psychology (New Brunswick, N.J.)*, *40*(12), 6308–6323. doi:10.100712144-021-01567-0 PMID:33746462

Kumaran, N., & Lugani, S. (2020). *Protecting against cyber threats during COVID-19 and beyond*. Google Cloud Blog. Retrieved on August 14, 2021 from: https://cloud.google.com/blog/products/identity-security/protecting-against-cyber-threats-during-covid-19-and-beyond

Kuss, D. J., Griffiths, M. D., & Binder, J. F. (2013). Internet addiction in students: Prevalence and risk factors. *Computers in Human Behavior*, *29*(3), 959–966. doi:10.1016/j.chb.2012.12.024

Laricchia, F. (2022). *Average number of connected devices in UK households 2020*. Statista. Retrieved on September 22, 2022 from: https://www.statista.com/statistics/1107269/average-number-connected-devices-uk-house/

LaRose, R., Lin, C. A., & Eastin, M. S. (2003). Unregulated Internet Usage: Addiction, Habit, or Deficient Self-Regulation? *Media Psychology*, *5*(3), 225–253. doi:10.1207/S1532785XMEP0503_01

Lavie, N., Beck, D. M., & Konstantinou, N. (2014). Blinded by the load: Attention, awareness and the role of perceptual load. *Philosophical Transactions of the Royal Society of London. Series B, Biological Sciences*, *369*(1641), 20130205. doi:10.1098/rstb.2013.0205 PMID:24639578

Li, W., Yang, Y., Liu, Z.-H., Zhao, Y.-J., Zhang, Q., Zhang, L., Cheung, T., & Xiang, Y.-T. (2020). Progression of Mental Health Services during the COVID-19 Outbreak in China. *International Journal of Biological Sciences*, *16*(10), 1732–1738. doi:10.7150/ijbs.45120 PMID:32226291

Mayhew, S. (2020). The COVID-19 vaccine development landscape. *Nature Reviews. Drug Discovery*, *19*(19). Retrieved October 14, 2022, from https://www.nature.com/articles/d41573-020-00073-5

Mcalaney, J., & Benson, V. (2020). Cybersecurity as a social phenomenon. *Cyber Influence and Cognitive Threats*, 1–8. Retrieved on April 24, 2021 from: https://www.sciencedirect.com/science/article/pii/B9780128192047000014

McKenna, K. Y. A., & Bargh, J. A. (1999). Causes and Consequences of Social Interaction on the Internet: A Conceptual Framework. *Media Psychology*, *1*(3), 249–269. doi:10.12071532785xmep0103_4

McKenna, K. Y. A., Green, A. S., & Gleason, M. E. J. (2002). Relationship Formation on the Internet: What's the Big Attraction? *The Journal of Social Issues*, *58*(1), 9–31. doi:10.1111/1540-4560.00246

Meerkerk, G.-J., Van Den Eijnden, R. J. J. M., Vermulst, A. A., & Garretsen, H. F. L. (2009). The Compulsive Internet Use Scale (CIUS): Some Psychometric Properties. *Cyberpsychology & Behavior*, *12*(1), 1–6. doi:10.1089/cpb.2008.0181 PMID:19072079

Mestre-Bach, G., Blycker, G. R., & Potenza, M. N. (2020). Pornography use in the setting of the COVID-19 pandemic. *Journal of Behavioral Addictions*, *9*(2), 181–183. doi:10.1556/2006.2020.00015 PMID:32663384

Meyer, C. (2022). *COVID-19 Fraud Could Cost UK Government Billions*. Retrieved on May 5, 2022 from: https://www.asisonline.org/security-management-magazine/latest-news/today-in-security/2022/february/covid19-fraud-could-cost-UK-government-billions/

Morahan-Martin, J., & Schumacher, P. (2000). Incidence and correlates of pathological Internet use among college students. *Computers in Human Behavior*, *16*(1), 13–29. doi:10.1016/S0747-5632(99)00049-7

Morgan, S. (2020). Global Cybercrime Damages Predicted To Reach $6 Trillion Annually By 2021. *Cybercrime Magazine*. Retrieved on September 18, 2021, from: https://cybersecurityventures.com/cybercrime-damages-6-trillion-by-2021/

Moukaddam, N. (2020). Psychiatrists Beware! The Impact of COVID-19 and Pandemics on Mental Health. *Psychiatric Times*. Retrieved on May 21, 2022, from: https://www.psychiatrictimes.com/view/psychiatrists-beware-impact-coronavirus-pandemics-mental-health

Moustafa, A. A., Bello, A., & Maurushat, A. (2021). The Role of User Behaviour in Improving Cyber Security Management. *Frontiers in Psychology*, *12*, 12. doi:10.3389/fpsyg.2021.561011 PMID:34220596

Mucci, F., Mucci, N., & Diolaiuti, F. (2020). Lockdown and Isolation: Psychological Aspects of Covid-19 Pandemic in the General Population. *Clinical Neuropsychiatry*, *17*(2), 63–64. Retrieved on April 4, 2022, from: https://www.ncbi.nlm.nih.gov/pmc/articles/PMC8629090/

Mudra Rakshasa, A., & Tong, M. T. (2020). Making 'Good' Choices: Social Isolation in Mice Exacerbates the Effects of Chronic Stress on Decision Making. *Frontiers in Behavioral Neuroscience*, *14*, 14. doi:10.3389/fnbeh.2020.00081 PMID:32523519

NCSC. (2020). *Advisory: COVID-19 exploited by malicious cyber actors*. Retrieved on January 30, 2022, from: https://www.ncsc.gov.uk/news/covid-19-exploited-by-cyber-actors-advisory

Nobles, C. (2018). Botching Human Factors in Cybersecurity in Business Organizations. *HOLISTICA – Journal of Business and Public Administration*, *9*(3), 71–88.

Nurse, J. R. C. (2018). Cybercrime and You: How Criminals Attack and the Human Factors That They Seek to Exploit. The Oxford Handbook of Cyberpsychology, 662–690.

Office for National Statistics. (2021). *Internet users, UK - Office for National Statistics*. Retrieved on January 22, 2022, from: https://www.ons.gov.uk/businessindustryandtrade/itandinternetindustry/bulletins/internetusers/2020

Olenik-Shemesh, D., Heiman, T., & Eden, S. (2012). Cyberbullying victimisation in adolescence: Relationships with loneliness and depressive mood. *Emotional & Behavioural Difficulties*, *17*(3-4), 361–374. doi:10.1080/13632752.2012.704227

ONS. (2021). *Business and individual attitudes towards the future of homeworking, UK - Office for National Statistics*. Retrieved on January 22, 2022, from: https://www.ons.gov.uk/employmentandlabourmarket/peopleinwork/employmentandemployeetypes/articles/businessandindividualattitudestowardsthefutureofhomeworkinguk/apriltomay2021

p, R. (2000). Examination of Psychological Processes Underlying Resistance to Persuasion. *Journal of Consumer Research*, *27*(2), 217–232.

Panda Security. (2020). *Is COVID-19 Making Cyberbullying Worse?* Panda Security Mediacenter. Retrieved on May 6, 2022, from: https://www.pandasecurity.com/en/mediacenter/mobile-news/covid-19-cyberbullying/

Papadatou, A. (2018). Workers are risking GDPR penalties by forwarding work emails to personal accounts. *HRreview*. Retrieved on August 4, 2020, from: https://www.hrreview.co.uk/hr-news/workers-are-risking-gdpr-penalties/114090#:~:text=Workers%20are%20risking%20GDPR%20pe nalties%20by%20forwarding%20work%20emails%20to%20personal%20 accounts

Pham, M. (2021). *Remote Work Security Survey Results: Is Remote Work Really Secure?* Retrieved on May 4, 2022, from: https://www.wrike.com/blog/remote-work-security-survey/

Pierce, M., Mcmanus, S., Hope, H., Hotopf, M., Ford, T., Hatch, S., John, A., Kontopantelis, E., Webb, R., Wessely, S., & Abel, K. (2021). Mental health responses to the COVID-19 pandemic: A latent class trajectory analysis using longitudinal UK data. *The Lancet. Psychiatry*, *8*(7), 610–629. doi:10.1016/S2215-0366(21)00151-6 PMID:33965057

Przepiorka, A., Blachnio, A., & Cudo, A. (2019). The role of depression, personality, and future time perspective in internet addiction in adolescents and emerging adults. *Psychiatry Research*, *272*, 340–348. doi:10.1016/j.psychres.2018.12.086 PMID:30599437

Przepiorka, A., Blachnio, A., & Cudo, A. (2020). Relationships between morningness, Big Five personality traits, and problematic Internet use in young adult university students: Mediating role of depression. *Chronobiology International*, *38*(2), 248–259. doi:10.1080/07420528.2020.1851703 PMID:33317359

Rawlings, R. (2020). *Password habits in the US and the UK*. Retrieved on May 5, 2022 from: https://nordpass.com/blog/password-habits-statistics/

Sadkhan, S. (2019). *Cognition and the future of information security*. Academic Press.

Schneier, B. (2015). *Digital Security in a Networked World*. Academic Press.

Scroxton, A. (2021). *UK loses £1.3bn to fraud and cyber crime so far this year*. Retrieved on July 4, 2022, from: https://www.computerweekly.com/news/252505825/UK-loses-13bn-to-fraud-and-cyber-crime-so-far-this-year#:~:text=Individual s%20and%20organisations%20in%20the

Servidio, R. (2014). Exploring the effects of demographic factors, Internet usage and personality traits on Internet addiction in a sample of Italian university students. *Computers in Human Behavior*, *35*, 85–92. doi:10.1016/j.chb.2014.02.024

Smith, S. (2022). *Human-Computer Interaction and Security*. Academic Press.

Spada, M. M. (2014). An overview of problematic Internet use. *Addictive Behaviors*, *39*(1), 3–6. doi:10.1016/j.addbeh.2013.09.007 PMID:24126206

Steinberg, L., & Morris, A. (2001). Adolescent development. *Annual Review of Psychology*, *52*(1), 83–110. doi:10.1146/annurev.psych.52.1.83 PMID:11148300

Su, W., Han, X., Jin, C., Yan, Y., & Potenza, M. N. (2019). Are males more likely to be addicted to the internet than females? A meta-analysis involving 34 global jurisdictions. *Computers in Human Behavior*, *99*, 86–100. doi:10.1016/j.chb.2019.04.021

Su, W., Han, X., Yu, H., Wu, Y., & Potenza, M. N. (2020). Do men become addicted to internet gaming and women to social media? A meta-analysis examining gender-related differences in specific internet addiction. *Computers in Human Behavior*, *113*, 106480. doi:10.1016/j.chb.2020.106480

Taylor, J., & Turner, R. J. (2002). Perceived Discrimination, Social Stress, and Depression in the Transition to Adulthood: Racial Contrasts. *Social Psychology Quarterly*, *65*(3), 213. doi:10.2307/3090120

Thatcher, A., & Goolam, S. (2005). Development and psychometric properties of the Problematic Internet Use Questionnaire. *South African Journal of Psychology. Suid-Afrikaanse Tydskrif vir Sielkunde*, *35*(4), 793–809. Retrieved May 9, 2022, from https://hdl.handle.net/10520/EJC98345. doi:10.1177/008124630503500410

Trzebiński, J., Cabański, M., & Czarnecka, J. Z. (2020). Reaction to the COVID-19 Pandemic: The Influence of Meaning in Life, Life Satisfaction, and Assumptions on World Orderliness and Positivity. *Journal of Loss and Trauma*, *25*(6-7), 544–557. doi:10.1080/15325024.2020.1765098

West, R. (2008). *The Psychology of Security | April 2008 | Communications of the ACM*. Retrieved on November 11, 2021, from: https://cacm.acm.org/magazines/2008/4/5436-the-psychology-of-security/fulltext

Whitty, M., Doodson, J., Creese, S., & Hodges, D. (2015). Individual Differences in Cyber Security Behaviors: An Examination of Who Is Sharing Passwords. *Cyberpsychology, Behavior, and Social Networking*, *18*(1), 3–7. doi:10.1089/cyber.2014.0179 PMID:25517697

Wiederhold, B. K. (2014). The Role of Psychology in Enhancing Cybersecurity. *Cyberpsychology, Behavior, and Social Networking*, *17*(3), 131–132. doi:10.1089/cyber.2014.1502 PMID:24592869

Wittenberg, M. T., & Reis, H. T. (1986). Loneliness, Social Skills, and Social Perception. *Personality and Social Psychology Bulletin*, *12*(1), 121–130. doi:10.1177/0146167286121012

Witteveen, D. (2020). Sociodemographic inequality in exposure to COVID-19-induced economic hardship in the United Kingdom. *Research in Social Stratification and Mobility*, *69*, 100551. doi:10.1016/j.rssm.2020.100551 PMID:32921869

World Economuc Forum. (2020). *A Preliminary Mapping and Its Implications*. Retrieved on October 14, 2021, from: https://www3.weforum.org/docs/WEF_COVID_19_Risks_Outlook_Special_Edition_Pages.pdf

World Health Organisations Europe. (2010). *Addressing socioeconomic and gender inequities in the WHO European Region Social and gender inequalities in environment and health*. Retrieved on September 22, 2022, from: https://www.euro.who.int/__data/assets/pdf_file/0010/76519/Parma_EH_Conf_pb1.pdf

World Health Organization. (2020). *Coronavirus Disease (COVID-19) - Events as They Happen*. Retrieved on September 14, 2022, from: https://www.who.int/emergencies/diseases/novel-coronavirus-2019/events-as-they-happen

Worldometer. (2022). *Coronavirus toll update: Cases & deaths by country*. Worldometers. Retrieved on September 14, 2022, from: https://www.worldometers.info/coronavirus/

Yen, J.-Y., Ko, C.-H., Yen, C.-F., Wu, H.-Y., & Yang, M.-J. (2007). The Comorbid Psychiatric Symptoms of Internet Addiction: Attention Deficit and Hyperactivity Disorder (ADHD), Depression, Social Phobia, and Hostility. *The Journal of Adolescent Health*, *41*(1), 93–98. doi:10.1016/j.jadohealth.2007.02.002 PMID:17577539

Young, S. (2008). The neurobiology of human social behaviour: An important but neglected topic. *Journal of Psychiatry & Neuroscience*, *33*(5). PMID:18787656

Zhang, P., Zhang, Y., Mu, Z., & Liu, X. (2017). The Development of Conformity Among Chinese Children Aged 9–15 Years in a Public Choice Task. *Evolutionary Psychology*, *15*(4), 147470491774363. doi:10.1177/1474704917743637 PMID:29169263

Zhou, M., & Kan, M.-Y. (2020). *The varying impacts of COVID-19 and its related measures in the UK: A year in review*. Academic Press.

Zhou, Y., Li, D., Li, X., Wang, Y., & Zhao, L. (2017). Big five personality and adolescent Internet addiction: The mediating role of coping style. *Addictive Behaviors*, *64*, 42–48. doi:10.1016/j.addbeh.2016.08.009 PMID:27543833

Zscaler. (2020). *30,000 Percent Increase in COVID-19-Themed Attacks*. Zscaler. Retrieved on May 6, 2022, from: https://www.zscaler.com/blogs/security-research/30000-percent-increase-covid-19-themed-attacks

Chapter 2
A Comprehensive Cybersecurity Framework for Present and Future Global Information Technology Organizations

Wasswa Shafik
https://orcid.org/0000-0002-9320-3186
School of Digital Science, Universiti Brunei Darussalam, Gadong, Brunei & Digital Connectivity Research Laboratory (DCRLab), Kampala, Uganda

ABSTRACT

This chapter examines how education, technology, national and international regulations contribute to a comprehensive cybersecurity framework for present and future global IT companies. IT-driven enterprises may utilize the following security recommendations. Businesses who seek to examine their external and internal security with security upload and establish settings for success regardless of location must solve these issues. To produce more effective legislation, education efforts, and technologies that are resistant to cyberattacks, this work explores fundamental research gaps in cybersecurity and demonstrates how cybersecurity may be divided into these three fundamental categories and integrated to tackle problems such as the creation of training environments for authentic cybersecurity situations. It will explain links between technology and certification and discuss legislative standards and instructional frameworks for merging criteria for system accreditation and cybersecurity. The study finishes with wireless network security recommendations.

INTRODUCTION

There is a common misconception that security and usability are mutually exclusive system goals (Nyarko & Fong, 2023). Studies even go so far as to ask whether the phrase "useful security" is an oxymoron or not. When it comes to passwords, one of the security methods that is utilized daily, we see a typical illustration of how the goals of these two notions are diametrically opposed to one another (Conchon,

DOI: 10.4018/978-1-6684-9018-1.ch002

2023; Montasari, 2023). From a security point of view, it's best to have long, complicated (hard to guess), unique passwords that are changed every so often. However, from a usability point of view, these requirements are often a big burden on users and, as a result, the usability of a system (Netshakhuma, 2023).

Most of these more general security concerns also arise in the context of cybersecurity, where the focus is on the digital environment (Shaikh & Siponen, 2023). Therefore, the challenge that is faced by the fields of cybersecurity Usability and comparable Human-Computer Interaction and Security concepts are bridging the conceptual and application gaps, emphasizing the importance of fusing these two concepts, resulting in usable cybersecurity interfaces and systems (Kamariotou & Kitsios, 2023). This is especially true as functions and features related to security become increasingly integrated into software programs and end-user systems as standard components.

Common examples of these user-facing applications and systems include word processing software (with tasks such as adding digital signatures to facilitate subsequent document authentication), document readers (which allow setting viewing, access, and printing permissions), personal devices (with activities such as applying security pins and locks to mobile phones), personal security firewalls, and email encryption tools (Bukauskas et al., 2023). All these applications and systems are designed to interact directly with the user. All of these are related in some way to the regular activities that take place in the online world.

The purpose of this chapter is to provide a brief overview of some of the most significant advancements that have been made in the fields of cybersecurity usability and HCISec, particularly the guidance and recommendations offered for highly usable cybersecurity systems. Because of this, one of the most important things this study does is bring together work that has already been published and make an initial core list of general principles (AlKalbani et al., 2023). This is important because it provides a starting point for designers, developers, and users alike to begin considering the impact of usable cybersecurity on their projects.

While we do appreciate specific advice given in areas such as authentication, access control, encryption, firewalls, secure device pairing, and safe interaction, at this moment we are concentrating more on general and, as a result, generally context-independent suggestions. A list that is focused on that general level is necessary because it will form a central part of future work. This work will, among other things, include assessing the applicability (and possible targeting) of guidelines for using technologies in the standard operating procedure of organization in security controls perspective (Rawal et al., 2023). In this manner, we can develop a better understanding of how different processes and technologies can be effectively used to create secure systems. A list focused on that general level is necessary because it will form a central part of future work. We also believe that this list may have a value that extends beyond our immediate intentions because it provides a helpful state-of-the-art review that can be utilized by academics, system designers, and IT professionals (Camgöz Akdağ & Menekşe, 2023; Solar, 2023).

A framework is required to implement cybersecurity in contexts that are both national and international and that handle hyperconnectivity. The Mission Framework offers a framework that may be used to bring together the three most important aspects of cybersecurity, which are education, policies, and technologies (Purwanto et al., 2023). The education review includes a discussion of the accrediting agencies for programs connected to IT or computer science. This discussion provides insight into creative approaches to teaching cybersecurity coursework. An organization needs to do a thorough examination of the governing policies, tools, and strategies that can be advanced in the field of cybersecurity education (English & Maguire, 2023). To build a portion of the model, it is necessary to conduct additional research into a variety of ideas, including simulation, virtualization, and engineering standards.

The overarching policy goal of the framework is reflected in its incorporation of a variety of directives, standards, mandates, legislation, and best practices. Policies from the Department of Defense (DoD), the National Institute of Standards and Technology (NIST), the United States military, and other agencies may fall under this category in the United States. These policies serve as a foundation upon which companies can build further guidance and direction when formulating their policies.

The technologies section of the framework collects information on developing technologies, such as those that incorporate Internet-enabled gadgets, and brings this information into the framework (Clinton, 2023). An examination of the security posture of these technologies, which also include mobile phones, operating systems, software, and other devices, is done to guarantee compliance with cybersecurity regulations (Childers et al., 2023). In addition, these regulations require organizations to implement measures to manage risk and protect their systems from cyberattacks (Girasa, 2023). The framework also addresses the need for continuous security assessment, monitoring, and testing of the information systems.

A specialized framework was developed that encompasses education, public policy, and technological advancement. This was accomplished by conducting a comprehensive and in-depth literature review. The result of this action is displayed in Figure 1, which shows the mission framework that was developed by analyzing the education, policy, and technology of that institution. This may be seen as the output of this activity. The specific entity may be a nation, an organization, or a collection of institutions working together as a consortium. The Mission Framework was developed to be able to work toward the creation of a cybersecurity environment in any country by considering these basic themes to shape demands and incorporate requirements that must be addressed to build a secure cyber infrastructure.

Figure 1. Proposed mission framework (technology, policy, and education)

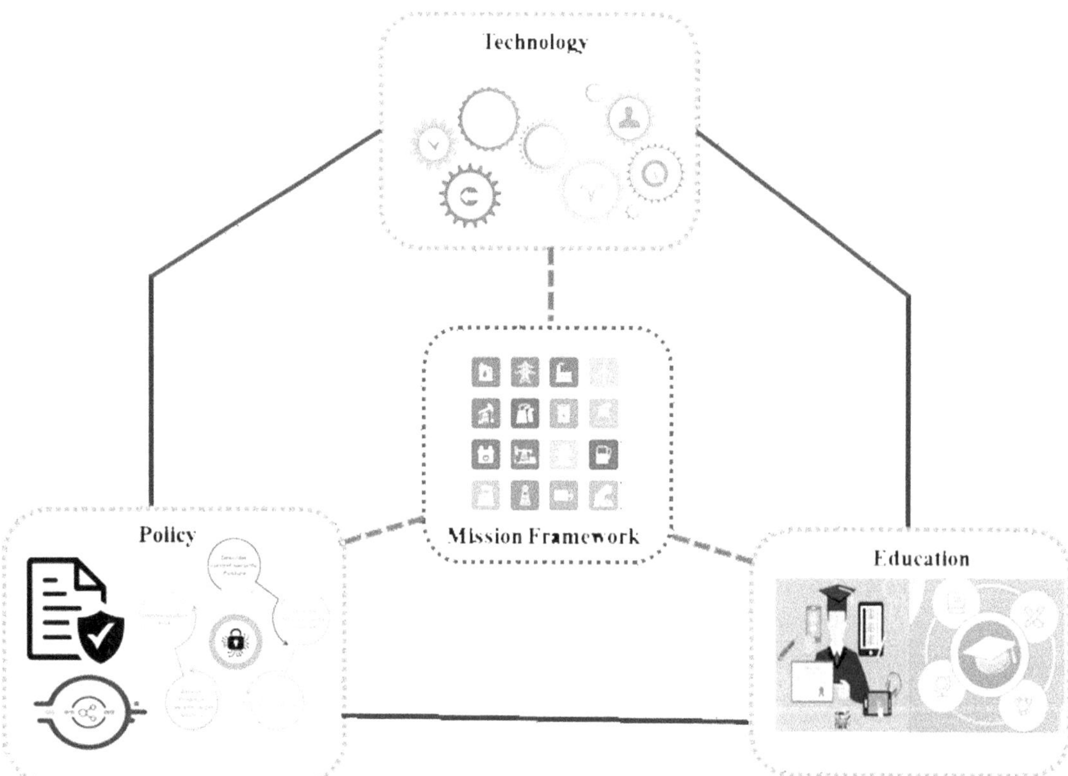

ENABLING TECHNOLOGIES

Secure computing is becoming increasingly important as environments become more entangled and hyperconnected (Girasa, 2023). As the Internet of Things (IoT), the Web of Things (WoT), and the Internet of Everything (IoE) continue to dominate the landscape of technological platforms, it is essential to ensure the safety of these intricate networks (Çubuk et al., 2023). Management must understand what it means to have more gadgets that can be linked and what potential risks they may be exposing themselves to as a result. To secure these environments, there is a need to employ enabling technologies such as encryption, identity management, access control, and authentication (Dykstra, 2023).

IoT is a global infrastructure for the information society that enables services by linking physical and virtual things using existing and evolving information communication technologies that are interoperable. The hype cycle for new technologies has been visualized by Gartner in the form of a figure that they generated. This hype circle plots the expectations along the y-axis, while the passing of time is represented along the x-axis (Figure 2). This point in time represents the inflection point for invention, the zenith of inflated expectations, the nadir of disillusionment, the ascent to enlightenment, and the plateau of productivity. The figure does not include any information regarding the safety of the technologies that are identified. The picture shows, in an easy-to-understand way, how technology changes over a period that matches expectations.

Figure 2. Emerging technologies in hype cycle
Source: Gartner (2014)

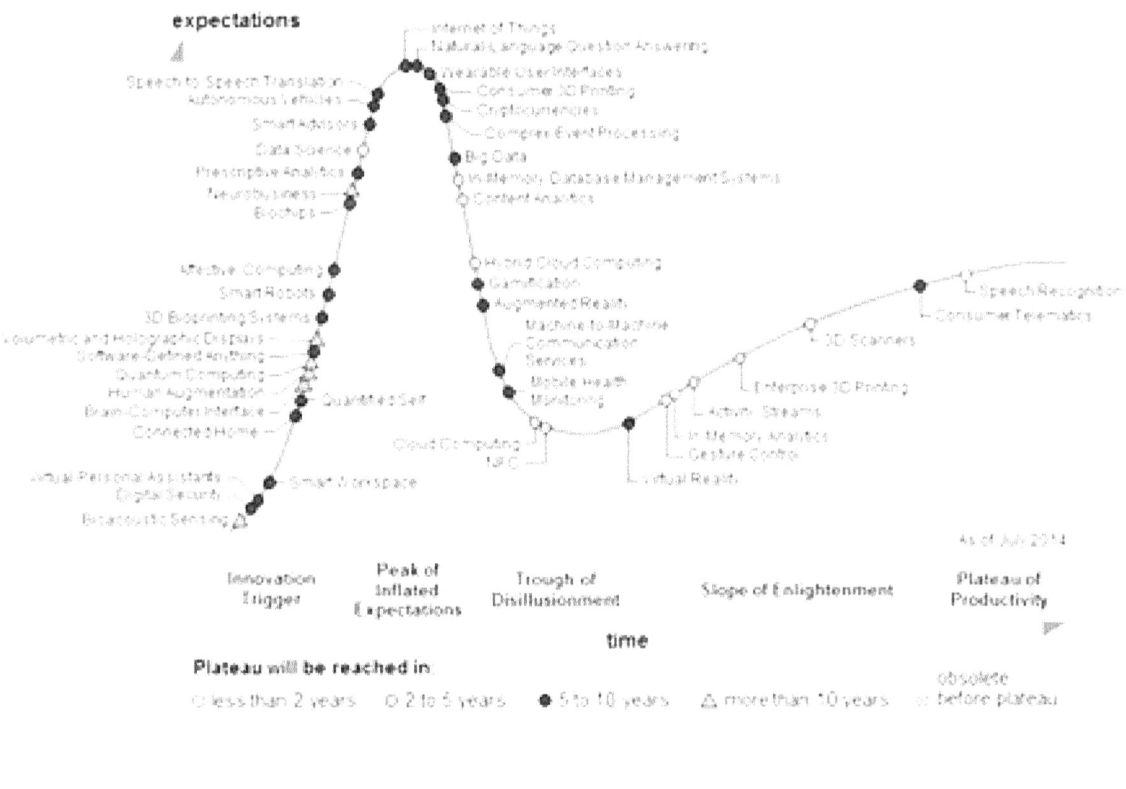

Hyper-connectivity is a developing trend that is prompting specialists in cybersecurity to build new security architectures for many platforms, such as mobile devices, laptops, and even wearable displays (Mohamed & Kamau, 2023). Such hyperconnectivity brings a new dimension to security challenges, as the more interconnected technologies become, the more vulnerable they become. These new security architectures must be compatible with multiple types of devices. During this condition of hyperconnectivity, it will be necessary to employ intricate preventative measures if there is to be any hope of preserving an appropriate security posture. This is true for both national and international security.

It is vital to understand existing and future threats to safeguard these systems from the exploitation of vulnerabilities. This understanding must include the instructions, laws, policies, regulations, and rules that drive the requirement for these systems to be secured. It is of the utmost importance to have a solid understanding of the potential dangers posed to one's safety by the usage of social media platforms, mobile devices, virtual worlds, augmented reality, and mixed reality (Shukla et al., 2023). Managers and those in executive suites need to examine what this greater Internet access means for their organization's IT policy as well as how the security posture is altered because of these additional capabilities.

A contributor to an article that was published by Forbes explains the idea of hyperconnectivity by using examples of six different situations (Turtiainen et al., 2023). These activities cover a wide spectrum, from hospitality to energy. Real-time monitoring, for instance, would be implemented in the medical field in the form of wrist monitors that the caregiving staff would be able to watch to obtain immediate real-time feeds on patients (Khan et al., 2023). Consider a pregnant woman who is experiencing early complications and can have her condition monitored by a wristband that transmits patient information wirelessly and in real-time. An attacker may begin compiling an intelligence profile on how to construct an attack most virtually and where it would receive the greatest resistance.

It is possible, for instance, that the devices that are being used on the lady to retrieve the child would experience a cyber assault and stop working in the middle of the procedure. Or there is the possibility that her medical records have been deliberately manipulated in such a way that she is receiving the incorrect therapy, putting her life in immediate jeopardy (Johri & Kumar, 2023; Shari, 2023). Changing the dosage quantities on the automated pill dispensers that ultimately dispense the medication to the patient might be as involved as it gets in this scenario.

When talking about hyperconnectivity, it is vital to study the concept of systems inside systems. Systems of systems are a collection of individual systems that have been interconnected to form a more intricate whole. When considering the potential of hyperconnectivity, the personal area network is a great example because it enables many technologies to be interconnected with different software programs (Faltermaier et al., 2023). Google glass may potentially be used for everything from the social media and global positioning system to digital terrain overlays and synchronization with other devices. Because of this, the system will become more complicated as it is added to bigger systems. This means that there will be more possible weak spots, the next section details the three main cybersecurity aspects of education, technology, directives, mandates, policies, and laws.

Education in the Cybersecurity Perspective

When developing a rigorous program to satisfy the need of being security while also participating offensively, if that is the objective of the company, it is necessary to have a thorough understanding of how successful cybersecurity is in teaching (Casey et al., 2023; Faltermaier et al., 2023). To meet the workforce requirements of a government entity, they can range from having a degree from a prestigious university to having a professional certification. One way to guarantee that the predetermined standards are being met is to gain an understanding of the requirements for the core technology program (Sadaghiani-Tabrizi, 2023). These requirements can include regional, national, or program-specific accreditation. For educational programs at institutions to be relevant to the needs of the labor force, these programs need to be developed, trained, updated, and eventually retired. The portion of the model that discusses how education must be analyzed to meet the requirements of cybersecurity education is depicted in Figure 3.

Figure 3. Proposed mission framework (education)

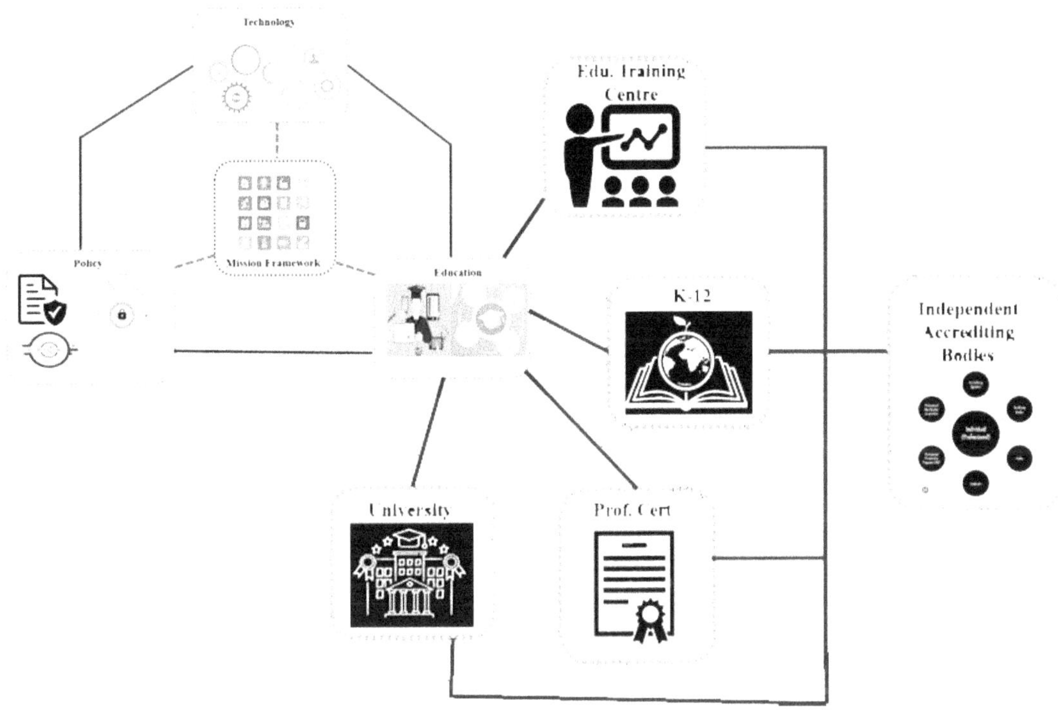

Cybersecurity programs need technology to build partnerships. Due to a lack of investment or a poor exchange rate, developing countries may have limited budgets, making technology expensive. Open-source software and cloud computing will make these operations global and affordable for all institutions. To share research, use open access (Zafar et al., 2023). Open access is best for collaborating with developing universities without large research databases. Training, education, video games, modeling, usability testing, and low-fidelity prototypes are all examples of the many forms that simulation can take. The efficiency of instruction can be improved using learning objects and other contemporary technologies like Google Glass when they are incorporated into simulations.

This section of the framework examines elementary and secondary education, as well as higher education, professional certification, executive education, and training. Independent accrediting agencies are essential to the operation of each of these educational approaches. Standards, education, and training are all things that are offered by these accrediting agencies (Johri & Kumar, 2023; Zafar et al., 2023). As an illustration, the American National Standards Institute and ISO 17024:2012 are both to be utilized as examples of organizations that are to serve as the standard for professional certificates. This enables an entity to establish minimum standards for the selection of education and training programs for cybersecurity, as well as the development of such programs.

Directives, Mandates, Policies, and Laws in the Cybersecurity Aspect

The events of September 11, 2001 not only altered policies in the United States but also altered policies in other countries regarding how they deal with and fight terrorism as a result of those events. Article 51 of the United Nations Charter was revised by the United Nations (Bada & von Solms, 2023). This article gives members of the United Nations the authority to defend themselves against violent assaults and so contributes to the maintenance of international peace and security.

Both the Prevention of Terrorism Act of 2005 and the Counter-Terrorism Act of 2008 were passed by the Parliament of the United Kingdom and became law as a result. The first act was enacted so that those suspected of being involved in terrorist acts may be detained. The Antiterrorism, Crime, and Security Act of 2001 was ruled to be unconstitutional, so it was expected that this act would replace it (Colomb et al., 2023). These acts appear to be a carbon copy of those passed in the United States to keep an eye on potential terrorists. The United States was also provided with information by the United Kingdom to facilitate the coordination of individuals who posed a potential threat.

To assure that there are no dangers on American territory, the procedures for national security in the United States have been strengthened. One of these alterations is an increase in the level of security at all entry points. The Homeland Security Act of 2002, often known as the "HS Act" (Public Law 07-296), was signed into law, which resulted in the establishment of an agency that was provided with financing and a significant number of resources to monitor the security posture of this country (Dedrick et al., 2023). Additional modifications include increased monitoring of people and residents within the country to prevent terrorist actions through the mention of terms such as bomb, terrorism, explosive, or Al-Qaeda. This monitoring is intended to take place within the country.

After the terrorist attacks of September 11, 2001, President George W. Bush rushed to have the USA Patriot Act passed into law 2001. This act was enacted as a response to the tragic events that occurred on September 11th, and it granted enhanced capabilities to several government entities (Moreta et al., 2023). Because of these improved capabilities, the government was granted the right to search various communications of individuals who were suspected of being involved in terrorist acts. Examples of these types of communications include e-mail, telephone records, and medical records. As a result, law enforcement agencies were able to get the upper hand and be more aggressive in their efforts to prevent possible attacks on US soil.

In the year 2011, former President Barack Obama gave his signature to a bill that would extend the authority of the USA Patriot Act. The public has voiced their disapproval of this act because it has the potential to be manipulated or used by people in authoritative positions. Because of this statute, government entities have been given the ability to violate constitutional rights. The Protecting Cyberspace as a National Asset Act of 2010 was a piece of legislation that, in addition to modifying other sections of the Homeland Security Act of 2002, also made changes to Title 11 (Reed et al., 2023). The resilience and safety of the United States cyberspace and communications infrastructure were both improved because of this act.

The fact that the President has stated that any form of cyberattack will be considered an act of war lends significance to this act. This is also extremely significant because the entirety of Estonia's digital infrastructure was brought to a halt by hackers who backed the rule of the old Soviet Union (Florackis et al., 2023). This kind of strike might cause severe damage to the infrastructure in the United States, leading to a loss of power that could last for days or even weeks, which in turn could cause people to die.

Israel is a nation that maintains some of the strictest policies in the world regarding both national and international security. This nation ensures its residents' safety by mandating that they all serve in the armed forces and establishing a few checkpoints at various locations across the land. Israel had already been conducting thorough security checks at its airports for a long time before the 9/11 attacks (Masmali & Miah, 2023). However, in the aftermath of those attacks, the nation has taken even more precautions to protect its citizens because it is surrounded by nations that have previously attempted to invade.

In case there is a threat to the border, Israel has also increased the number of unmanned aerial vehicles and unmanned ground vehicles that patrol the border. In a location such as the Huntsville Metro, there might be multiple nuclear facility meltdowns, loss of ISR capabilities, and loss of contact with the warfighter that the US is supporting (Masmali & Miah, 2023). Additional modifications from this act include the power to carry out a research and development program to improve cybersecurity infrastructure. At the time, all government enterprises had to comply with the Federal Information Security Management Act of 2002. This act has revealed some flaws in the cybersecurity architecture of the United States, particularly in those organizations that are leaders.

In the fall of 2010, numerous news articles and headlines asserted that Stuxnet was a significant step forward in terms of cyberwarfare. This dangerous worm was complicated, and it was meant to attack only a particular computer system. This worm was able to determine location, system type, and possibly other information (Agrawal et al., 2023). And this worm would only assault the system if it satisfied certain criteria that had been predetermined in the program's coding. At Natanz, the software of a programmable logic controller, which was used to control the centrifuges, was compromised by the Stuxnet computer worm. This tampering ultimately disrupted the Iranian nuclear program.

Cyberattacks against critical infrastructure, such as supervisory control and data acquisition (SCADA) systems, are a source of worry for the Department of Homeland Security. SCADA stands for supervisory control and data acquisition, and it refers to the types of systems that are used in critical infrastructures like electricity grids and nuclear power plants to automatically monitor and adjust switches, among other activities (Lamba & Kandwal, 2023). The Department of Homeland Security is concerned about these systems since they are typically unmanned and can be accessed remotely.

The fact that they can be accessed online could make it possible for anyone to take control of vital infrastructure assets remotely. There has been a rise in the number of mandates and directives that must be followed to guarantee that any system that is implemented satisfies severe standards. Figure 4 illustrates how connected devices must comply with both policy and technology to maintain a secure environment. This integrates technology and policy for the life cycle of a product, the use of a product, and the development of policies surrounding the application of technology.

Figure 4. Proposed mission framework (connected devices)

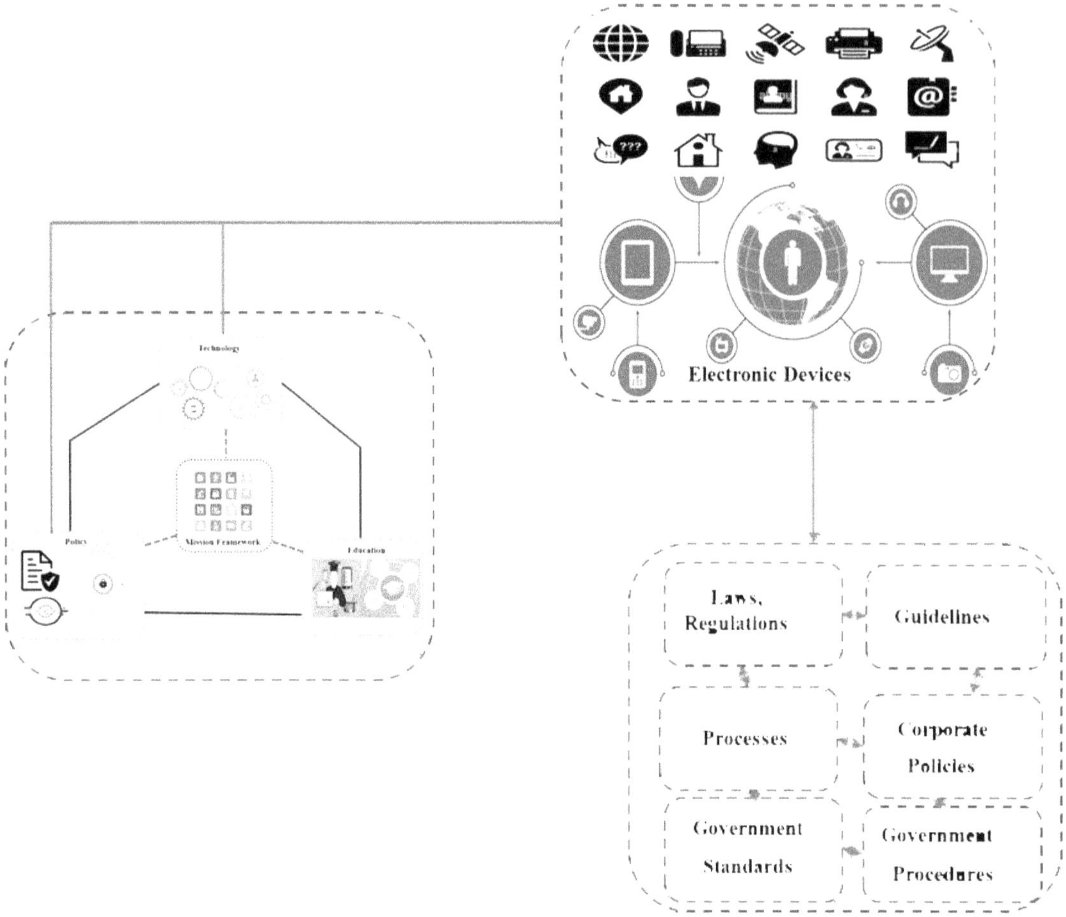

In the case of a laptop, a script that installs preapproved software removes applications regarded to be a danger by the company and configures firewalls and antivirus settings that would be run on the device. This would entail writing the results of the program to a file with an extension of.txt or.html, which the administrator of the system can read later while performing an audit of the system (Seaman, 2023). If the file ends in.txt or.csv, then it can be examined using the R programming language to look for irregularities or trends.

Testing is an essential part of the life cycle of developing software and systems. Even though NIST has provided some guidance in the form of SP 800-15 (Seaman, 2023), there is nothing that addresses the process of developing tests on commercial devices that provide an analysis that considers risks. As a result, there is a demand for the creation of testing applications, such as built-in tests, that give consumers the ability to determine the level of risk that they are willing to take. An example of a testing procedure for various devices is presented in Figure 5.

Location information can be retrieved from the devices to investigate the laws, regulations, and policies that are in effect in the given location. After ensuring that all the requirements have been met, step 3 involves performing a handshake that enables devices to connect. The capacity to do inspections as frequently as feasible is included in the devices so that they can remain safely attached. In order for this process to be carried out, a software application that enables connectivity to the Internet will need to be installed on each of the devices (Ghiasi et al., 2023). For an organization to successfully implement this process, the risk management framework and the common weakness enumeration database need to be updated daily (Alismail et al., 2023; Torroglosa-Garcia et al., 2023). This is done to ensure that the owner of the device is aware of any pertinent risks before deciding to connect or pair the device in question.

Figure 5. Risk management framework

Certificates and Accreditation Implementation

It is vital to establish a Certification and Accreditation (C&A) procedure that is focused on IT products and systems under governing regulations. When an organization deploys systems that make use of baseline regulation and security measures, it eliminates the need for the organization to establish controls from the ground up (Estrada & Reyes Álvarez, 2023; Lad, 2023). The C&A process in an organization needs to be measured using a system that has a solid foundation for the organization to be successful.

Two procedures, both of which will be discussed below, should be considered by companies as potential candidates for alteration to better fulfill the needs of globalized IT businesses.

The Common Criteria (CC), which is an internationally recognized collection of security criteria, offers an analysis that is transparent and trustworthy of the security capabilities of IT solutions. Customers can have a greater level of trust in the security of the products they purchase because of the CC's capacity to provide an independent review of a product's ability to fulfill security standards, which in turn leads to better-informed decision-making (De Arroyabe et al., 2023; Eltahir & Ahmed, 2023).

Customers who are concerned about their data's safety, such as the federal government of the United States, are increasingly demanding that CC certification be used as a deciding element in purchase decisions. Because the requirements for certification have been set transparently, manufacturers are able to cater to highly precise security needs while still offering a diverse range of products. Users in other countries can make purchases of IT products with the same level of confidence because certification is recognized across all nations that comply with the CC thanks to the international scope of the CC, which is now implemented by over fifteen nations (Pratama et al., 2023). To evaluate a product based on its level of security, it is necessary to first determine the customer's specific security requirements and then examine the product's existing capabilities. Customers receive assistance in both procedures because of the CC's two primary features, which are protection profiles and evaluation assurance levels (Perakslis & Knechtle, 2023).

The National Institute of Standards and Technology (NIST) developed a methodology for dealing with risk management called the Risk Management Framework (RMF) (NIST, 2012). The RMF employs a risk-based methodology for the selection and design of security controls. This methodology considers factors such as efficacy, efficiency, and limits brought on by relevant laws, directives, executive orders, policies, standards, or regulations. The RMF categorization process is broken down into six parts, which serve as the foundation for this NIST advice (Siegel et al., 2023). Phase 1: categorize. An effect study serves as the foundation for the evaluation and classification of the system. Phase 2: Make your choice. During this time, the organization is obligated to determine the security and privacy controls necessary to protect the system and the organization, as well as to select, tailor, and document them in accordance with the level of risk posed to organizational operations and assets as well as individuals. These controls are the result of high-level requirements that were broken down into lower-level requirements, and they need to be addressed in the design; phase 3 does the implementation.

The controls that were chosen in step 2 are installed into the system during this stage, along with the accompanying environment of operation that goes along with it. Assessing is the fourth phase. It is necessary to evaluate the controls that have been put in place to determine whether they are performing as expected and whether the desired outcome satisfies the security requirements for the system. Authorizing is the fifth phase. Obtain authorization for the system to operate based on a determination that is acceptable regarding the level of risk that is acceptable for the system. Phase 6 monitoring is managed there. Evaluate the effectiveness of the system's security controls on a consistent and continuous basis. This may entail carrying out security inspections on an annual basis to assess compliance.

CYBERSECURITY RISKS COMMUNICATION

The field of risk communication is one that has been studied for a considerable amount of time and is quite mature. This is particularly true in the fields of health and natural disasters. It is possible to describe risk communication as the interactive process of providing information about risk (its nature, meaning, repercussions, likelihood, and response options) to persons to enable those individuals to make informed decisions (Ghiasi et al., 2023). This exercise can be broken down into three different goals: advancing or changing information and attitudes; modifying risk-relevant behavior; and fostering cooperative dispute resolution and decision-making.

For any of these objectives to be achieved, individuals must first "digest" or "perceive" the risk information. Because of this, risk perception is one of the essential first stages in the process of risk communication. This stage takes into consideration the numerous ways in which an individual genuinely interprets a risk as well as the various circumstances that influence their perspective. The processes of risk analysis, risk appraisal, and risk treatment are some of the other processes fundamental to risk communication. These processes are implicit in the aims that were discussed before. These tasks, when combined, give a person the mental capacity to comprehend the danger, evaluate it, and arrive at a well-informed judgment for how the risk should be managed cognitively (Shari, 2023). When one considers the expansive scope of risk communication as well as its connection to human perception and decision-making, it should not come as a surprise that many people consider this to be a difficult topic with multiple aspects that affect and influence its processes.

The perceptual and subjective aspect of risk itself is a major factor that contributes to the complexity of risk communication. The health and terrorist sectors refer to risk as a socially and psychologically built and oriented entity. The subjectivity of this topic has been discussed at length in the academic literature, which has also provided some key examples, such as the fact that actual risk and perceived risk can be quite different, and the fact that an individual's appetite for risk and acceptability of risk depends heavily on that person's priorities and values (Hill et al., 2023). Both points are important to remember.

Most prominent and significant assessments on the topic of risk perception. He draws from a variety of domains to validate the arguments made previously and to emphasize how challenging, yet vital, it is to examine risk communication and perception. Given this complexity, it is essential that any method for conveying the risks associated with cybersecurity have adequate knowledge of the possible obstacles and strategies to prevent them, which will result in more effective communication of security information (Lourenço et al., 2023).

Considering this, we look at the fundamental characteristics of the well-established domains of natural disasters and health that have been discovered to affect risk communication. It is envisaged that developments in these areas will allow for considerably more rapid progress in the field of cybersecurity risk communication research. To organize this review, we will be using the three potential trouble spots in risk communication that were outlined in Kolar et al. (2023). These trouble spots are the risk message itself, the communicator or source of the message, and the recipient of the message.

Risk Message

Most relevant issues have complex risk data. The risk message content is a decision that is both fundamental and crucial. The knowledge that is not valued can lead to detrimental acts. The precision of risk information could impede communication. in the context of terrorism to demonstrate that imprecise communications can heighten dread without increasing awareness. After obtaining the correct information, it is essential to convey a warning message. The format of risk messages is a popular subtopic. The three fundamental modalities of presentation are numerical (percentages, frequencies, and probabilities), verbal (terms such as "unlikely," "possible," and "certain"), and visual (drawings, graphs, charts, and diagrams) (Almatari et al., 2023). Each risk communication format has advantages and disadvantages. Formats may be combined.

Numeric risk statements are accurate, exact, and simple to transform. This format's main flaw is that it assumes mathematical and probabilistic literacy that even highly educated people lack. Number formats are also difficult. Probabilities, frequencies, relative risks, reference classes, and the notion of risk are discussed by the authors. Probabilities of a single event, conditional probabilities, and relative risks are baffling since it is difficult to determine to which event category a percentage or probability relates (Jaber & Fritsch, 2023).

Verbal communication is uncommon but advantageous. These include being natural, simple to use, and effective at conveying the source, magnitude, and imprecision of uncertainty in regular risk communication. The greatest disadvantage of this method is its significant interpretation variability. The term "likely" may not be understood by all when defining danger (Jaber & Fritsch, 2023). This issue impacts those who communicate at risk. Interpretation is influenced by experience, knowledge, and expectations.

Risk Source or Communicator

We will now shift our attention to the risk communicator or source and the challenges they encounter. This will bring us back to the previously stated broad regions. The major impediment in this regard is the fact that communicators themselves struggle to comprehend and evaluate risk. The research on quantitative risk communication conducted, reveals several instances in which key information sources (such as physicians, judges, and specialists) incorrectly or inconsistently appraised rather serious dangers (Buchanan & Kronk, 2023). Based on their research on numeracy in risk communication in the health profession, provide additional evidence for this view. It has also been established that prominent sources, such as the media, contribute to the problem by misinterpreting and disseminating hazard statistics. This is a result of the media's neglect of the issue.

Message Receiver

The recipient adds another obstacle. Personal risk perception is crucial. Culture, beliefs, needs, knowledge, awareness, risk familiarity, feeling of control, voluntariness, and risk effect and dread are influential factors. Literacy and numeracy levels also affect risk communication (several studies across many areas support this) (Lourenço et al., 2023; Siegel et al., 2023). Emotion (for example, fear, wrath, and anxiety), attitude, and affect (a good or unpleasant feeling about something) can potentially affect risk perception and decision-making. Humans generally base their perceptions and decisions on their emotions and moods.

The affect heuristic is crucial to risk communication and this field. Other prominent heuristics (for instance, availability, anchoring and adjustment, representativeness) have been studied for their pros and cons in risk assessment. The receiver must trust the risk communicator. In case a person does not believe the source, they may overestimate or underestimate the risk (Masmali & Miah, 2023). These points require more research. This general link to trust supports the paper's use of trustworthiness research for cybersecurity-risk communications.

Based on this brief overview of risk communication's challenges, one of the field's leading proponents has called risk assessment, a crucial aspect of communication that groups analysis and evaluation, a "battlefield." These problems demonstrate that providing correct risk information does not guarantee that people will understand and act on it (De Arroyabe et al., 2023; Kamariotou & Kitsios, 2023; Purwanto et al., 2023). One-size-fits-all risk communication solutions don't work. The literature then provides risk communication guidelines. These include presentation, source association, cognition optimization, and communicating with specific groups, including low-numeracy people.

COMMUNICATION OF CYBERSECURITY RISKS

Risk communication in cybersecurity explores how to communicate security-risk information to system users to improve understanding and decision-making. Persuading users to take a certain action may be a cybersecurity goal. Security communications research is still young and can be divided into perception and decision-making, like early risk-communications research (Buchanan & Kronk, 2023). Our review focuses on these two topics. This assessment covers cybersecurity-risk communications, not security usability. These notions may overlap, but our attention is on the former.

Security Risks Perceptions

The authors begin their examination of ideas on information security, emphasizing the human aspect. They employ established literature on risk perception. Knowledge, impact, severity, controllability, possibility, and awareness, according to their research, define the information security perspective. Studies reveal factors that influence individuals' risk perceptions of internet security issues. The authors found that consumers evaluate online risks based on four critical factors: their ability to control or avoid the risk, their dread of the repercussions, their unfamiliarity with the dangers, and the immediacy of the consequences or impact (Dedrick et al., 2023). According to the authors, these characteristics may help researchers forecast how individuals would respond to online threats.

Additionally, perceptions of security risk have been investigated. A novel risk perception measurement paradigm. The model distills common perception elements and is based on two security-risk characteristics: an individual's perception of a threat and its consequences, with a scale that reflects distinct values and measures. For a particular solution at a particular time, a person may have a low grasp of a hazard and see the probable outcomes as severe (AlKalbani et al., 2023; Mohamed & Kamau, 2023). Total scores can be used to characterize a group's risk perception, track individual risk perception changes, or both.

Several authors have directly influenced the perception of security risk to enhance risk communication. To enhance the procedure, the authors of (Conchon, 2023) integrate graphics and symbols in information security communications. This method of knowledge delivery was learned in the classroom. Contrary to their predictions, the authors' study revealed no statistically significant differences between the graphical and text-only test groups. This is relevant because it means that not all features are easily transferable between sectors and that material must be continuously researched and provided with caution. When expressing information regarding security threats, the authors also evaluate vocabulary, structure, meaning, and color. All of them pertain to research on risk perception, which demonstrates once again that cybersecurity-risk communication should benefit from these guidelines.

Decision-Making on Security Risks

Users' security risk-reward decisions are studied. Risk perception, security competence, and culture affect risk decision-making, their study revealed. Applying and evaluating these insights in security is encouraging. Satisficing, cognitive biases including the representativeness heuristic and base rate and response bias, time pressure, and inattentional blindness are examples (Estrada & Reyes Álvarez, 2023). That and other research indicated that customers don't think they're at risk, are uninspired, think safety is abstract, and lose more than they win. The authors advise raising security-risk awareness, modifying risk messages or dialogues to capture attention, or removing users from security decisions. This useful work promotes risk perception and communication.

Online dangers are often assessed without all the facts. Four risk "knowability" levels result in known certainty, known uncertainty, unknown uncertainty, and unknowable uncertainty. Due to strict security, a supplier guarantees no identity theft from online transactions. Unknowable uncertainty is when no one knows what percentage of online supplier transactions lead to identity theft. These levels affect decision-making differently, as the authors show (Shari, 2023). Risk expression affects choices.

Physical security, medical infections, criminal behavior, economic failure, and conflict were examined. These methods address security communication concerns. These models aren't perfect, but they can improve communication (Khan et al., 2023). Targeted security-risk communication uses mental models. Movie mental models and activity identification techniques offer timely alerts related to video stills. Video may enhance comprehension more than words. This innovative method needs user testing. However, users will need to see a film before utilizing the system, and activity detection and logic must be added to the software or system schemas (Khan et al., 2023; Zafar et al., 2023). These include interface designs that match users' mental models, an elegant and simple design, standard colors to draw attention, icons as visual indicators, particular wording to indicate risk levels, and consistent, meaningful terminology.

Designers should use many presentation and interaction methods to convey information, relevant messages, and user-appropriate and adjustable interfaces and alerts in security communications. Other security managers' and administrators' policies don't address security-risk communication. Cybersecurity risk is now communicated by the industry. Since technology communicates cyberattack risk, our research is important to intrusion detection (Camgöz Akdağ & Menekşe, 2023; Montasari, 2023). Many graphical and textual solutions appear to be pragmatic applications of well-known human cognition and perception principles rather than sophisticated analyses of how to maximize cyber risk communication for information system monitors.

Cybersecurity analysts' real-time incident-management performance is enhanced by the authors' visualization and suggestion systems. Cybersecurity experts classify incidents better. This study addresses important cybersecurity alerting system issues such as visual versus tabular displays and information presentation sequences, which helps our research. This article will influence our recommendations.

USABLE CYBERSECURITY GUIDELINES

We began by conducting a search of the published research for general recommendations that had been proposed to improve the usability of cybersecurity interfaces and systems. Our research allowed us to establish the most applicable guidelines that were in keeping with the objectives of this research. After finding it, we proceeded to develop an initial set of guidelines for the analysis. Following that, we evaluated the list by contrasting the various articles' recommendations, and, if feasible, we grouped extremely similar recommendations together, renaming the groupings as required. During our article, we also took notice of recurring rules within the body of research. Recommendations that appear more than once may be seen as having more compelling arguments in their favor. Following is a revised list of general principles that have been gleaned from previous research and are based on the findings of our investigation and analysis.

Security Management Interfaces

Security is no longer seen as an afterthought in terms of management interfaces for cybersecurity (Conchon, 2023; Nyarko & Fong, 2023). Because of this, there are a few other features that are unique to usable cybersecurity and have demonstrated that they are deserving of study. These capabilities include the capacity to evaluate a cybersecurity system from a variety of encapsulation levels, the facilitation of the understanding and diagnosis of potential risks, and the encouragement of management personnel to respond quickly and effectively to critical security issues.

Separate and Distinct Concepts

Combining disparate ideas can easily lead to misunderstanding. Because of this, it might be beneficial to keep user values and security policies distinct from one another, as well as to keep security policies and security implementation distinct (Netshakhuma, 2023; Shaikh & Siponen, 2023). Therefore, it is no longer necessary for end users to have a solid understanding of security processes to develop commensurate and appropriate policies. In addition, one action that would be of great assistance to a user in the process of system setup would be the automation of the step that goes from policy to implementation.

Tools Are Not Solutions

Tools such as Secure Sockets Layer (SSL) and Internet Protocol Security (IPsec) are not solutions to user concerns by themselves; rather, they are building blocks (Purwanto et al., 2023). To supplement these and other lower-level technologies, there is a need for high-level building blocks that can be drawn upon by system designers to create systems that are more user-focused and contain usable security. These blocks would be available to system designers as a resource.

Design It Such That Security Does Not Reduce Performance

System performance is another essential factor that must be prioritized while also striking a balance between usability and cybersecurity (Childers et al., 2023). It is the responsibility of the designers to ensure that the software application and system can make effective use of the built-in security measures by employing algorithms that are both efficient and carefully designed.

Model Security Into Each Layer of Applications

An alternative strategy to concentrating on security just at the lower and more technical levels of the networking stack is to design security into all an application's layers, with a particular emphasis on the application's top layers (Sadaghiani-Tabrizi, 2023). This could be a helpful approach. The purpose of this recommendation is to make it such that a user's duties and, more broadly, their high-level goals automatically incorporate the underlying security measures. If this seamlessness is provided, then the system has a better chance of being perceived as being more user-friendly. For this strategy to be successful, the designers behind it will need to have a solid comprehension of the mental models held by users and the ways in which they reason concerning the system.

Create an Appropriate Mental Model

A user's internal representation or understanding of a system and how it operates can be termed that user's "mental model" (Siegel et al., 2023). It is important for designers to try to establish systems that consider the mental model of a user and, as a result, encourage the construction of models that accurately depict the interface and functionality of cybersecurity systems.

Reduce Security and Technical Jargon

Users need to be able to comprehend the functions of the security features before they can make use of them. As a result, designers should use technical and security-specific phrases rarely, and when they do, they should carefully consider whether to include definitions. This is especially helpful for end-user systems and people with little to no experience.

Design for Learnability

The user interfaces for cybersecurity tools ought to be intuitive (Dedrick et al., 2023). Based on the reference above, it is hypothesized that familiarity and consistency are among the factors that influence learnability. When it comes to cybersecurity, key aspects that might increase usability include the use of metaphors (relating the real world to system functions to exploit familiarity) and consistent terms and dialogues within the system. Both things are important because they have the potential to make the system more user-friendly to avoid confusion.

Minimalistic Design

Even though it is generally understood that certain aspects of cybersecurity functionality (for example, configurations) may be somewhat complicated (Ziadia et al., 2023), especially for an inexperienced user, designers should still strive to keep interfaces simple, reduce the likelihood of information overload, and steer clear of awkward interface setups.

Focus on System Satisfaction and User Experience

The goal of cybersecurity interfaces should be to provide users with a pleasant and fulfilling experience to the greatest extent that is practically possible. This could consist of activities such as making tiny modifications to the interface to benefit user preferences or allowing for some degree of security interface or action customization. Alternatively, this could also refer to the user being able to customize their own security settings.

Assist Users With Their Tasks and Offer Suggestions

Users need to be made aware of the cybersecurity responsibilities they are responsible for, and when appropriate, systems need to provide them with direction on how to complete those operations (Shari, 2023). This guidance also includes recommended help for situations in which users are unsure about decisions and the ramifications of those decisions. Both systems designed for security experts, which places a heavy emphasis on recommendations and respective justifications, and those designed for end-users, in which security is typically a secondary aim, have a role to play in the process of raising awareness and providing direction to individuals.

Reduce System-Related Cognitive Load

Interfaces for cybersecurity should be developed to reduce the amount of mental strain placed on users when they are interacting with the system. Many studies conducted over the years on human cognition have shed light on the constraints of working memory and the necessity of providing help to users while still working within the confines of their memory and mental limitations (Eltahir & Ahmed, 2023). This may involve automating security activities or configurations, making it easy to set up system security without placing unreasonable demands on users' memories in general. When considering cybersecurity, several general perception and communication issues should also be taken into consideration. These aspects are related to cognition and should be studied.

Display Security Features

In the same vein as the other aspects of the program, security should be simply accessible and visible (Clinton, 2023). The practice of concealing cybersecurity functionality behind more advanced or otherwise unrelated elements of an interface is likely to make the work at hand more challenging for the user and, as a result, reduce the system's overall usability.

Showing System State

Users need to be informed of the current level of security that the system possesses. This is a sort of passive feedback regarding cybersecurity in many ways (Camgöz Akdağ & Menekşe, 2023; Solar, 2023; Zafar et al., 2023). Some easy-to-understand examples include the word "Secured" appearing on some password-protected or encrypted documents, the appearance of active icons whenever a system is performing security functions, and the display of padlocks within browsers to indicate that the user is browsing using Secure Sockets Layer (SSL) or Transport Layer Security (TLS).

Preventing, Managing, and Recovering Errors (Undo)

It is important for systems to be constructed in such a way that they can predict and prevent mistakes made by users (Masmali & Miah, 2023). If errors do occur, however, they should be dealt with in a dignified manner, provided instructive prompts, and measures for recovery should be outlined. When users make mistakes and enter undesired program states, this guideline recommends that cybersecurity interface designs offer to undo and rapid exit functions. Users of the program should be able to rely on it and not feel lost when using it.

Help, Advise, and Document

Users should be able to quickly find and access help and advice manuals, as well as system documentation, for cybersecurity functions whenever they are required to do so. If users are unable to locate these features and determine how to utilize them, it is likely that they will be ignored.

Informative Feedback

Useful system feedback is an essential component for several of the other recommendations for usable cybersecurity that are included below (for example, help (Siegel et al., 2023), error handling (Ghiasi et al., 2023), and visibility of the condition of the security system (Reed et al., 2023)). The feedback that is provided ought to be understandable, informative, adequate, and not overly technical; if it is pertinent, it should include suggestions for moving forward.

Accept All Users

The functionality of cybersecurity should be created in such a way that it is adaptable and can accommodate both inexperienced and experienced users. Expert users should be able to swiftly access essential functionality via system shortcuts, hotkeys, and other such things, whereas rookie users may at times require assistance and step-by-step guidance (Pratama et al., 2023). This instruction, in general, places an emphasis on the necessity of diverse ways for systems to interact with one another.

Early Cybersecurity Usability Considerations

At the beginning of the process of designing and developing a system, there should be discussion and analysis of cybersecurity, usability, and the connection between these three ideas (Perakslis & Knechtle, 2023). Bolting on or retrofitting cybersecurity usability just toward the end of a system's development is likely to be detrimental to the system overall and lead to additional usability and security difficulties.

CONCLUSION

In this contribution, an original approach to thinking about cybersecurity is presented in the form of a framework that brings education, policy, and technological advancements together. The education evaluation showed new ways to teach cybersecurity courses and talked about the groups that accredit programs in IT, computing technologies, and computer science. The guidelines, resources, and strategies that can be utilized moving forward in the field of cybersecurity education were also examined in further detail. Several other ideas, including simulation, virtualization, U-Learning, and engineering standards, were investigated. In the section on policies, there should be a requirement to examine and make use of a variety of directives, standards, regulations, legislation, and best practices.

These policies came from the Department of Defense, the National Institute of Standards and Technology, the United States military, and other organizations. These serve as the foundation for additional guidance and direction that can be provided to organizations that are creating policies. The purpose of the technologies section is to collect information about developing technologies, such as those that incorporate Internet-enabled devices and similar products. Mobile phones, operating systems (OS), software packages, and other devices all need to be reviewed individually, with special attention paid to how the security posture shifts once they are integrated into a system context.

The application of these three components can be utilized to drive policies at the federal or state level, and for the commercial sector, this results in an effect that lasts for an extended period in the fight against cybercrime. According to the findings of this body of collective research, a comprehensive vision of cybersecurity must prioritize education, policies, and technological advancements. Previous viewpoints have investigated these topics in isolation rather than capturing them as a whole; however, this research may be utilized to bring these themes together with the explicit goal of targeting the deployment of IT systems to specific locations worldwide.

REFERENCES

Agrawal, A., Khan, R. A., & Ansari, M. T. J. (2023). Empowering Indian citizens through the secure e-governance: The digital India initiative context. In *Emerging Technologies in Data Mining and Information Security* (pp. 3–11). Springer. doi:10.1007/978-981-19-4676-9_1

Alismail, A., Altulaihan, E., Rahman, M. M., & Sufian, A. (2023). *A Systematic Literature Review on Cybersecurity Threats of Virtual Reality (VR) and Augmented Reality*. Data Intelligence and Cognitive Informatics.

AlKalbani, A., AlBusaidi, H., & Deng, H. (2023). Using a Q-Methodology in Demystifying Typologies for Cybersecurity Practitioners: A Case Study. In *Intelligent Sustainable Systems* (pp. 291–303). Springer. doi:10.1007/978-981-19-7660-5_26

Almatari, O., Wang, X., Zhang, W., & Khan, M. K. (2023). *VTAIM: Volatile Transaction Authentication Insurance Method for Cyber Security Risk Insurance of Banking Services*. Academic Press.

Bada, M., & von Solms, B. (2023). A cybersecurity guide for using fitness devices. *The Fifth International Conference on Safety and Security with IoT*, 35–45. 10.1007/978-3-030-94285-4_3

Buchanan, J., & Kronk, H. (2023). *The Slow Adjustment in Tech Labor: Why Do High-Paying Tech Jobs Go Unfilled?* The Center for Growth and Opportunity.

Bukauskas, L., Brilingaitė, A., Juozapavičius, A., Lepaitė, D., Ikamas, K., & Andrijauskaitė, R. (2023). Remapping cybersecurity competences in a small nation state. *Heliyon*, *9*(1), 12808. doi:10.1016/j.heliyon.2023.e12808 PMID:36685367

Camgöz Akdağ, H., & Menekşe, A. (2023). Cybersecurity Framework Prioritization for Healthcare Organizations Using a Novel Interval-Valued Pythagorean Fuzzy CRITIC. In *Intelligent Systems in Digital Transformation* (pp. 241–266). Springer. doi:10.1007/978-3-031-16598-6_11

Casey, E., Jocz, J., Peterson, K. A., Pfeif, D., & Soden, C. (2023). Motivating youth to learn STEM through a gender inclusive digital forensic science program. *Smart Learning Environments*, *10*(1), 1–24. doi:10.118640561-022-00213-x

Childers, G., Linsky, C. L., Payne, B., Byers, J., & Baker, D. (2023). K-12 educators' self-confidence in designing and implementing cybersecurity lessons. *Computers and Education Open*, *4*, 100119. doi:10.1016/j.caeo.2022.100119

Clinton, L. (2023). *Fixing American Cybersecurity: Creating a Strategic Public-private Partnership*. Georgetown University Press.

Colomb, Y., White, P., Islam, R., & Alsadoon, A. (2023). Applying Zero Trust Architecture and Probability-Based Authentication to Preserve Security and Privacy of Data in the Cloud. In *Emerging Trends in Cybersecurity Applications* (pp. 137–169). Springer. doi:10.1007/978-3-031-09640-2_7

Conchon, E. (2023). Cyber Security Strategies While Safeguarding Information Systems in Public/Private Sectors. *Electronic Governance with Emerging Technologies: First International Conference, EGETC 2022, Tampico, Mexico, September 12–14, 2022, Revised Selected Papers*, 49.

Çubuk, E. B. S., Zeren, H. E., & Demirdöven, B. (2023). The role of data governance in cybersecurity for E-municipal services: Implications from the case of Turkey. In *Handbook of Research on Cybersecurity Issues and Challenges for Business and FinTech Applications* (pp. 410–425). IGI Global.

De Arroyabe, I. F., Arranz, C. F., Arroyabe, M. F., & de Arroyabe, J. C. F. (2023). Cybersecurity capabilities and cyber-attacks as drivers of investment in cybersecurity systems: A UK survey for 2018 and 2019. *Computers & Security*, *124*, 102954. doi:10.1016/j.cose.2022.102954

Dedrick, J., Perrin, K. A., Sabaghian, E., & Wilcoxen, P. J. (2023). Assessing cyber attacks on local electricity markets using simulation analysis: Impacts and possible mitigations. *Sustainable Energy, Grids and Networks*, 100993.

Dykstra, J. (2023). *The Slippery Slope of Cybersecurity Analogies*. Academic Press.

Eltahir, M. E., & Ahmed, O. S. (2023). *Cybersecurity Awareness in African Higher Education Institutions: A Case Study of Sudan*. Academic Press.

English, R., & Maguire, J. (2023). Exploring Student Perceptions and Expectations of Cyber Security. In Computing Education Practice (pp. 25–28). doi:10.1145/3573260.3573267

Estrada, S., & Reyes Álvarez, J. (2023). Conclusions: The Challenge Towards the Future Is Digital and Sustainable Transformations from a Systemic Perspective in a Changing COVID World. In *Digital and Sustainable Transformations in a Post-COVID World* (pp. 475–502). Springer. doi:10.1007/978-3-031-16677-8_18

Faltermaier, S., Strunk, K., Obermeier, M., & Fiedler, M. (2023). *Managing Organizational Cyber Security–The Distinct Role of Internalized Responsibility*. Academic Press.

Florackis, C., Louca, C., Michaely, R., & Weber, M. (2023). Cybersecurity risk. *Review of Financial Studies*, *36*(1), 351–407. doi:10.1093/rfs/hhac024

Gartner. (2014). *Gartner's 2014 Hype Cycle for Emerging Technologies Maps the Journey to Digital Business*. https://www.gartner.com/newsroom/id/2819918

Ghiasi, M., Niknam, T., Wang, Z., Mehrandezh, M., Dehghani, M., & Ghadimi, N. (2023). A comprehensive review of cyber-attacks and defense mechanisms for improving security in smart grid energy systems: Past, present and future. *Electric Power Systems Research*, *215*, 108975. doi:10.1016/j.epsr.2022.108975

Girasa, R. (2023). Taxation of Virtual Currencies; Environmental, Social and Governance Considerations; Protection of Intellectual Property Rights; Antitrust; and Cybersecurity. In *Regulation of Cryptocurrencies and Blockchain Technologies* (pp. 261–311). Springer. doi:10.1007/978-3-031-21812-5_7

Hill, C., James, B. I., & Sahyoun, N. (2023). *What is Missing in Data Governance? Regulation, Board Oversight, and a New Role for Accountants*. Academic Press.

Jaber, A., & Fritsch, L. (2023). Towards AI-powered Cybersecurity Attack Modeling with Simulation Tools: Review of Attack Simulators. *International Conference on P2P, Parallel, Grid, Cloud and Internet Computing*, 249–257.

Johri, A., & Kumar, S. (2023). Exploring Customer Awareness towards Their Cyber Security in the Kingdom of Saudi Arabia: A Study in the Era of Banking Digital Transformation. *Human Behavior and Emerging Technologies*, *2023*, 2023. doi:10.1155/2023/2103442

Kamariotou, M., & Kitsios, F. (2023). Information Systems Strategy and Security Policy: A Conceptual Framework. *Electronics (Basel)*, *12*(2), 382. doi:10.3390/electronics12020382

Khan, N. F., Ikram, N., Murtaza, H., & Javed, M. (2023). Evaluating protection motivation based cybersecurity awareness training on Kirkpatrick's Model. *Computers & Security*, *125*, 103049. doi:10.1016/j.cose.2022.103049

Kolar, M., Fernandez-Gago, C., & Lopez, J. (2023). Trust Negotiation and Its Applications. In *Collaborative Approaches for Cyber Security in Cyber-Physical Systems* (pp. 171–190). Springer. doi:10.1007/978-3-031-16088-2_8

Lad, S. (2023). Creating a Security Culture. In *Azure Security For Critical Workloads* (pp. 201–207). Springer. doi:10.1007/978-1-4842-8936-5_8

Lamba, T., & Kandwal, S. (2023). Global Outlook of Cyber Security. *Proceedings of the Third International Conference on Information Management and Machine Intelligence*, 269–276.

Lourenço, J., Morais, J. C., Sá, S., Neves, N., Figueiredo, F., & Santos, M. C. (2023). Cybersecurity Concerns Under COVID-19: Representations on Increasing Digital Literacy in Higher Education. In *Perspectives and Trends in Education and Technology* (pp. 739–748). Springer. doi:10.1007/978-981-19-6585-2_65

Masmali, H. H., & Miah, S. J. (2023). Emergent Insight of the Cyber Security Management for Saudi Arabian Universities: A Content Analysis. *Proceedings of Seventh International Congress on Information and Communication Technology*, 153–171. 10.1007/978-981-19-1610-6_14

Mohamed, A. Y., & Kamau, S. K. (2023). A Continent-Wide Assessment of Cyber Vulnerability Across Africa. ArXiv Preprint ArXiv:2301.03008.

Montasari, R. (2023). Cyber Threats and the Security Risks They Pose to National Security: An Assessment of Cybersecurity Policy in the United Kingdom. *Countering Cyberterrorism*, 7–25.

Moreta, N., Aragon, D., Oña, S., Jaramillo, A., Ibarra, J., & Jahankhani, H. (2023). Comparison of Cybersecurity Methodologies for the Implementing of a Secure IoT Architecture. In *Cybersecurity in the Age of Smart Societies* (pp. 9–29). Springer. doi:10.1007/978-3-031-20160-8_2

Netshakhuma, N. S. (2023). Cybersecurity Management in South African Universities. In *Cybersecurity Issues, Challenges, and Solutions in the Business World* (pp. 196–211). IGI Global.

Nyarko, D. A., & Fong, R. C. (2023). Cyber Security Compliance Among Remote Workers. In *Cybersecurity in the Age of Smart Societies* (pp. 343–369). Springer. doi:10.1007/978-3-031-20160-8_18

Perakslis, E., & Knechtle, S. J. (2023). Information design to support growth, quality, and equity of the US transplant system. *American Journal of Transplantation*, *23*(1), 5–10. doi:10.1016/j.ajt.2022.10.005 PMID:36695621

PratamaA. R.AlshaikhM.AlharbiT. (2023). Increasing cybersecurity awareness through situated e-learning: A survey experiment. Available at SSRN 4320165. doi:10.2139/ssrn.4320165

Purwanto, W., Dodge, B., Arcaute, K., Sosonkina, M., & Wu, H. (2023). DeapSECURE Computational Training for Cybersecurity: Progress Toward Widespread Community Adoption. *Journal of Computational Science Education.*

Rawal, B. S., Manogaran, G., & Peter, A. (2023). Cybersecurity for Beginners. In *Cybersecurity and Identity Access Management* (pp. 1–20). Springer. doi:10.1007/978-981-19-2658-7_1

Reed, J., Shimizu, A., & Shifflett, J. (2023). *Cost Effectiveness Analysis of the use of Colorless Appropriations in Navy and DoD Software Development Pilot Programs* [PhD Thesis]. Acquisition Research Program.

Sadaghiani-Tabrizi, A. (2023). Revisiting Cybersecurity Awareness in the Midst of Disruptions. *International Journal for Business Education*, *163*(1), 6.

Seaman, J. (2023). Zero Trust Security Strategies and Guideline. In Digital Transformation in Policing: The Promise, Perils and Solutions (pp. 149–168). Springer. doi:10.1007/978-3-031-09691-4_9

Shaikh, F. A., & Siponen, M. (2023). Information security risk assessments following cybersecurity breaches: The mediating role of top management attention to cybersecurity. *Computers & Security*, *124*, 102974. doi:10.1016/j.cose.2022.102974

Shari, A. M. J. (2023). *Knowledge, Attitude, and Practices Towards Internet Safety and Security Among Generation Z in Malaysia: A Conceptual Paper*. Academic Press.

Shukla, M., Ziya, F., Arun, S., & Singh, S. P. (2023). Cyber Security Techniques Management. In *Holistic Approach to Quantum Cryptography in Cyber Security* (pp. 155–178). CRC Press.

Siegel, D., Bogers, M. L., Jennings, P. D., & Xue, L. (2023). Technology transfer from national/federal labs and public research institutes: Managerial and policy implications. *Research Policy*, *52*(1), 104646. doi:10.1016/j.respol.2022.104646

Solar, C. (2023). *Cybersecurity Governance in Latin America: States, Threats, and Alliances*. State University of New York Press.

Torroglosa-Garcia, E., Palomares, A., Song, H., Brun, P.-E., Giampaolo, F., Van Landuyt, D., Michiels, S., Podgorelec, B., Xenakis, C., & Bampatsikos, M. (2023). A Holistic Approach for IoT Networks' Identity and Trust Management–The ERATOSTHENES Project. *Internet of Things: 5th The Global IoT Summit, GIoTS 2022, Dublin, Ireland, June 20–23, 2022, Revised Selected Papers, 13533*, 338.

Turtiainen, H., Costin, A., & Hämäläinen, T. (2023). Defensive Machine Learning Methods and the Cyber Defence Chain. In *Artificial Intelligence and Cybersecurity* (pp. 147–163). Springer. doi:10.1007/978-3-031-15030-2_7

Zafar, H., Williams, J., & Gupta, S. (2023). *Toward an Effective SETA Program: An Action Research Approach*. Academic Press.

Ziadia, M., Mejri, M., & Fattahi, J. (2023). Semantics for Security Policy Enforcement on Android Applications with Practical Cases. In *Advances in Computational Intelligence and Communication* (pp. 115–133). Springer. doi:10.1007/978-3-031-19523-5_8

Chapter 3
Examining Data Privacy Through the Lens of Government Regulations

Biodun Awojobi
https://orcid.org/0000-0002-8461-1719
University of Dallas, USA

Brett J. L. Landry
https://orcid.org/0000-0002-0408-2408
University of Dallas, USA

ABSTRACT

Privacy and security have common elements but are different. Digital privacy choices are made based on the beliefs and perceptions of what can be shared and what should be kept discreet during communication. There has been a proliferation in the use of social networking sites. As a result, many individuals, firms, and communities view a loss in privacy as the result of a cybersecurity incident. However, not all cybersecurity incidents result in a privacy loss and not all privacy loss is the result of a cybersecurity incident. Privacy regulations provide the building blocks to ensure that sufficient data privacy standards are abided and that there are consequences for non-compliance, which in most cases are fines and levies to the defaulting organization. These regulations should provide guardrails to protect individuals and organizations by requiring data owners to be better stewards of that data. The problem is that technology changes at a faster pace than regulations can be created, so there is always a lag in the implementation.

INTRODUCTION

The privacy of digital information is one of the most complicated issues to address as it transcends many directions. Data Privacy and cybersecurity have common elements but are different concepts. Privacy choices are made based on the beliefs and perceptions of what should be shared and what should be kept discreet during communication. Cybersecurity protects the confidentiality, integrity, and availability of

DOI: 10.4018/978-1-6684-9018-1.ch003

systems and data. It is the common areas that provide a "conceptual blurring of boundaries between privacy and security" (Conger & Landry, 2008, p. 3). As a result, many individuals, firms, and communities view a loss of privacy as the result of a cybersecurity incident. A cybersecurity incident can lead to a breach of privacy, which may result in the loss of personal data which also includes Personally Identifiable Information (PII). This incident may result in the loss of confidentiality, integrity, or availability. The general principle is that once one of these tenets is compromised, there has been a breach of security of the organization or individual. Stevens (2010) proposes that "a data breach occurs when there is a loss or theft of, or other unauthorized access to, data containing sensitive personal information that results in the potential compromise of the confidentiality or integrity of data."

However, not all cybersecurity incidents result in a privacy loss, and not all privacy loss results from a cybersecurity incident. "Privacy and cybersecurity risk overlap concerning concerns about the cybersecurity of PII, but there are also privacy concerns without implications for cybersecurity and cybersecurity concerns without implications for privacy" (Boeckl et al., 2019). The best way to illustrate the overlap and differences is with the Venn diagram, as shown in Figure 1. Data privacy issues can be addressed from ethical, legal, and technological viewpoints. This chapter will examine data privacy through the lens of government regulations in technology. Examples of social media, Internet of things (IoT), voice-based assistants, and tracking will facilitate this examination to review technology and privacy concerns.

Figure 1.

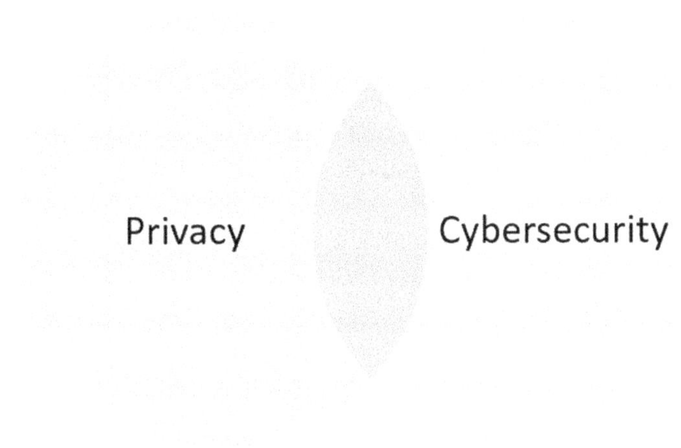

GOVERNMENT REGULATIONS FOR PROTECTING PRIVACY

Government regulations should provide the building blocks to ensure that sufficient data privacy standards are abided-by and that there are consequences for non-compliance, which in most cases are fines and levies to the defaulting organization. For example, a 2019 Pew Research Center survey discovered that "Over 60% of U. S. adults reported that they did not think it was possible to go a day without the government or companies collecting data from them" (Brown, 2019). Determining if the government collects more data than private organizations is challenging. The government keeps and processes data for its citizens and has jurisdiction to collect data from private companies. In addition, the government is involved in surveillance activities using government-owned assets like cameras and partnerships with private organizations like telecommunication companies.

Suppose digital privacy is a modern-day issue that gets addressed using common-law principles. How does the government step up to fill the void of abuse of personal information within social networking sites? The problem of perception of the citizens of the government interfering in what is supposed to be their business. Can governments work with companies that own and manage social media sites to ensure they correctly classify data and restrict or hash out personally identifiable information used within their platform to better protect individuals' right to digital privacy? To what extent can the government dictate what gets posted on a social networking site? Primarily when that social media site may be owned and operated in another country. One can argue that the government's interaction with technology can impact innovation; however, without controls in place, the companies that hold and control the social media platforms can potentially leverage the data for their own gains.

With regulations, the government should adopt information dissemination techniques used for important announcements to educate individuals on the government's commitments to privacy perception. The main difference between government regulation is the concept of opt-in versus opt-out strategies. These differences will be explored by examining GDPR and U. S. state privacy laws.

EU General Data Privacy Regulation (GDPR)

Unlike the United States, that are yet to adopt a national data privacy regulation, the European Union (EU) has led customer privacy efforts by enacting the EU General Data Privacy Regulation (GDPR). GDPR is built around the opt-in strategy. IAPP defines opt-in as a "…means an individual makes an active affirmative indication of choice; i.e., checking a box signaling a desire to share his or her information with third parties" (IAPP, 2023a). At the core of the GDPR is a set of interpretations, including the right to be forgotten or the right to erasure (GDPR.EU, 2023). The design of the EU GDPR was to accomplish these three goals:

1. Harmonize data privacy laws across Europe.
2. Protect and empower all EU citizens' data privacy.
3. Reshape the way organizations across the region approach data privacy.

With the GDPR Article 17 Right to erasure, an individual has the right to have their data deleted under the following circumstances as listed in Table 1 (Intersoft Consulting, 2023).

Table 1. Article 17 GDPR excerpt- right to erasure

1	The data subject shall have the right to obtain from the controller the erasure of personal data concerning him or her without undue delay and the controller shall have the obligation to erase personal data without undue delay where one of the following grounds applies:
A	the personal data are no longer necessary in relation to the purposes for which they were collected or otherwise processed;
B	the data subject withdraws consent on which the processing is based according to point (a) of Article 6(1), or point (a) of Article 9(2), and where there is no other legal ground for the processing;
C	the data subject objects to the processing pursuant to Article 21(1) and there are no overriding legitimate grounds for the processing, or the data subject objects to the processing pursuant to Article 21(2);
D	the personal data have been unlawfully processed;
E	the personal data have to be erased for compliance with a legal obligation in Union or Member State law to which the controller is subject;
F	the personal data have been collected in relation to the offer of information society services referred to in Article 8(1).

There are exceptions to the GDPR request by an individual to erase their data. Organizations can override the request for the deletion of an individual's data when the following list applies (GDPR.EU, 2023).

1. The data is being used to exercise the right of freedom of expression and information.
2. The data is being used to comply with a legal ruling or obligation.
3. The data is being used to perform a task that is being carried out in the public interest or when exercising an organization's official authority.
4. The data being processed is necessary for public health purposes and serves in the public interest.
5. The data being processed is necessary to perform preventative or occupational medicine. This only applies when the data is being processed by a health professional who is subject to a legal obligation of professional secrecy.
6. The data represents essential information that serves the public interest, scientific research, historical research, or statistical purposes and where erasure of the data would likely to impair or halt progress towards the achievement that was the goal of the processing.
7. The data is being used for the establishment of legal defense or in the exercise of other legal claims.

U.S. Individual State Privacy Laws

Unlike the European Union, regulations in the U. S. are not as protective of customer privacy (Strahilevitz, 2012). As of 2023, only five states have passed privacy plans; California, Colorado, Connecticut, Virginia, and Utah. Mississippi has an inactive bill, 19 states have introduced bills, and the remaining 25 states do not have comprehensive bills introduced (IAPP, 2023c). For the five states with privacy plans, there are two different plans. Colorado, Connecticut, Virginia, and Utah follow the proposed State of Washington plan, which differs from the California plan. However, it has been predicted that not having a single federal U.S. and having 50 different disjointed state laws could create out-of-state costs exceeding $1 trillion over a ten-year period (Castro et al., 2022).

All of the U.S. state-passed plans follow the opt-out strategy, which IAPP defines as " … an individual's lack of action implies that a choice has been made; i.e., unless an individual checks or unchecks a box, their information will be shared with third parties" (IAPP, 2023b). This means that by default, individuals must make a choice and take action to ensure privacy.

THE PRIVACY OF DIGITAL INFORMATION

Enforcing privacy in a non-digital age is more straightforward as there are fewer loopholes to information disclosure. For example, a writer of a manuscript that exists only in print form can ensure that the content of the paper gets preserved and kept private by not disclosing the content and keeping it locked in a safe. This approach has apparent advantages, such as the author's intellectual property will be protected and will only get disclosed on a need-to-know basis.

Computers have reimagined the concept of information storage and retrieval with the digitalization of content. This is especially true with shared cloud computing and storage. With this wave of digitization, the scope of privacy has changed. The days when an individual has an end to end control over what gets shared with others are fading quickly. However, the benefits associated with digitization are so enormous that the risks in the form of privacy are often ignored or unknown.

The increased computing processing and storage capabilities means we can store metadata on almost any object, which can be instantly retrieved whenever needed. In most developed countries, digital transformation has already reached its climax. Personal records have made their way into a variety of databases. Our personal preferences, habits, driving patterns, when we go to sleep, and when we wake up are all information recorded in databases due to our exposure to computing devices, information, and interactions with other humans. Typically, these forms of data do not get collected in one transaction or interaction. Instead, they get collected through multiple transactions and interactions with several systems. For example, many developed countries operate cashless systems. When a customer pays a vendor with a credit card, some of their information is shared with the vendor. In addition, some vendors will request that customers sign-up for a loyalty program. Loyalty programs usually require the customer's phone numbers and other personal information to be collected, which is then used for tracking purposes.

The convenience individuals receive through their exposure to Internet-connected services has far-reaching consequences. As humans, we start out trusting technology and expecting our interactions with technology to be private so long we have a username and password or other forms of authentication. Interestingly, however, we must be aware that information metadata can lead to targeted attacks such as phishing. Threat actors can easily steal intellectual property from computers and other devices, and a privacy breach is irreversible because you can never recover all copies of the data. Unauthorized physical access and software compromise of the device are just some of the ways the privacy of a voice-based assistant can be compromised.

Another reason why smart home devices have become popular is because of the cost of the devices. The relatively low price point of the devices compared to enterprise-grade devices comes at a cost. Manufacturers of IoT devices adopt mass device production strategies, which could involve skipping quality and security vulnerability checks to reduce the production cost of the devices. It is also becoming increasingly common for rental properties like apartments and homes to install IoT devices like smart door locks instead of traditional ones with a physical key. Apartments want to be able to control door access of the tenant when they default on their rent payment, and a smart lock can achieve this. Smart locks also collect logs of user access into the homes.

Privacy and Technology

Every individual will have a specific definition of privacy. Privacy for certain individuals is about the context of what is acceptable as information that can be shared and the information that should be kept discreet. Problems arise when attempting to conclude because "privacy means different things to different people" (Sears & Jacko, 2007). Warren and Brandeis (1890) proposed that privacy is the right to be withdrawn from the external world and "the right to be left alone." It is often misconstrued that privacy is a thing of perception when it is one of choice. Private information is what we choose not to share with the public or limit to a group of people. Each person has the choice to choose what information is private. For example, one person may choose to share their complete medical history, while another one will consider this to be their private data.

Individuals need the ability to control the amount of information transmitted or shared with others. As a result, technology should provide variable control of private information shared with other individuals. Technology adoption should have a cost-benefit justification and use variable controls. When an individual adjusts privacy settings, the system should intuitively display the benefit or penalties resulting from the change. Another concern is that an individual's current needs influence privacy decisions. Since these needs are constantly changing, privacy decisions are in constant negotiation.

Social Media

Social media sites have been successful at helping individuals connect with various forms of media – articles, blog posts, pictures, videos, etc. that are posted by people they may or may not know. While some social media sites offer ways to limit information exposure to unintended recipients, not all individuals leverage the features.

Individuals should be able to completely delete their data from any social media site that stores them. Since mobile devices are a convenient means of access to social media platforms, customers might presume that uninstalling the mobile application will address the exhaustive data tracking and collection. Social media platform developers like Facebook have partnerships with mobile operating system vendors like Google's Android platform to preinstall the social media mobile app on a brand-new device. The partnership may also extend to making the social media app a native app, ensuring the user cannot uninstall the application (Cuthbertson, 2019; Santos, 2018). The inability of a phone user to delete applications from a mobile device is similar to individuals not being able to opt out of store tracking devices. This is a violation of privacy, mainly because the only option the customers have is to refrain from buying the smartphone or visiting the store. Privacy should be an individual decision. The choice to share data should be up to the device's owner.

Some individuals find it easy to disclose their information publicly within their online social community based on the artificial fence provided by Facebook. LinkedIn is another example of a power player social media site that collects information about individuals. While some of the personal data collected are for system improvements, if the data gets to the hand of an unintended recipient with evil motives, the breach's impact will be severe.

Internet of Things and Voice-Based Assistants

IoT devices have tremendous privacy concerns because of their rapid adoption, often with little regard for data privacy. Regardless of the manufacturer, all voice-based assistants are designed to respond to a specific wake word. The wake word is, however, different, and the server that transcribes, processes, and stores the interactions are other. Eavesdropping cases are not just notorious to Amazon's Alexa and Apple's Siri voice assistants. The researchers at VRT NWS found that Google has been eavesdropping on conversations of customers using the Google Home smart assistant and the Google smart assistant app on mobile devices as well (Van Hee et al., 2019). In their research, they listened to over a thousand recordings and found signs of sensitive information in the recordings. They also identified that of the "more than a thousand excerpts, 153 of which were conversations that should never have been recorded and during which the command 'Okay Google' was clearly not given" (Van Hee et al., 2019). This is another blurred line that is crossed with smart assistants. It is difficult to prove if the customer triggered the wake word before the smart assistant started the recording because the smart assistant triggers random recording without the customer directly activating the wake word.

The rise in the adoption of the smart doorbell system has allowed Police departments to access video footage without the owner's knowledge or permission (Burgess, 2022). One of the ways the government encourages the public to buy Ring is by providing subsidies for the product. The subsidies, however, come at a cost to the public. The privacy of the public gets traded for the subsidized device price. The more installed surveillance system in the community and the more the public subscribes to Ring's Neighbors app, the more the police can stay current on security alerts around the neighborhood. The premise of the Neighbors app is to foster awareness and a strong relationship between a geofenced community around security. The Neighbors app also helps alert the police on ongoing threats. The privacy line, however, gets drawn when the customers are mandated to share the feeds from their devices with the police in return for subsidies or if the police have a backdoor to intercepting the feeds from the users' devices.

Voice-based assistants like Amazon Alexa and Google Home are ubiquitous in most homes because they are cheap, easy to set up, and can do a wide range of activities. However, voice-based assistants introduce a more comprehensive range of privacy issues. Since they are always on and listening for their wake word and connected to the manufacturer's cloud service, the risk of unauthorized PII being sent to unsanctioned servers is high. When a user issues a wake word to Amazon's Alexa, the user's voice interaction is recorded and immediately transcribed to a text, then played to the voice-based assistant as a command. Depending on the command, Alexa will either issue a response or control other embedded devices that respond accordingly. Amazon lets users delete the voice recordings, giving the user a false sense of privacy. The company retains the data, however, just not as a sound bite. Amazon keeps the text logs of the transcribed audio on its cloud servers, and there is no option for the user to delete them (Ng, 2019). However, a customer could explicitly submit a request their to have their data erased per GDPR.

Also, when the privacy terms of these voice-based assistants change, customers are often not aware of these changes as the notices are usually updated on websites or sent by email. There are multiple ways to breach the privacy of a voice-based assistant. The perception of privacy of a user of voice-based assistants will continue to evolve based on the known and unknown privacy risks and the user's level of awareness. Awojobi and Landry (2023) found that there are also differences in privacy perceptions based on demographics, level of education, smartphone adoption, and technical awareness and expertise.

Forensic evidence for voice-based assistants can also be collected from the customer's mobile devices. This is because most voice-based assistants, notably Google Home and Amazon Alexa, have apps on mobile devices that mirror the functionality of the always-on devices at the customer's homes. Like most mobile applications, apps for embedded devices run in the background collecting data on the mobile device and activating the smartphone microphone when the customer triggers the wake word. Users could disable the tracking features on mobile devices to protect privacy (Valentino-DeVries & Singer, 2018). Eavesdropping, data retention, and data re-ingestion as part of a machine learning model are some of the known privacy issues with voice-based assistants today. These problems have not reduced the proliferation of voice-based assistants in the marketplace. There is a need for a better understanding of the human perception of privacy to identify if these known issues matter to consumers of voice-based assistants.

Physical Tracking

One of the metadata collected from exposure to the digital computing space is location information. Connectivity to the Internet requires that the device used as a host gets assigned an Internet Protocol (IP) address. IP addresses can be used to track usage location, address owner, and more. Misuse of geographic information because of Internet use is a digital privacy issue. With the advancements in computer and mobile operating systems using Global Positioning System (GPS) and other software-based location tracking features, the exact location of individuals on social media can be tracked. As early as 2013, Li and Goodchild (2013) recognized that "it is possible to impose certain regulations on government agencies regarding the use and disclosure of individual geographic data. This issue is complicated since "data collection is no longer a process monopolized by the government, it is difficult to trace every piece of geographic information by its origin and transformation, as well as to identify data providers."

Radio Frequency Identification (RFID) readers connect with tags in cars, wallets, passports, and other items without us knowing. Landry and Blanke (2011) describe that RFID tags can be read by rogue readers, which means anyone in proximity could read the contents and track the tag. Additionally, passive RFID tags never need to be charged, making them truly stealth devices. Retailers are also culprits of organized data mining of customer behavior and tracking customers' shopping experiences. Retailers use RFID devices without individuals' knowledge. RFID tags can be followed before a sale, during the sales transaction, and after the transaction. Kwet (2019) describes in-store tracking using Bluetooth beacons to connect with apps on the customer's smartphone. The use of beacons allows the tracking of customers in the store and can even track customers between visits. When customer data is collected and used to create intelligence that organizations profit from, the user should have the option to opt-in or opt-out of the data collection and processing. However, beacons are not only used in retailers such as Walmart and Target; they are also used in airports, hotels, cinemas, sports events, museums, and even in front of billboards. There are also third-party marketing firms that are using this data to profile users.

Device manufacturers of voice-based devices collect data about the device's location, to which the device is registered, and the usage patterns – like voice commands the device is being asked to act. Voice-based assistants are not confined to a specific room, meaning underage children are exposed to the devices. The exposure of underage children to voice-based assistants is a severe privacy risk because the device manufacturers can harvest the communication by the kids and exploit the data. Adults, children, organizations, and any individual, should be in complete control of their data and the privacy of their data.

The Issue of Consent

The issue of privacy has been closely related to consent. Adults can make privacy decisions by themselves when presented with privacy options; however, manufacturers of voice-based assistants should not make privacy decisions for minors. For example, Amazon has been unlawfully recording the voices of minors with its Alexa for Kids (Webb, 2019). Data collected from minors or devices specially designed for minors with these devices are subject to privacy laws protecting minors, like Children's Online Privacy Protection Rule (COPPA) (FTC, 2023) and the European Union General Data Privacy Regulation (GDPR). COPPA is a U.S. act that focuses on protecting the privacy of children under the age of 14. Payne, Landry, and Dean discussed (2015) the ethics of data mining and its role in data privacy and found that choice is a common characteristic of GDPR and U. S. regulations. Expressly, consumers must consent to how their data is used and shared.

DISCUSSION

Changing physical to digital assets requires better privacy because data is more transient. At the same time, technological advances cause a lag in government regulations. The differences are opt-in, as in Europe, and opt-out, as in the United States, is significant contributors to how privacy regulations are developed and how companies collect and maintain data. Companies operating in opt-out environments will more aggressively collect individual data than opt-out environments.

Government regulations can provide standardization for how security and privacy controls are deployed. However, government regulations do not stop privacy violations. They only offer deterrent controls for privacy protection. For example, Ivanova (2018) described an incident where an E.U. resident's data, which were recordings from using Alexa, was sent to another user who had never previously used the product. The recordings sent to the wrong user were already downloaded, and the unintended recipient could listen to all the recordings made from another user's home. Issues like these are a breach of privacy and cause distrust within the user community. Additionally, companies may hide behind end-user license agreements (EULA) and maintain that data collection is retained for training purposes. In the AI world, this now includes machine learning in addition to human training.

Like those listed above, Amazon's data and transparency practices are against the Children's Online Privacy Protection Rule (COPPA) instituted by the Federal Trade Commission (FTC). COPPA imposes specific privacy protection requirements on online services and websites used by children under the age of 13 (FTC, 2023). According to the FTC data retention and deletion requirement guidelines regarding COPPA, "An operator of a Web site or online service shall retain personal information collected online from a child for only as long as is reasonably necessary to fulfill the purpose for which the information was collected. The operator must delete such information using reasonable measures to protect against unauthorized access to or use of the information in connection with its deletion" (FTC, 2023). While the requirement does not state the exact time the data needs to be collected, the law stipulates that data should only be kept for a reasonable use duration. Amazon has an Alexa device that is targeted at children, and a case was reported "where a group of 19 consumer and public health advocates filed a complaint with the Federal Trade Commission claiming that the Amazon Echo Dot Kids Edition was retaining children's data even after parents deleted the voice recordings. The data stored on Alexa's remember feature was not deleted until the parents called customer service to delete the entire profile" (Ng, 2019). Events like these go against trust and privacy principles; unfortunately, laws can be interpreted and applied in multiple ways. Despite the public allegations, Amazon issued a statement stating that the Amazon Echo Dot Kids Edition complies with COPPA. When a consumer deletes their online record stored on the servers of a cloud-based assistant, the system returns a successful deletion prompt to the end-user. In contrast, the deletion only led to a partial deletion within the device manufacturer's storage network and is a breach of integrity and a violation of the cybersecurity triad. Amazon violates the integrity component of the cybersecurity triad – confidentiality, integrity, and availability tenets in this scenario.

Apple and Google claimed that they do not store user data in an un-anonymized format, and the data gets deleted after the user initiates a delete action. "A Google spokesman said both the audio and text entry becomes removed when a person deletes that data. For Apple, which uses Siri as a voice assistant, the company said voice recordings are never associated with a person or an account and get tied to a random identifier that you can delete." (CNet, 2019). Apple also posted on its website that "When you turn Siri and Dictation off, Apple will delete the User Data associated with your Siri identifier, and the learning process will start all over again" (CNet, 2019). However, the information has since been modified after Apple got sued for the unauthorized recording of users (Gurman & Burnson, 2019). Unauthorized collection, retention, or access to customer data, whether anonymized or not, is a breach of privacy and trust of consumers, especially when the company had previously come out publicly that they delete user-associated data accordingly.

Apple's Siri, like Google Home and Amazon Alexa, records voice interaction to improve the speech recognition capability of the devices. Apple indicated that the voice recordings they use to train their speech recognition models are anonymized; however, because humans are in charge of reviewing the sample recording, the voice of a public figure may be easily recognized, which is a violation of privacy. As a result, Apple has been sued for violating user privacy under the California Privacy law (Ng, 2019). The lawsuit was "filed in federal court in San Jose by the adult guardian of a child in California whom both use iPhones; Apple was accused of violating a California privacy law that prohibits the recording of people without their permission" (Gurman & Burnson, 2019). Like most cloud-based assistants, Apple's user agreement gives the company the right to record users when they activate Siri with the wake word, which is the "Hey Siri" command. Nevertheless, Siri "can be activated by nearly anything," including the sound of a zipper or a user raising an arm, according to the complaint. Apple's privacy and security policy with regards to voice recording by Siri states that "user recordings from Siri queries are saved for six months "so that the recognition system can utilize them to understand the user's voice better." After six months, another copy of the recording "without its identifier" is saved for up to two years by Apple in order to "improve and develop" Siri functions" (Apple, 2019). According to the information contained in the policy by Apple and written answers to questions regarding Apple's privacy policies to the U. S. Congress, the accusers questioned if Apple lied to the U. S. Congress and asked: "Do Apple's iPhone devices can listen to consumers without a clear, unambiguous audio trigger?" (Gurman & Burnson, 2019). Apple, Amazon, and Google employ contractors to review the voice recordings captured by the cloud-based assistants to improve the quality of the product, a process Apple refers to as grading.

While confidentiality agreements bind these contractors, an anonymous contractor reported that they "regularly hear confidential medical information, drug deals, and recordings of couples having sex" (Perper, 2019). The news and the lawsuit against Apple have led to the company halting the grading program. Following legal actions against Apple, Amazon reviewed its privacy policies and granted consumers the ability to opt out of the grading with Alexa (Drozdiak & Turner, 2019). Control of privacy and sharing should be within the power of the consumer. Consumers should be able to retrieve and replay recordings that the manufacturers of the cloud-based assistants have on them. Consumers should also be able to securely and completely delete their data from Apple's, Google, and Amazon's server. No technical details were given concerning the anonymization technique used by Apple and Google to conceal customer identity before their contractors review the voice recording. If the anonymization is based on an algorithm, it is possible that the algorithm is reversible and could lead to the anonymized data being remapped to an actual customer.

Humans as the Weakest Link

Concerning security and privacy, humans remain the weakest link (Harbert, 2021). The government cannot control individuals' choices concerning the privacy of their information. As discussed earlier, an individual may choose to share all of their medical information online. Another person may choose to do so only within the 'fence' of a social media application. Government policies can address digital privacy issues. An easy example is how GDPR has changed the use of web browser cookies usage and notification. However, government policies are not enough. A government can, however, layout plans, frameworks, awareness campaigns, and guidelines to help protect citizens' privacy. Governments can also limit access to certain websites, social media, or other sources of data.

Privacy can be an individual's preference stance. Individuals' technical expertise sometimes does not matter when making privacy-related choices. A technologically savvy and privacy-aware individual may decide to share information on a social media site, even with the consequences of the exposure of such information being known. The blurred lines between privacy awareness and emotional influence on irrational decisions are dynamic.

With all of this in mind, are government privacy regulations useless? No. Government regulations direct individuals, organizations, and governments to better privacy practices. This chapter only examined GDPR and U. S. State laws, and it is worth mentioning that there are over 80 other national privacy regulations. These include Australia's Privacy Legislation Amendment, Brazil's Lei Geral de Proteção de Dados (LGPD), Canada's PIPEDA, India's Personal Data Protection, and South Africa's Protection of Personal Information Act (POPIA). However, as discussed, the significant differences between opt-in and opt-out strategies will determine the strength of the privacy regulations.

CONCLUSION

There are many intricate and intriguing issues regarding data privacy. In this chapter, you learned about some data privacy issues that cut across stakeholders like individuals, businesses, technology companies, and the government. Each stakeholder has its unique requirements, needs, and interests. For example, government organizations like the police need intelligence to keep citizens safe; however, collecting user information may pry into an individual's privacy limits. Also, in the pursuit of product improvement, technology companies collect data to tune product performance better. When the data collected here is mismanaged, or standard user privacy protection policies do not back the access to the data, the data can compromise individual privacy, hence having unforeseen consequences.

Misuse and abuse of sensitive information is a consequence of data classified as private getting into the hands of bad actors. The major challenge with digital information is the irreversibility of a data compromise once it has occurred. In other words, when user data has been compromised and accessed by bad actors, even a containment and remediation of the source of a breach cannot prevent the consequences of the compromised data. Without the right technology controls and policies in place, once an unauthorized user has established sensitive data access, it is almost impossible to revoke the access. This is the leading cause of identity theft, fraud, ransom, and other crimes. It is also the reason why organizations that have suffered from a breach offer identity theft monitoring solutions to alert users of existing and future compromises to their private information.

The lack of a global data privacy standard or, at a minimum, a baseline is another challenge that makes data privacy difficult to address at scale. Laws and regulations governing privacy vary from country to country. In some countries like the United States, laws and regulations vary from state to state. This can make it difficult for businesses to comply with all of the relevant laws and make it difficult for individuals to know their rights.

Despite the challenges, it is essential to protect the privacy of digital information. There are a number of things that individuals, businesses, and governments can do to help protect privacy, including:

1. Being careful about what information you share online.
2. Using strong authentication and security measures.
3. Being aware of the privacy policies of the businesses with whom you do business.
4. Supporting laws and regulations that protect privacy.
5. Think and implement privacy principles in all product design decisions.

Implications for Practitioners

1. Practitioners must have a broad understanding of the various government regulations across continents. As of the time this book was published, the United States does not have a single federal privacy law; however, several state laws have been enacted. Practitioners should stay up-to-date and aware of the specific regulations that apply to their business and take steps to comply with them.
2. Practitioners should take proactive steps in educating their employees about the importance of data privacy and why it matters. Educating employees about the importance of data privacy ensures that protecting sensitive data is a top priority.
3. Practitioners should promote transparency about their data collection and use practices. Let customers know what data was collected and how it would be used. This will help to build trust and confidence.
4. Be responsive to data privacy incidents. If a data breach does occur, be sure to respond quickly and effectively. This will help to minimize the damage.

REFERENCES

Awojobi, B., & Landry, B. J. L. (2023). An examination of factors determining user privacy perceptions of voice-based assistants. *International Journal of Management, Knowledge and Learning*, *12*, 53–62. doi:10.53615/2232-5697.12.53-62

Boeckl, K., Fagan, M., Fisher, W., Lefkovitz, N., Megas, K., Nadeau, E., Piccarreta, B., O'Rourke, D. G., & Scarfone, K. (2019). *Considerations for managing internet of things (IoT) cybersecurity and privacy risks.* National Institute of Standards and Technology, NISTIR 8228.

Brown, S. (2019). *Most Americans don't think it's possible to keep their data private, report says.* https://www.msn.com/en-us/news/technology/most-in-us-don-t-think-it-s-possible-to-keep-data-private/ar-BBWUn0z?ocid=anah
eimntp

Burgess, M. (2022, July 16). Amazon handed Ring videos to cops without warrants. *Wired.* https://www.wired.com/story/amazon-ring-police-videos-security-roundup/

Castro, D., Dascoli, L., & Diebold, G. (2022). *The looming cost of a patchwork of state privacy laws.* https://www2.itif.org/2022-state-privacy-laws.pdf

Conger, S., & Landry, B. J. L. (2008). The intersection of privacy and security. In *Sprouts: Working Papers on Information Systems* (pp. 1-7). Academic Press.

Cuthbertson, A. (2019). *Facebook deal makes it impossible to delete app from Android smartphones.* https://www.independent.co.uk/tech/facebook-app-delete-android-smartphones-samsung-galaxy-a8719081.html

Drozdiak, N., & Turner, G. (2019). *Tech giants risk privacy probes over Alexa, Siri reviewers.* https://www.bloomberg.com/news/articles/2019-08-05/tech-giants-risk-privacy-probes-over-alexa-siri-eavesdropping

French, A. (2017, Jan 5). *Q&A: Alexa may be listening, but will she tell on you?* https://www.latimes.com/business/technology/la-fi-tn-amazon-echo-privacy-qa-20170105-story.html

FTC. (2023). *Children's Online Privacy Protection Rule (COPPA).* FTC. https://www.ftc.gov/legal-library/browse/rules/childrens-online-privacy-protection-rule-coppay-protection-rule

GDPR.EU. (2023). *Everything you need to know about the "Right to be forgotten".* https://gdpr.eu/right-to-be-forgotten/

Gurman, M., & Burnson, R. (2019). *Apple sued over Siri's unauthorized recording of users.* https://www.msn.com/en-us/news/technology/apple-sued-over-siris-unauthorized-recording-of-users/ar-AAFu9gi

Harbert, T. (2021). *The weakest link in cybersecurity.* SHRM. https://www.shrm.org/hr-today/news/all-things-work/pages/the-weakest-link-in-cybersecurity.aspx

IAPP. (2023a). *Opt-In.* https://iapp.org/resources/article/opt-in/

IAPP. (2023b). *Opt-Out.* https://iapp.org/resources/article/opt-out/

IAPP. (2023c). *U.S. state comprehensive privacy laws.* https://iapp.org/media/pdf/resource_center/us_state_privacy_laws_overview.pdf

Intersoft Consulting. (2023). *Art. 17 GDPR – Right to erasure ('right to be forgotten').* General Data Protection Regulation (GDPR). https://gdpr-info.eu/art-17-gdpr/

Kwet, M. (2019). *In stores, secret surveillance tracks your every move.* https://www.nytimes.com/interactive/2019/06/14/opinion/bluetooth-wireless-tracking-privacy.html

Landry, B. J. L., & Blanke, S. J. (2011). Enumerating RFID networks. In *Proceedings of the Decision Sciences Institute Southwest Region* (pp. 201-209). Academic Press.

Li, L., & Goodchild, M. F. (2013). Is privacy still an issue in the era of big data? - Location disclosure in spatial footprints. In *21st International Conference on Geoinformatics* (pp. 1-4). IEEE. 10.1109/Geoinformatics.2013.6626191

Ng, A. (2019). *Amazon Alexa transcripts live on, even after you delete voice records.* https://www.cnet.com/home/smart-home/amazon-alexa-transcripts-live-on-even-after-you-delete-voice-records/

Payne, D., Landry, B. J. L., & Dean, M. (2015). Data mining and privacy: An initial attempt at a comprehensive code of conduct for online business. *Communications of the Association for Information Systems*, *37*(34), 482–504. doi:10.17705/1CAIS.03734

Perper, R. (2019). *Apple will suspend and review a global program that allows contractors to listen to Siri recordings.* https://www.businessinsider.com/apple-suspends-siri-contractors-listen-privacy-system-2019-8

Santos, J. (2018). *Facebook app impossible to delete from Samsung phones.* https://www.ibtimes.com/facebook-app-impossible-delete-samsung-phones-users-complain-2750257

Sears, A., & Jacko, J. A. (2007). *The human-computer interaction handbook: fundamentals, evolving technologies and emerging applications.* CRC Press. doi:10.1201/9781410615862

Stevens, G. (2010). *Federal Information Security and Data Breach Notification Laws.* Library of Congress. Congressional Research Service. https://digital.library.unt.edu/ark:/67531/metadc505501/

Strahilevitz, L. J. (2012). Toward a positive theory of privacy law. *Harvard Law Review*, *126*, 2010.

Valentino-DeVries, J., & Singer, N. (2018, Dec 10). *How to stop apps from tracking your location.* https://www.nytimes.com/2018/12/10/technology/prevent-location-data-sharing.html

Van Hee, L., Van Den Heuvel, R., Verheyden, T., & Baert, D. (2019). *Google employees are eavesdropping, even in your living room, VRT NWS has discovered.* VRT NWS.

Warren, S., & Brandeis, L. (1890). The right to privacy. *Harvard Law Review*, *4*(5), 193–220. doi:10.2307/1321160

Webb, K. (2019). *Amazon just got hit with a lawsuit that claims it's putting children's privacy at risk by recording what they say to Alexa.* Business Insider. https://www.businessinsider.com/amazon-accused-of-violating-child-privacy-laws-alexa-recordings-lawsuit-2019-6

Chapter 4
Zero Day Vulnerability Assessment:
Exploit Detection and Various Design Patterns in Cyber Software

Vidhant Maan Thapa
University of Petroleum and Energy Studies, India

Sudhanshu Srivastava
University of Petroleum and Energy Studies, India

Shelly Garg
University of Petroleum and Energy Studies, India

ABSTRACT

In this technology-driven era, software development and maintenance are rapidly growing domains and are predestined to thrive over the coming decade. But the growing demand for software solutions also brings its own implications, and software vulnerabilities are the most crucial of these. Software vulnerabilities can be referred to as weaknesses or shortcomings of software solutions, which increase the risks of exploitation of resources and information. In the past few years, the number of exploits has been increasing rapidly, reaching an all-time high in 2021, affecting more than 100 million people world-wide. Even with the presence of existing vulnerability management models and highly secure tools and frameworks, software vulnerabilities are harder to identify and resolve as they may not be independent, and resolving them may cause other vulnerabilities. Moreover, a majority of the exploits are caused by known vulnerabilities and zero-day vulnerabilities.

DOI: 10.4018/978-1-6684-9018-1.ch004

INTRODUCTION

Zero-day vulnerabilities are the vulnerabilities that were previously unknown to the vulnerability management team (Dougherty et al., 2009). They have a high risk of being exploited even before identification. These turn into zero-day exploits, if vulnerabilities are exploited before mitigation (Bilge & Dumitraş, 2012). 2021 experienced exponential growth in these exploits with an estimate that more than 40 percent of these attacks occurred in the last year. From the 2006 Stuxnet attack to the 2019 Facebook and 2021 LinkedIn zero-day attacks, zero-day vulnerabilities are the cause of the majority of cyber attacks compromising the resources and information of millions of users (Chen et al., 2018; Kaushik et al., 2023; Khan & Mailewa, 2023; Nafees et al., 2018; Park et al., 2023; Yin et al., 2023).

Causes of Increased Zero-Day Exploits/Vulnerabilities

A major reason for an increasing number of zero-day vulnerabilities is the rising number of software solutions and updates that occur regularly. Although, these vulnerabilities are harder to detect before being exploited due to their unknown nature but often times developers do not really resolve these implications even identification as it may break other existing programs. This usually occurs due to ineffective design patterns or the existence of anti-patterns in the software solution. Moreover, large software solutions have hundreds (if not thousands) of existing vulnerabilities which may have higher risks of exploitation (Jaber & Fritsch, 2023). Furthermore, as a result of the increasing number of private companies that provide offensive cyber tools and services and malware vendors, global ransomware activity has escalated to a massive extent. This accessibility to developed exploit kits has hiked the number of zero-day exploits over the past few years (Blumbergs et al., 2023).

Handling Zero-Day Vulnerabilities

Due to the unknown nature and increasing existing presence in legacy and current software solutions, it's impossible to completely eradicate zero-day vulnerabilities but with specific practices and tools, we can reduce their growth, and codependencies and tackle these exploits much more effectively in the long run (Pérez-Díaz et al., 2023). For a secure software solution in regard to vulnerabilities and exploits we should successfully incorporate the following steps:

1. Preventing zero-day vulnerabilities to occur in the first place
2. Finding Existing Zero-day Vulnerabilities
3. Quick Recovery from zero-day exploits

Preventing Zero-Day Vulnerabilities to Occur in the First Place

One of the major reasons for the existence of zero-day vulnerabilities in software solutions is the implementation of improper or too co-dependent software/ architectural design patterns which often hinder troubleshooting or debugging processes. A suitable architectural design pattern can help mitigate security vulnerabilities. The basic procedure to choose a secure architectural design pattern for your software solution (Aryal et al., 2023).

Secure Design Patterns

Secure design patterns help in minimizing the accidental insertion of vulnerabilities into the codebase and mitigate the consequences of these vulnerabilities.

Secure design patterns addressing security issues during the architectural design phase and the code-implementation phase (Yang, Dong, Xiao, Cheng, Shi, Li, & Sun, 2023). A design pattern is a reusable solution partial solution to a commonly occurring problem in the designing phase. Secure design patterns differ a lot from security patterns which deal with access control, authorization, and authentication (AAA). These assist in the facilitation of secure development processes and govern the existence and configuration of current security systems.

There are three general classes of secure design patterns:

ÿ **Architectural-Level Design Patterns:** Architectural level design patterns primarily focus on high-level administration of roles and responsibilities between different components of the software solution and also define the interaction between these components. Distrustful Decomposition, Privilege Separation, and Defer to Kernel are some of the most widely used architectural-level secure design patterns (Anand et al., 2022; Aoudni, Donald, Farouk, Sahay, Babu, Tripathi, & Dhabliya, 2022; Aoudni, Donald, Farouk, Sahay, Babu, Tripathi, & Dhabliya, 2022; Kumar & Subbiah, 2022; Mohammed, 2022; Redino et al., 2022; Yang, Dong, Xiao, Cheng, Shi, Li, & Sun, 2023).

ÿ **Design-Level Patterns:** Design level patterns help in addressing internal design issues of these high-level components and not the interaction between these components. Example: Secure State Machine and Secure Visitor (Mubaiwa & Mukosera, 2022).

ÿ **Implementation-Level Patterns:** Implementation level patterns involve low-level security issues and are usually applicable for implementing a specific functionality or feature to the software solution. Secure Directory, Pathname Canonicalization, and RAII (Runtime Acquisition Is Initialization) are some of the widely used Implementation level patterns (Le, Chen, & Babar, 2022).

There can be many secure design pattern solutions depending on software susceptibilities and problem statements, although for preciseness and to avoid divergence from the current subject matter we will cover the following secure design patterns in detail (Abri et al., 2019; Ahmed, 2022; Blaise et al., 2020; Garg & Baliyan, 2019; Martins et al., 2022; Singh et al., 2019; Vetterl & Clayton, 2019; You et al., 2019).

Distrustful Decomposition

Distrustful decomposition is an architectural-level secure design pattern that primarily focuses on dividing the system into many small independent processes where each process has its own set of privileges. IPC mechanisms (Inter-Process communication) such as Remote Procedure calls (RPCs) and Unix domain sockets help in facilitating communication between these processes. The primary objective of the Distrustful decomposition design pattern is to move separate functions into mutually untrusting programs (Kim et al., 2019). This helps in reducing the attack surface and prevents other processes to be affected when one or more processes are compromised. This prevents the attacker from compromising the entire system due to the exploitation of the single process/component because no other process trusts the information dispatched by the compromised component (Garre et al., 2021).

Incorporating a Distrustful Decomposition pattern during the software development cycle can largely reduce the number of zero-day exploits by minimizing co-dependencies between processes and also by containing the attack only at a single component level. This not only minimizes damages from zero-day exploits but also provides a better environment for troubleshooting and fixing vulnerabilities as each component is independent and directly does not affect other components without the use of IPC protocols (Le, Chen, & Babar, 2022). Some of the prominent known application of the Distrustful decomposition pattern was in Windows vista for running applications safely with administration privileges, in the mail system, and also inspired the creation of a similar pattern used in the Postfix mail system (Meira et al., 2020).

PrivSep (Privilege Separation)

Privilege Separation (PrivSep) is another architectural-level pattern whose intention is to avoid limiting the overall functionality of the program while largely reducing the amount of code running with special privileges (Zhou et al., 2020). The primary goal is to ensure that only a small, safe necessary subset of the entire code base requires elevated privileges code base, while the remaining larger set of complex and error-prone operations runs on standard user privileges (Jacobs et al., 2020).

This pattern is useful for services that require users to authenticate themselves and then run the standard system operations with normal user privileges. This helps in reducing exploits like SQL injections and reducing the scope of zero-day exploits by limiting the attacker to only access user privileges and preventing exploitation of resources using elevated user access (Liu et al., 2020). This basically means that if an adversary gain controls over the child's processes, it is only confined to the current set of privileges that may not be of a higher degree and fails to gain control over the parent, thereby minimizing the amount of damage that an attacker could inflict (Mercaldo & Santone, 2020). PrivSep Secure design pattern was implemented in OpenBSD, X Window server, and other Linux/Unix-based applications (Vishwakarma & Jain, 2019).

Defer to Kernel

Defer to Kernel is a secure design pattern that utilizes and takes advantage of existing verification kernel functionality and focuses on separating functionalities that require elevated user privileges from the existing user privileges. The primary objective of this secure design pattern is to reduce or avoid the use of user elevated privileges that are much more susceptible to privilege escalation attacks. The Key difference between the Privilege separation pattern is that the Differ to kernel pattern primarily utilizes existing kernel functionalities for user verification. Before execution of any operations that require root or super user privileges, the system needs to verify and validate whether the current user is allowed to execute functionality or not.

The following secure design pattern is widely used in Linux/Unix-based systems and also in securable objects in windows. The Defer to Kernel pattern has a client-server architecture. Existing applications must be re-architectured as a client-server system which adds ups additional complexity to the system because of communication between the client and the server. The server receives the request from the client which also includes the identity of the client, which is then validated by the existing verification functionalities of the kernel, which further determines whether to authorize the user's request or to reject it (Dionísio et al., 2019; Nagendran et al., 2019; Schwarz, Lackner, & Gruss, 2019; Suciu et al., 2022).

Vulnerability Anti-Patterns

Anti-patterns are poor software practices of implementing certain design patterns that can have negative consequences. Developers should have operating knowledge of these anti-patterns to successfully avoid their inclusion in the codebase. These are highly error-prone and are susceptible to creating loopholes thereby making the program more vulnerable (Efstathopoulos et al., 2019). Many well-known anti-patterns can increase the risks of exploitable bugs and vulnerabilities. A few of these include:

God Object Anti-Pattern

The anti-pattern refers to the excessive concentration of functions in a single class, allowing the object of that class to have multiple functionalities. It supersedes the idea of "single responsibility". This means the responsibilities of too many functionalities are designated to a single class or object. This makes the code hard to debug, test, and maintain. From a zero-day perspective, it becomes very difficult to recover from zero-day exploits as functionalities are codependent (i.e., fixing a bug can transpose other parts of the code). Moreover, if an attacker gains control over a god object, it will comprise the security of the entire system (Khan et al., 2019).

Boat Anchor Anti-Pattern

Boat anchor anti-pattern is another common software anti-pattern. It happens when developers leave a lot of unused (non-functional) code in the codebase for future use-case purposes. It overtime piles up, ending up creating a hulky mess of obsolete code in the code base which makes it harder to debug and unit test. This often leads to another design pattern known as "dead code". It not only hinders the patching process but also slows down execution speed due to excessive technical debt. Moreover, these boat anchors (obsolete codes) often contain a backdoor to the re-invented functionalities which an attacker can exploit and compromise certain parts of the program, if not the entire system (Afianian et al., 2019; Redini et al., 2020; Wang et al., 2020).

FINDING EXISTING ZERO-DAY EXPLOITS

It is quite challenging to successfully identify and unravel zero-day vulnerabilities due to their unknown nature, but with optimal techniques and resources, it is possible to detect and identify exploitable zero-day vulnerabilities (Malhotra et al., 2021).

Common Vulnerability and Exposure Database and Third-Party Associations

Common Vulnerability and Exposure database (CVE) is an open-source project by MITRE corporation whose primary goal is to define, recognize and categorize publicly disclosed vulnerabilities. These vulnerabilities are reported to the database by bug hunters, security activists, and white-hat hacker groups. This acts as a formal notice to the manufacturer of the software informing them to fix those exploitable vulnerabilities. Another popular database is the National Vulnerability Database (NVD) which harmonizes with the MITRE CVE list (Schwarz, Weiser, & Gruss, 2019). But often, big tech giants prefer getting information from third parties or directly from bug hunters offering a higher incentive and keeping a non-disclosure agreement until the vulnerabilities are fixed. Companies like google have one of the finest security teams called *Project Zero* whose mission is to detect and catalog zero days vulnerabilities.

Project Zero internally has a Threat Analysis Group (TAG) which tracks parties involved in government-backed hacking, disinformation campaigns, and financially motivated abuse. Once it is suspected that bad actors are using exploitable bugs, they report it to the manufacturer for quick recovery. Google's thread analysis group (TAG) doesn't only addresses zero-day vulnerabilities in google's tool but also discloses zero-day exploits in other software solutions too, with a primary objective of creating a secure world. For example, google recently disclosed a zero-day vulnerability targeting Windows operating system and reported it to Microsoft.

Monkey Testing (Extensive Fuzzing)

Monkey testing refers to the execution of random actions or inputs in a program until a crash or error occurs exposing any exploitable vulnerabilities. The idea behind monkey testing is if we generate random inputs (text prompts or either simulating random touches on the screen) it can cover all possible test cases given that we do it long enough and with enough randomness.

The figurative "monkey" refers to the infinite monkey theorem that states that if an army of monkeys is hitting random inputs on a typewriter for an infinite amount of time, it will eventually type out the entire works of William Shakespeare. Although apart from time and randomness, the intelligence of the monkey also plays a vital role in generating valid enough inputs that are not directly rejected by the parser but do create unforeseen behaviors that are invalid enough to expose or trigger some exploitable part of the code. So, the ultimate zero-day tool kit revolves around having a supercomputer powerful enough to bombard an application with all possible combinations of actions/inputs.

In the real world, monkey testing is practiced through a popular penetration testing framework known as fuzzing. Fuzzing is an automated software testing method that breaks the system by injecting random, malformed, and invalid inputs to find exploitable vulnerabilities. A fuzzer is a tool that allows us to inject these sem-random or random inputs. Google OSS-Fuzz, FuzzDB, Ffuf (fuzz faster u fool), Google ClusterFuzz, and radamsa are some of the open-source fuzzing tools prominently used by software testers.

Prominent Use-Cases

One-Fuzz: Microsoft open-sourced its fuzzing tool "One Fuzz" which is used by Microsoft edge to identify exploitable vulnerabilities. The fuzzer can create thousands (if not millions) of web pages and load them in the web browser. It was used to load all possible combinations of HTML and JavaScript files to see how the Microsoft Edge browser responds to it. After running the automated fuzzer for a certain amount of time says days or weeks the organization would log thousands of crash reports that exposed some exploitable vulnerabilities in the browser.

OSS-FUZZ: Google's open-source fuzzing tool which routinely examines over 700 critical open-source projects for vulnerabilities was launched in 2016. It is widely known for its effort to detect almost all Log4shell vulnerabilities over a certain amount of time. It continues to improve java fuzzing and has successfully reported over 10,000 exploitable vulnerabilities in open-sourced projects.

IMPLEMENTATION

In the upcoming Discussion, we will try to imitate monkey testing (Extensive fuzzing) using an open-source fuzzer called radamsa. It functions by reading samples of valid file inputs and generating similar test cases. The main objective is to break the program using semi-random inputs and find any exploitable vulnerabilities. We tried to generate test-suite (set of test cases) for a simple c program which we will try to break (input sanitization) by giving random inputs for N number of test cases or until a crash occurs.

To achieve this, we created a basic shell script for creating random inputs (numbers) is fed to the above-mentioned C file and test-cases are recorded accordingly for errors. Our objective behind this implementation is to provide a general idea of a zero-day toolkit which revolves around having a super computer powerful enough to bombard the system with all possible combinations of inputs in a relatively small times (say days or weeks).

Quick Recovery From Zero-Day Exploits

Figure 1. Handling zero-day exploits

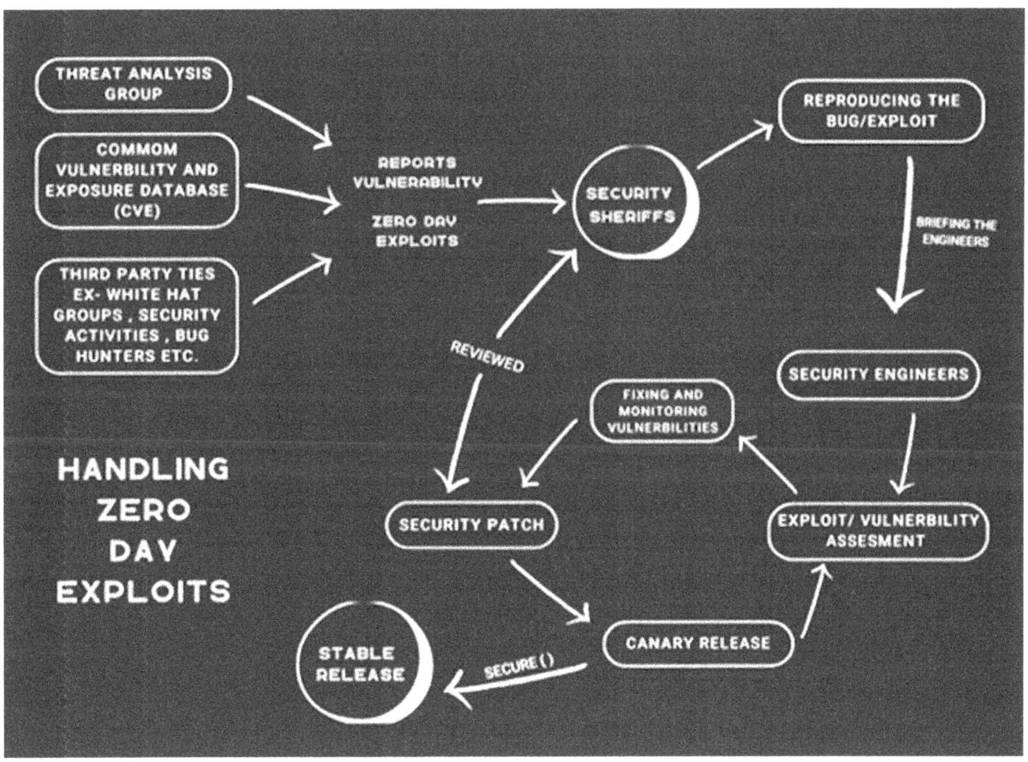

Due to the unforeseen nature of zero-day exploits, it is not possible to provide an optimal model or pipeline for handling zero-day exploits. Most organizations follow the traditional way method of fixing exploits. Zero-day exploits need to be handled in a tightly bounded time frame in order to reduce the amount of damage that is inflicted during the lifecycle of the exploit which can incur heavy financial and technical debts to the system.

Large Tech giants like Google have designated teams for solely handling zero-day vulnerabilities. Google has a queue of security sheriffs which facilitates the overall bug-fixing process and guides the security engineers. Due to the lack of a concrete way for handling zero-day exploits, we proposed our own general model to handle these exploits which is based on google's zero-day project. Although, optimal results cannot be achieved as each zero-day attack may differ from the other.

General Zero-Day Model

Explanation:

The organization receives reports of a zero-day attack or exploitable vulnerabilities from threat analysis groups (TAG), CVE databases, or other third-party ties like white-hat hacker groups and bug-hunters. These reports are accessed by the Security sheriffs who are responsible for resolving these vulnerabilities and securing the software along with security engineers. The security sheriffs try to reproduce the bug in a secure environment to gain major information and brief the security engineers about the issues.

The security engineers then follow the standard exploit measures, essentially starting with a vulnerability assessment. Vulnerabilities are fixed and monitored in the next stage to ensure that it does not affect other parts of the code. A security patch is released which undergoes automated testing and is reviewed by the security sheriffs. After this, a canary release is deployed. After a few iterations of these processes authenticating the security standard of these patches, a stable release is deployed for the general public.

CONCLUSION AND FUTURE SCOPE

Even with potent present-day technological growth zero-day exploits still continues to be an impenetrable feat. Although, many tech companies have fabricated their own solutions with hopes of mitigating the damages inflicted by them but have failed to provide an optimal solution. An exponential growth related to supercomputers and mainframes is required to significantly improve present-day solutions to zero-day exploits. Although, it is possible to facilitate hassle-free patching of these vulnerabilities and significantly reduce zero-day vulnerabilities by implementing secure design patterns and avoiding poor software practices like anti-patterns. Moreover, organizations like Google's threat analysis group (TAG) and Common vulnerabilities and exposure (CVE) database have continued their quest to create secure software solutions by regularly identifying and reporting exploitable vulnerabilities.

The success of any zero-day model relies largely on continuous adaptability as each zero-day exploit can bring forth unanticipated challenges oftentimes making prior principles and practices susceptible.

As for us, we should recognize that there are no optimal solutions to zero-day problems as strategies, principles, and practices can always be improvised to accommodate uncertain events. There is no golden model or pipeline that works for every organization as each organization may face different zero-day exploits depending on its software solution, therefore each needs to analyze its requirements and ongoing hazards to amalgamate strategies from different methodologies to figure out what works for them.

REFERENCES

Abri, F., Siami-Namini, S., Khanghah, M. A., Soltani, F. M., & Namin, A. S. (2019, December). Can machine/deep learning classifiers detect zero-day malware with high accuracy? In 2019 IEEE international conference on big data (Big Data) (pp. 3252-3259). IEEE.

Afianian, A., Niksefat, S., Sadeghiyan, B., & Baptiste, D. (2019). Malware dynamic analysis evasion techniques: A survey. *ACM Computing Surveys*, *52*(6), 1–28. doi:10.1145/3365001

Ahmed, O. (2022). *Behaviour Anomaly on Linux Systems to Detect Zero-day Malware Attacks* [Doctoral dissertation]. Auckland University of Technology.

Anand, P., Singh, Y., & Selwal, A. (2022). Learning-Based Techniques for Assessing Zero-Day Attacks and Vulnerabilities in IoT. In *Recent Innovations in Computing* (pp. 497–504). Springer. doi:10.1007/978-981-16-8248-3_41

Aoudni, Y., Donald, C., Farouk, A., Sahay, K. B., Babu, D. V., Tripathi, V., & Dhabliya, D. (2022). Cloud security based attack detection using transductive learning integrated with Hidden Markov Model. *Pattern Recognition Letters*, *157*, 16–26. doi:10.1016/j.patrec.2022.02.012

Aoudni, Y., Donald, C., Farouk, A., Sahay, K. B., Babu, D. V., Tripathi, V., & Dhabliya, D. (2022). Cloud security based attack detection using transductive learning integrated with Hidden Markov Model. *Pattern Recognition Letters*, *157*, 16–26. doi:10.1016/j.patrec.2022.02.012

Aryal, K., Gupta, M., & Abdelsalam, M. (2023). *Analysis of Label-Flip Poisoning Attack on Machine Learning Based Malware Detector.* arXiv preprint arXiv:2301.01044.

Bilge, L., & Dumitraş, T. (2012, October). Before we knew it: an empirical study of zero-day attacks in the real world. In *Proceedings of the 2012 ACM conference on Computer and communications security* (pp. 833-844). 10.1145/2382196.2382284

Blaise, A., Bouet, M., Conan, V., & Secci, S. (2020). Detection of zero-day attacks: An unsupervised port-based approach. *Computer Networks*, *180*, 107391. doi:10.1016/j.comnet.2020.107391

Blumbergs, B., Dobelis, E., & Paikens, P. (2023). WearSec: Towards Automated Security Evaluation of Wireless Wearable Devices. *Secure IT Systems: 27th Nordic Conference, NordSec 2022, Reykjavic, Iceland, November 30–December 2, 2022 Proceedings*, *13700*, 311.

Chen, C., Cui, B., Ma, J., Wu, R., Guo, J., & Liu, W. (2018). A systematic review of fuzzing techniques. *Computers & Security*, *75*, 118–137. doi:10.1016/j.cose.2018.02.002

Dionísio, N., Alves, F., Ferreira, P. M., & Bessani, A. (2019, July). Cyberthreat detection from twitter using deep neural networks. In 2019 international joint conference on neural networks (IJCNN) (pp. 1-8). IEEE. doi:10.1109/IJCNN.2019.8852475

Dougherty, C., Sayre, K., Seacord, R. C., Svoboda, D., & Togashi, K. (2009). *Secure design patterns.* Carnegie-Mellon Univ.

Efstathopoulos, G., Grammatikis, P. R., Sarigiannidis, P., Argyriou, V., Sarigiannidis, A., Stamatakis, K., . . . Athanasopoulos, S. K. (2019, September). Operational data based intrusion detection system for smart grid. In *2019 IEEE 24th International Workshop on Computer Aided Modeling and Design of Communication Links and Networks (CAMAD)* (pp. 1-6). IEEE. 10.1109/CAMAD.2019.8858503

Garg, S., & Baliyan, N. (2019). A novel parallel classifier scheme for vulnerability detection in android. *Computers & Electrical Engineering*, *77*, 12–26. doi:10.1016/j.compeleceng.2019.04.019

Garre, J. T. M., Pérez, M. G., & Ruiz-Martínez, A. (2021). A novel Machine Learning-based approach for the detection of SSH botnet infection. *Future Generation Computer Systems*, *115*, 387–396. doi:10.1016/j.future.2020.09.004

Jaber, A., & Fritsch, L. (2023). Towards AI-powered Cybersecurity Attack Modeling with Simulation Tools: Review of Attack Simulators. In *International Conference on P2P, Parallel, Grid, Cloud and Internet Computing* (pp. 249-257). Springer.

Jacobs, J., Romanosky, S., Adjerid, I., & Baker, W. (2020). Improving vulnerability remediation through better exploit prediction. *Journal of Cybersecurity*, *6*(1), tyaa015. doi:10.1093/cybsec/tyaa015

Kaushik, B., Sharma, R., Dhama, K., Chadha, A., & Sharma, S. (2023). Performance evaluation of learning models for intrusion detection system using feature selection. *Journal of Computer Virology and Hacking Techniques*, 1-20.

Khan, H. A., Sehatbakhsh, N., Nguyen, L. N., Prvulovic, M., & Zajić, A. (2019). Malware detection in embedded systems using neural network model for electromagnetic side-channel signals. *Journal of Hardware and Systems Security*, *3*(4), 305–318. doi:10.100741635-019-00074-w

Khan, S., & Mailewa, A. B. (2023). Discover Botnets in IoT Sensor Networks: A Lightweight Deep Learning Framework with Hybrid Self-Organizing Maps. *Microprocessors and Microsystems*, *97*, 104753. doi:10.1016/j.micpro.2022.104753

Kim, T., Kim, C. H., Rhee, J., Fei, F., Tu, Z., Walkup, G., . . . Xu, D. (2019). {RVFuzzer}: Finding Input Validation Bugs in Robotic Vehicles through {Control-Guided} Testing. In *28th USENIX Security Symposium (USENIX Security 19)* (pp. 425-442). USENIX.

Kumar, R., & Subbiah, G. (2022). Zero-Day Malware Detection and Effective Malware Analysis Using Shapley Ensemble Boosting and Bagging Approach. *Sensors (Basel)*, *22*(7), 2798. doi:10.339022072798 PMID:35408413

Le, T. H., Chen, H., & Babar, M. A. (2022). A survey on data-driven software vulnerability assessment and prioritization. *ACM Computing Surveys*, *55*(5), 1–39. doi:10.1145/3529757

Liu, X., Lin, Y., Li, H., & Zhang, J. (2020). A novel method for malware detection on ML-based visualization technique. *Computers & Security*, *89*, 101682. doi:10.1016/j.cose.2019.101682

Malhotra, P., Singh, Y., Anand, P., Bangotra, D. K., Singh, P. K., & Hong, W. C. (2021). Internet of things: Evolution, concerns and security challenges. *Sensors (Basel)*, *21*(5), 1809. doi:10.339021051809 PMID:33807724

Martins, I., Resende, J. S., Sousa, P. R., Silva, S., Antunes, L., & Gama, J. (2022). Host-based IDS: A review and open issues of an anomaly detection system in IoT. *Future Generation Computer Systems, 133*, 95–113. doi:10.1016/j.future.2022.03.001

Meira, J., Andrade, R., Praça, I., Carneiro, J., Bolón-Canedo, V., Alonso-Betanzos, A., & Marreiros, G. (2020). Performance evaluation of unsupervised techniques in cyber-attack anomaly detection. *Journal of Ambient Intelligence and Humanized Computing, 11*(11), 4477–4489. doi:10.100712652-019-01417-9

Mercaldo, F., & Santone, A. (2020). Deep learning for image-based mobile malware detection. *Journal of Computer Virology and Hacking Techniques, 16*(2), 157–171. doi:10.100711416-019-00346-7

Mohammed, V. (2022). Automatic Static Vulnerability Detection Approaches and Tools: State of the Art. *Advances in Information, Communication and Cybersecurity: Proceedings of ICI2C'21, 357*, 449.

Mubaiwa, T. G., & Mukosera, M. (2022). *A hybrid approach to detect security vulnerabilities in web applications*. Academic Press.

Nafees, T., Coull, N., Ferguson, I., & Sampson, A. (2018, November). Vulnerability anti-patterns: a timeless way to capture poor software practices (vulnerabilities). In *24th Conference on Pattern Languages of Programs* (p. 23). The Hillside Group.

Nagendran, K., Adithyan, A., Chethana, R., Camillus, P., & Varshini, K. B. S. (2019). Web application penetration testing. *International Journal of Innovative Technology and Exploring Engineering, 8*(10), 1029–1035. doi:10.35940/ijitee.J9173.0881019

Park, N. E., Lee, Y. R., Joo, S., Kim, S. Y., Kim, S. H., Park, J. Y., Kim, S.-Y., & Lee, I. G. (2023). Performance evaluation of a fast and efficient intrusion detection framework for advanced persistent threat-based cyberattacks. *Computers & Electrical Engineering, 105*, 108548. doi:10.1016/j.compeleceng.2022.108548

Pérez-Díaz, N. W., Chinchay-Maldonado, J. O., Mejía-Cabrera, H. I., Bances-Saavedra, D. E., & Bravo-Ruiz, J. A. (2023). Ransomware Identification Through Sandbox Environment. In *Proceedings of the Future Technologies Conference* (pp. 326-335). Springer.

Redini, N., Machiry, A., Wang, R., Spensky, C., Continella, A., Shoshitaishvili, Y., ... Vigna, G. (2020, May). Karonte: Detecting insecure multi-binary interactions in embedded firmware. In *2020 IEEE Symposium on Security and Privacy (SP)* (pp. 1544-1561). IEEE. 10.1109/SP40000.2020.00036

Redino, C., Nandakumar, D., Schiller, R., Choi, K., Rahman, A., Bowen, E., . . . Nehila, J. *(2022). Zero Day Threat Detection Using Graph and Flow Based Security Telemetry*. arXiv preprint arXiv:2205.02298. doi:10.1109/ICCCIS56430.2022.10037596

Schwarz, M., Lackner, F., & Gruss, D. (2019, February). JavaScript Template Attacks: Automatically Inferring Host Information for Targeted Exploits. NDSS.

Schwarz, M., Weiser, S., & Gruss, D. (2019, June). Practical enclave malware with Intel SGX. In *International Conference on Detection of Intrusions and Malware, and Vulnerability Assessment* (pp. 177-196). Springer.

Singh, U. K., Joshi, C., & Kanellopoulos, D. (2019). A framework for zero-day vulnerabilities detection and prioritization. *Journal of Information Security and Applications*, *46*, 164–172. doi:10.1016/j.jisa.2019.03.011

Suciu, O., Nelson, C., Lyu, Z., Bao, T., & Dumitraş, T. (2022). Expected exploitability: Predicting the development of functional vulnerability exploits. In *31st USENIX Security Symposium (USENIX Security 22)* (pp. 377-394). USENIX.

Vetterl, A., & Clayton, R. (2019, November). Honware: A virtual honeypot framework for capturing CPE and IoT zero days. In *2019 APWG Symposium on Electronic Crime Research (eCrime)* (pp. 1-13). IEEE. 10.1109/eCrime47957.2019.9037501

Vishwakarma, R., & Jain, A. K. (2019, April). A honeypot with machine learning based detection framework for defending IoT based botnet DDoS attacks. In *2019 3rd International Conference on Trends in Electronics and Informatics (ICOEI)* (pp. 1019-1024). IEEE. 10.1109/ICOEI.2019.8862720

Wang, Y., Jia, X., Liu, Y., Zeng, K., Bao, T., Wu, D., & Su, P. (2020, February). Not All Coverage Measurements Are Equal: Fuzzing by Coverage Accounting for Input Prioritization. NDSS.

Yang, S., Dong, C., Xiao, Y., Cheng, Y., Shi, Z., Li, Z., & Sun, L. (2023). *Asteria-Pro: Enhancing Deep-Learning Based Binary Code Similarity Detection by Incorporating Domain Knowledge.* arXiv preprint arXiv:2301.00511.

Yin, J., Tang, M., Cao, J., You, M., & Wang, H. (2023). Cybersecurity Applications in Software: Data-Driven Software Vulnerability Assessment and Management. In *Emerging Trends in Cybersecurity Applications* (pp. 371–389). Springer. doi:10.1007/978-3-031-09640-2_17

You, W., Wang, X., Ma, S., Huang, J., Zhang, X., Wang, X., & Liang, B. (2019, May). Profuzzer: On-the-fly input type probing for better zero-day vulnerability discovery. In 2019 IEEE symposium on security and privacy (SP) (pp. 769-786). IEEE.

Zhou, S., Yang, Z., Xiang, J., Cao, Y., Yang, M., & Zhang, Y. (2020, August). An ever-evolving game: Evaluation of real-world attacks and defenses in ethereum ecosystem. In *Proceedings of the 29th USENIX Conference on Security Symposium* (pp. 2793-2809). USENIX.

Chapter 5
Pragmatic Risk-Based Approach to Cybersecurity: Establishing a Risk-Enhanced Unified Set of Security Controls

Stephen G. Fridakis
https://orcid.org/0009-0005-7436-7213
Oracle Health, USA

ABSTRACT

Sometimes security and technology professionals confuse their state of compliance with their security posture. While an organization can meet the requirements to any regulatory standard (HIPAA, SOC, etc.), doing so should not be construed as meeting the requirements to defend a potential cyberattack, provide data protection during business processing, or maintain a highly secure development environment. In this chapter, the authors discuss how security and compliance can co-exist. They associate each one of these with controls that are either derived from formal frameworks or meet custom operational or other requirements of an organization. They explore how each control needs to be implemented with a risk perspective in mind, and finally, they suggest methods on how to manage such a control catalog.

WHY COMPLIANT DOES NOT MEAN SECURE

Compliance guidelines are provided as a generalized method to define common minimum standards for a specific area of concern such as payment industry, healthcare, financial information and so on. Given the high degree of interpretation that each guideline is subject to, any blind strict adherence will not result in any material improvements in security or operations. There are many factors that can still cause a security failure despite an organization's adherence to the standard. Lack of skilled staff, human error, availability of information to support breach detection, dysfunctional organizational structures are all contributors to bad security despite meeting the compliance standards.

DOI: 10.4018/978-1-6684-9018-1.ch005

Establishing a framework is a very complicated undertaking. As Table 1 suggests, most frameworks are updated in regular intervals, yet keeping up with the pace and implementation of certain updates can be challenging.

Table 1. Popular frameworks and their latest version/release date

Framework	Current Version	Release Date
NIST	1.1	April 2018
ISO 27001/27002	35.030 -35.030	October 2022 - March 2022
CIS	8	May 2021
SOC2	Oct 2022	Oct 2022
PCI-DSS	4	Mar 2022
COBIT	2019	2018
HiTrust	11	Jan 2023
Cloud Control Matrix (CSA)	4	Jan 2021
CMMC	2	Nov 2021
HIPAA	2023	Jan 2023

In their 2018 (GAO, 2018) report titled "Critical Infrastructure Protection: Additional Actions are Essential for Assessing Cybersecurity Framework Adoption", the US Government Accountability Office (GAO) stated that while there may be regular updates of a certain framework such as NIST, their timely adoption may be hindered by conflicting and overlapping standards or tools that have not kept up with the updates. Despite that, using a framework is useful, not to say essential. One can argue that the tools, other frameworks and lack of necessary knowledge challenge strict adherence to what is specified. HIPAA establishes the minimum security controls for administrative, physical and technical safeguards. The standard itself provides no guidance regarding the implementation of specific methods (the "how"). Instead it uses open ended suggestions to implement what is "reasonable" or what is "a best practice" reducing security posture to mere concepts.

Another such example relevant to medical - life sciences applications that include hardware and sensors is ISO27034 (IEC, 2022). This standard devotes significant space in application security controls which it defines as "data structure containing a precise enumeration and description of a security activity and its associated verification measurement to be performed at a specific point in an application's lifecycle." Furthermore it defines the targeted Level of Trust as "name or label of a set of Application Security Controls deemed necessary by the application owner to lower the risk associated with a specific application to an acceptable (or tolerable) level, following an application security risk analysis." Implementing such a standard is quite overwhelming, and any organization's ability to associate the standard with its own operations and perform a risk analysis based on it is quite challenging.

There is more vagueness and ambiguity that suggest the need for close review and customization with other controls as well. NIST 800-53 control AU-11 addresses the matter of log retention in the following terms (NIST, 2022): "Retain audit records to provide support for after-the-fact investigations of incidents and to meet regulatory and organizational information retention requirements. Organizations retain audit records until it is determined that the records are no longer needed for administrative, legal, audit, or other operational purposes." While this control is a general best practice, it leaves a lot of organizational level work that needs to be performed, especially if an organization also needs to comply to other frameworks (e.g., FISMA, PCI, etc.) while trying to specify the retention period for various log categories that need to be retained.

PCI applies to anyone who is storing, processing or transmitting any card holder data or sensitive authentication data associated with credit cards. There is a lot of confusion around PCI. Security professionals in organizations that do not store, transmit or process credit cards, have to defend their opinion that they do not need to meet PCI repeatedly. That is because even though they may not deal directly with credit cards, their clients do!

Referring to PCI section 12.8.2 (PCI, 2022) we see that the specific requirement is to: "Maintain a written agreement that includes an acknowledgement that the service providers are responsible for the security of cardholder data the service providers possess or otherwise store, process or transmit on behalf of the customer, or to the extent that they could impact the security of the customer's cardholder data environment". It is practically impossible to ascertain whether using credit card information for multi-factor authentication purposes or acting as a hosting provider to an application with credit card information subjects someone to PCI compliance.

We could devote many pages describing similar examples of vague or contradicting controls while trying to establish that security and compliance are equally important albeit their different scope and perspectives. Security is tasked with protecting information from various threats. Compliance is a point-of-time report of how an organization interprets and meets standards established by the applicable security framework(s).

While frameworks such as NIST CSF and ISO 27001 are complementary, they can also be quite conflicting with one another. Our key suggestion is to utilize controls that satisfy an organization's business priorities and risk profile and build a set of unified - common controls to satisfy regulatory priorities while also measuring the state of the organization's security posture.

Both NIST CSF and ISO recommend maintaining an asset registry or inventory. Similarly about seventy-five percent of their controls are complementary. At the same time, NIST is primarily provided by and for US federal agencies while ISO is not. NIST is voluntary while ISO relies on auditors. Arguably ISO is not particularly technical, giving more emphasis on risk.

The Covid pandemic has exasperated the gap between compliance and security. During that time certain organizations may have shifted their attention to use cases and controls that emphasize how end points are managed. Allowing one's own device (BYOD) on the network was probably exhaustively debated given working-from-home or taking residence in many remote locations. Some organizations looked at zero-trust in earnest, implementing controls that do not trust the user, the device they were using, or the network from which they were accessing corporate applications and data.

In principle, networks and associated logging, monitoring and other utilities can be fully compliant to many frameworks - HIPAA, ISO, or NIST. However, we can clearly argue that such a highly compliant no-trust network (a world play on zero-trust) can be breached, and for this reason, organizations in a post-covid era may not trust even an authenticated user to be whom they claim to be.

The traditional trust-and-verify method is questionable when you realize that you cannot trust even an insider with a trusted account. Furthermore, even an authenticated user can be afforded very limited access to anything while in other framework driven scenarios, a trusted insider has access to all levels of corporate systems and sensitive data.

Organizations that operate the majority of their applications in a cloud environment or in multiple clouds come to realize that the old notion of perimeter protection[1] has become redundant. Using phones to access applications, or working remotely in some cases using the employee's own computers. Add to that wearables and other IoTs. Utilizing a compliance framework suggests that there is an identifiable perimeter that can be hardened, monitored and managed.

Compliance audits invariably include evidence but usually come down to some sort of a binary "yes-or-no" answer to a very oversimplified - complex issue. The same audits are peppered with questions such as how often to update antivirus signatures or change passwords. Frameworks such as NIST and ISO are useful as guidelines for compliance and security, but for security to be effective, their controls have to be customized and applicable to the organization, and considered through a risk based approach. This is the focus of the remainder of this chapter.

IMPLEMENTING A UNIFIED CONTROLS FRAMEWORK

An organization should adhere to the controls mandated by those frameworks that best complement its business and operations. These controls should address cybersecurity and privacy principles in a strategic, operational and tactical context. The complete set of controls would be a common set between the frameworks chosen, extracted directly from them, complemented by several customer controls.

How can an organization select controls and ensure that there is "enough" of them is the subject of this discussion. The purpose of controls is to make security features understood and to enable review of their effectiveness. Controls also exist to protect a company's data, applications and network. One of the motivations for a unified controls framework is to make audits and collection of compliance evidence reasonably easy and to align business practices and audit requirements. The last one can be quite challenging.

Establishing a map between various framework controls is quite easy. There are many tools that can achieve that including the Center for Internet Security (CIS, 2022) or the National Initiative for Cybersecurity Careers and Studies (NICCS, 2021) or the American Institute of Certified Public Accountants (AICPA, 2022) that has already mapped the trust services criteria (TSC) of SOC 2 to ISO 27001, NIST CSF, GDPR, and certain other frameworks.

Adopting a common set of controls is quite beneficial. Evidence of compliance is collected once and is applicable to each audit for the various frameworks. These controls are identified as they best suit our business, avoiding control overlap. It is important to realize that requesting the same or even similar evidence from the same stakeholders multiple times a year is very time consuming and a huge burden that takes them away from their own job responsibilities. By eliminating duplicative controls, a Unified Control Framework reduces that burden.

While we explore the concept that compliance does not equal security, we can only reflect on the ease of validation of the various controls when a unified framework is used. We believe that a set of standard and custom controls that are risk weighted and managed can actually be very effective for security. We will also discuss a method to determine whether an organization has sufficient control coverage that satisfies security objectives. Controls are the bridge mechanism between compliance and practical security implementation. Implementing a set of controls also suggests additional capabilities related to governance and risk management.

We cannot discount the fact that a unified set of controls makes audits and the associated collection and verification of evidence easier. We think that 50-60% of controls are common across NIST, ISO, and in certain cases other frameworks, making possible an overall reduction of audit costs to even half their combined price.

Figure 1. Sample services/controls catalog for a medical technology organization

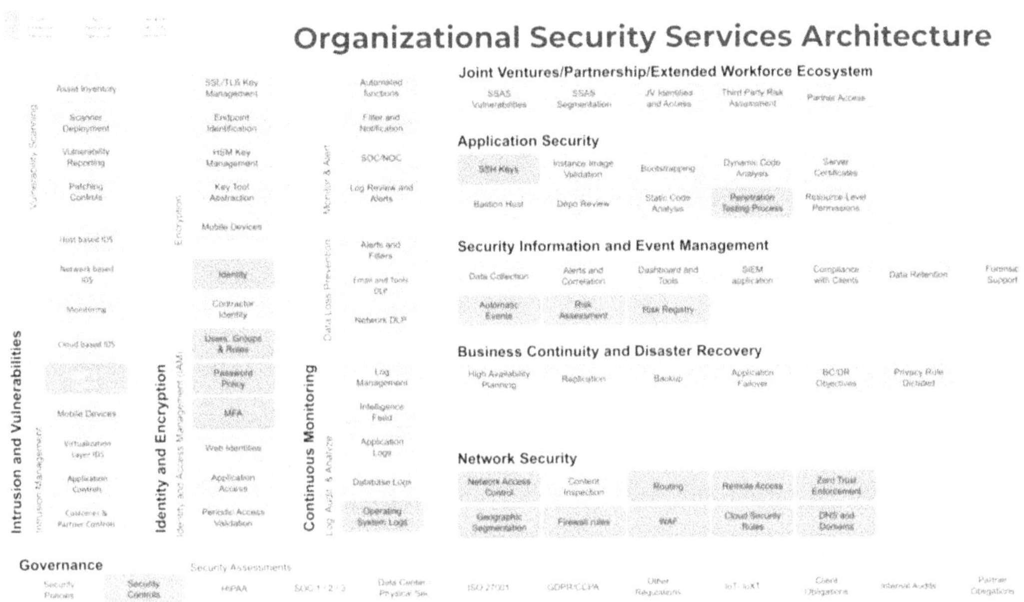

CUSTOM CONTROLS TO CONSIDER

While reviewing the sample security controls catalog provided above, we may recognize that several of these controls are directly adopted from ISO, NIST or even HIPAA. Roughly 20% are custom. They have been developed because we needed to formalize the implementation of certain features, make them accountable, and formally monitor their effectiveness. Organizations fall victims to common vulnerabilities due to lack of certain controls or bad interpretation of existing ones. For example:

- **SQL Injection:** Failure to use parameterized query. One of the most common practices to protect the code against SQL Injection is encapsulating and parameterizing SQL commands. Parameterized queries is a technique that aims to separate the SQL query from the user input values. The user input values are passed as parameters. They can no longer contain an executable code since the parameter is treated as a literal value and checked for the type and length.
- **Cross Site Scripting (XSS):** Failure to do context-sensitive escaping on data.
- **Cross Site Request Forgery (CSRF):** Failure to use a token on state-changing requests.
- **Direct Object Reference (DOR):** Failure to strictly validate a direct object reference. Such a vulnerability occurs when an application uses a reference to an internal object. The application can reveal the real identifier and format or pattern used of the element in the backend.

Establishing custom controls to perform static or dynamic code analysis or mandating the use of tools such as Struts Validator, Java Cryptography Extension, ESAPI Encoder, will materially help reduce exposure to such vulnerabilities. After considering the frameworks mentioned above we would suggest that certain controls are insufficient or totally absent from popular frameworks. Any organization therefore should consider implementing some sort of custom controls for these subjects:

These controls are:

- **Contingency Planning:** We did not find a framework that provides any mandate to consider business recovery and contingency documentation or how such plans are developed and validated.
- **Information Security Management:** How are threats addressed and linked to remediation.
- **Skills and Training:** What kind of capabilities to maintain and source them.
- **Governance:** How are security policies, and other management matters addressed.
- **Risk Management:** How are identified issues managed, remedied, and reported and the methodology to perform risk assessments.
- **Access Management:** Link between various features and how they affect access to applications, data sets and other assets.
- **Cyber Insurance:** Discussion about recommendations or scenarios that would mandate cyber liability insurance.
- **Cloud Service Operations:** Controls associated with a split security responsibility model, multi-tenancy utilization, ephemeral facilities and network deployed as software.
- **Web Application or Other Firewall (WAF):** Handling of dynamic application security issues using a WAF and other uses of conventional firewalls.
- **Data Loss Protection:** Implementation of such a feature or alternative IDS/IPS implementation.
- **Ransomware Protection:** Methods to secure or deter ransomware attacks.
- **Email Security:** Encryption, impersonation protection, digital signatures as part of email protection.
- **Multi-Factor Authentication:** Broad controls including conventional MFA but also combination of hardware authentication or elevated rights management.
- **Third Party Library Management:** Controls associated with the use of third-party software such as open source but also firmware and hardware components.
- **File Management:** Controls associated with the monitoring and validation of key files.

Some of these controls are part of the ISO or NIST frameworks or special guidelines associated with them. The reason for stating these here is that they do not seem explicitly mandated or having any specific controls dedicated to their deployment and management.

CONTROL SUFFICIENCY

Knowing how many controls are enough to implement is a matter of identifying and managing risk. Only once security requirements are known, articulated, and quantified, they can be addressed with adequate controls. At a minimum, an organization will identify its key assets and establish controls. In order to articulate applicable risks, they may use a threat model or other method. There is also a set of threats, known as residual risk, that an organization will just accept. These can be documented and managed over time.

Adequate security is defined as: "The condition where the protection and sustainability strategies for an organization's critical assets and business processes are commensurate with the organization's tolerance for risk" (Augustine & Millstein, 2023). A list of assets is first established to determine whether enough controls have been implemented. Assets include intellectual property, data, technology, servers, facilities and many intangibles such as knowledge and contracts. Assets are classified to establish whether they are essential to the organization or not.

The organization's risk tolerance is the next thing that needs to be defined. This is a variable perspective that affects budget, headcount, operations and other methods of doing business. It is variable as it may change depending upon an organization's performance, partnerships, and other factors. Establishing the appetite for risk is both a qualitative and a quantitative metric that can be established by a series of event/result/impact statements. One easy example to consider is the introduction of an application that is supported by a client services organization.

Current applications have established a request-to-resolution time and resolution accuracy time that the organization would love to maintain. To achieve this, management will need to allocate resources, processes, and technology. Upon allocation of these resources, the organization needs to determine how much variation they are willing to tolerate. For example, is slipping the response time by two hours acceptable? Or what would be the impact to reputation and client satisfaction if the accuracy of the response falls by 10%?

Extending this thought process to security brings up two key questions - "How many controls are enough?" and the closely associated "What do I have to lose?". A similar process to the one explored above will arrive to an acceptable response.

Given our definition of assets we will have to establish all those and the associated business processes that are essential to the organization in order for it to meet its obligation and success in its mission. Following that, we will need to establish the appetite and acceptable risk as it relates to those assets.

To avoid this exercise becoming overly stochastic and unmanageable we will suggest an easily implementable method. It will rely on historical references of events and an understanding of the current environment. It will also extend the risk profile with an associated remediation strategy that will allow us to have a dimension of the risk itself and the potential impact and remedy cost. We will refrain from utilizing Return on Investment of a certain implementation, or Value at Risk as they can also be rather confusing. We will establish how much security we can afford based on understanding of our key assets and the threats that will affect our business most.

Once an organization's assets have been determined we will establish the key threats and associated controls to address them. It is necessary to note any controls do not exist for each purpose.

Table 2. Sample association of asset types to threats and mitigating controls

Asset Type	Potential Threats	Controls
Data	Data Leak Sensitive Information exposure Data manipulation	Data encryption Backup, Restoration Perimeter Defence
Human Resources	Identity theft Man in the middle attack Social engineering - Whaling, etc. Unauthorized access	Access Control Monitoring, Log Review Awareness Training Background Screening Formal Certifications
Infrastructure	Denial of Services, DoS/DDoS Hardware, Firmware attack BotnetVirus Attack	Privileged Access Management Audit Log Intelligence Malware, Antivirus Network Scanning Asset Inventory Hardening Vulnerability Assessment
Applications	Unauthorized software Denial of service Application access/slow-down	Avoid email impersonation (DKIM) Application code review Configuration management Vulnerability Assessment Cloud configuration Asset tagging

Cloud implementations have made asset management quite difficult due to the ephemeral nature of their assets, but at the same time tagging and labeling have introduced many new capabilities where assets can easily be allocated to projects or other components allowing measuring and attributing resources and cost. Allocating individuals to access profiles allows an understanding of who has access to what asset under what circumstance (device used, network accessed and other variables).

This small set of threats can now be considered from both a quantitative and qualitative perspective which will establish the importance and priority for the employment of the associated controls. The problem with this analysis is that most of the time it is highly subjective.

In our suggested review each threat should be viewed from two perspectives - how big can the loss be (size) and what is the chance that it will actually occur? All these values are also influenced by historical references to past events.

Table 3. Qualitative and quantitative assessment of threats

Potential Threats	Size			Chance		
	Downtime	Equipment Cost	Other Fees	Has It Occurred in the Last Year	Ease to Attempt	Existing Control Effectiveness
Data Leak						
Identity theft						
etc.						

This table can vary widely depending on the information available. One thing is absolutely certain: Quantitative metrics reduce bias and inconsistency when they are used consistently throughout the threat model. Following the adage of "garbage in - garbage out" it is absolutely necessary to consider the numbers used in this analysis. The reason we evaluate the effectiveness of existing controls is that past successful attacks may have led to the implementation of technologies that now makes the same attacks more difficult to be successful while leaving other potential vulnerabilities.

Implementing controls is associated with assets. Establishing a service catalog should not imply that ALL controls apply to ALL network segments, applications or end points. It is the threat model that links controls to assets and establishes the importance and risk associated with each control. As a result, processes to plan for, monitor, review, report, and update an organization's threat assessment and control deployment must be part of normal day-to-day business conduct, risk management, and security governance.

IMPLEMENTING A RISK-BASED CONTROLS FRAMEWORK

In the previous section we discussed a risk assessment approach that links assets to threats and assigns both qualitative and quantitative values to each threat. We will now further explore this idea of a risk enhanced controls framework for cybersecurity. The basis for any such implementation lies in an organization's ability to effectively manage risk. By design, businesses are risk-averse.

Risk assessments are now mandated by multiple regulatory oversight agencies including the Securities and Exchange Commission (SEC), Federal Financial Information Examination Council (FFIEC), Office of the Comptroller of the Currency (OCC), Health Insurance Portability and Accountability Act (HIPAA), Presidential Directives on Critical Infrastructure Protection, Payment Card Industry Data Security Standards (PCI-DSS). Failure to execute an assessment and demonstrate ongoing management of any identified risks can cause very material penalties.

While the quality of the assessments themselves is debatable we have seen an increase in penalties levied for lack of a risk management program. Here is a small example:

- **2016:** Athens Orthopedic Clinic fined $1.5 million for "longstanding and systemic noncompliance with HIPAA privacy and security rules, including the failure to conduct a risk analysis, implementation of risk management and audit controls, failure to maintain HIPAA policies and procedures, failure to secure business associate agreement with multiple vendors, and failure to provide training to workforce members."
- **2018:** Anthem Healthcare fined $16 million for "failure to conduct a comprehensive, organization-wide risk analysis to identify potential risks to the confidentiality, integrity, and availability of ePHI" (HHS - Anthem, 2020).
- **2020:** CHSPSC LLC (Business Associate) fined $2.3 million for "longstanding and systemic noncompliance with HIPAA security rules, including the failure to conduct a risk analysis and failures to implement information system activity review, security incident procedures, and access controls."
- **2020:** Primera Blue Cross fined $6.5 million for "systemic noncompliance with the HIPAA rules, including the failure to conduct an enterprise-wide risk assessment and the failure to implement risk management and audit controls" (HHS - Premera, 2020).

- **2020:** USAA Federal Savings Bank fined $85 million by the OCC for "risk management inadequacies" (OCC, 2020).
- **2020:** Citibank fined $400 million by OCC for "risk management failures" (OCC, 2020).

All of these penalties were associated with data breaches or other incidents. What was the problem though? Would an assessment have deterred the hackers? Would an assessment have led to management of those issues identified? Managing a risk presupposes some sort of assessment, but they are distinctly different. As we previously discussed, an assessment associates a threat with an asset and determines the likelihood and impact of an occurrence in a very specific context.

Once a risk and its impact has been identified, magnitude and other parameters of management determine whether the risk will be remedied, absorbed, ignored, or handled. Management also includes how it is communicated and monitored. Management typically employs:

- A method rendering a common handling of risks and an ability to determine over time improvement or degradation of the risk posture if an organization
- An understanding of the organization's tolerance for risk
- An indication of who has the ability and authority to make decisions related to specific risks

Even the most sophisticated and comprehensive assessment will be ineffective or just a paper-exercise if there is a lack of appropriate management.

Risk management is an integral part of sound security practices and consists of:

Asset Inventory: The organization needs to establish a list of assets including technology, knowledge, staff, and other. Each asset will then need to be associated with potential threats. To aid this process, rely on historical references ("has this happened before") and an allocation of true likelihood and impact ("how easy is it to enact the threat", "if a hacker is successful what would the tangible and intangible impact be"). The result of this exercise is referred to as Inherent Risk.

Control Assessment: A controls catalog cannot stand on its own. It is quite rare that an organization deploys all possible controls against all different assets. Arguably not every single application utilizes multi factor authentication or fine-grained access control. Therefore we need to always refer to our controls in the context of assets they are deployed against. Once we validate the controls in place and identify whether they truly reduce the risk we are left with what is called Residual Risk. We then compare the residual risk with our risk appetite and tolerance levels to determine if it exceeds the appetite and tolerance thresholds. If so, then a decision has to be made as to the handling of the residual risk.

Risk Remediation: Risk can be accepted, avoided, shared or transferred in order to be mitigated.

Ongoing Monitoring: Similar to the notion of a car losing a significant part of its value once it has been driven off the lot, a risk assessment is outdated the moment it has been published. Ongoing risk assessment is a good but an expensive goal. In several organizations the process is repeated (re-validation, not a full assessment) every time there is an application launch, acquisition of a new technology, significant upgrades, an incident of any kind, a launch of a new policy or procedure, or a new SOP.

Despite all that, an organization may still find significant breaches or penalties for inadequate assessment or management. This may happen for the following reasons:

- Bad understanding or lack of awareness of assets. It can be quite challenging to account for all the applications that may contain sensitive data. Add to that shadow-IT or data extracts unbeknownst to IT and the problem is quite tough.
- A misconception that a control needs to equally apply to all systems. Starting from the understanding that hackers are already inside we cannot practically address all vulnerabilities. Our priority should then be to deploy controls to safeguard critical data and applications.
- The risk assessment process is performed in haste and it is not based on any historical evidence or rational review of the threats. This results in entire areas of risk being ignored. For example, an organization may discuss the deployment of mobile device management and MFA for employees but ignore consultants and partners who may be using their own computers and have access to the same data. This important issue will be further discussed in this chapter.
- The risk assessment is performed by a part of the organization that is not directly involved with security, or even IT, and does not have the knowledge or awareness to perform a valid and accurate assessment

IDENTIFYING ALL POSSIBLE ASSETS OF YOUR ORGANIZATION

Establishing and maintaining a list of assets is quite integral to appropriate controls allocation and risk management. While we are not going to discuss technical e-discovery methods or other techniques, we need to consider certain challenges that lead to incomplete or inadequate risk assessments when whole asset categories have been ignored. The use of cloud-computing, virtualization, devices, extended partner based networks and federated access makes it very difficult to know everything that is running on our networks. While the answer to many of these issues is automation, we also need to ensure that certain fundamental issues are addressed.

Organizations have the capability to deploy e-discovery systems that can also reveal applications or integrations of which one may not be familiar or aware. The asset inventory that will be compiled using these methods should include:

- Hardware and Software (mostly identified by contracts, known integrations or licenses)
- Code repositories (identified by interviewing the development organization and partners)
- Endpoints (laptops, desktops, peripherals, devices acquired on behalf of the organization). For the purposes of risk management and security controls a detail inventory is not required for these other than an endpoint-class understanding by operating system, ownership and other such high level characteristics
- SSAS and cloud computing (other than known integrations solicit the assistance of Finance and/or Procurement)
- Subscriptions
- Data repositories
- Publications, documentation, and intellectual property
- Software licenses
- Cryptographic artifacts (private/public keys and other encryption components)

Unless one establishes a future-proof method, maintaining such an inventory is challenging. Additionally, there has to be some automated reconciliation of hardware and software that several commercial tools can facilitate.

DEFINING THE RIGHT THREATS AS PART OF A RISK ASSESSMENT

Security professionals rely on accurate threat assessments to deploy the necessary controls. This task covers a broad range of threats associated with offices, data center facilities, accidents, supplies, reliance on critical infrastructure, partners and vendors. Following the determination of assets at risk we identify two kinds of threats: those threats that are inherent to an asset by means of its attractiveness and those that are a result of active threat assessment.

While there are multiple kinds of threats that may be applicable to a data center facility (fire, flood, etc.) we felt that we should devote this section to discuss how someone can arrive at an exhaustive list of potential cyber threats. Relying solely on historical reference is not advisable. We did state that an historical perspective to incidents and control effectiveness is essential, but we cannot ignore a hacker's creativity and resourcefulness.

We established a long list of potential threats recognizing that our most important asset is most likely data. Addressing these threats is aspirational in nature but it is unlikely. While considering their applicability now and in the future, you need to think analytically and mostly be concerned about monitoring and diagnostics as controls rather than determent, especially for emerging threats. This list was compiled by taking into consideration several Security Information and Event Management (SIEM) out-of-the-box vulnerability monitoring and management capabilities.

The list below should prompt several discussions including whether such a threat applies to a certain asset. Please note, we do not ask whether it applies to a whole organization because controls are explicitly deployed against assets. Whether there is some history associated with similar exploits, and their impact should be considered next. Finally, whether there are controls in place associated with the asset examined to monitor for, detect and defend against such an attack.

- Advanced Persistent Threat (sophisticated attack requiring multiple technologies and intelligence)
- Application/Federation Credentials (exploiting SAML, OAuth or other methods to access applications)
- Brute Force Attack (stealthy attack exploiting combinations of words/numbers to gain access)
- Cloud Attacks (special attention to GCP, AWS, and Azure environments especially regarding access to credentials and open buckets or other cloud components that may be misconfigured)
- Cloud IAM (cloud access for individuals or applications can utilize certain features including passwords, tokens, or cryptographic credentials that hackers attempt to exploit)
- Cookie Compromise (compromise a cookie and affect how an application is behaving)
- Credentials Hijacking (using social engineering or technology to steal one's user id and password)
- Credential Reuse (finding a list of compromised credentials and using them to access another site)
- Cross-Site Scripting (inject malicious code into a trusted web site)
- Crypto Attacks (crypto mining or taking over a computer for unauthorized crypto activities)
- Database/Repo Mining (accessing information portal and getting access to confidential information)

- Device and IoT Threats (using a device to gain access to a network and data)
- Distributed Denial of Service Attack (using several automated methods to flood and overwhelm a company's systems)
- DNS Attacks (amplification, hijacking, tunneling) - taking over, redirecting or altering DNS information
- Man-in-the-Middle Attack (applications are susceptible to a hacker embedding themselves between the app and the user)
- Hardware component attack (firmware, chip, or other component specific to hardware device)
- Insider Threat (access to sensitive or confidential information by a trusted party)
- Network Sniffing (unauthorized scanning of the network to identify open ports, devices that can be compromised or unpatched components)
- Phishing (combination of social engineering and technical methods aiming at obtaining credentials or other sensitive information)
- Privileged User Compromise (elevated access or obtaining system/management level credentials)
- Ransomware (hijacking of a system, forced encryption)
- Router and Infrastructure Security (taking over a wifi hotspot or other network equipment)
- Security Tool Attack (disabling security defenses)
- Shadow IT (unauthorized storage of data, use of applications or cloud components without the appropriate corporate security)
- SQL Injection (inserting SQL query in the input structure of an application)
- Stolen Credentials (getting unauthorized access to User Id, passwords)
- System Misconfiguration (a catch-all threat for unpatched and poorly configured systems)
- Third Party Software Attack (utilize a trusted vendor software to attack receiving systems or their interfaces)
- Unauthorized Download or Software Installation (installing malicious software)
- Viruses (defeating antivirus control and install a virus on a platform)
- Website Impersonation (fake website pretending to be a legitimate one)

THE EVOLUTION OF RISK ASSESSMENTS (MATURITY TO RISK TO CONTINUOUS MONITORING)

Maturity based risk assessments are still in use today. This approach consists of establishing a level of maturity by building, documenting and managing certain activities like code review or log monitoring. When starting a new security program, it may be helpful to differentiate the various controls and capabilities using a maturity scale in order to differentiate what is truly at its infancy versus something that is in place and needs to be documented, versus something that is well documented and repeatable. As the program matures, such an approach becomes unsuitable.

A maturity based program does not complement the approach discussed in this chapter. The emphasis of matching controls to assets and measuring their effectiveness is contrary to a maturity based approach that is applicable to "everything controls". It is important to note that given the different risk posture of various assets any improvement can be made with each asset in mind. Aspiring to raise the maturity level of an organization can be very costly and has the potential to render all the controls ineffective.

Identifying an organization's risk appetite and associating assets to controls and to risks allows risk management to become a primary goal for the organization. As such, an investment becomes tangible and metrics become easily obtainable and familiar (KPI, KRI, etc.). A risk-based approach suggested here allows for the implementation and improvement of controls for each asset and allows for adjustments as the threat landscape changes.

There are some business-wide tasks that will need to be put in place to complement the risk-based assessment.

1. Formalize risk assessment at the corporate level and make cybersecurity risk part of it
2. Coordinate the asset inventory across all departments and partners
3. Communicate vulnerabilities across the organization to improve awareness and get agreement in impact
4. Understand threats and the applicability and effectiveness of controls
5. Understand how controls and vulnerabilities change over time and make adjustments
6. Map assets to controls and threats and make a risk assessment accordingly
7. Plot risks against the organization's tolerance
8. Monitor risks and controls using practical metrics such as key risk indicators (KRIs), and key performance indicators (KPIs).

DYNAMIC VALIDATION OF CONTROLS EFFECTIVENESS

It is essential that controls are tested regularly to validate their efficiency and effectiveness and to establish any new vulnerabilities to which that particular asset may be susceptible. Organizations sometimes perform pen tests and vulnerability assessments, to test and see if those controls are working together properly and can actually deter an attack.

Another essential measure is to perform phishing and awareness campaigns. Despite sophisticated techniques and expensive protections, a hacker can still rely on an employee clicking a link that they should not. This method supports the goal of i\Improving controls and reducing risk. It should be promoted.

CONCLUSION

Checking-the-box may satisfy some rudimentary short term goals of an audit. Making decisions about security controls, spending, and vulnerabilities should be risk-based which will result in better compliance. We provided practical and relatively easy to implement approaches to achieve a risk-based allocation of controls to assets. Our goal is to meet a balance between compliance and security posture, recognizing that while complementary, they are quite different.

We placed all of our emphasis on sound risk management. Identifying threats using historical perspective but also real validation of vulnerabilities addresses the applicability of controls and provides for prioritization of their deployment. The risk-based approach is highly interactive. Linking business risks to controls allows executives to understand the purpose of cybersecurity investment and its value in meeting regulatory obligations.

Aiming at reducing risk is centerplace and the subject of frequent reporting. Regulatory compliance gives a false sense of security. Security can suffer by using a single framework with a standard set of controls. The best security plan for our environment is a mixture of all these activities and a risk oriented approach that can be easily understood.

REFERENCES

AICPA. (2022). *SOC Service Organizations: Information for Service Organizations*. AICPA. https://us.aicpa.org/interestareas/frc/assuranceadvisoryservices/serviceorganization-smanagement

Augustine, N., & Millstein, I. (2023). *Governing for Enterprise Security*. SEI Digital Library. https://resources.sei.cmu.edu/asset_files/technicalnote/2005_004_001_14513.pdf

CCM. (2023). *CSA Cloud Controls Matrix (CCM)*. https://cloudsecurityalliance.org/research/cloud-controls-matrix/

CIS. (2022). *Mapping and Compliance*. CIS Center for Internet Security. https://www.cisecurity.org/cybersecurity-tools/mapping-compliance

CIS. (2023). *CIS Center for Internet Security*. https://learn.cisecurity.org/cis-controls-download

CMMC. (2022). *About CMMC*. DoD CIO. https://dodcio.defense.gov/CMMC/About/

COBIT. (2022). *Control Objectives for Information Technologies*. ISACA. https://www.isaca.org/resources/cobit

GAO. (2018). *Reports Challenges and Successes in Cybersecurity Framework Adoption*. Van Ness Feldman LLP. https://www.vnf.com/gao-reports-challenges-and-successes-in-cybersecurity-framework

HHS - Anthem. (2020). *Pays OCR $16 Million in Record HIPAA Settlement Following Largest U.S. Health Data Breach in History | Guidance Portal*. HHS.gov. https://www.hhs.gov/guidance/document/anthem-pays-ocr-16-million-record-hipaa-settlement-following-largest-us-health-data-breach

HIPAA. (2022). *HIPAA for Professionals*. HHS.gov. https://www.hhs.gov/hipaa/for-professionals/index.html

HITRUST Alliance. (2023). *Information Risk Management and Compliance*. https://hitrustalliance.net/

IEC. (2022). *IEC 27001:2022 - Information security, cybersecurity and privacy protection — Information security management systems — Requirements*. https://www.iso27001security.com/html/27034.html

NewsH. H. S. (2023) https://public3.pagefreezer.com/content/HHS.gov/31-12-2020T08:51/https://www.hhs.gov/about/news/2020/09/21/orthopedic-clinic-pays-1.5-million-to-settle-systemic-noncompliance-with-hipaa-rules.html#:~:text=Athens%20Orthopedic%20Clinic%20PA%20

NICCS. (2021). *NICE Framework Mapping Tool | NICCS*. https://niccs.cisa.gov/workforce-development/nice-framework-mapping-tool

NIST. (2018). *Framework for Improving Critical Infrastructure Cybersecurity, Version 1.1*. NIST Technical Series Publications. https://nvlpubs.nist.gov/nistpubs/CSWP/NIST.CSWP.04162018.pdf

NIST. (2022). *Special Publication (SP) 800-53 Rev. 5, Security and Privacy Controls for Information Systems and Organizations*. NIST Computer Security Resource Center. https://csrc.nist.gov/publications/detail/sp/800-53/rev-5/final

OCC. (2020). *Assesses $85 Million Civil Money Penalty Against USAA*. Office of the Comptroller of the Currency (OCC). https://www.occ.gov/news-issuances/news-releases/2020/nr-occ-2020-135.html

PCI. (2022). *Official PCI Security Standards Council Site - Verify PCI Compliance, Download Data Security and Credit Card Security Standards*. PCI Security Standards Council. https://www.pcisecuritystandards.org/about_us/

Premera, H. H. S. (2020). *Health Insurer Pays $6.85 Million to Settle Data Breach Affecting*. HHS.gov. https://www.hhs.gov/hipaa/for-professionals/compliance-enforcement/agreements/premera/index.html

ENDNOTE

1 There are numerous guidelines regarding perimeter protection. CNSSI 4009-2015 states: "Monitoring and control of communications at the external boundary of an information system to prevent and detect malicious and other unauthorized communications, through the use of boundary protection devices (e.g., gateways, routers, firewalls, guards, encrypted tunnels)." while NIST SP800-53 Rev 5. States "Monitoring and control of communications at the external interface to a system to prevent and detect malicious and other unauthorized communications using boundary protection devices."

Chapter 6
HES:
A Case Study on Cybersecurity and Privacy Risks in Health Surveillance Systems

Fatma Dogan Akkaya
Kastamonu University, Turkey

ABSTRACT

The COVID-19 pandemic has led to the implementation of digital health surveillance systems worldwide, including Turkey's Hayat Eve Sığar (HES) platform. While effective in monitoring and tracing the virus, these systems also raise concerns about data privacy and cybersecurity risks. This chapter examines potential risks such as data breaches, malware attacks, unauthorized access, misuse of personal health information, and inadequate security protocols. To mitigate these risks, healthcare organizations must implement strong security measures and adopt a culture of security with a focus on continuous improvement and proactive risk management. The HES in Turkey provides a valuable case study for understanding these risks and measures to mitigate them. The chapter highlights the growing trend of digital health services invading individuals' private spaces and regulating their lives, emphasizing the importance of data privacy and security in safeguarding personal health information.

INTRODUCTION

Our Ford himself did a great deal to shift the emphasis from truth and beauty to comfort and happiness. Mass production demanded the shift. Universal happiness keeps the wheels steadily turning; truth and beauty can't. (Huxley, 1932, p. 201)

Mass behaviour control policies, such as mass surveillance, restrictions, and limitations on movement, which we are used to seeing in dystopian novels and movies, have abruptly and daringly entered our lives with the peak of the COVID-19 epidemic in 2020. Many countries have developed various networked disease monitoring systems to monitor and control the spread of the disease, leveraging their technological infrastructure and capabilities. The introduction of these systems has been sudden and

DOI: 10.4018/978-1-6684-9018-1.ch006

without prior notice, highlighting the urgency of the situation and the need for effective measures to contain the pandemic.

The COVID-19 pandemic has prompted the deployment of digital health surveillance systems globally, one of which is Turkey's *Life Fits Home*, Hayat Eve Sığar (HES), platform. HES is a digital platform developed by the Turkish Ministry of Health in response to the COVID-19 pandemic. From 2020 to 2022, the HES was heavily utilized as a tool for monitoring and tracking the spread of the virus during the pandemic. It offers individuals the most current information on their COVID-19 situation and enables them to report any symptoms and contacts they may have had. Individuals can use the platform as a mobile application, a website, and a call centre to report their symptoms and receive guidance on whether to seek medical attention or get tested for COVID-19. This data is used to identify and notify individuals who may have been exposed to the virus. One of the key features of the HES platform is its QR code system. Individuals who have tested negative for COVID-19 can generate a QR code that can be used to access public spaces such as shopping centres, restaurants, and public transportation. The QR code is scanned by officials at the entrance to these spaces, verifying the individual's COVID-19 status and allowing them to enter if they are not infected. The HES platform also includes a range of other features, such as real-time updates on the number of COVID-19 cases, hospital bed availability, and information on COVID-19 testing centres. The platform is updated regularly with new information and guidance as the situation around the pandemic evolves. Although the HES platform is still operational, the data it provides no longer results in restrictions in public spaces. Nevertheless, this system contains a range of software and quantitative data that can be rapidly activated in the event of any potential epidemic.

In this paper, the HES system will serve as a case study for analysing these cybersecurity risks in health surveillance systems. Between 2020 and 2022, it was obligatory to display the HES code in public areas and events such as workplaces, schools, hospitals, intercity buses, shopping centres, football matches or various events. It means that HES, an app that manages digital apps and QR codes on smartphones, collects vast amounts of personal data and health records from millions of people for the first time and in a cyber program of this scale. From the point of view of health surveillance systems, the HES program has shown how technology-supported health services can be provided instantly by reaching the recipients and has proven that it will make a great contribution to increasing the quality of public health. However, on the other hand, what precautions are taken in case of data breaches regarding users' information, which security protocols are adhered to, or how and where the huge data stored, are possible weaknesses of HES and all digital health surveillance systems using the same method in the world. Additionally, the chapter will examine the challenges faced by the Turkish government in implementing the HES system, including public trust, data privacy concerns, and limiting personal rights. In order to gain a comprehensive understanding of the use and implications of digital health surveillance systems, it is necessary to examine not only the example of Turkey, but also similar applications implemented worldwide in response to the COVID-19 pandemic. Therefore, the discussions of privacy and data security concerns developed around the HES and other similar digital applications will lead us to examine the repercussions of the suspension of basic human rights for the benefit of public health in the global arena.

The theoretical foundation of surveillance phenomena is crucial in understanding the operation of surveillance practices, their societal and cultural ramifications, and the power dynamics involved. Therefore, this chapter will commence by examining the theoretical discourse on the healthcare context, where digital health surveillance systems have become indispensable in the monitoring and management of public health. This chapter will further explore the potential risks associated with digital health surveillance systems, including data breaches, malware attacks, unauthorized access, misuse of personal medical information, and insufficient security protocols. Finally, the chapter also explores ethical and practical considerations, including providing cybersecurity training, regularly monitoring and testing, transparency and accountability. To address above mentioned risks, it will emphasize the necessity for healthcare organizations to implement robust security measures and foster a culture of security, emphasizing continuous improvement and proactive risk management.

THE THEORETICAL BACKGROUND OF SURVEILLANCE PHENOMENA: EXPLORING POWER DYNAMICS AND SOCIAL IMPLICATIONS

For centuries, surveillance has been a significant regulating instrument for societies, serving multiple purposes such as maintaining law and order, protecting national security, and controlling pandemics. With the emergence of new technologies and the increased availability of data, digital surveillance systems have evolved. Now it is capable of collecting, analysing, and storing enormous amounts of data. We currently live in a fast-paced era where innovations and transformations occur rapidly, and even the most recent technological developments quickly become outdated. To put it simply, surveillance refers to the act of monitoring individuals, groups, or societies, while in a scientific context, it involves monitoring all processes within a specific ecosystem. While traditional surveillance involved the observed and the observer, self-monitoring has emerged as an independent theme, facilitated by tools such as pregnancy tests, smart watches, and breathalysers that enable individuals to monitor their health status (Marx, 2016). Software-based daily tracking is also used for personal and academic development. Therefore, it is intriguing to contemplate how the technological capability of collecting and processing vast amounts of data will impact human society in the future, both positively and negatively.

The theoretical background of surveillance phenomena is complex and multidimensional. When delving into the contemporary discourse on surveillance, one is confronted by a diverse array of studies. It draws on a range of disciplines, including sociology, political economy, law, criminology, and public health. The study of surveillance phenomena examines issues related to power, social control, privacy, and social order, and explores the ways in which surveillance practices can shape social norms and values, and its implications on societies.

In the modern age of fluid communication and information (Bauman, 2000), is there anyone or anything that can truly remain hidden from surveillance? The phenomenon of surveillance, which is a different reflection of the relationship between the individual and society, has been the subject of extensive research and inquiry in recent decades, seeking answers to numerous related questions. In this context, Georg Simmel (1906), a prominent figure in classical sociology, examined the sociology of secrecy and aimed to uncover the emotional, symbolic, and positional features of human relationships on both interpersonal and societal levels. He argued that secrecy is a social phenomenon, and agreements on privacy at both interpersonal and institutional levels serve to protect the social identities of individuals. According to Simmel (1950), secrecy is essential for individuals to avoid getting lost in the masses, particularly in urban areas where everyone depends on one another for division of labour, and for maintaining social order from the state's perspective, as long as it is not become extreme.

Michel Foucault (1977) is a renowned theorist who is known for observing the transformations and increasing control of states in post-industrial societies, alongside other scholars such as Nisbet (1977), Ericson and Haggerty (1997), Deflem (2000). He benefited the term "panopticon" as a metaphor for the all-encompassing culture of surveillance in contemporary societies, drawing on the 18th-century philosopher Jeremy Bentham's prison design. Bentham's panopticon was a circular building with a central tower, enabling guards to observe all the prisoners in their cells without them knowing whether they were being watched. Foucault used the panopticon as a symbol for the subtle, pervasive, and effective new form of power that pervades modern society, as people are continually monitored and controlled through various social institutions, including schools, hospitals, factories, and prisons. Foucault contended that the panopticon was not only a physical design, but also a mode of social organization and control that operated through discourses and practices of surveillance, normalization, and discipline. Foucault's idea of the panopticon served as inspiration for writers like George Orwell (1987), and helped to pioneer the dystopian narrative style, which explores the ways in which totalitarian regimes and manipulation-based systems like Big Brother erode freedoms and subject individuals to constant surveillance and control. Jeremy Bentham, who famously left behind his skeleton to be displayed in public, now sits on a stool at University College London, gazing out at the audience from within his inspection glass box. In today's world, all forms of surveillance, represented by the metaphor of the panopticon, are being revisited through digital surveillance systems and tools. However, as Gary T. Marx (2016) argues, we must move beyond traditional forms of surveillance to address the new modes of surveillance that have emerged. Rather than localized and segmented views, we must focus on more centralized and expansive forms of surveillance that rely on communication and technology.

In modern times, surveillance has evolved with the development of new technologies, particularly those related to digital information and communication. Digital surveillance systems have become increasingly sophisticated and powerful, capable of collecting and analysing vast amounts of data from multiple sources. Therefore, the study of the evolution of surveillance practices in modern society become a crucial area of inquiry. David Lyon (1994) has contributed significantly to the study of surveillance practices in contemporary society, examining the emergence and expansion of surveillance technologies and practices, including closed-circuit television (CCTV), biometric identification, and computer databases. He argues that these technologies have fundamentally altered the nature of surveillance, making it more pervasive, invisible, and difficult to resist. In his work, Lyon (2001) defines the concept of the "surveillance society" and argues that it has become a pervasive and normalized aspect of modern society across various institutional domains. These include the military, nation-states, workplaces, policing, and even consumption, where personal information is collected and analysed through technologies such as RIFT (Radio-frequency identification technology), barcode systems, and customer loyalty programs (Lyon, 2007). Lyon emphasizes that the consequences of such practices go beyond privacy concerns, affecting power dynamics and social control. He suggests that it is not only states but also other entities that engage in surveillance practices, highlighting the need for greater scrutiny and regulation of these activities.

In the healthcare sector, digital health surveillance systems have become essential tool for monitoring and managing public health. These systems can track disease outbreaks, monitor the spread of infectious diseases, and enable healthcare authorities to respond more quickly to public health emergencies. However, the use of digital health surveillance systems also raises concerns about privacy, data security, and potential misuse of collected data. Several theoretical and conceptual frameworks can aid in our understanding of surveillance in the realm of health. One such framework is "surveillance capitalism", a term coined by Shoshana Zuboff (2019) to describe a type of capitalism that relies on the collection and analysis of personal data for commercial gain. Zuboff (2019) argues that in our current era, where the ideal of a liberal and egalitarian world has been abandoned, companies with enormous capital resources gather and sell personal data to advertisers under the guise of data consumption. Additionally, state institutions expand their surveillance capabilities by justifying it as a measure to combat terrorism. According to Zuboff (2019), surveillance capitalism commodifies personal data and uses it for profit, leading to privacy violations and exploitation. This framework highlights the risks associated with the use of personal data for commercial purposes and the need to ensure that individuals' privacy and rights are protected. While surveillance capitalism is not limited to the realm of health, it has important implications for the collection and use of personal health data. Therefore, it is important to consider the ethical implications of digital health surveillance systems and to implement appropriate safeguards to prevent the exploitation of personal health data.

The concept of "technological determinism", attributed to mostly Thorstein Veblen, can be another theoretical framework that suggests that technology drives societal change and shapes social relationships and institutions. Karl Marx also recognized this influence of technology on society but emphasized that technological development is shaped by social relations and economic structures (Feldman, 2016). In the context of health surveillance systems, it posits that advances in technology can revolutionize public health surveillance. However, a critical perspective is necessary to recognize the broader social, cultural, and political factors that shape the development and use of these systems, as technological determinism can oversimplify the complex relationships between technology and society. On the other hand, unequal distribution of technology and internet access results in a "digital divide" that hinders the reach of health systems to various socioeconomic groups and geographic areas. This digital divide can lead to health outcome disparities among different groups and impede the development of effective public health policies, such as the collection and analysis of data for health system improvements (Saeed and Masters, 2021). Furthermore, unequal access to technology and the internet may worsen existing power imbalances as those with access to technology may have greater control over health data collection, analysis, and distribution. This can further marginalize disadvantaged groups and limit their involvement in health decision-making. To address the digital divide in health surveillance and steer technological determinism towards a positive direction, equal access to technology and the internet must be ensured and the development of inclusive and innovative health surveillance systems that consider the unique needs and perspectives of different populations are encouraged. In this sense, critical theory which examines the ways in which power relations are embedded in social structures and practices, offers a comprehensive theoretical framework for comprehending the economic, political, and cultural patterns of inequality and marginalization (Todic et al., 2022).

Finally, actor-network theory (ANT) can be useful in understanding how various actors, such as healthcare providers, patients, public health officials, and technological devices, interact to shape the development and implementation of health surveillance systems. ANT is a theoretical framework that focuses on the relationships between actors, both human and non-human, and how these relationships shape social and technological systems. It was initially developed by Bruno Latour, Michel Callon, and others in the 1980s and aimed at understanding the production of scientific facts and technology. By analysing the relationships between actors and the ways in which they shape the development and implementation of these systems, we can gain insight into how to design and implement more effective and equitable health surveillance systems. For example, the design and functionality of health surveillance technologies can shape the behaviours and decisions of healthcare providers and patients, ultimately influencing the effectiveness of the system (Bilodeau and Potvin, 2018).

Surveillance is seen as an unavoidable aspect of the modern world, as different theoretical perspectives share a common understanding. According to Lyon (2001), the information society is synonymous with the surveillance society, while Weber (1987) portrayed individuals as trapped in the iron cage of bureaucracy -or shell as hard as steel as for some scholars (Baehr, 2001)- in overcapitalized societies. Ball and Webster (2003) argued that Weber actually considered surveillance a necessary by-product of the world's increasing rationalization. Throughout our study, we will revisit these frameworks periodically to deepen our understanding of the complex network of actors and factors that shape digital health surveillance systems. By examining these analytical lenses, we can gain insight into how digital health surveillance systems operate and the implications they have for public health and individual privacy. The following chapter will analyse the cybersecurity risks inherent in health surveillance systems, particularly Turkey's HES health monitoring program, as well as health surveillance systems worldwide that involve the collection and management of sensitive personal health information.

RISKS ASSOCIATED WITH DIGITAL HEALTH SURVEILLANCE SYSTEMS

The COVID-19 pandemic has indeed accelerated the adoption and implementation of various digital technologies to enhance the public health response. These technologies are playing a crucial role in monitoring populations, identifying cases, tracing contacts, and assessing the impact of interventions through the use of mobility data. Moreover, digital technologies are being utilized to engage with the public, disseminate vital information, and provide telemedicine services (Greenhalgh, Koh, & Car, 2020). Budd et al. (2020) provided a comprehensive overview of the various digital technologies utilized during the Covid-19 epidemic, including online syndromic monitoring, smartphone applications, digital diagnostics and genomics, visualization tools, wearable devices and sensors, computer vision, SMS and instant messages, technologies that protect security and privacy, and machine learning and natural language processing. Thanks to these technological advancements, the public health response has become more streamlined and efficient, resulting in improved outcomes in the fight against the pandemic.

The purpose of digital health applications developed to combat COVID-19 is to provide quick and efficient access to diagnosis and test results, monitor health data, schedule appointments, and facilitate communication between doctors and patients. Almalki and Giannicchi (2021) conducted a review of digital health applications related to COVID-19 and identified they have five main purposes, which included raising awareness, managing exposure, monitoring health by healthcare professionals, conducting research studies (67,5% in total), and primarily tracking personal health (31%). One of the prominent finding of the research was that numerous apps aimed at personal health monitoring were developed by governments or national authorities (67%). This situation shows that state authorities have a significant responsibility in ensuring that personal data is collected, processed, and used in a manner that respects individuals' privacy and protects them from harm. This responsibility includes creating and enforcing laws and regulations that govern the collection and use of personal data, as well as investing in cybersecurity measures to prevent unauthorized access to sensitive information. In the United Kingdom, the European Union and the United States, app-based contact tracing has shown high public acceptance (Altman et al., 2020; Milsom et al., 2021). However, in their study conducted in the US, Ioannou and Tussyadiah (2021) express concerns of their participants regarding the potential invasion of privacy resulting from the collection and use of personal information through mobile applications, as well as the monitoring of people's online activities by authorities. A different study conducted in Canada has revealed that the public is concerned about the invasion of privacy resulting from contact tracing applications and other digital surveillance technologies, despite the social benefits they provide through collaboration between government and companies (Westerlund et al., 2021). The study suggests that transparency from government and companies in data collection and use, coupled with effective supervision, can increase the level of trust in the use of these technologies. Additionally, Dowthwaite et al. (2021) discovered that the acceptance rate of using such applications and their continued use in later periods is very low, particularly among sensitive groups such as members of Black, Asian, and minority ethnic communities, as well as older adults aged 65 years, who may not fully understand the technology. Unfortunately, there is insufficiency in studies that prioritize social acceptance and practice of digital surveillance, which makes it challenging to draw comparisons across different contexts. In summary, these digital data collection applications have the ability to easily access personal information, have flexible rules, and use smart tools to quickly analyse big data. However, consumers who use these applications lack sufficient knowledge about their personal health metrics, as well as a clear roadmap for what to do if their sensitive data is exploited for financial gain.

A range of digital data sources are used to develop and interpret data collected for COVID-19 by public health authorities and companies around the world. In Turkey experience, The HES platform developed by the Turkish Ministry of Health for COVID-19-related health services has been effective in tracking the spread of COVID-19 and providing up-to-date information on the pandemic. However, concerns have been raised about the collection and storage of personal data, sensitive health and travel information. Drawing on the literature, institutional announcements published online, and media coverage, I intend to analyse potential cybersecurity risks from various countries, along with HES. Regarding the HES, it is not directly related to cybersecurity risks from various countries. However, it is essential to highlight the security and privacy of personal and sensitive health data collected through the app. Some of the significant risks and related ethical concerns to consider, both for HES and other health surveillance applications around the world, are:

Data Breaches and Malicious Attacks

Health surveillance systems collect a large amount of sensitive personal health information, which makes them an attractive target for hackers looking to steal valuable data. If a data breach occurs, it can lead to the exposure of patients' personal and medical information, including their health history, prescriptions, and lab results. This information can then be sold on the black market or used to commit identity theft. Kruse et al. (2017) notes that healthcare organizations often have limited resources to dedicate to cybersecurity, which can make it difficult to prevent and respond to cyber threats.

In response to the Covid-19 pandemic, many countries established health surveillance systems that relied largely on contact tracing applications. However, due to the urgent nature of the situation, it was foreseeable that these applications, which were quickly developed by either state agencies or private companies, would be vulnerable to attacks from the outset. As expected, security concerns and data breaches have been reported in contact tracing apps in many countries. In May 2021, Amnesty International reported that a vulnerability in the Qatar COVID-19 contact tracing app had put the personal data of more than a million people at risk (Hern, 2020). The app, which used a centralized system, had collected sensitive personal information such as names, health status, and location data, making it an easy target for hackers. As a result of such incidents, countries such as the UK announced that they were shifting to a decentralized system to reduce the security risks of centralized systems (GOV.UK, 2022). In August 2022, reports emerged that the personal data of 48.5 million users of Shanghai's COVID-19 app, Suishenma, was being sold by hackers (Baptista, 2022). The app, which is used by all residents and visitors in Shanghai to access public places, collect parcels, and order food, had collected sensitive personal information, including names, national identities, health status, and location data. The incident once again highlighted the security and privacy risks associated with collecting sensitive personal data through mobile devices and the need for stronger security measures to protect user data.

The contact tracing app used in Turkey, called HES, stands out from other similar apps used in different countries because it collects user information in a centralized manner, unlike the decentralized approach used in apps like Singapore's *TraceTogether* (but the app is an exception with a hybrid decentralized-centralized approach) or the European consortium's *PEPP-PT*, *COVIDSafe* in Australia and *ABTraceTogether* in Canada. Furthermore, while most decentralized apps rely on Bluetooth technology to ensure user privacy (Hogan et al., 2021), HES utilizes GPS to track users' location information, similar to China's *Alipay/WeChat*, South Korea's *Self-quarantine Safety Protection App* and Israel's *HaMagen* contact tracing apps. The Apple-Google contact tracking app, which was developed jointly by the industry, also utilizes Bluetooth proximity tracking. However, there are apprehensions about how private companies handle sensitive health data, and this has sparked a debate about the new role that big tech companies are assuming in the domain of public health (Sharon,2020).

Although HES has not reported any data breaches so far, the fact that it collects user data such as names, identification numbers, phone book, health data, location, phone camera and even files video, audio, image files from phone memory in a centralized system raises concerns about potential privacy and security breaches. Ministry of Health of Turkey declares the security of HES application users on their personal data in accordance with Law No: 6698 on the Protection of Personal Data (KVKK), Article 10 "Data Supervisor's Responsibility to Inform" (saglik.gov.tr). In the case of Turkey's contact tracing app, HES, it has been designed to indicate an individual's risk status based on their COVID-19 test results or their contact with someone who has tested positive for COVID-19. Due to this, the HES code and query results are classified as special quality personal data, as they relate to health data. However, there are concerns regarding the app's extensive access to users' personal data on their phones, and the fact that all this information is processed and stored in a single centre. These concerns have heightened security implications. The recent data theft event in Shanghai serves as a reminder of the potential risks associated with the collection and storage of sensitive personal information through mobile apps in one centre. In order to ensure the highest level of security, it is important for health surveillance applications like HES to take necessary measures and implement frequent updates to maintain security protocols.

Malware is another highly sophisticated threat to digital data systems, and it has consistently ranked among the top 15 threats over the past decade, according to ENISA, the European Union Cyber Security Agency, report (2020). Despite its prevalence, many security systems are still unable to detect and prevent malware attacks. Health surveillance systems may be vulnerable to malware attacks, which can result in the disruption of system operations or the theft of personal health information. Malware, short for 'malicious software', refers to software designed to harm computer systems, steal sensitive information, or gain unauthorized access to computer networks (Joint Security and Privacy Committee, 2003). The data breaches mentioned earlier are typically the result of an internal agent. However, malicious attacks can be attributed to external entities or sources, which may include a variety of fraudulent activities involving hacking or IT incidents, such as scams, malware attacks, ransomware attacks, phishing, spyware, scams or stolen cards (Seh et al., 2020).

Malware attacks can be especially dangerous in healthcare settings, as they can compromise the confidentiality, integrity, and availability of patient data. Malware can also infect electronic health records systems, leading to the loss or corruption of patient data. The urgent need for contact monitoring applications during the pandemic led to their rapid deployment, but security experts have raised concerns about the vulnerabilities in these apps or have discovered various vulnerabilities that can leave them open to attacks. According to BBC News (2020), India has made it compulsory for citizens to download *Aarogya Setu*, a contact tracing application developed to combat the spread of Covid-19. This has made it the world's largest and most controversial biometric-based identity database. A software engineer from India announced his intention to expose the application's vulnerabilities by hacking into it, which raised concerns about the app's security (Dixit, 2020). Similar concerns have been raised about Qatar's mandatory contact tracing app, *ETHARAZ*, as reported by The Guardian (Hern, 2020). Turkey also has its own mandatory contact tracing program called HES, which may face similar security vulnerabilities and concerns.

These potential security concerns that have emerged raise important considerations in the current context. Governments are facing pressure to manage the pandemic by keeping health records under control, but this raises potential security concerns. Digitizing health records and constant surveillance has become the norm for both public and private institutions. This requires significant resources, including a trained team, to handle the workload and ensure the safety of sensitive information. However, only nations with adequate technological education and means can handle this situation. This aligns with Veblen's concept of technological determinism, where technological superiority drives social, economic, and political change, resulting in development. Therefore, the world is moving towards a digital health landscape where countries that can produce or afford technology are likely to have an advantage.

This also includes addressing issues of digital divide and discrimination, which can have significant implications for data security and patient protection. The digital divide refers to disparities in access to technology and internet connectivity, which can put certain populations at a disadvantage in terms of data security. Through this process, it has once again become apparent that countries in the Western and Asian regions, who have embraced technology as a means for economic advancement, have made considerable strides in the development and commercialization of tracking devices. However, this is not the case in less developed countries, where resources and infrastructure are limited, and the adoption of technology for healthcare and surveillance purposes may be more challenging. In the context of healthcare, the digital divide also refers to the disparities in access to technology and internet connectivity among different populations, which can affect their ability to benefit from healthcare services and put them at a disadvantage in terms of data security. Even in the UK, which is one of the highest developed countries, the digital divide persists, with one-third of households lacking access to mobile broadband. A survey found that the significant portion of the population, including 30% of seniors aged 55 and above and 21% of young adults aged 18 and above, do not have access to smartphones (ONS, 2019). This divide results in many people not being able to benefit from healthcare technologies, such as contact tracing apps, which can lead to health inequalities. Healthcare organizations must take steps to address these inequalities, such as providing access to technology and internet connectivity for underprivileged communities, to ensure that all patients are able to receive equal protection for their sensitive personal health information. Singapore, recognized for its technological advancements, addressed this inequality by distributing wearable devices to individuals who lacked access to smart mobile devices (Asher, 2020). Additionally, discrimination can also be a concern when it comes to cybersecurity in healthcare. Certain groups may be at higher risk of cyberattacks or data breaches due to their race, ethnicity, gender, or other characteristics. Numerous reports and studies worldwide have indicated that various disadvantaged groups have been unable to accurately contribute to statistical health records due to factors such as criminalization (Davis, 2020), fear of minority status (Marsh, Deng and Gan, 2020), stigmatization (news.un.org), and religious (Yasir, 2020) or racial discrimination (Shapiro, Jingnan and Benincasa, 2020). Healthcare organizations must ensure that their security measures do not disproportionately harm or disadvantage these groups, and that they are taking steps to address any potential biases or discriminatory practices that may arise.

The implementation of effective cyber security measures for health surveillance technology can be challenging due to various technical barriers and different approaches used by countries. However, the sharing, processing, and necessary handling of sensitive personal data by government or private companies raises also intellectual discussions. Most of the Covid-19 monitoring applications were developed using trial and error methods, with different protocols and consent declarations. Disease monitoring practices worldwide have tested the continuity of the system with technological tools and social motivation, leading to the development of action plans for a 'digital surveillance society'. The utilization of drones for city surveillance, thermal and infrared cameras for diagnosis, and wearable technology for mobile surveillance have generated worries about civil liberties, including violations of privacy and "the institutionalization of mass surveillance capabilities" (Nothias et al., 2021:3). The developing of online symptom reporting, initially implemented in Singapore and the UK, and the mandatory PCR testing based on self-reporting for entrance into public spaces and travel in Turkey, aligns with Foucault's metaphor of panopticon, in which individuals being observed without their awareness, resulting in self-monitoring and adherence to societal standards.

Overall, the contact tracing systems reflects the complex trade-offs between public health, individual privacy, and social norms in modern societies. While there may be concerns about privacy and surveillance, it is essential to balance these with the need to prevent the spread of disease and ensure the safety of individuals in public spaces. Each responsible governing body must take all necessary measures and provide adequate clarification to alleviate concerns regarding potential infringements on civil liberties, along with the issues such as data breaches, theft, or security breaches.

Unauthorized Access and Misuse of Personal Health Information

Unauthorized access is second important healthcare disclosure type after hacking incidents (Seh et al. 2020). Health surveillance systems often contain personal health information that should only be accessed by authorized personnel, such as healthcare providers or researchers. However, if these systems are not properly secured, unauthorized individuals may be able to access this information. This can lead to serious privacy violations and compromised patient care. Illegitimate access to patient data can result in various types of abuse, such as identity theft and fraud, and can also damage the reputation of healthcare providers and erode trust among patients. As a result, patients may suffer significant financial losses when their sensitive personal information is sold on the dark web (Chernyshev, Zeadally and Baig, 2019). Meanwhile, the healthcare industry, which is less equipped to handle such security breaches compared to other data-driven industries, is likely to experience the most significant impact (Liu, Musen and Chou, 2015).

In some cases, individuals with authorized access to health surveillance systems may misuse patients' personal health information. For example, they may share this information with unauthorized parties, use it for personal gain, or use it to discriminate against patients based on their health status. (Gerke, Minssen, and Cohen (2020) note that the misuse of personal health information can have serious consequences for patients, including damage to reputation, financial loss, and even physical harm. Another form of misuse is third-party data sharing (Trinidad, Platt and Kardia, 2020). When healthcare organizations share patient data with third-party entities, there is a risk that the data will be used for purposes other than what was intended. This can happen if healthcare organizations do not adequately review third-party assets or have inadequate contracts to ensure the appropriate use and protection of patient data. Sharing recorded patient information with third parties is recently popular practice among public health authorities who aim to enhance their services and provide better care for their patients using advanced technical capabilities. However, such initiatives are often met with apprehension due to the potential security risks involved.

According to the Financial Times, NHS (National Health Service) England has announced its intention to share medical data from around 55 million patients with third-party researchers, encompassing various types of sensitive information such as mental and sexual health, abuse and criminal records (Murgia, 2021). Patients have the option to opt-out of the plan, but in the absence of such action, their data will be integrated into a unified database that includes all registered GP (general practitioner) patients in the country (Murgia, 2021). Moreover, the collaboration between established technology companies and non-profit organizations come under heightened scrutiny. In 2019, Google and Ascension, the largest non-profit healthcare system in the United States, disclosed that they had transferred identifiable patient records to Google's cloud servers for the purpose of analysing data from Ascension's 50 million patient population in their joint project, called "Nightingale" (Valinsky, 2019). This agreement sparked widespread public backlash and prompted a federal investigation (Copeland and Needleman, 2019). The following words of Elizabeth Denham from ICO - an independent organization dedicated to safeguarding information rights - encapsulates the ethical principles governing the interface between patient rights and technological advancement in the UK and beyond: "There's no doubt the huge potential that creative use of data could have on patient care and clinical improvements, but the price of innovation does not need to be the erosion of fundamental privacy rights." (Shead, 2017).

The Covid-19 pandemic has brought about a global adoption of contact tracing apps, reigniting debates about the balance between individual rights and government surveillance, as well as the interests of data-collecting companies. These discussions are further complicated by institutional differences that make it challenging to implement effective privacy measures and develop a roadmap that satisfies both the public interest and the need to combat a potentially fatal pandemic.

Some countries, such as Hong Kong, Taiwan, and China, have implemented centralized practices that limit access to public spaces and isolate infected individuals. These measures are often enforced by the government, with mandatory participation required. In contrast, other countries, such as Australia, the UK, France, and Ireland, have adopted decentralized monitoring practices to identify close contacts of infected individuals. In countries like Germany, Switzerland, and Italy, the emphasis is on informing individuals about possible exposure to infected people to encourage behavioural changes (Hogan et al., 2021). Some of the countries using the decentralized system have announced that they will use the contact tracing technology, which is a joint venture between Google and Apple (Dave, 2020). The table shows that many countries prioritize privacy by collecting data with the consent of individuals. In contrast, some countries have prioritized public health welfare by mandating data collection to respond quickly to the epidemic. However, these measures allowed to contain the disease quickly, while raising privacy concerns.

As previously discussed, Turkey's HES contact monitoring application is a state-developed service that collects data in a centralized repository and mandates isolation for individuals entering public spaces or diagnosed with COVID-19. The personal data collected through the HES during the pandemic has been subject to the KVKK (Personal Data Protection Authority), which has issued periodic information messages. In a statement dated 27/03/2020, the KVKK emphasized the importance of personal data security for data controllers and processors, even in exceptional circumstances such as a pandemic. Processing of personal data related to COVID-19 measures must be limited, necessary, and proportional to the purpose (kvkk.gov.tr, 2020a). In a statement dated 09/04/2020, the KVKK recognized the potential serious harm to individuals if their location data and health status were captured by third parties and emphasized the need for relevant institutions and organizations to take necessary measures to ensure data security. The KVKK also highlighted that personal data should be deleted or destroyed when administrative measures are taken and the reasons for data processing disappear (kvkk.gov.tr,2020b). However, these statements are advisory in nature, and it is unclear whether specific measures have been implemented to address data breaches, misuse, or mishandling of personal data.

The mandatory implementation of COVID-19 follow-up applications has been subject to varying degrees of control in different countries due to cultural differences. In China, the widespread use of the app has proven to be more effective than in South Korea, where only those diagnosed with the virus or close contacts are required to download the app. In Turkey, mandatory adoption has been viewed as necessary to increase the effectiveness of the measure, given that the country has a history of using a centralized digital service platform carried out by the Presidency of the Republic of Turkey Digital Transformation Office since the early 2000s. The platform provides various digital services to citizens including identity, health, social security, education, tax, property, and legal-related services, and the public is familiar with the system of storing, processing, and sharing personal information. As a result, any security concerns regarding the HES, which has been easily integrated to this broader platform, did not cause much public reaction in Turkey.

However, there are criticisms that the HES system was hastily prepared, contains too much information, and does not adequately protect individual rights for the benefit of the broader population. The *Smittestopp* application in Norway, as highlighted by Hogan et al. (2021), serves as a similar example in this regard. The rushed development of the contact tracing application has proved it has significant security risks, but it is essential to note that this should not undermine the high level of trust that Norwegian citizens have in their government and new technologies, which are deeply ingrained in the country's culture (Hogan et al. 2021). Similarly, while Turkey's HES system is compatible with the country's digital surveillance culture, it is essential to address the concerns raised and take concrete measures to protect individual rights.

Until now, we discussed how various countries have implemented different strategies regarding the collection of personal data during the pandemic. These strategies were either based on individual consent or compulsion, depending on their priorities for contact tracing practices. However, a research group from the World Economic Forum have proposed an alternative approach to managing personal data that strikes a balance between public welfare and individual rights under state supervision (Okamoto and Fujita, 2020). This approach is called Authorized Public Access (APPA), which allows access to personal data for a specific, widely agreed upon public purpose, without the need for explicit individual consent. The core governance question then becomes who should be granted access to the data and under what conditions, instead of focusing on data ownership. It aims to balance the interests of three key factors: individual rights, data holders, and the public interest. This approach seeks to provide a solution that considers these factors and addresses the issue of data collection for public purposes while respecting individual rights. The APPA framework can be significant because it shifts the focus from data ownership to determining who should have access to data and under what circumstances. However, it's important to ask a more fundamental question: aside from predictable disease measures, what purpose will all of this collected data serve?

In the initial stages of the pandemic, Singapore developed the *TraceTogether* contact tracing app with the intention of safeguarding its citizens, presenting it as a tool for the people's sake (Lee and Lee, 2020). This Bluetooth-based app served as inspiration for similar contact tracking applications worldwide. However, after a short while, the government of Singapore caused controversy by passing a law that permitted the use of Covid-19 tracking data in specific criminal investigations, going against their promise to only use the collected data for containing the coronavirus (Lee and Tarabay, 2021). On the other hand, there is a growing concern about the ability of nation-states to safeguard sensitive personal health information, particularly in Western countries, when using the contact tracing infrastructure created by global tech giants like Google and Apple. To address these concerns, the Google and Apple contact tracing Application Programming Interface (API) is designed to collect as little personal information as possible. The API only collects anonymous Bluetooth signals from nearby devices, and no location data or personally identifiable information is stored on the user's device or on central servers. However, Michael Veale (2020), an academic specializing in data law, criticizes the unwillingness of such firm-driven decentralized systems to respond to the unique demands of countries using the system, as in the UK (which aims to avoid false notifications, while applying the self-report system during the disease process) and France (which seeks a partial centralized system despite possible snooping risk from neighbouring countries). However, Veale underlines that the main problem that will cause everyone to lose their sleep is the centralized control of the computing infrastructure held by these companies. According to him, data is simply a tool with a specific purpose, and these companies possess new cryptographic tools that can be used to design roadmaps capable of influencing the behaviour of particular individuals, events, communities, or even entire countries, without privacy-invading tools.

The Covid-19 pandemic was an unprecedented ordeal for humanity, and now it has become a measure of the capacity of nations to enhance their surveillance on populations. We witness how the utilization of contact tracing devices as a surveillance tool demonstrates the different manifestations of power and dominance that arise in unique ways within various countries. In this respect, Gjerde (2021) analysed the Norwegian government's response to the COVID-19 pandemic and contended that the state employed both liberal and authoritarian measures called for increased focus by governmentality scholars on the state's ability to influence power, including at the micro level. On the other hand, there is a tension wherein technology developers are frequently equated with nation-states, yet they do not face any sanctions for their actions and responsibilities. In both cases, societies are either under the grip of 'surveillance society' or 'surveillance capitalism'. The ever-evolving world has adapted to the 'new normal' and continues to be shaped by deeply ingrained power dynamics that surpass the concepts of Weber's iron cage (1987), Foucault's panopticon (1977), Deleuze's control society (1992), and Mattelart's cultural imperialism phenomenon (2010). The COVID-19 pandemic has led to the widespread use of Bluetooth, GSM, and Apple/Google app-based technologies, resulting in the need for novel definitions of surveillance and policies governing the interactions between governments, private technology companies, and civilian audiences. This has substantially transformed the traditional framework of surveillance capitalism and its association with the state. As described by Zuboff (2019), surveillance capitalism's influence has expanded to encompass every aspect of every individual's life and continues to erode their free will and autonomy. To mitigate the various risks associated with surveillance and data privacy, it is crucial to implement strict protocols and sanctions that apply to both public and private institutions. These measures should be accompanied by clear public expectations to ensure their effectiveness.

Inadequate Security Protocols

Inadequate security protocols refer to the absence or weakness of security measures designed to protect personal health information. If these protocols are inadequate or poorly implemented, the systems may be vulnerable to attack. This can include a lack of encryption or data access controls, weak passwords, or insufficient network segmentation. Without proper security measures in place, personal health information can be easily accessed or stolen by unauthorized individuals. This can lead to identity theft, financial loss, and damage to reputation for patients, as well as legal and financial consequences for healthcare organizations.

Personal health data is a type of personal information that, if processed improperly, can lead to discrimination and have severe consequences for the individual. Therefore, the collection, storage, and processing of personal health data is considered a fundamental human right and is subject to legal protection protocols at both regional and international levels. Many countries have taken steps to safeguard their citizens' privacy by enacting domestic laws and signing international agreements.

The European Union (EU) have the most comprehensive provisions on data protection and privacy, although over 120 countries currently have privacy laws in place, as stated by Thales Group (2022). Data protection regulations are becoming increasingly important worldwide, with many countries implementing their own laws to protect the personal data of their citizens. The General Data Protection Regulation (GDPR) has had a significant impact on organizations processing personal data of EU citizens, with hefty fines and reputational damage resulting from non-compliance. The European Data Protection Authority (EDPB, 2020a) released a statement in March 2020, suggesting that public authorities should attempt to process location data in a manner that maintains individuals' anonymity and prevents their re-identification. Moreover, in April 2020, EDPB (2020b) issued a directive for contact tracing apps. The practices to be followed, including individuals having full control over their data, contact tracing using technologies such as Bluetooth, only collecting mandatory data in case of positive cases, observing data minimization, and not collecting additional health or personal data or tracking user movements. The European Commission (EC, 2020) issued a directive in April 2020 on data protection standards for tracking applications used in fighting the pandemic. Along with the EDPB directive, the EC also recommends not using location data in contact tracing. Europe, which has a strong commitment to human rights, places significant importance on privacy compared to other regions. This is reflected in GDPR, which has a significant impact on data privacy within the European Union.

However, the implementation of tracking apps in certain European countries has raised concerns about privacy and security risks. For example, France's *StopCovid* and its updated version *TousAntiCovid* apps have faced criticism for technical issues and the use of a central server. Despite this criticism, the French government has upgraded its technological infrastructure while being overseen by the French Data Protection Authority (CNIL) to address these concerns (Norton Rose Fulbright, 2021). Similarly, the *Immuni* app in Italy, developed in partnership with Apple-Google, was met with scepticism due to concerns about private companies accessing personal information, and the app is no longer in use (Reuters, 2020). Austria's *Stopp Corona-App* also faced criticism, with public acceptance remaining low compared to Switzerland and Germany (Amann, Sleigh, & Vayena, 2021), and the app has been discontinued (EC, n.d.). In contrast, Germany's *Corona-Warn-App*, developed by SAP and Telecom for the government, is considered to have minimal privacy and security risks due to adherence to the Privacy-Preserving Contact Tracing (PEPP-IT) protocol and supervision by the German government. As a result, the app has been well-received in Germany and is viewed as a model for contact tracing apps in other European countries (Simon & Rieder, 2021).

The United States (US) is another actor that strives to adhere to various protocols regarding contact tracing applications. The US has implemented the Health Insurance Portability and Accountability Act (HIPAA), a federal law that protects the privacy and security of health data for all entities within the country. HIPAA establishes guidelines for the use and disclosure of health information by covered entities, and grants individuals' specific rights related to their health information. The law also mandates covered entities to implement safeguards to protect the confidentiality and integrity of health data (cdc.gov, n.d.). To address COVID-19 data privacy concerns, there are two bills that aim to protect individuals' health information and ensure privacy standards for COVID-19 contact tracing apps. Additionally, Apple and Google have collaborated on an (Application Programming Interface (API) that tracks the location of users to alert potential exposure to COVID-19, which has been adopted by several state health departments, but this approach could work well if consent is obtained and the encryption implementation by Apple and Google is secure (Norton Rose Fulbright, 2021).

The decision to use the Apple/Google API for contact tracing was based on its privacy-friendly protocol and decentralized data collection model, which met the basic requirements for privacy-preserving contact tracing. However, some experts, including Sharon (2020), argue that it represents a power play where sovereign states have limited say. Additionally, it is unclear how the ready-made API will be adapted to comply with the legal frameworks in the United States and Europe. The United Kingdom can also be included as an example in this context. Initially, the UK used a centralized system for contact tracing, but later switched to the Apple-Google infrastructure. However, the government still faced criticisms regarding oversight, trust, and accountability issues (Norton Rose Fulbright, 2021).

The exponential growth in data creation and storage has made enhanced data protection crucial and irreplaceable. Several countries have implemented data protection laws to safeguard personal information. Brazil has the General Data Protection Law that supplements over 40 data privacy-related laws and requires companies to adopt Data Protection Officers and security protocols. South Africa has the Protection of Personal Information Act, while Bahrain has the Data Protection Law, the first of its kind in the Middle East. The Philippines has the Data Privacy Act, and Canada has the Personal Information Protection and Electronic Documents Act. In the UK, the GDPR applies until July 2021, after which the Data Protection Act 2018 and the Data Protection, Privacy, and Electronic Communications (DPPEC) Regulations of 2019 will apply. India has enacted the Personal Data Protection bill, while other countries with data protection laws include Australia, Angola, British Virgin Islands, Denmark, Finland, Nigeria, and Israel. Governments around the world have implemented measures to contain the spread of COVID-19, including tracking and tracing measures. However, some of these measures have raised concerns about privacy violations and lack of transparency. According to OECD report (2020), while some countries such as Italy, Germany and France have implemented frameworks to support these measures in compliance with existing privacy regulations, others such as the Republic of Korea, Singapore and Israel have collected and processed data without the need for new legislation.

Turkey, like other countries, has implemented both similar and distinct security protocols to safeguard privacy and data protection during the pandemic. Turkey is legally bound by the Personal Data Protection Law (KVKK), which is a regional law, as well as the text of Fundamental Rights and Freedoms protected by the Turkish Constitution. To combat Covid-19, the Ministry of Health developed the HES application, which can provide location-based tracking of people, and it has made it mandatory to enter public areas and kept infected individuals under surveillance. To protect people's health information, a temporary code has been created using the pseudonymisation technique, which is used in social activities. While the measures taken to protect personal data are understandable, the penalties imposed on those who do not comply with the isolation rules during the crisis have raised concerns about the rights of individuals protected by law. The Ministry of Interior announced that "9,974 people/businesses were fined, and 178 businesses were temporarily suspended within the scope of three or more violations" in September 2020 due to non-compliance with isolation conditions (Bulur,2020). However, it has been announced that the fines imposed between March 2020 and November 9, 2022 will be deleted after the relaxation of pandemic rules (ntv.com.tr). Even for the sake of public health, finding or creating a legal basis that restricts the freedom of movement of people could lead to serious rights violations and pressure in the future.

The most criticized point about contact tracing systems is the collection of data in a central system. However, this system is also respected in a sense, as it was very effective in preventing the spread of the disease, especially in Asian countries. In this sense, the rough definition actually turned into a question of whether we should prioritize individual rights or public health. Turkey has implemented data storage and processing practices in a central system by following Asian countries that have taken fast and drastic measures. However, as Hogan et al. (2021) emphasizes, it should not be strange to observe a formation suitable for countries' local cultures regarding the privacy-benefit balances, especially during crisis periods such as epidemics. As we mentioned before, Turkish citizens have been using a digital database where they can do all their transactions from a single centre for a long time, and no one was surprised because the HES was integrated into this system. The issue that researchers, security experts and even the public should raise is that countries like Turkey that use centralized data storage systems should be informative and accountable about how they develop different ways for data security. Countries can choose and localize experiences like those seen in France, where the government using a central system is constantly monitored and updated by the authorities, or like in Germany, where continuous informing of the public and the adoption of a transparent communication system are implemented.

Actor-network theory (ANT) could be proposed as a framework for understanding the complex interconnections between different actors involved in the security of health surveillance data both in Turkey and worldwide. This theory emphasizes the role of non-human actors such as technology and material objects in shaping human behaviour and decision-making. By applying ANT to the study of healthcare providers' security measures, it may be possible to identify the specific technological and material factors that contribute to inadequate security protocols, as well as the social and organizational factors that may influence these decisions. By understanding the complex web of actors and factors that contribute to inadequate security protocols, healthcare organizations can develop more effective strategies for protecting health surveillance data. This may involve investing in more robust technical solutions, such as encryption and access controls, as well as improving training and education for staff on best practices for data security. Additionally, by identifying the social and organizational factors that contribute to inadequate security protocols, healthcare organizations can implement changes to their policies and culture to create a more secure environment (Potvin, 2005). Overall, applying ANT as a framework for understanding healthcare data security can help healthcare organizations to identify and address vulnerabilities and improve their security protocols.

RECOMMENDATIONS AND FUTURE RESEARCH

Recognizing potential cybersecurity risks associated with health surveillance systems is significant in order to construct robust steps should be taken to mitigate them. By taking some precautions, healthcare organizations can better protect patients' sensitive personal and health information. To mitigate the risks associated with inadequate security measures, healthcare organizations must implement solid security measures such as strong access controls and encryption, requiring third-party entities to adhere to strict privacy and security standards, and providing users with clear and transparent information about how their data will be used and shared (Ahmed et.al. 2020). In addition to technical measures, healthcare organizations must also adopt a culture of security, with a focus on continuous improvement and proactive risk management. This includes regular security assessments, incident response planning, and ongoing training and awareness campaigns.

Throughout the chapter, legal and ethical considerations surrounding the global collection and management of sensitive personal health information through contact tracing apps during the Covid-19 pandemic were extensively discussed. The chapter compared various applications from around the world, and the HES system in Turkey was used as a specific example to provide some possible solution suggestions while considering the theoretical issues in the background. However, it is important to emphasize and promote some recommendations that should be supported by various disciplines and platforms to encourage future research and public opinion formation. These recommendations include adhering to principles and values such as strong universal security protocols, providing cybersecurity education for the staff, regularly monitoring and testing the systems for vulnerabilities, promoting transparency and accountability, fostering a culture of cybersecurity, and considering the human aspect in all aspects of the system.

By implementing *strong universal security protocols*, healthcare organizations can protect patients' sensitive personal and health information. This includes encryption and access controls, as well as requiring third-party entities to adhere to strict privacy and security standards. Providing cybersecurity training to staff is also important to ensure that they are aware of potential risks and can take appropriate action to prevent security breaches.

Regularly monitoring and testing the system for vulnerabilities is also crucial in order to identify and address potential security threats before they can be exploited by malicious actors. This can include vulnerability assessments, penetration testing, and ongoing monitoring of network traffic and user activity.

Transparency and accountability in data management is also important to build trust with patients and ensure that their personal information is being handled responsibly. This includes providing clear and transparent information about how their data will be used and shared, as well as taking responsibility for any security incidents that may occur.

Creating a *culture of cybersecurity* within organizations is another important but often neglected premise. The European Union Agency for Cybersecurity (ENISA, 2019) has produced a report that highlights the importance of addressing not only the technical aspects of cybersecurity, but also the behavioural and cultural aspects that can affect an organization's overall security posture. It notes that the need for a shared understanding of cybersecurity risks and threats, and for all employees to be engaged in the effort to protect against them.

Finally, *considering the human aspect* of cybersecurity is crucial in order to foster a culture of security within healthcare organizations. This includes ongoing training and awareness campaigns, incident response planning, and a commitment to continuous improvement and proactive risk management.

Additionally, it is important to note that considerations related to the human aspect of cybersecurity also encompass issues of digital divide and discrimination. Healthcare organizations must take steps to address the inequalities arising from digital divide, such as providing access to technology for underprivileged communities. Discrimination can also be a concern, as certain groups may be at higher risk of cyberattacks or data breaches. Healthcare organizations must ensure that their security measures do not disproportionately harm or disadvantage these groups, and that they are taking steps to address any potential biases or discriminatory practices that may arise. This requires ongoing education and training for staff on issues of diversity, equity, and inclusion, as well as regular reviews of security protocols to identify and address any potential disparities or biases.

Overall, this book chapter aim to provide insights into the cybersecurity risks involved in health surveillance systems and the importance of data privacy and security in protecting personal health information. The most important innovation brought by digital surveillance systems like HES is the growing acceptance that digital health services penetrate private spaces of individuals and regulate the lives of health recipients. The trend suggests that in the future, more individuals will be willing to share their personal data to benefit from digital health systems. Digital health tools are becoming increasingly popular for monitoring vital metrics, medications, fertility, sleep, fitness, mental health, and other health markers, with the potential to become even more functional in the future. Health monitoring processes will not only be limited to private initiatives but also professionalized by the state. One example of this is the *Datenspende-App* developed by Germany, which collects general movement and fitness data from a user's fitness tracker and sends it to the Robert Koch Institute (RKI) for analysis. Unlike pandemic-era contact tracing devices, this app does not track contacts but looks for anomalies in the data related to pulse rate, sleep rhythm, and activity level that may indicate the presence of an acute respiratory disease such as Covid-19. Such state-run health monitoring practices may become more prevalent in the future. This type of mobile device-supported applications, considered perhaps the first step of advanced technology digital health services that we will encounter in the future, contain positive and negative examples that will provide infrastructure to health organizations in terms of cybersecurity, data accuracy, and respect for privacy.

REFERENCES

Ahmed, N., Ahmed, N., & Nafees, A. (2020). Cybersecurity challenges in healthcare: A systematic review. *International Journal of Healthcare Management*, *13*(1), 33–41.

Almalki, M., & Giannicchi, A. (2021). Health Apps for Combating COVID-19: Descriptive Review and Taxonomy. *JMIR mHealth and uHealth*, *9*(3), e24322. Advance online publication. doi:10.2196/24322 PMID:33626017

Altmann, S., Milsom, L., Zillessen, H., Blasone, R., Gerdon, F., Bach, R., Kreuter, F., Nosenzo, D., Toussaert, S., & Abeler, J. (2020). Acceptability of app-based contact tracing for COVID-19: Cross-country survey study. *JMIR mHealth and uHealth*, *8*(8), e19857. Advance online publication. doi:10.2196/19857 PMID:32759102

Amann, J., Sleigh, J., & Vayena, E. (2021). Digital contact-tracing during the Covid-19 pandemic: An analysis of newspaper coverage in Germany, Austria, and Switzerland. *PLoS One*, *16*(2), e0246524. Advance online publication. doi:10.1371/journal.pone.0246524 PMID:33534839

Baehr, P. (2001). The "Iron Cage" and the "Shell as Hard as Steel": Parsons, Weber, and the Stahlhartes Gehäuse Metaphor in the Protestant Ethic and the Spirit of Capitalism. *History and Theory*, *40*(2), 153–169. doi:10.1111/0018-2656.00160

Ball, K., & Webster, F. (2003). *The Intensification of Surveillance: Crime, Terrorism and Warfare in the Information Age* (K. Ball & F. Webster, Eds.). Pluto Press.

Baptista, E. (2022). *Hacker offers to sell data of 48.5 million users of Shanghai's COVID app*. https://www.reuters.com/world/china/hacker-offers-sell-data-485-mln-users-shanghais-covid-app-2022-08-12/

Bauman, Z. (2000). *Liquid Modernity*. Polity Press.

BBC News. (2020). *Aarogya Setu: Why India's Covid-19 contact tracing app is controversial*. https://www.bbc.com/news/world-asia-india-52659520

Bilodeau, A., & Potvin, L. (2018). Unpacking complexity in public health interventions with the Actor–Network Theory. *Health Promotion International*, *33*(1), 173–181. PMID:27492825

Budd, J., Miller, B. S., Manning, E. M., Lampos, V., Zhuang, M., Edelstein, M., Rees, G., Emery, V. C., Stevens, M. M., Keegan, N., Short, M. J., Pillay, D., Manley, E., Cox, I. J., Heymann, D., Johnson, A. M., & McKendry, R. A. (2020). Digital technologies in the public-health response to COVID-19. *Nature Medicine*, *26*(8), 1183–1192. doi:10.103841591-020-1011-4 PMID:32770165

Bulur, S. (2020). *İçişleri Bakanlığı: 22 Ağustos'tan bu yana 20 bin 94 kişinin izolasyon koşullarına uymadığı belirlendi* [Ministry of Interior: Since August 22, it has been determined that 20,094 people have not complied with the isolation conditions]. https://www.aa.com.tr/tr/turkiye/icisleri-bakanligi-22-agustostan-bu-yana-20-bin-94-kisinin-izolasyon-kosullarina-uymadigi-belirlendi/1974931

CDC. (2022). *Health Insurance Portability and Accountability Act of 1996 (HIPAA)*. https://www.cdc.gov/phlp/publications/topic/hipaa.html

Chernyshev, M., Zeadally, S., & Baig, Z. (2019). Healthcare data breaches: Implications for digital forensic Readiness. *Journal of Medical Systems*, *43*(7), 7. Advance online publication. doi:10.100710916-018-1123-2 PMID:30488291

CNN. (2020). *Africans in Guangzhou Are on Edge, After Many Are Left Homeless Amid Rising Xenophobia as China Fights a Second Wave of Coronavirus*. https://edition.cnn.com/2020/04/10/china/africans-guangzhou-china-coronavirus-hnk-intl/index.html

Copeland, R., & Needleman, S. (2019). Google's 'Project Nightingale' triggers federal inquiry. *The Wall Street Journal*. https://www.wsj.com/articles/behind-googles-project-nightingale-a-health-data-gold-mine-of-50-million-patients-115735718
67

Dave, P. (2020). *Apple-Google contact tracing tech draws interest in 23 countries, some hedge bets.* https://www.reuters.com/article/us-health-coronavirus-apps-tracing-idUSKBN22W2NW

Davis, S. L. M. (2020). Contact Tracing Apps: Extra Risks for Women and Marginalized Groups. *Health and Human Right Journal.* https://www.hhrjournal.org/2020/04/contact-tracing-apps-extra-risks-for-women-and-marginalized-groups/#_edn17

Deflem, M. (2000). Bureaucratization and Social Control: Historical Foundations of International Police Cooperation. *Law & Society Review*, *34*(3), 601–640. doi:10.2307/3115142

Deleuze G., (1992). Postscript on the societies of control. *October, 59*, 3–7.

Dixit, P. (2020). *India's Contact Tracing App Is All But Mandatory. So This Programmer Hacked It So That He Always Appears Safe.* https://www.buzzfeednews.com/article/pranavdixit/india-aarogya-setu-hacked

Dowthwaite, L., Fischer, J., Perez Vallejos, E., Portillo, V., Nichele, E., Goulden, M., & McAuley, D. (2021). Public Adoption of and Trust in the NHS COVID-19 Contact Tracing App in the United Kingdom: Quantitative Online Survey Study. *Journal of Medical Internet Research*, *23*(9), e29085. Advance online publication. doi:10.2196/29085 PMID:34406960

EC. (2020). *Coronavirus: Guidance to ensure full data protection standards of apps fighting the pandemic.* https://ec.europa.eu/commission/presscorner/detail/en/ip_20_669

EC. (n.d.). *Mobile contact tracing apps in EU Member States.* https://commission.europa.eu/strategy-and-policy/coronavirus-response/travel-during-coronavirus-pandemic/mobile-contact-tracing-apps-eu-member-states_en

EDPB. (2020a). *Statement on the processing of personal data in the context of the COVID-19 outbreak.* https://edpb.europa.eu/sites/default/files/files/news/edpb_statement_2020_processingpersonaldataandcovid-19_en.pdf

EDPB. (2020b). *Guidelines 04/2020 on the use of location data and contact tracing tools in the context of the COVID-19 outbreak.* https://edpb.europa.eu/sites/default/files/files/file1/edpb_guidelines_20200420_contact_tracing_covid_with_annex_en.pdf

ENISA. (2019). *Cybersecurity Culture Guidelines: Behavioural Aspects of Cybersecurity.* https://www.enisa.europa.eu/publications/cybersecurity-culture-guidelines-behavioural-aspects-of-cybersecurity

ENISA. (2020). *Threat Landscape Report: From January 2019 to April 2020.* https://www.enisa.europa.eu/publications/enisa-threat-landscape-2020-main-incidents/at_download/fullReport

Ericson, R., & Haggerty, K. (1997). *Policing the Risk Society*. University of Toronto Press. doi:10.3138/9781442678590

Feldman, J. M. (2016). Technology, Power and Social Change: Comparing Three Marx-Inspired Views. *Socialism and Democracy*, *30*(2), 28–72. doi:10.1080/08854300.2016.1184913

Gerke, S., Minssen, T., & Cohen, I. G. (2020). Ethical and legal challenges of artificial intelligence-driven healthcare. In A. Bohr & K. Memarzadeh (Eds.), *Artificial Intelligence in Healthcare* (pp. 21–36). Academic Press., doi:10.1016/B978-0-12-818438-7.00012-5

Gjerde, L. E. L. (2021). Governing humans and 'things': Power and rule in Norway during the Covid-19 pandemic. *Journal of Political Power*, *14*(3), 472–492. doi:10.1080/2158379X.2020.1870264

gov.uk. (2020). *Next phase of NHS coronavirus (COVID-19) app announced. Department of Health and Social Care.* https://www.gov.uk/government/news/next-phase-of-nhs-coronavirus-covid-19-app-announced

Greenhalgh, T., Koh, G. C. H., & Car, J. (2020). Covid-19: A remote assessment in primary care. *British Medical Journal*, 368. PMID:32213507

Hayat Eve Sigar. (n.d.). *Republic of Turkey Ministry of Health Hayat Eve Sığar (HES) Application.* https://hayatevesigar.saglik.gov.tr/gizlilik_politikasi_eng_index_V2.html

Hern, A. (2020). *Qatari contact-tracing app 'put 1m people's sensitive data at risk'.* https://www.theguardian.com/world/2020/may/27/qatar-contact-tracing-app-1m-people-sensitive-data-at-risk-coronavirus-covid-19

Joint Security and Privacy Committee NEMA/COCIR/JIRA. (2003). *Defending Medical Information Systems Against Malicious Software.* https://www.medicalimaging.org/wp-content/uploads/2011/02/medical-defending.pdf

Kruse, C. S., Frederick, B., Jacobson, T., & Monticone, D. K. (2017). Cybersecurity in healthcare: A systematic review of modern threats and trends. *Technology and Health Care*, *25*(1), 1–10. doi:10.3233/THC-161263 PMID:27689562

Kumaraguru, P., Acquisti, A., Cranor, L. F., Hong, J., & Nunge, E. (2010). Privacy in mobile and social computing. Synthesis Lectures on Information Security. *Privacy and Trust*, *3*(1), 1–131.

KVKK. (2020). *Kamuoyu Duyurusu (Public Announcement).* https://www.kvkk.gov.tr/Icerik/6721/KAMUOYU-DUYURUSU-Covid-19-ile-Mucadele-Surecinde-Kisisel-Verilerin-Korunmasi-Kanunu-Kapsaminda-Bilinmesi-Gerekenler-

Lee, T., & Lee, H. (2020). Tracing surveillance and auto-regulation in Singapore: 'smart' responses to COVID-19. *Media International Australia, Incorporating Culture & Policy*, *177*(1), 47–60. doi:10.1177/1329878X20949545

Lee, Y., & Tarabay, J. (2021). *Singapore Passes Law to Use Covid Tracing in Criminal Probes.* https://www.bloomberg.com/news/articles/2021-02-02/singapore-passes-law-to-use-covid-tracing-for-criminal-probes#xj4y7vzkg?leadSource=uverify%20wall?leadSource=uverify%20wall

Liu, V., Musen, M. A., & Chou, T. (2015). Data breaches of protected health information in the United States. *Journal of the American Medical Association, 313*(14), 1471–1473. doi:10.1001/jama.2015.2252 PMID:25871675

Lyon, D. (1994). *The Electronic Eye.* The Polity Press.

Lyon, D. (2001). *Surveillance Society: Monitoring Everyday Life.* Open University Press.

Lyon, D. (2007). *Surveillance Studies: An Overview.* Polity Press.

Marx, G. T. (2016). *Windows into the Soul: Surveillance and Society in an Age of High Technology.* The University of Chicago Press. doi:10.7208/chicago/9780226286075.001.0001

Mattelart, A. (2010). *The globalization of surveillance.* The Polity Press.

Milsom, L., Abeler, J., Altmann, S., Toussaert, S., Zillessen, H., & Blasone, R. (2020). *Survey of acceptability of app-based contact tracing in the UK, US, France, Germany, and Italy.* https://osf.io/7vgq9/

Murgia, M. (2021). *England's NHS plans to share patient records with third parties.* https://www.ft.com/content/9fee812f-6975-49ce-915c-aeb25d3dd748

Nisbet, R. (1977). *Twilight of Authority.* Random House.

Norton Rose Fulbright. (2021). *Contact tracing apps: A new world for data privacy.* https://www.nortonrosefulbright.com/en-fr/knowledge/publications/d7a9a296/contact-tracing-apps-a-new-world-for-data-privacy#Germany

Nothias, T., Jasper, K., Vavrovsky, A. S., Beauvoir, S., & Bernholz, L. (2021). Digital Surveillance, Civil Society and The Media During The Covid-19 Pandemic. *Digital Civil Society Lab Stanford Center on Philanthropy and Civil Society.* https://pacscenter.stanford.edu/wp-content/uploads/2021/10/Digital-Surveillance-COVID-Report.pdf

NTV. (2022). *Pandemi cezaları nasıl silinecek?* [How will pandemic fines be deleted?]. https://www.ntv.com.tr/turkiye/ogrenim-kredisi-ve-covid-19-cezalarina-iliskin-tahsilat-genelgesi,OkYyOaRKdkOSBBpFifd6Zw

OECD. (2020). *OECD Policy Responses to Coronavirus (COVID-19). Ensuring data privacy as we battle COVID-19.* https://www.oecd.org/coronavirus/policy-responses/ensuring-data-privacy-as-we-battle-covid-19-36c2f31e/

Okamoto, M., & Fujita, T. (2020). *A new data governance model for contact tracing: Authorized Public Purpose Access.* https://www.weforum.org/agenda/2020/08/contact-tracing-apps-privacy-framework-appa-data-governance/

ONS. (2019). *Internet access—households and individuals.* https://www.ons.gov.uk/peoplepopulationandcommunity/householdcharacteristics/homeinternetandsocialmediausage/bulletins/internetaccesshouseholdsandindividuals/2019#main-points

Orwell, G. (1987). *Nineteen Eighty-Four.* Penguin Books.

Potvin, L., Gendron, S., Bilodeau, A., & Chabot, P. (2005). Integrating social theory into public health practice. *American Journal of Public Health, 95*(4), 591–595. doi:10.2105/AJPH.2004.048017 PMID:15798114

Reuters. (2020). *Italy to launch contact-tracing app to fight coronavirus.* https://www.reuters.com/article/us-health-coronavirus-italy-app-idUSKBN2383EW

Saeed, S. A., & Masters, R. M. (2021). Disparities in Health Care and the Digital Divide. *Current Psychiatry Reports, 23*(9), 61. doi:10.100711920-021-01274-4 PMID:34297202

Seh, A. H., Zarour, M., Alenezi, M., Sarkar, A. K., Agrawal, A., Kumar, R., & Khan, R. A. (2020). Healthcare Data Breaches: Insights and Implications. *Health Care, 8*(2), 133. doi:10.3390/healthcare8020133 PMID:32414183

Shapiro, J., Huo, J., & Benincasa, R. (2020). *In New York Nursing Homes, Death Comes to Facilities with More People of Color.* https://www.npr.org/2020/04/22/841463120/in-new-york-nursing-homes-death-comes-to-facilities-with-more-people-of-color

Sharon, T. (2020). Blind-sided by privacy? Digital contact tracing, the Apple/Google API and big tech's newfound role as global health policy makers. *Ethics and Information Technology, 23*(S1), 1–13. doi:10.100710676-020-09547-x PMID:32837287

Shead, S. (2017). *Google DeepMind's first deal with the NHS was illegal, UK data regulator rules.* https://www.businessinsider.com/ico-deepmind-first-nhs-deal-illegal-2017-6

Simmel, G. (1906). The Sociology of Secrecy and of Secret Societies. *American Journal of Sociology, 11*(4), 441–498. doi:10.1086/211418

Simmel, G. (1950). The Metropolis and Mental Life. In K. Wolff (Ed.), *The Sociology of Georg Simmel* (pp. 409–424). Free Press.

Simon, J., & Rieder, G. (2021). Trusting the Corona-Warn-App? Contemplations on trust and trustworthiness at the intersection of technology, politics and public debate. *European Journal of Communication, 36*(4), 334–348. doi:10.1177/02673231211028377

Thales Group. (n.d.). *Beyond GDPR: Data Protection Around the World.* https://www.thalesgroup.com/en/markets/digital-identity-and-security/government/magazine/beyond-gdpr-data-protection-around-world

Todic, J., Cook, S. C., Spitzer-Shohat, S., Williams, J. S. Jr, Battle, B. A., Jackson, J., & Chin, M. H. (2022). Critical Theory, Culture Change, and Achieving Health Equity in Health Care Settings. *Academic Medicine*, *97*(7), 977–988. doi:10.1097/ACM.0000000000004680 PMID:35353723

Trinidad, M. G., Platt, J., & Kardia, S. L. R. (2020). The public's comfort with sharing health data with third-party commercial companies. *Humanities & Social Sciences Communications*, *7*(1), 149. doi:10.105741599-020-00641-5 PMID:34337435

UN News. (2020). *COVID-19 stoking xenophobia, hate and exclusion, minority rights expert warns.* https://news.un.org/en/story/2020/03/1060602

Valinsky, J. (2019). *Google is collecting health data on millions of Americans.* https://edition.cnn.com/2019/11/12/business/google-project-nightingale-ascension/index.html

Veale, M. (2020). *Opinion: Privacy is not the problem with the Apple-Google contact-tracing app.* https://www.ucl.ac.uk/news/2020/jul/opinion-privacy-not-problem-apple-google-contact-tracing-app

Weber, M. (1987). The Protestant Ethic and the Spirit of Capitalism. Academic Press.

Westerlund, M., Isabelle, D. A., & Leminen, S. (2021). The Acceptance of Digital Surveillance in an Age of Big Data. *Technology Innovation Management Review*, *11*(3), 32–44. doi:10.22215/timreview/1427

Yasir, S. (2020). *India is Scapegoating Muslims for the Spread of the Coronavirus.* https://foreignpolicy.com/2020/04/22/india-muslims-coronavirus-scapegoat-modi-hindu-nationalism/

Zhao, H., Zhang, J., Wu, Q., & Guo, Y. (2019). Inadequate security measures of health surveillance data: A survey of healthcare providers in China. *International Journal of Environmental Research and Public Health*, *16*(12), 2131. PMID:31208146

Zuboff, S. (2019). *The Age of Surveillance Capitalism: The Fight for a Human Future at the New Frontier of Power*. Public Affairs.

Chapter 7
Imperatives of Risk Analysis and Asset Management on Cyber Security in a Technology-Driven Economy

Godwin Emmanuel Oyedokun
Lead City University, Ibadan, Nigeria

Omolara Campbell
Lead City University, Ibadan, Nigeria

ABSTRACT

As the relevance of the digital economy increases, the need for secured cyberspace increases. Cyber threats are inescapable in digital progress. In the growth of cyber dominance, cybersecurity is necessary and very essential. Risk analysis is the process of assessing the likelihood of an adverse event occurring within the corporate, government, or environmental sectors. This chapter, therefore, explores the imperatives of risk analysis and asset management on cyber security in a technology-driven economy from the existing body of knowledge in the field. The chapter is divided into five sections, where the first section has to do with the introduction. The remaining four sections deal with the concepts of risk and risk analysis, asset management, factors determining attainment of continuous improvement of an asset performance management (APM) solution, cyber-crime and cyber-security, and conclusion and recommendations.

INTRODUCTION

Most companies are subject to millions of cyber-attacks as a result of the prevailing diversity of cyber-crimes and unethical project risk analysis which has hindered the economy from being technology-driven. Asset management and cyber security strategy put in place must help to prevent most attacks and recover quickly from any that might have succeeded. Understanding risk as a possibility of loss in a scenario is a critical concept in Asset Management and is a key function and area of competence. The idea that

DOI: 10.4018/978-1-6684-9018-1.ch007

the productivity of capital is determined by the rate of return we anticipate receiving over some future period serves as the foundation for evaluating capital investment projects. Cyberspace needs to be more secure as the importance of the digital economy grows.

The threat of cyberattacks is unavoidable as technology advances. Cybersecurity is essential as cyber domination increases. A national policy is created to provide the framework and infrastructure needed to protect cyberspace so that nations can profit from and prosper in the digital economy. A key component of national security is cybersecurity. Nations must strike a compromise between ensuring the dependability and security of cyberspace and the needs of digital economies. Nations around the world now place a high focus on protecting themselves from cyber-attacks.

The connected world offers amazing opportunities as the global population is shifting to cyberspace, related risk analysis, and asset management. Businesses must innovate and be online if they want to remain relevant and competitive in the digital economy. Technology and the economy came together to change how businesses operate so they may reach new markets and generate money. Information is a catalyst for business innovation and an agent of integration. It is time to embrace innovation and disruptive technologies because they are unheard of in business.

The linked world is changing our social fabric in terms of politics, economy, technology, and culture as the social transformation takes place right now. This digital revolution has a wide range of effects on the world, from e-economy, social movements, government elections, and awareness of global issues swiftly. This chapter critically examines the imperatives of risk analysis and asset management on cyber security in a technology-driven economy and makes some recommendations in the concluding part.

RISK AND RISK ANALYSIS

Risk is an exposure to the possibility of loss, injury, or other adverse or unwelcome circumstances; a chance or situation involving such a possibility. Management of risk within asset management is critical because asset managers are responsible for optimizing outcomes for the good of their organization, and therefore need to make judgements about which actions best achieve the right blend of outcomes based on organizational objectives.

To make these judgements, they need to predict how their actions will impact the future performance of the assets. They need to quantify both the probability of their actions (or inactions) causing a change in performance and then they need to determine the impact or consequences of that change in performance.

Risk = Probability X Consequence

(of failure) (of failure)

Risk analysis is the process of assessing the likelihood of an adverse event occurring within the corporate, government, or environmental sector. A project's likelihood of success or failure, the variation of portfolio or stock returns, the likelihood of future economic conditions, and the uncertainty of predicted cash flow streams are all examples of fundamental uncertainties that are studied through risk analysis.

To reduce potential unfavorable unanticipated outcomes, risk analysts frequently collaborate with forecasting experts. All businesses and people take risks; rewards or gains are less likely to occur without risk. The issue is that taking on too much risk can fail. By using risk analysis, it is possible to strike a balance between incurring risks and minimizing them. When considering risk, the following factors could be considered:

1. A project, investment, or business may face a variety of risks that need to be identified, assessed, and mitigated.
2. In quantitative risk analysis, the risk is assigned a numerical value using simulations and mathematical models.
3. A person's subjective judgement is a key component of qualitative risk analysis, which uses it to create a theoretical model of risk for a specific scenario.
4. Often, risk analysis is a combination of art and science.

Assuring that the risks being taken are commensurate with the targeted risks involves the processes of recognizing, monitoring, and managing risk. Models are used extensively in the process of mitigating market risk. A model is a condensed version of an actual phenomenon. Financial models make an effort to include the crucial components that affect pricing and sensitivity in the financial markets. By doing this, they offer crucial information needed to control investment risk.

For instance, investment risk models assist a portfolio manager in determining how much a change in a particular risk element is expected to affect the portfolio's value. Additionally, they shed light on the potential profits and losses the portfolio could incur as well as the likelihood of large losses (CFA, 2022). Risk management is a fairly recent phenomenon. Managers started to discuss risk after the '90s. This is the reason why only departments that made financial transactions with derivative instruments had to implement a risk management system.

The introduction of risk management in the financial sector implies several stages (Olteanu & Olteanu, 2011). Subsequently, these systems were extended to other financial services. Today, market risk management or credit risk represents a combined concept. Financial risk management is quite complex because implied risks are independent and dynamic. For example, a recession might generate effects both on the market risk and volatility, but it might induce bankruptcy as well by increasing operational and systemic risk. If risk management implies these interrelations, we deal with integrated risk management (Olteanu & Olteanu, 2011).

Today the risk is analyzed and measured with complex computerized systems. Ironically, they generate a new type of risk: model risk. Implementation of these models quite often represents black boxes; consequently, they may be implemented only by specialists who need an enormous quantity of data and who must be aware of the limits implied by these models. The use of derivative financial instruments through Stock Exchanges simplifies and increases the efficiency of risk management; specialists offer consultancy for understanding the functioning of mechanisms and for ensuring continuous financial flows (Sharpe, 1970).

To benefit from a competitive risk management system, organizations are up to date with the latest implementation models. Organizations must have a proactive policy for the implementation of risk management at all decision-making levels. The setting up of a risk management department requires high costs, which may only be supported by large organizations.

TYPES OF RISK ANALYSIS

Risk analysis can be quantitative or qualitative.

Quantitative Risk Analysis

In quantitative risk analysis, the risk is given numerical values by creating a risk model through simulation or deterministic statistics. A risk model is given inputs that are primarily assumptions and random variables. The model generates a range of outputs or outcomes for each given set of inputs. Risk managers evaluate the model's results using graphs, scenario analysis, and/or sensitivity analysis before deciding how to reduce and manage the risks.

A variety of potential outcomes of a choice or action taken can be generated using a Monte Carlo simulation. The quantitative technique called simulation uses a distinct set of input values each time it calculates the results for the random input variables. Each input's result is noted, and the model's final output is a probability distribution of all potential outcomes.

A distribution graph that displays some measures of central tendencies, such as the mean and median, and evaluates the variability of the data using standard deviation and variance can summarize the results. Using risk management methods like scenario analysis and sensitivity tables, the results can also be evaluated. The best, median and worst outcomes of any occurrence are displayed in scenario analysis.

For a risk manager, separating the outcomes into categories of best to worst offers a reasonable range of knowledge. A portfolio manager might, for instance, utilise a sensitivity table to analyse the effects of changes to the various values of each investment in a portfolio on the variance of the portfolio. Decision trees and break-even analysis are two other categories of risk management methods.

Qualitative Risk Analysis

A qualitative risk analysis is a type of analysis that does not identify and rate hazards using numbers and statistics. A formal characterisation of the uncertainties, an assessment of the potential consequences (should the risk materialise), and contingency preparations for adverse events are all components of qualitative analysis. SWOT analysis, cause and effect diagrams, decision matrices, game theory, and other techniques are examples of qualitative risk tools. An organisation may use a qualitative risk technique to assess the effect of a security breach on its servers to better plan for any potential revenue loss. Even though the majority of investors are worried about downside risk, mathematically speaking, the risk is the variance of both the upside and the downside.

Example of Risk Analysis

Value at Risk (VaR): *It is a statistic that gauges and assesses the degree of monetary risk present in an organisation, portfolio, or position over a given period. Investment and commercial banks most frequently use this indicator to assess the size and frequency of prospective losses in their institutional portfolios. VaR is a tool used by risk managers to gauge and manage the degree of risk exposure. VaR calculations can be used to calculate the risk exposure of individual holdings, entire portfolios, or an entire company.*

VaR is determined by reversing the order of historical returns from the worst to the best, presuming that returns will repeat themselves, particularly when it comes to risk. One crucial point to remember is that VaR doesn't give analysts complete assurance. Instead, it's a probability-based estimate. If you take into account the greater returns rather than just the poorest 1% of returns, the probability increases.

Ex-Post Risk: Ex-post risk is a term used to describe a risk measuring method that forecasts future hazards connected to an investment using historical results. It is a method of measuring risk that makes use of past performance to forecast future investment risk.

These risks are those that are controlled by investment returns after the event. The statistical deviation from the historical relative mean of long-term returns for a certain asset is used to calculate future risk. If there are no unexpected occurrences or situations, using the ex-post risk strategy can assist investors and financial professionals in estimating the maximum potential for losses during any particular trading session.

Limitations of Risk Analysis

Since risk is a probabilistic measure, it can never tell you with certainty how much risk you are exposed to at any particular time; all it can tell you is how likely it is that potential losses will be distributed, if and when they may be known. Additionally, there are no accepted techniques for estimating and assessing risk, and even VaR has a variety of methodologies for doing so. Normal distribution probabilities, which are infrequent in reality and cannot take into account severe or "black swan" events, are frequently used to presume that risk will occur. For instance, the financial crisis of 2008 revealed that VaR calculations significantly underestimated the likelihood of risk events caused by portfolios of subprime mortgages. Limitations of risk analysis could be stated as follows:

Empirical Adjustments: Adjusting the variables that affect a decision's outcome is extremely challenging. To decrease the risk that we would make a "poor" investment, we would like to change these elements. How can we accomplish that, though, without jeopardising our ability to make a "good" investment? What is the rationale behind the modification, in any case? We make adjustments for bias rather than uncertainty.

Revising Cutoff Rates: To mitigate against uncertainty, choosing larger cutoff rates achieves similar results. The likelihood of a return in proportion to the risk taken is something the management would like to have. A high calculated return on investment might be an incentive to take a risk when there is a lot of uncertainty in the numerous estimations of sales, costs, prices, and other factors. In actuality, this is a very sound position. The main issue is that the decision-makers still need to be aware of the risks they are accepting and the likelihood that they will receive the anticipated return.

More Accurate Forecasts: The reduction of estimation error is a worthwhile goal. No matter how many projections of the future are used to make a capital investment choice, the future still exists in the end. Therefore, regardless of how accurate the forecast is, we are still left with the awareness that there will always be some level of unpredictability.

Selected Probabilities: The probability of certain elements have been factored into return calculations using a variety of techniques. A mathematical calculation known as probability can be used in several contexts. The possibility of an event occurring divided by the number of anticipated outcomes of the event is another way to define probability. For instance, probability can be used to estimate sales growth or to calculate the likelihood that a particular marketing plan will be successful in bringing in new clients.

L.C. Grant spoke about a tool for predicting discounted cash flow rates of return when the service life is prone to deterioration and obsolescence. He determined the probability that the investment will fail at any point after it is made using the service-life factor's probability distribution. He estimated an overall expected rate of return after computing these components for each year from the maximum service life.

Edward G. Bennion proposed using game theory to account for different market growth rates since they would affect the rate of return for various solutions. To create the best possible strategy, he used the calculated probability that particular growth rates would occur.

It should be noted that both of these procedures produce an expected return and that each is based on just one uncertain input factor, in this example, service life, and market growth, respectively. Both are beneficial and help the executive see investment possibilities more clearly, but neither significantly narrows the range of "risk is taken" or "return is anticipated for" to aid in the difficult capital planning decisions.

ASSET MANAGEMENT

Asset management is a resource that has an economic value attached to it. Asset Management could be defined as follows:

1. The process of creating, operating, managing, and profitably selling assets. It is the process of gradually building up overall wealth through the purchase, upkeep, and trading of investments with the potential for appreciation.

2. It is a methodical approach to the management and value realization of the items that a group or entity is in charge of, across their entire life cycle. It may apply to both tangible and intangible assets (physical things like buildings or equipment) (such as human capital, intellectual property, goodwill, or financial assets).
3. Asset management is a methodical procedure for creating, using, maintaining, improving, and getting rid of assets in the most economical way possible (including all costs, risks, and performance attributes).
4. Asset management explicitly focuses on helping organizations to achieve their defined objective and optimizes available benefits, thus ensuring the best blend of activity to achieve the best balance for the organization.
5. Asset management improves decision-making throughout the life cycle of the asset in the areas of resulting in the lowest total cost of ownership in terms of acquisition, operation, maintenance, and renewal.
6. Asset management aims to both increase value and reduce risk.
7. It is also increasingly employed in both the private sector and public infrastructure sectors to ensure a coordinated approach to the optimization of costs, risks, service/performance, and sustainability.

On the other hand, Information Technology Asset is identified as a company-owned information system or hardware used in business activities while IT Asset Management (ITAM) refers to a set of business practices that ensure optimum utilization of resources within an organization through the reduction of risks, elimination of wastages, and minimization of costs in the long run. The expected outcome is supporting effective long-term management procedures of an organization and efficiency while maintaining strategic decision-making. With ITAM, improvement in communications and understanding of the modus operandi in the various departments and units of the organization is ensured. Additionally, the organisation is given the ability to enforce compliance with regulatory standards and cybersecurity regulations thanks to ITAM. This helps to increase productivity by providing technical support and putting a cap on the overhead costs associated with managing the organisation's IT environment.

ITAM has always been identified as a continued and systematic process that ensures activities within the organization attain optimum performance through proper alignment with the focus and core values of the organization. Thus, effective implementation of ITAM is a must for any organization to successfully realize its set goals and objectives.

Therefore, it becomes crucial for an organization's management to use the right technologies to assess the present needs of asset management. Identification of the best operational practices for reliable asset monitoring, system documentation, and best use of the system becomes crucial for the organisation. Creating a schedule for updating and reviewing existing assets of the organization also comes to the fore.

Importance of Asset Management

There are several reasons why businesses should be concerned about asset management. Such include:

Risks Identification: Asset management encompasses the identification and management of risks that arise from the utilization and ownership of certain assets. It implies that an organization will always be equipped to handle any risks that may arise.

Easy Assets Control: The process of asset management makes it easy for organizations to keep track of their assets, whether liquid or fixed. Firm owners will be aware of the locations of their assets, how they are being used, and whether any alterations have been completed. Increased returns result from the ability to recover assets more effectively.

Amortization Accuracy: The method of asset management makes sure that assets are accurately recorded in the financial statements since assets are verified frequently.

Removes Ghost Assets: There are instances where stolen, lost, or destroyed assets are improperly documented in the records. The owners of the company will be aware of the lost assets using a strategic asset management strategy and will remove them from the books.

Asset management is also important because it can help organizations to:

1. Reduce the total costs of operating their asset;
2. Reduce the capital costs of investing in the asset base;
3. Enhance the efficiency of their assets' operations (reduce failure rates, increase availability, etc.);
4. Reduce the potential health impacts of operating the assets;
5. Reduce the safety risks of operating the assets;
6. Minimize the environmental impact of operating the assets;
7. Maintain and improve the reputation of the organization;
8. Improve the regulatory performance of the organization; and
9. Reduce legal risks associated with operating assets.

Developing a Strategic Asset Management Plan

Any business, whether public or private, must own its assets. A business owner must create a strategic plan to handle the resources efficiently. The process to be followed in the strategic plan is presented below:

Complete an Asset Inventory: A business owner must first take inventory of all of his possessions before doing anything else. He will not successfully manage the assets in his inventory if he doesn't know the precise number of assets there are. The following items ought to be listed in an inventory of the company's possessions: the total number of assets, location of assets, value of each asset, date of acquisition, and estimated lifespan of assets.

Compute Life-Cycle Costs: To ensure the accuracy of his asset management strategy, a business owner should calculate each asset's total life-cycle costs. It is a common mistake for business owners to only take into account the cost of the initial acquisition. Throughout the asset's life cycle, it is expected that additional expenditures will arise, such as maintenance fees, condition and performance modeling, and disposal costs.

Set Levels of Service: Calculating life-cycle costs is followed by setting service levels. To put it simply, it entails outlining the full scope, caliber, and purpose of the numerous services that the assets provide. The business owner can then choose the necessary maintenance, operations, and replacement steps to keep the assets in good working order.

Exercise Long-Term Financial Planning: A business owner's asset management plan should ideally be straightforward enough to be incorporated into long-term financial planning. With a sound financial plan in place, the owner may decide which objectives can be accomplished and which ones need to be prioritised.

Benefits of Asset Management

There are many benefits of adopting an asset management strategy. These are presented below:

Improving Acquisition and Use: By monitoring a company's assets throughout its life cycle, a business owner can enhance the process of asset acquisition and utilization. A prominent example of this is Cisco Systems, which uses personal computer asset management to save costs. When putting such a plan into action, the business uncovered wasteful purchase habits, which it fixed by creating a better procedure for obtaining the tools that employees needed.

Improving Compliance: Governmental entities, charitable organizations, and businesses are required to submit reports outlining the acquisition, use, and disposal of assets. To make reporting simpler, the majority of them keep track of their asset information in a centralized database. When they need to prepare the reports after their fiscal year, they can easily obtain all the information they need through this method.

Double-Barreled Goal: Asset management is to increase an investment portfolio's worth over time while keeping a manageable level of risk, that is, maximising value while minimising risk.

Types and Classifications of Asset Management

Financial Asset Management (FAM)

The term "portfolio manager" (sometimes known as "asset manager") most frequently refers to the area of financial services that manages investment funds and segregated customer accounts. Asset management is a department of a financial organisation that hires professionals to handle client investments and money management. This is done either actively or passively. Financial asset management can be categorized into two:

1. **Active Asset Management:** This entails active responsibilities like examining the client's assets to planning and managing the investments. Asset managers are in charge of all of these, and suggestions are given based on each client's financial situation. Due to the additional labor required, active asset management costs more for investors.
2. **Passive Asset Management:** Assets are divided here to reflect an industry or market index. Passive asset management requires much less work than active asset management does. Additionally, it needs less customization and oversight, making it less expensive for investors.

Physical and Infrastructure Asset Management

The mix of managerial, economic, financial, engineering, and other disciplines used by physical assets to deliver the best value level of service for the expenses involved is known as infrastructure asset management (Malley & Patterson, 1998). It entails managing each stage of the life cycle of tangible assets, such as buildings and infrastructure, including design, construction, commissioning, operation, maintenance, repairs, replacement, and decommissioning/disposal. A priority system is necessary for the operation and upkeep of assets in a budget-constrained setting. For example, the rapid growth of renewable energy has led to the emergence of proficient asset managers engaged in the administration of solar systems (solar parks, rooftops, and windmills).

These groups frequently work with financial asset managers to provide investors with turnkey solutions. Since the majority of industrialised nations' infrastructure networks were nearly complete in the 20th century and they need to be managed to run and maintain them cost-effectively, infrastructure asset management has become crucial in the 21st century. Software asset management is one kind of infrastructure asset management. The International Organization for Standardization published the management system standard for asset management in 2014. The ISO 55000 series offers definitions, specifications, and instructions for setting up, sustaining, and enhancing an efficient asset management system. The formation of such a framework depends heavily on local governance. It can be further categorised into the following:

1. **Physical Asset Management:** The process of managing a physical asset's entire life cycle, including design, construction, commissioning, operation, maintenance, repair, modification, replacement, and decommissioning/disposal. Examples of such assets include buildings, production and service plants, water and waste treatment facilities, distribution networks, transportation systems, and other physical assets. The ideas of Total Cost of Ownership can now be applied to facility management of a single system, a building, or a campus. Thanks to the increasing availability of data from asset systems. Asset health management and physical asset management are related.
2. **Infrastructure Asset Management:** This focuses on the public sector, utilities, real estate, and transportation systems as it develops this theme. Asset management can also refer to the collaborative and evidence-based decision-making processes that will shape the future interfaces between the built, natural, and human environments.
3. **Fixed Assets Management:** This is an accounting process that seeks to track fixed assets for financial accounting. Organisations can keep an eye on their machinery and vehicles, evaluate their condition, and keep them in good operating order with the help of fixed asset management. By doing this, they reduce lost inventory, equipment breakdowns, and downtime, improving the lifetime value of the items.
4. **IT Asset Management:** This involves the collection of business procedures that integrate accounting, contracting, and inventory management to enable IT environment life cycle management and strategic decision-making.
5. **Digital Asset Management:** This is a type of digital asset management for media material on smart devices. DAM is the process of putting all of an organisation's media assets in one place so that everyone may access them as needed. Large audio or video files that must be worked on concurrently by numerous teams of workers typically use this.

Enterprise Asset Management (EAM)

Enterprise Asset Management (EAM) systems are asset *information* systems that support the management of an organization's assets. An EAM combines a computerized maintenance management system (CMMS), various modules, and an asset registry (an inventory of assets and their characteristics such as inventory or materials management), geographically dispersed, networked, or integrated assets. The use of geographic information systems (GIS) is frequently used to portray them as well.

A GIS-centric asset registry standardizes data and enhances interoperability, giving users the capacity to efficiently and effectively reuse, coordinate, and exchange information. The traditional departmental function silos are broken down with the aid of a GIS platform and data on both "hard" and "soft" assets.

The soft assets can include rights-of-way, permissions, licenses, branding, patents, and other entitlements, whereas the hard assets are the traditional physical assets or infrastructural assets.

Only one of the "enables" of effective asset management is the EAM system. To achieve their organizational goals, asset managers must make informed decisions. To do this, they need access to good asset information as well as leadership, clear strategic priorities, competencies, cross-departmental co-operation and communication, workforce and supply chain engagement, risk and change management systems, performance monitoring, and ongoing improvement.

Public Asset Management (PAM)

The definition of Public Asset Management (PAM) broadens the scope of Enterprise Asset Management (EAM) by including the management of any assets that are valuable to a municipal authority and its constituents. Planning and development of land use make use of PAM.

Intellectual and Non-Physical Asset Management

The use of assets when the user's rights are restricted by a licensing agreement is becoming more common among both consumers and organisations. Examples include software, music, books, and other items. The restrictions on these licenses, such as a time frame, would be identified by an asset management system. A license is frequently granted for a specific amount of time when purchasing software, for instance. There are time-based software licenses available from both Adobe and Microsoft.

There is a difference between the ownership of software and software updates in both the corporate and consumer worlds. A version of the programme may be owned, but not later releases. To push customers to buy newer hardware, producers of cellular phones frequently fail to upgrade their products. Large corporations that license software to customers, like Oracle, make a distinction between the right to use and the right to maintenance and support.

Asset Performance Management (APM)

APM is a collection of tools and services made to improve the effectiveness of operations and maintenance for every fleet, plant, and equipment. APM offers special value to contemporary industrial operations. Thanks to its integration of General Electric industry expertise, work process automation, and Digital Twin analytics. For a holistic approach to asset and O&M management, APM's Solutions for Health, Reliability, Strategy, Integrity, and Safety can be used separately or in tandem. APM is offered as on-premises software and as a cloud-based service.

Asset Managers

Asset managers are subject to fiduciary obligations. They must act in good faith while making judgments on behalf of their customers. They must perform a thorough study using both macro- and micro-analytical techniques. This involves reviewing corporate financial records, statistical research of current market patterns, and anything else that might help achieve the stated objective of client asset appreciation. Financial organizations that cater to high-net-worth people, governmental bodies, businesses, and institutional investors like colleges and pension funds offer asset management as a service.

Functions of Asset Managers

To achieve the client's financial objectives while remaining within the client's risk tolerance, the asset manager's role is to decide which investments to make or avoid. Among the most well-known options for investing include stocks, bonds, real estate, commodities, alternative investments, and mutual funds. They may be referred to as financial advisors or portfolio managers. Professionals in asset management provide the following services to clients:

Developing Policy: The organizational plan, which is a company's top-level "business plan," and the Asset Management Strategy are connected by the Asset Management Policy. To meet the goals of the organization, it is often a set of principles or rules that direct Asset Management work. It covers the "what" and the "why" in particular.

Developing Strategy: The Asset Management Strategy directs the organization's asset management activity; it will determine the high-level asset management objectives that are needed from the activity to deliver the organization's objectives; it will define the approach to planning that will be taken.

Asset Management Planning: Asset Management Planning looks at considering all the options for activities and investments going forward and then putting together a set of plans which describe what will be done when and by whom. The asset manager ensures that the plan delivers what is required of it by the strategy.

Delivering the Plans: This is the bit where work is done on the assets, whether assessing or monitoring them, maintaining or repairing them, refurbishing or replacing them. This activity needs to include the appropriate controls to ensure the work is done efficiently and that information gathered is fed back into the strategy and planning activities.

Developing People: This activity is specifically about developing the skills and competencies of people to improve asset management activities. It spans from the board room to the toolbox and also through the supply chain. It looks at the culture within an organisation and how change can be managed to achieve optimal results for that organisation.

Managing Risk: Understanding risk is a critical concept in asset management and is a key function and area of competence. Its focus is on being able to assess the risk of action or inaction on the performance of assets in the context of the organization's corporate objectives.

Managing Asset Information: Collecting and collating the right information to inform Asset Management decisions is crucial to achieving Asset Management success. When there is insufficient data, decisions are made in the dark (or, at best, in the twilight!). it is critical to ensure that the right people have the right information to make the best decisions.

Types of Asset Managers

Asset managers can be categorised according to the kind of asset they manage and the level of service they offer. Before investing, it's critical to comprehend a manager's responsibilities because each sort of asset management has a varied level of accountability to the customer. The following are some types of asset managers:

Registered Investment Advisors: An organization that offers clients advice on stock trading or even administers their portfolios is known as a registered investment advisor (RIA). RIAs are subject to stringent regulation, and if they oversee more than $100 million in assets, they must register with the Securities and Exchange Commission (SEC).

Investment Broker: A broker is a person or business that serves as a middleman for its clients by purchasing stocks and other securities and managing client assets. Since brokers typically don't have a fiduciary commitment to their clients, it's crucial to conduct extensive research before making a purchase.

Financial Advisor: A financial advisor is a specialist who can buy and sell securities on behalf of their clients or recommend investments to them. Asking first is always important because financial advisors may or may not have a fiduciary duty to their clients. Many financial advisors have a particular area of expertise, like tax law or estate planning.

Robo-Advisor: The cheapest form of an investment manager is not even a human. A Robo-advisor is a computer algorithm that automatically monitors and rebalances a portfolio of assets by buying and selling securities by predetermined objectives and risk tolerances. Robo-advisors are substantially less expensive than individualised investment services because there is no human involvement.

Challenges of Asset Management in Organisation

The following among others are the challenges of Asset Management in the organisation:

1. Little to no visibility.
2. It does not keep management edicts.
3. It does not respond to the economy or politics.
4. It does respond to how it is treated and used.

Furthermore, Service Channel (2022) posited Seven Challenges of Asset Management as follows:

1. Little to No Visibility
2. Warranty Leakage
3. Lack of Information Sharing
4. Difficult Repair or Replace Decisions
5. Asset Servicing Errors
6. Time Sink
7. Difficult Strategic Decision Making.
    1. Little to No Visibility

Without visibility, it is impossible to accurately determine the asset inventory at each location(s). Without a historical record of the assets and information, it is impossible to track crucial information for future support and service needs, such as the serial or model number of an item. Smaller assets, such as equipment and appliances, are frequently relocated between locations for a variety of reasons, which makes the situation much worse. In other words, without knowledge of what you already have in place and where everything is, it is impossible to be making wise asset-related decisions.

2. Warranty Leakage

It is quite likely that a firm is not tracking the warranty status or availability of its assets if it is not tracking them at all. This could result in the business spending real money on frivolous maintenance.

According to a study by the Service Channel, organisations waste up to 35% of potential warranty savings by having to pay for repairs on equipment that is still covered by the original warranty.

3. Lack of Information Sharing

Data management is essentially what asset tagging is. It is challenging, if not impossible, to build a dynamic data profile of the major assets without modern asset tagging, even at the most basic level, such as with repair and cost histories. As a result, the Facility Manager and other users are left with no effective means of holding suppliers responsible for decisions about repairs and maintenance.

4. Difficult Repair or Replace Decisions

For financial managers (FMs), deciding whether to replace or repair an asset is a regular decision. Making the wrong choice might cost the company a lot, either in terms of overpaying or paying for equipment downtime. These repair-or-replace decisions could end up being little better than a coin flip without the appropriate levels of data to assess and direct the FMs.

5. Asset Servicing Errors

Without a way to quickly and confidently identify a certain asset, it is impossible to ensure that the on-site team is selecting the right piece of machinery when putting together a work order. When it comes to emergency or on-demand services, time is of the essence, and prices can soar if the service provider makes the wrong choices about which asset to fix or maintain while on the job site. If periodic maintenance is carried out on the wrong asset, even planned maintenance might be ineffective or put assets at risk.

6. Time Sink

The time needed to just keep things as they are is the primary issue with any operational complexity. Without effective asset tagging solutions, this is unquestionably the case for facility managers who are attempting to manage essential assets. The time spent manually managing assets may end up being the most expensive, given all the duties a facility manager possesses.

7. Difficult Strategic Decision Making

Every budget includes a significant amount for capital expenditures, which have a significant financial influence on a company's bottom line. To guarantee that the firm is behaving strategically and wisely when making major decisions like investing in new capital equipment, comprehensive, accurate, and clean asset data across a site portfolio is required. A firm must be aware of its asset inventory, its service history, and the cost-per-asset throughout its lifecycle for anything from new location build-outs to future capital budgeting. And without a precise method of capturing, maintaining, and tracking equipment across the entire firm, it is impossible to do that.

CYBER-CRIME AND CYBER-SECURITY

Cybercrime is defined as any unauthorized activity involving a computer, device, or network. The main objectives are to gain access to, alter, or destroy sensitive data, demand money from users, or obstruct regular corporate operations. Cybercrime can be divided into three categories: computer-assisted crimes, offenses in which computers themselves are targets, and offenses in which computers are only incidental to the crime rather than the primary focus (Mulligan, 2017).

According to a 2020 study by McAfee and the Canadian Security Intelligence Service, based on data collected by Vanson Bourne, the world economy loses more than $1 trillion each year due to cybercrime. Political, ethical, and social incentives can also drive attackers. Any organisation's security is built on three guiding principles: confidentiality, integrity, and availability. This is known as the CIA, and it has been the industry standard for computer security since the first mainframes were created. Today technology plays a bigger role in daily life than ever before. The advantages range from having almost immediate access to information on the internet to the contemporary conveniences offered by concepts and technology for smart home automation.

Cybersecurity is a field that deals with ways to protect systems and services from malicious online actors including spammers, hackers, and cybercriminals. While certain cyber security components are built to launch an assault immediately, the majority of modern specialists are more concerned with figuring out how to safeguard all assets, from computers and cellphones to networks and databases, against attacks (Solon & Hern, 2017).

Cybersecurity is necessary for everyone with an internet connection. This is because the majority of cyberattacks are automated and focus on common vulnerabilities as opposed to targeting particular websites or businesses. Utilizing regular cyber security risk assessments to identify and analyze hazards is the most effective and cost-effective strategy to secure your firm. A risk-based approach to cyber security will guarantee that resources are concentrated where they are most needed (Mulligan, 2017).

Cybersecurity can be defined as follows:

1. The use of technology, procedures, and controls to defend against cyberattacks on systems, networks, programs, devices, and data is known as cyber security.
2. The lowering of the danger of cyberattacks and safeguard against the unlawful use of technologies, networks, and systems.
3. The defense of internet-connected devices and services against nefarious hacking, spamming, and cybercrime attacks. Companies employ the procedure to safeguard themselves against phishing scams, ransomware attacks, identity theft, data breaches, and monetary losses.

CYBER SECURITY AND INFORMATION SECURITY

Information security and cyber security are dissimilar but are frequently used interchangeably. Information security is a broader category that safeguards all information assets, whether in hard copy or digital form and focuses on protecting computer systems from illegal access as well as from being otherwise damaged or rendered unavailable.

CYBER SECURITY THREATS

Despite society's generally positive attitude toward modern advancements, cyber security concerns posed by contemporary technology is a serious threat. We proceed to present the types of cyber threats as follows:

Malware: This is a category of software that includes programmes like ransomware, botnet software, RATs (Remote Access Trojans), rootkits and bootkits, spyware, Trojans, viruses, and worms that aim to harm computers or gain unwanted access to them. It may also obstruct access to your computer's resources, cause system instability, or covertly send data from your data storage.

Trojans: This is similar to the mythical Trojan Horse. This deceives victims into believing they are opening a secure file. After being installed, the trojan targets the system, generally creating a backdoor that gives hackers access.

Formjacking: This inserts malicious code into online forms.

Cryptojacking: It installs illicit cryptocurrency mining software.

DNS (Domain Name System) Poisoning Attacks: This compromise the DNS to redirect traffic to malicious sites.

Cyberterrorism: This danger consists of a political attack against computers and information technology to cause harm and widespread societal unrest.

Botnets: These are large-scale cyberattacks carried out by remotely controlled, malware-infected machines which are used in this particularly heinous operation. It is a network of computers managed by a single, coordinated cybercriminal. It is noteworthy that hacked computers join the botnet network.

Adware: This is frequently referred to as software with advertising. The adware infection is a potentially unwanted programme (PUP) that was put in without your consent and creates annoying web adverts automatically.

SQL Injection: A Structured Query Language attack inserts malicious code into a SQL-using server.

Phishing: It is the practice of sending fraudulent emails that resemble emails from reputable sources. The intention is to steal private information, including login credentials and credit card numbers. This is the most typical kind of Cyberattack. Through education or a technological solution that filters harmful emails, you can be better protected. Hackers use false communications, notably e-mail, to trick the recipient into opening and following instructions that frequently require personal information. In some phishing scams, malware must have been downloaded.

Man-in-the-Middle Attack (Mitm): As part of Mitm attacks, hackers insert themselves into a two-person online transaction. Frequently, Mitm attacks take place on unprotected public Wi-Fi networks.

Denial of Service: A network or computer is subjected to a denial-of-service attack (DoS) by being overwhelmed with "handshake" activities, which effectively overload the system and prevent it from responding to user requests.

Social Engineering: A strategy used by opponents to get someone to provide sensitive information is social engineering. They can demand money from you or access your private information. Any of the aforementioned dangers can be paired with social engineering to increase the propensity to open harmful links, download malware, or believe in phishing emails.

Ransomware: This a destructive software used to demand payment by preventing users from accessing files or the computer system until the ransom is paid. Even if the ransom is paid, there is no guarantee that the system will be fixed or the files will be restored.

TYPES OF CYBERSECURITY

In the media, the phrase "cyber security" has become a catch-all for the process of preventing every type of cybercrime, from identity theft to the deployment of international digital weapons. These classifications are accurate, but they fall short of describing the full nature of cyber security for persons without a background in computer science or the digital sector. Cyber security could be classified as follows:

Critical Infrastructure Cyber Security: Due to the fact that SCADA (supervisory control and data acquisition) systems sometimes rely on outdated software, critical infrastructure firms are frequently more susceptible to attack than other organisations. The Network Information System (NIS) Regulations apply to those who operate vital services in the UK's energy, transportation, health, and water sectors as well as those that supply digital services. Organisations must use the proper organisational and technical controls to manage their security risks by the regulations.

Network Security: Network security entails fixing flaws in your operating systems, network architecture, wireless access points, servers, hosts, firewalls, and network protocols.

Cloud Security: Securing data, applications, and infrastructure in the cloud is the focus of cloud security. For businesses using cloud service providers like Amazon Web Services, Azure, Google Rackspace, and others, it refers to developing safe cloud architectures and applications.

IoT (Internet of Things) Security: IoT security entails protecting networks and smart devices connected to the IoT. IoT devices are objects that connect to the Internet automatically, such as smart lighting, thermostats, fire alarms, and other equipment.

Application Security: This addresses the integration of various defenses into the software and services of an organisation against a variety of threats. To reduce the possibility of unwanted access or manipulation of application resources, this subdomain necessitates cyber security professionals to create secure code, design secure application structures, implement robust data input validation, and more.

Identity Management and Data Security: This subdomain covers the procedures, protocols, and methods used to let authorised users access an organization's information systems. These procedures entail putting in place strong information storage systems that protect the data while it is in transit or stored on a server or computer. Additionally, this sub-domain employs two-factor or multi-factor authentication techniques more frequently.

Mobile Security: As more people rely on mobile devices, mobile security is becoming increasingly important. This sub-domain guard against dangers including unauthorised access, device loss or theft, malware, viruses, and more for both organisational and individual data kept on portable devices like tablets, smartphones, and laptops. Mobile security also makes use of authentication and training to strengthen security.

Disaster Recovery and Business Continuity Planning (DRBCP): Threats do not always come from people. The DRBCP subdomain includes procedures, alerts, monitoring, and plans that can be used by organisations to keep their mission-critical systems operational before, during, and after any incident (including fires, explosions, and other natural disasters), as well as to resume and recover any lost operations and systems.

However, information is power, and staff awareness of cyber threats is important in the context of cyber security. It is therefore essential to provide corporate workers with training in the principles of computer security to increase understanding of organisational procedures and policies, industry best practices, and monitoring and reporting of suspicious or malicious activity. Classes, programmes, and certifications relating to cyber security are covered in this subdomain.

MANAGEMENT OF CYBER SECURITY MEASURES

1. Effective cyber security management must come from the top of the organization.
2. It must also have a robust cyber security culture, reinforced by regular training.
3. It must ensure that every employee recognizes cyber security as their responsibility.
4. Good security and effective working practices must go hand in hand.

RELEVANT APPROACH TO CYBER SECURITY

A cyber security strategy will ensure that your efforts are focused where they are most needed. The most economical and effective method of preventing an organization is to do routine cyber security risk assessments to identify and evaluate threats. Cyber security measures to boost cyber defenses are as follows:

User Education: Data breaches are most often caused by human error. As a result, there is a need to equip employees with the knowledge they need to counter threats. Employees will learn how security dangers influence them and how to apply best practises guidance to practical scenarios through staff awareness training.

Application Security: Web application flaws are a frequent entry point for cybercriminals. Web application security must be a top priority because applications are becoming more and more important to companies.

Network Security: Protecting the integrity and usefulness of your network and data is the process of implementing network security. A network penetration test can be used to do this by evaluating the network for security flaws and vulnerabilities.

Leadership Commitment: The secret to cyber resiliency is leadership commitment. Without it, it is challenging to set up or enforce efficient procedures. Top management must be willing to incur expenditure in the right cyber security tools, such as awareness training.

Password Management: A set of principles and best practices to be followed by users while storing and managing passwords efficiently to secure passwords as much as they can to prevent unauthorized access. Every organisation should implement a password management policy to guide staff to create strong passwords and keep them secure.

CYBER SECURITY EXPERT

Cyber Security experts are the security professionals that individuals and companies rely upon to identify potential threats and protect valuable data from hackers and other cybercrimes.

FUNCTIONS OF CYBER SECURITY EXPERTS

1. Identifying, testing, and fixing a company's infrastructure's vulnerabilities.
2. Keep an eye on harmful information and spot network intrusions.
3. Install firewalls, antivirus software, and frequent software updates.
4. strengthen areas that may have been attacked.

Cyber Security Experts work in one or more of these common Cyber Security domains to keep data safe:

1. **Asset Security:** Analyze wireless access points, computers, networks, and routers.
2. **Security Architecture and Engineering:** Ensure consistency in security policies and practises.
3. **Communication and Network Security:** Control cloud storage and data transmission.
4. **Identity and Access Management:** Monitor user identification and responsibility.
5. **Security Operations:** keeping an eye on security to spot attacks.
6. **Security Assessment and Testing:** To guarantee compliance with industry requirements, test security policies.
7. **Software Development Security:** Create and repeatedly test code.
8. **Security and Risk Management:** Determine potential hazards and put in place the necessary security measures.

Different strategies are used by cyber security experts to protect computer systems and networks. Some of the best practices include:

1. Using two-way authentication.
2. Running antivirus software.
3. Using firewalls to disable unwanted services.
4. Securing passwords.
5. Installing regular updates to avoid phishing scams.
6. Securing domain name servers (DNS).
7. Employing cryptography, or encryption.

EFFECT OF RISK ANALYSIS AND ASSET MANAGEMENT ON CYBER SECURITY IN A TECHNOLOGY-DRIVEN ECONOMY

Businesses, mindsets, innovations, and entire economies can all be characterised as being technology-driven. Technology, design and purpose, culture, profit, supply and demand, and many other aspects can form the basis of a technology-driven economy or socioeconomic activity. Processes that are motivated by the possibilities of currently available technology are said to be technology-driven. For instance, the latest scientific discoveries may spur technological innovation. This fresh technology can then result in fresh goods and services.

Another illustration is economies that decide to utilise cutting-edge technologies. They let technology drive at least some of the value that their economy generates. Technology has recently emerged as one of the most important forces driving change and innovation. Therefore, many economies ought to think about what advantages they might derive from giving internal technology a higher priority.

Asset management has a double-barrel goal: increasing value while mitigating risk. In other words, the client's risk tolerance is the first thing to be discussed. Risk aversion is (or should be) a characteristic of both the retiree who depends on portfolio income and the pension fund administrator who manages retirement assets. Any adventurous person, especially a young person, would wish to experiment with high-risk ventures. Using both micro and macro analytical techniques, the asset manager is expected to perform thorough research. These consist of studies of firm financial records, statistical research of current market patterns, and anything else that might assist in achieving the stated objective of client asset appreciation.

Different methods can be used to evaluate the risk and reward tradeoff of a possible investment opportunity using the information provided by risk analysis. A risk analyst begins by determining what might go wrong. These drawbacks must be compared to a probability meter that assesses the probability that the event will occur. It also makes an effort to determine the magnitude of impact the incident will have. Hedging or buying insurance can decrease the number of identified risks, including market risk, credit risk, currency risk, and others. It's crucial to understand that risk analysis enables experts to recognize and reduce hazards, but not entirely avoid them.

CYBER SECURITY RISK ASSESSMENT IN INFORMATION TECHNOLOGY SECTOR

The Information Technology (IT) Sector provides both products and services that support the efficient operation of today's global information-based society. These products and services are integral to the operations and services provided by other Critical Infrastructure and Key Resource (CIKR) sectors. Threats to the IT sector are complex and varied. They are likened to the risks presented by criminals and hackers some of which are manmade and known to be cyber-attacks or cybercrimes that exploit known and unknown vulnerabilities in products and services developed by the IT Sector.

The management of the platforms on which information is processed and transmitted should ensure the confidentiality, integrity, and availability of information as well as the avoidance of financial loss and reputation risk, among other things, for cyber security to be safe and sound in the modern era. Due to the IT sector's high degree of interdependency with other CIKR sectors and the continuously evolving threat landscape, assessing vulnerabilities and estimating consequences is difficult (ENISA, 2015).

Therefore, these issues must be dealt with in a collaborative and flexible framework. This will enable the public and private sectors to enhance resiliency and security by taking proactive steps to secure their critical information assets and other information that are accessible from cyberspace. Cyber security resilience is considered an organization's ability to maintain normal operations despite all cyber threats and potential risks in its environment. Resilience provides an assurance of sustainability for the organization using its governance, interconnected networks, and culture.

TECHNOLOGY AND THE ECONOMY

Many nations are considering strategies which will spur economic growth and create jobs for both the youth and the working population at large. Information Communication Technology is not the only source of generating a rapid rate of economic growth, rather it's directly responsible for the creation of millions of new jobs. Furthermore, it plays a significant role in enabling innovation and growth. With 40% of people on the planet now online, the number of mobile subscriptions (6.8 billion) is getting close to the worldwide population estimates. The competitiveness of economies in this new environment is reliant on their capacity to take advantage of emerging technologies. The five most typical economic impacts of ICT are listed below.

CONCLUSION AND RECOMMENDATIONS

Risk analysis determines the potential dangers and estimates the possibility that they may materialize. Risk analysis is a tool used by investors while making investment decisions. It makes it possible for businesses, governments, and investors to determine the likelihood that a negative event will have a detrimental effect on a project, the economy, or an investment. Risk assessment is crucial for figuring out the value of a particular project or investment and the appropriate process(es) to manage such risks.

Innovation is constant in the digital economy. Due to the ongoing testing and redefining of boundaries, the digital revolution presented new challenges to both corporations and countries. The digital economy makes use of cyberspace, and evolving cyber threats go hand in hand. The trust and confidence of the stakeholders, including the government, business sector, and individuals, are essential for nations to succeed in the digital economy in terms of readiness in the technical environment and network infrastructure. The enablers of the digital economy are the stakeholders' trust and confidence.

To create a safe and secure cyberspace for the people, cybercrime defense is crucial. The internet has given criminals a platform to engage in cybercrime swiftly and broadly while remaining anonymous. No country is an island in cyberspace since the globe is now a networked global village. To protect the country and fight cybercrime, international cooperation is essential. Collaboration and knowledge-sharing efforts among nations are essential to reducing the impact of cyberattacks. The close ties and partnerships between states improve and expand global cybersecurity.

Opportunities through risk analysis and asset management on cyber security in a technologically driven economy go hand in hand with analyzing risks, managing available assets, cyber risks, and cyber threats. Cybersecurity is a need in the progress and growth of the digital economy. As nations capitalize on the digital revolution, cybersecurity is a national priority to foster economic welfare. Based on North Atlantic Treaty Organisation and European Union Agency for Cybersecurity, from 2013 to 2016, there was a total of 48 national cybersecurity strategies (NCSS) released.

The broad objectives of NCSS are to handle ICT risks, maintain a safe, reliable, and trusted electronic operating environment, promote economic and social prosperity, and promote trust, business development, and economic progress. The extent and depth of each National Council of State Society differs, with the primary goals being roles and responsibilities in cybersecurity, situational awareness, legal issues, training, research, and development, secured ICT products and services, and international collaboration. This chapter however rounds off with the following recommendations:

1. Countries should implement national cyber security strategies to address cybersecurity issues to foster economic growth.
2. Government should make risk analysis a matter of policy for every project before the award of the contract.
3. Every organization should make strategic asset management plans available to every stakeholder.

REFERENCES

ENISA. (2015). *ENISA Threat Landscape*. ENISA.

Malley, O. L., & Patterson, M. (1998). Vanishing point: The mix management paradigm re-viewed. *Journal of Marketing Management, 14*(8), 829–851. doi:10.1362/026725798784867545

McAfee. (2014). *Net losses: Estimating the global cost of cybercrime*. McAfee.

Mulligan, C. (2017). *Cybersecurity: Cornerstone of the digital economy*. Imperial College Business School.

Olteanu, C. & Olteanu, F. M. (2011). *Market portfolio and risk management of financial securities*. Publishing Foundation "Andrei Şaguna", Constanţa.

Republic, C. (2015). *National Cyber Security Strategy of the Czech Republic (2015-2020)*. Academic Press.

Sharpe, W. F. (1970). *Portfolio theory and capital markets*. McGraw-Hill.

Solon, O., & Hern, A. (2017). 'Petya' ransomware attack: what is it and how can it be stopped? *The Guardian*.

KEY TERMS AND DEFINITIONS

Asset Management: Asset management is the practice of increasing total wealth over time by acquiring, maintaining, and trading investments that have the potential to grow in value.

Cyber Security Framework: Cyber security framework is a set of rules and procedures designed to enhance a company's cyber security measures, not some flashy software application or hardware appliance.

Cybersecurity: Cybersecurity is the protection of internet-connected systems such as hardware, software, and data from cyber threats. The practice is used by individuals and enterprises to protect against unauthorized access to data centers and other computerized systems.

Enterprise Asset Management (EAM): Enterprise Asset Management (EAM) systems are asset information systems that support the management of an organization's assets.

Information SECURITY: Information security is a broader category that safeguards all information assets, whether in hard copy or digital form and focuses on protecting computer systems from illegal access as well as from being otherwise damaged or rendered unavailable.

IT Asset Management: IT asset management is the process of ensuring an organization's assets are accounted for, deployed, maintained, upgraded, and disposed of when the time comes. It is the process of making sure that the valuable items, tangible, and intangible, in the organization are tracked and used.

Risk: Risk is an exposure to the possibility of loss, injury, or other adverse or unwelcome circumstances; a chance or situation involving such a possibility.

Risk Analysis: Risk analysis is the process of assessing the likelihood of an adverse event occurring within the corporate, government, or environmental sectors.

Risk Assessment: Risk assessment is a process or method of Identifying hazards and risk factors that have the potential to cause harm (hazard identification). It is the process of analysing and evaluating the risk associated with that hazard (risk analysis, and risk evaluation).

Risk Management: Risk management is the process of identifying, assessing, and controlling financial, legal, strategic, and security risks to an organization's capital and earnings.

Technology-Driven Economy: Technology-driven economies are economies driven by the potential of available technology.

Chapter 8
Cybersecurity Disclosure and Corporate Reputation:
Rising Popularity of Cybersecurity in the Business World

Arpita Lenka
CHRIST University (Deemed), India

Madhurima Goswami
CHRIST University (Deemed), India

Harmandeep Singh
CHRIST University (Deemed), India

Harsha Baskaran
Compose Corner, India

ABSTRACT

This chapter emphasizes the importance of cybersecurity for a corporation as today's organizations are more vulnerable than ever and their enemies are in the form of viruses and malware. The work provides evidence that cybersecurity can have an impact on brand value, market value, and overall corporate reputation. It focuses on depicting the global scenario with reference to cybersecurity disclosures by corporations and how it is important in today's digitized era where data is the most valuable and vulnerable asset. With rapid digitalization, cybersecurity has become a major concern for all businesses, especially when there is financial and reputational damage to cybersecurity breaches and incidents. Even in the absence of clear cybersecurity laws and regulations, corporations are opting for voluntary disclosure. Existing literature explains this as an attempt to mitigate any potential risk or occurred risk through increased transparency which will build the trust of all stakeholders.

DOI: 10.4018/978-1-6684-9018-1.ch008

INTRODUCTION

Digitalisation is not a new word as it has been used for several decades now. "Digitalisation" is the "process of transforming from an analog to a digital format," which refers to the conversion of analog texts, photos, or sounds into a digital format that can be processed by a computer, according to Gartner's IT Glossary (Blieberger et al. 1996, p. 18). This definition would have sufficed if we were in the early 2000s. Unfortunately, the Covid-19 pandemic of 2020 showed the world the actual definition of digitalisation when that was the only way to survive and thrive. Digitalisation is using digital technologies to change a business model and provide new revenue and value-producing opportunities. It is the process of moving to a digital business (Gartner IT Glossary, 2019).

An online global survey of executives was conducted by Mckinsey (2020). From July 7 to July 31, 2020, a total of 899 C-level executives and senior managers representing a wide range of geographies, industries, firm sizes, and functional specialisations responded to this online survey. From the responses received, it was estimated that adoption of digital technologies by companies for supply chain and customer interaction was accelerated by 3-4 years due to the Covid-19 pandemic. Places like North America took the most significant stride towards digitalisation, with 60% of its products and services now entirely or partially digital.

Digitalisation has not only helped with survival, but it has also enabled opportunities to make businesses better and more efficient. That is why spending $2 trillion by businesses on digital transformation in 2019 does not come as a surprise. At a CAGR (Compound Annual Growth Rate) of 20.9%, it is predicted that the global market for digital transformation will increase from $1.79 trillion in 2022 to $6.78 trillion in 2029 (Fortune Business Insights, 2022). The insane amount of investment makes sense when it directly contributes to the company's growth. Companies with higher levels of digital maturity reported revenue growth of 45% compared to 15% for companies with lower levels (Deloitte, 2020). 45% of businesses suffering declining revenues as a result of COVID-19 stated they are putting more of a focus on digital transformation (McKinsey, 2020).

Digitalisation is doing wonders for businesses across the globe. Unfortunately, there is no rose without a thorn. Businesses have a sharp and poisonous thorn to deal with before they reap the benefits of digitalisation, that is, cybersecurity risks. Public Safety Canada (2014) defines cybersecurity as "The body of technologies, processes, practices and response and mitigation measures designed to protect networks, computers, programs and data from attack, damage or unauthorised access to ensure confidentiality, integrity, and availability." According to DHS (2014), it is "The activity or process, ability or capability, or state whereby information and communications systems and the information contained therein are protected from and/or defended against damage, unauthorised use or modification, or exploitation."

A decade ago cybersecurity was an alien concept. Businesses didn't consider it to be a significant factor in their business environment that could affect their strategic position. A majority of businesses had an "it won't happen to me" mindset and were unwilling to completely rethink their strategies to counter this possible danger (James, 2021). The scenario has completely changed now. With the emergence of big data, the shortage of skilled professionals to run and implement big data is not the only challenge that is faced by organisations. Security of such data is also stressful ("Companies Are Satisfied With Business Outcomes From Big Data and Recognize Big Data as Very Important to Their Digital Transformation, Accenture Study Shows | Accenture," 2014). Since COVID-19, the number of attacks has surged five-fold (Williams et al., 2020).

No business can afford to turn a blind eye to cybersecurity and its damages. Security breach damages include the cost of a clean-up, regulatory fines levied by authorities, or the loss of the firm's data. But the damage brought on by such breaches goes far beyond all these. There are several hidden costs, such as harm to the brand's reputation, loss of intellectual property, or economically sensitive data that is beneficial to a rival. It also includes the cost of going back to the ordinary course of business, post-attack disruption, forensic investigation, restoration, and deletion of hacked data and systems. All these can affect a company's capacity for differentiation and, consequently, its ability to compete in the market. These expenses are hard to quantify, calculate and analyse.

Therefore, the consequence includes:

1. Revenue Loss
2. Damage to Brand Reputation
3. Loss of Intellectual Property
4. Hidden Cost
5. Online vandalism is like changing a few words in the website or database. Such minute changes are hard to identify and often need to be noticed. This can affect the company in many ways.
6. Damage to a relationship with internal and external stakeholders.

There are multiple costs a company must incur when faced with cybercrime and not just the losses in the market but some internal costs as well. These costs can be of physical nature that involves the replacement costs of the equipment that was compromised leading to such an attack or the replacement cost spent on acquiring up-to-date software and replacing the outdated software which was responsible for the non-detection of the breach. The company also has to undergo staff cost which includes the hiring of more technically superior individuals who are more reliable as well as competent to handle such breaches as well as setting up a risk management team which is particularly costly as well as time-consuming for a company to prevent such an event from ever happening again.

A company also incurs time cost which is generally the amount of loss of productivity which is lost due to such a cyber-attack and a lot of time is invested by the management to recover from such an event and in setting up the preventive measures to tackle these problems in the future effectively and efficiently. Cybercrimes take a toll on companies not just in the market but on the overall performance of the company, hence making a recovery for the company so hard in the short as well as in the long run.

REPUTATIONAL AND FINANCIAL DAMAGE

In the growing age of technological advancement, the internet has played a vital role in developing every significant aspect of life and quality of life. The internet has made it easier to connect people and has made things more accessible to the public which has its own merits and demerits. The internet has also played a vital role in society's economic development, especially in finance and markets. If we address the topic of share market and finance, it can be observed that more than 90% of the market functions, tools, and processes cannot be performed without the accessibility of the internet.

This dependency of the markets and financial world on the internet and cyberspace has increased tremendously in the past decade. This increased dependency on cyberspace also comes with its vulnerability to being attacked and breached by data hackers which places a huge question mark on the security of such data. Data breaches adversely affect the company's performance and reputation in the market.

In an analysis of companies between 1995 to 2015, it was observed that the public always shows an adverse reaction towards the news of data or security breaches in any company leading to future losses and an eventual fall in the share price. Data hackers or cyber criminals show their involvement often in the selling of sensitive customer information or sensitive company information to different companies or show their major influence in insider trading activities to manipulate the market to make profits.

Such data and security breaches can severely damage the company's reputation and performance in the market. These breaches primarily impact the technological and financial sectors in the worst possible way. Any breach in these industry sectors leads to a long phase of diminishing returns and losses in the market. The severity of data breaches and their effects and consequences on the goodwill, reputation, internal management activities, and the company's customers, no matter the size of the breach, are tremendous. A significant amount of attention is put into the aspect of the reaction of the investors towards such data breaches occurring in companies and how these companies get punished for their lack of proper maintenance of proper and authentic cyber security measures causing such unprofessional behaviour and breach of sensitive information of the company as well as customer data.

Analysis and research on various companies to determine how data-breached companies are affected in Wall Street and other stock marketing platforms in the long and short run to determine the consequences or punishments of such breached companies were carried out. The key results of such research were that these breached companies within three to four months were noted to be underperforming in the market and fell below average. After six months, the performance worsened as they could not perform well in the market. After a year or so, the companies experienced a drop in share prices and a significant underperformance in the market due to the data breach.

The article's researchers noted that the more sensitive the data, the more severe the breach would be and the more severe the impact of such a breach would be on the company. The article also analyses how the impact increased as the time of the breach passed, deriving and concluding that recently breached companies face fewer consequences than companies that have faced such data breaches in a prior period. This research also explored the impact of data breaches on their stock market performance according to the industries these companies operate in, broadly categorising them into finance, healthcare, media, and hospitality. The observation suggested that it had a minimalistic effect as the much more critical aspect of such an impact on the market was how sensitive the nature of the breach was and the magnitude of such a data breach (Bischoff, 2021).

Cybercrime is one of the significant threats that exist in the world that is so dependent on cyberspace at the current time, therefore, awareness and essential steps must be taken by each and every company to mitigate such a cyber risk by investing in risk management systems and teams in their organisation. The Cybercrime industry grows rapidly day by day with more techniques to breach the data arising. It is easier for hackers to extract data from a company if it doesn't implement proper cyber security measures and software and a proper responsive risk management team to pacify such cyber criminals.

Financially speaking, cybercrimes cost a fortune annually to the global economy, so it is to be treated as a priority global-level threat to every sector and every individual forming part of the economy. Particularly referring to the stock market the strongest reaction, as well as the highest losses incurred by the stock market in the past decade, has been because of cybercrime as this data or security breach information when disclosed to the public invokes a drastic adverse reaction by the public leading to such damaging abnormal losses in the years.

Researchers of cybercrime and financial markets have observed a pattern or a relationship between the fall of share price and future losses after a company's data have been breached by cybercriminals. But much to the surprise of researchers, not all companies face such a decline in performance and share prices, which is to be expected by the average market statistics. Some businesses can quickly recover their losses and reputation after a data breach and stabilise their standing in the market. This makes it difficult for researchers to determine a fixed relation between data theft and share price impacting the market, so it has been determined as a causal relationship.

Other factors are present in the market such as the market news, the severity of the kind of cyberattack, the type of data stolen as well as the industry which was attacked by cyber criminals, the sentimental value of the market towards the company and the customers of the company all these factors come into consideration while determining the fall or rise of share prices in the market. Therefore, researchers have concluded that these types of drops in share prices due to data and security breaches can lead to abnormal returns for a company as these events cannot be anticipated by the company.

Statistically speaking, most companies have negative abnormal returns after a data or security breach for many consecutive years. Still, with the proper response and risk management teams being properly invested and set up in such companies these outcomes can be minimised to a much greater extent, and recovery can be made as early as possible. Therefore, companies should invest adequate time and money in their cyber security projects and risk management teams to tackle such cyber-crime events as effectively and efficiently as possible. This is the sole reason why strong companies with proper cyber-infrastructure and organisation can recover at a faster rate while companies with weak infrastructure fail to do so (Spanos & Angelis, 2016).

A company must maintain a strong cyber security system where the probability of cyber risk is reduced to a minimum to prevent such breaches from occurring. A company should first aim at improving the technological factor by acquiring upgraded anti-virus software and a strong firewall so that the data can be as protected as possible. Then, it should focus on the human factor by hiring professionally trained employees to counter such hackers effectively. The company should also maintain a routine checkup to see whether the systems are operating as planned or not and to prepare for the worst possible scenarios companies should also formulate a risk management team that looks after the department of cyber risks and the countermeasures that are to be taken when such a risk appears (Brogi et al., 2018).

There is no slowing down in cybercrime. Cybercrime is extremely persistent as it is very lucrative and rewarding and cybercriminals have a slim chance of getting caught and penalised. The global cost of falling prey to cyber breaches and cyber incidents is exceptionally high in terms of loss of business confidential information, business-sensitive information, theft of Personally Identifiable Information (PII), manipulation of financial data, loss of data regarding the potential acquisition or merger or leak of insider strategies of listed companies which insensitively causes damage to stock value and sneaking into encrypted payment data as well as opportunity costs related to disruption in production and operational fundamentals of a company, as mentioned previously.

The reputational damage also costs a lot to companies that have sustained cyber attacks. The loss of intellectual property ranges from theft of product design to information regarding technological features. Such loss can lead to the launch of substitute products in the market or even disrupt the company's forward or backward linkages. This leads to a decline in revenue for the company and a loss of customers.

Banking and other financial institutions are said to be the most vulnerable sectors for cyber crimes and outright theft. Companies incur considerable costs to buy insurance against cyber crimes and protect and strengthen their firewalls against cyber criminals.

Thus it is of utmost importance in this era of digital evolution for companies to implement uniform security measures across their company and in every possible way insulate their data essential for the functioning of the business in the long run and stabilise such security measures (Economic Impact of Cybercrime, n.d.).

Every two in three Small and Medium Scale businesses suffered over Rs. 3.5 Crore business loss in post-pandemic cyber attacks in terms of customer data, internal emails, employee data, data associated with intellectual property, and even the loss of financial information. With an excessive emphasis on keeping pace with the changing digital world, being technologically sound and efficient has been the motto of every small business. Thus, there has been an equivalent increase in concerns related to cyber security risks. Around 62% of SMBs in India suffered cyber security breaches in some way or another, and 13% of them, which were able to sustain themselves from such cyber incidents suffered a loss of over Rs. 7 Crore.

In a survey by CISCO, where over 3,700 SMBs have been studied across the Asia/Pacific region that includes Australia, China, Hong Kong, India, Indonesia, Japan, New Zealand, Malaysia, Singapore, South Korea, Taiwan, Thailand, the Philippines, and Vietnam, business and IT experts were assigned with cyber security responsibilities reported losses more than just concerning customer data loss. All such losses resulted in upsetting disorder in the operational functions of the companies, an unsettling negative impact on the company's image and reputation as well as a tremendous loss of customer trust, confidence, and faith in the companies.

In the pre-pandemic scenario, businesses considered digitalisation a means to effective cost reduction, although now it has gained the utmost importance for sustainable survival and controlling damage. Thus, most small businesses have adopted automation through digitalisation but this increasingly made them vulnerable to cyber security threats. Therefore, during the covid post-period, they have stressed strengthening their cyber security solutions and defence mechanisms. As it has been reported that cyber security breach incidents have increased rapidly by 193% from 2019 to 2020 in India alone (data from Indian Computer Emergency Response Team (CERT-In)), strategic initiatives have been employed to defend SMB systems against malware attacks and phasing activities which have also contributed equally as that of cyber attacks in loss of customer-centric, financial, employee-related and data related to intellectual property (Soni, 2021).

The "contagion effect," which occurs when negative news about one firm tends to have an adverse influence on investors' perceptions of all companies in an industry, is one of the financial world's most well-documented effects. If a significant financial services business, for instance, recently suffered a significant data breach, there is cause for concern that other financial services organisations may also be vulnerable to a data breach or cyber assault. This somewhat mirrors the mindset and behaviour of threat actors, who will continue to take advantage of opportunities once they have discovered a soft target or a security flaw until the necessary cyber defences are in place to prevent such an attack.

What can businesses do in light of that paradigm to avoid becoming "contaminated" by the effects of a significant data security breach? To become absolutely open and honest about cybersecurity risk, according to Robin Pennington, co-author of the article "Do Voluntary Disclosures Mitigate the Cybersecurity Breach Contagion Effect?" that was published in the Journal of Information Systems. This entails open discussion of management controls in place, voluntary disclosure of risk variables, and upfront analysis of threat scenarios the organisation may face. It was also discovered that the contagion effect could be significantly reduced by early, pre-breach disclosure of cybersecurity risk. A company can also be protected from contagion by increasing transparency after a breach (Lindsey, 2020).

VOLUNTARY DISCLOSURES

When a company's management decides to share information outside the bounds of regulations like generally accepted accounting principles and Securities and Exchange Commission rules because they believe it will help users of the company's annual reports make better decisions, this is known as voluntary disclosure. This raises the question: why will a company provide information about its cyber security policies, measures, and breaches to the public?

In a study of the disclosure of cybersecurity information in Dutch annual reports, such as cybersecurity measures and cyber incidents, from a financial law and economics perspective it is seen that even in the absence of stringent regulations or governance concerning cyber security disclosures, most of the companies, have had started to include data about the cyber security or any related concerns and their measures; as such inclusiveness in annual reports resulted in providing greater apprehensiveness about the company's perspective regarding social welfare.

It was noticed that most companies in the study disclose minor information. It can be as minor as mentioning cybersecurity as an essential area and not mentioning anything specific about the company. Various studies show that cybersecurity disclosures worldwide have been consistently low, extremely general, and seldom company-specific. Therefore, it was prudently concluded that company-specific cybersecurity disclosure and extensive openness are yet to be standard practice. Ultimately such an approach effectively leads to an increase in the sustainability status of the companies (Eijkelenboom & Nieuwesteeg, 2021).

It has often been found that voluntary disclosure of information pertaining to cyber security, risk, and the breach has positively impacted the market value of corporate bodies. People tend to build greater trust in such business houses as they strive towards resolving their shortcomings, plugging the loopholes in the system, and building an even more robust firewall to restrict intruders from gaining entry into the system.

When a firm voluntarily discloses information concerning cybersecurity in its annual report, it gives the marketplace a signal that the firm is actively engaged in preventing, detecting, and correcting security breaches. It is the acceptance and admission of potential risk and what the firm is doing to tackle or minimise it. Voluntary disclosures regarding the cyber security of a firm will also result in a reduction of information asymmetry between a firm's management and its investors. This could lower the firm's cost of capital.

Cybersecurity risk disclosures are said to play a key role in enhancing the market valuation of a company. On average, voluntary disclosure concerning information security affects firms' stock prices by more than 6%. According to recent studies, top management understands the need to disclose information voluntarily concerning cybersecurity (Gordon et al., 2010).

A study by Berkman et al. (2018) examines the effects of two additional indicators of cybersecurity awareness, namely IT corporate governance and a company's historical history of data breaches, on market valuation. We discover that companies with superior IT corporate governance have higher market valuations, and companies that previously had a cyber breach incident have higher business valuations. This latter finding might mean that following a breach, management will take steps to reduce the possibility of such and that investors will perceive these moves as adding to the company's worth.

The findings generally demonstrate that the market places a high value on cybersecurity awareness. Salient, extensive, and frequent cyber risk disclosures and management policies help instil trust in the people about the company and thus show a positive association between market valuation and information about cyber security disclosure. Nevertheless, a strong market reputation is established through such disclosures. It is known that public and external stakeholders like investors have a substantial interest in such disclosures as their financial decision-making depends on such crucial statistics. Economic consequences of cyber breaches have been observed in many cases due to the under-reporting of potential threats by companies (Hilary et al., 2016).

There have been considerable advances in the voluntary disclosures of cyber attacks by companies, as, over time, companies have realised that withholding information on such sensitive content, which has enormous implications on investors and customers, can ultimately have a severe negative impact on the market value and reputation of the company if discovered by external resources. It was found that withheld cyber-attacks are associated with a decline of approximately 3.6% in equity values in the month the attack is discovered and disclosed attacks with a substantially lower decline of 0.7%. It was inferred that managers release information on cyber-attacks when investors already suspect a high likelihood (40%) of an attack (Amir et al., 2018).

Research from Gao et al.(2020) revealed that cybersecurity breaches often have a negative impact on the reputation or image of the company, along with customer relationships. The direct cost attributable to such cyber attacks is much less than the hidden costs incurred due to the confidential data breach. It is thus important to inform the customers and investors about such attacks and system breaches to help them make informed decisions, otherwise, they might feel cheated. Hence, information about the nature of the risk that a company is exposed to and the impact of each risk on the company should be disclosed along with the probable costs and repercussions of such cyber incidents.

It also revealed that most US companies used fewer words to talk about risks associated with inadequate insurance coverage for cyber security risks, as they did not have insurance coverage for the same. However, during the period 2011- 2018, to draw a veil over the same they started to mention identified predictions about future cyber security threats that a company might face due to the changing business environment. Since then, the inclusion of such progressive statements in the annual reports has seen a rising trend.

Public disclosures concerning cybersecurity governance and risk management contribute to increasing stakeholder confidence by giving clarity about how boards carry out their cybersecurity risk oversight obligations. In the dynamic environment of today's cyber risk, gaining the trust of investors and other stakeholders requires strong cybersecurity governance and disclosures.

According to a study by Ernst & Young (E&Y) conducted by Seets and Niemann (2022) on cybersecurity risk disclosure and oversight, businesses are improving their cybersecurity disclosures and giving more information on issues including director expertise, management reporting to the board, and committee oversight. We also observe new patterns in applying external frameworks or standards and considering cybersecurity in CEO compensation. However, there are still opportunities for businesses to improve their cybersecurity disclosures to show stakeholder trust that cybersecurity is prioritised, controlled, and watched over as a crucial corporate risk and strategic opportunity.

Cybersecurity has become an unavoidable business obligation for the corporate world, and accountability is a way of fostering trust and guaranteeing resilience against cyber risks and high-impact cyber-attacks. The Organisation of American States (OAS) promotes cybersecurity activities in Latin America through various programs that encourage regional and global cooperation. Countries have steadily embraced international policy directives at the national level.

Some have made significant advancements, including adopting national strategies, accepting the Budapest Convention, and passing data protection laws, among others. From 2016 to 2022, most of the companies in Latin American companies have observed growth in the disclosure pattern of cybersecurity facts in a company-specific manner (Ramírez et al., 2022). This shows the advancement in cybersecurity disclosures and measures taken by companies.

Along with perceived benefits, it is equally crucial to understand how management and corporate governance play a role in the degree of voluntary disclosure made by a firm. Cyber Security: The Changing Role of the Board and the Audit Committee (2016) by Deloitte digs into the changing role of the Board and Audit committees to be effective and well-balanced by securing the cyber defence system and being vigilant and resilient. Companies with adequate information security risk management practices often delegate control of their security policies to the highest levels of the business.

When it comes to identifying, managing, and minimising risks, management has ownership, responsibility, and accountability. From a governance standpoint, one of the board's most crucial duties is to confirm that management has a clear understanding of how the business could be seriously impacted and that management has the necessary expertise, resources, and strategy in place to reduce the likelihood of a cyber incident and that management has the capacity to mitigate any potential harms.

Depending on the organisation and industry, the audit committee's level of involvement in cybersecurity matters varies greatly. While there may be a distinct risk committee in certain firms, the audit committee is directly responsible for managing cyber security risk in others. A specialised cyber risk committee focusing solely on cyber security is frequently present in organisations where technology is the foundation of their operations. Regardless of the formal framework chosen, the rapid advancement of technology, the growth of data, and the risks that come with it—risks that have recently been brought to light by security breaches—show how crucial it is to recognise cyber security as a real, enterprise-wide business risk.

With regards to emerging economies, cybersecurity disclosure is not voluntary. In research from Mazumder and Hossain (2022), the extent and determinants of cybersecurity disclosures in banking companies in Bangladesh are explored. This study mainly focuses on how the board composition characteristics (i.e., the board size, independence, and gender diversity) impact cybersecurity disclosure in the listed commercial banks in Bangladesh. The board of directors is expected to play a crucial role in the overall risk governance process.

Based on agency theory and resource-based theory's theoretical justifications, this study asserts that banks with bigger board sizes, more independent directors, and more gender-diverse boards are more likely to have a favourable effect on cybersecurity disclosure. The study discovers a growing trend of cybersecurity disclosure among listed banks in Bangladesh based on longitudinal data over a 7-year period (2014-2020). According to the study, banks provide more cybersecurity disclosures and vice versa when independent directors make up a larger portion of the board.

The study further demonstrates a strong correlation between cybersecurity disclosures and the percentage of female board members. Independent directors and female directors enable effective oversight and bring resources like competence, current information, risk awareness, and accountability, which favourably influence cybersecurity disclosure procedures, in line with the ideas of both agency theory and resource-based theory. This analysis was unable to determine whether the size of the boards is regularly linked to cybersecurity disclosures in the annual reports of listed banks.

Another study of the listed companies in Toronto, almost in the same line as that of the study that took place in Bangladesh, confirms a positive association between the presence of cybersecurity-related disclosure and gender diversity in corporate governance. Women are reported to enhance board decision-making, resulting in improved disclosure, thanks to their diverse skill sets, experience, and knowledge.

By providing a fresh perspective to complex problems and more effectively assessing shareholders' needs, women on boards have an overall positive impact.

Due to their conservatism and greater risk aversion than men, women provide more risk-related information, such as cybersecurity information. As evidenced by their cyber-related disclosure, heterogeneous boards do better in cybersecurity issues than homogeneous boards. The results support the theoretical underpinnings of gender difference in psychology as proposed by earlier research. Which contends that diverse groups operate and behave in ways that differ from those of homogeneous groupings. The participation of women impacts the board's cohesion and cognitive conflicts, and these changes in group dynamics improve the board's decision-making (Radu & Smaili, 2021).

Calderon and Gao (2020) consider the relationship between audit fees and the cybersecurity risk disclosures made by businesses. It was discovered that a company's audit fees are influenced by the language (readability and litigious language) and the content (word count) revealed in their cybersecurity risk disclosures. Additionally, audit companies assess audit risks by looking at general cybersecurity risk disclosures and sporadic cyber-breach occurrences. The implication is that the auditor considers cybersecurity risk disclosures when determining their risk assessments and, consequently, their fee schedules.

Auditor work may be reduced if cybersecurity disclosures are easier to understand and have less of an impact on how auditors determine the client's inherent risk and control risk. Additionally, it's conceivable that clearer and more accurate cybersecurity disclosures result in better-informed judgments of the necessity to alter the detection risk to accomplish the proper level of total audit risk.

A CASE STUDY ON VOLUNTARY DISCLOSURE TRENDS IN INDIAN COMPANIES

India lacks the necessary institutional framework to compel companies to disclose cyber security information. The Indian government is significantly underfunded when it comes to creating and enforcing cybersecurity-related rules, legislation, and guidelines. India does not have a comprehensive cybersecurity law, but it promotes cybersecurity norms through the Information Technology (IT) Act and numerous other sector-specific rules. It also offers a legal foundation for India's crucial information infrastructure. To prevent sensitive information from being compromised, damaged, exposed, or misused, Indian enterprises and organisations must follow "reasonable security standards and procedures," as stated in Section 43A of the Information Technology Act.

Over the years, several amendments and additions to the Information Technology Act have been made. Unfortunately, none of these provide clarity on cybersecurity disclosure. Lack of policies or regulation that mandates cybersecurity disclosure, it is assumed that the current disclosures made by Indian companies are voluntary. The authors conducted a study on the Bombay Stock Exchange (BSE) 200 index non-financial companies on 31st March 2022 to measure the rate of voluntary disclosure in the annual reports starting from the financial year 2017-18 to 2021-22. The Bombay Stock Exchange (BSE) 200 index was chosen because its component companies represent more than 70% of the Bombay Stock Exchange's market capitalisation.

Five-year annual reports were collected for all the companies from National Stock Exchange (NSE) corporate filing. Fifty-nine keywords were selected from the research paper titled 'Cybersecurity Awareness and Market Valuations' authored by Henk Berkman, Jonathan Jona, Gladys Lee, and Naomi

Soderstrom in the year 2010. A few variations of the keywords were added later after analysing several annual reports to ensure no keyword was missed due to variation in writing style.

Python software was used to extract keywords and give the occurrence count of each keyword in an annual report. From the data collected, the following trendline was created for five years. From the graph, we can see that the cybersecurity disclosure for most of the companies has increased over the study period. The authors noticed a significant increase in the disclosure in the year 2020-21, denoted by the red trendline. The year 2020 was when the Covid-19 pandemic started, and the world witnessed a rapid acceleration in digitalisation. The disclosure rate continued to increase in the following financial year of 2021-22, denoted by the purple trendline.

Figure 1. The figure shows the trendline of year-wise cybersecurity disclosure in the annual reports of BSE 200 non-financial companies. The disclosure rate is measured through the occurrence of selected keywords in the annual report and their count.

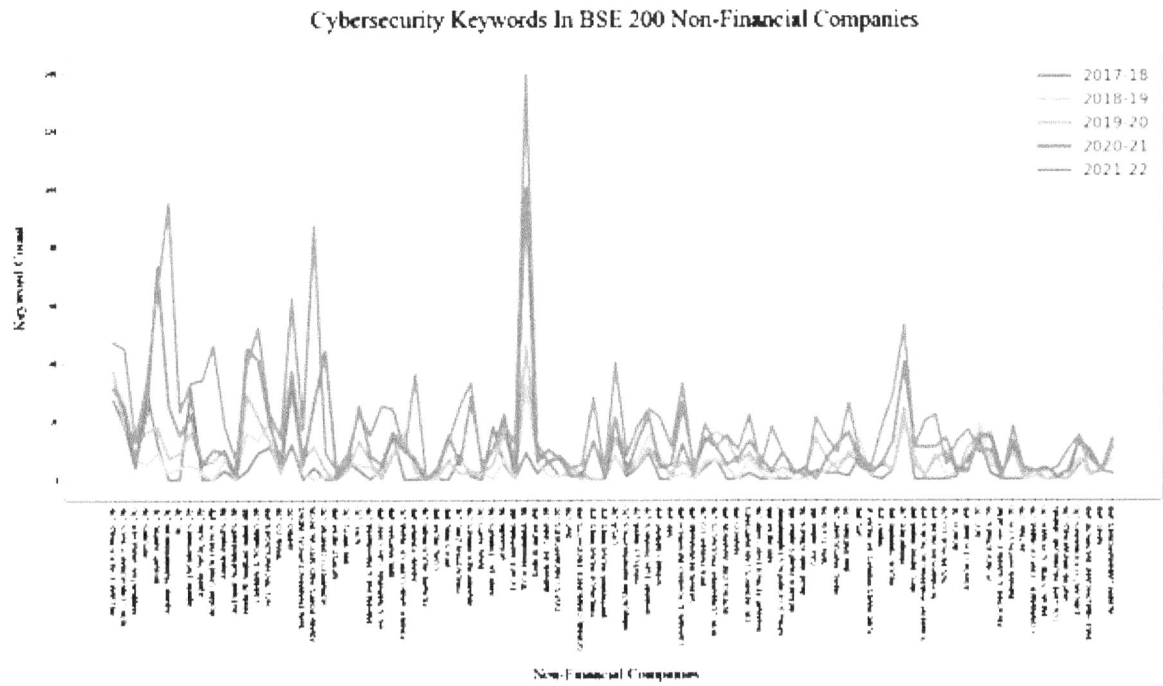

In the study, it was seen that some companies whose annual report had zero keywords relating to cybersecurity in pre-covid years suddenly started using it in the year 2021-21 when the Covid-19 pandemic began. The most used keyword was 'cyber', which occurred 1313 times during the 5-year study period followed by 'cyber security', 'information security', and 'data privacy'.

Figure 2. The vertical bar graph shows the year wise count of total keyword occurrence by all the non-financial companies of Bombay Stock Exchange (BSE) 200 as on 31st March, 2022

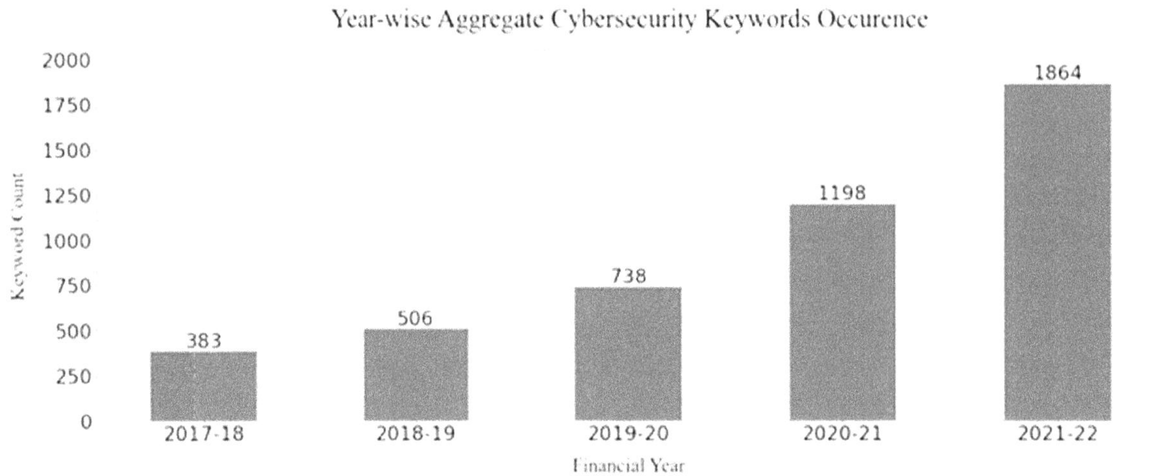

From Figure 2 it is clear that, collectively, also the keyword occurrence is constantly increasing. Hence, it can be inferred the increased digitalisation due to the pandemic resulted in increased voluntary cybersecurity disclosures in the annual reports. The increased voluntary disclosure also signifies the companies' increased interest in cybersecurity in general.

CONCLUSION

Around the globe, cybersecurity regulation and guidelines is majorly lagging yet we see that the degree of disclosure concerning cybersecurity is constantly increasing. It could only mean the business world has finally understood the benefits of such disclosures and the reward associated with transparency with their stakeholders. Data is the most important component for digitising an economy and bringing about innovation. However, the malevolence or animosity around it is equally prevalent. Study reveals that cybercrime can end up costing the world $10.5 Trillion annually by 2025.

Even though the year-over-year increase in cyber security growth is about 12- 15%, which is undoubtedly a significant increase, it falls flat compared to the increase in the costs incurred from cyber breach incidents. Cybercrime costs incurred root from damages caused due to the destruction of data, monetary theft, decreasing efficiency of productivity, robbing of intellectual property, pilferage of personal information and financial data, embezzlement, treachery, deception, a post-attack disorder in operational functions, forensic investigation, reinstatement of data, removal of hacked information and mostly reputational loss.

The Board plays a crucial role in being the most vital link to cyber security as the company's core value depends on how well it secures its data, strengthens its cyber defence programs, and the intensity of its pliability to sustain cyber threats and incidents (Freeze, 2021). Cybersecurity incidents not only lead to monetary losses but also the loss of public confidence as the general public starts to doubt whether their money or data is safe with the companies or not and this can lead to chaos in the business and the market.

REFERENCES

Amir, E., Levi, S., & Livne, T. (2018). Do firms underreport information on cyber-attacks? Evidence from capital markets. *Review of Accounting Studies*, *23*(3), 1177–1206. doi:10.100711142-018-9452-4

Berkman, H., Jona, J., Lee, G., & Soderstrom, N. (2018). Cybersecurity awareness and market valuations. *Journal of Accounting and Public Policy*, *37*(6), 508–526. doi:10.1016/j.jaccpubpol.2018.10.003

Bischoff, P. (2021, February 9). How data breaches affect stock market share prices. *Comparitech*. Retrieved on May 22, 2022, from: https://www.comparitech.com/blog/information-security/data-breach-share-price-analysis/

Blieberger, J., Klasek, J., Redlein, A., & Schildt, G.-H. (1996). *Informartik 3. Auflage*. Springer Verlag.

Brogi, M., Arcuri, M. C., & Gandolfi, G. (2018). The effect of cyber-attacks on stock returns. *Corporate Ownership and Control*, *15*(2), 70–83. doi:10.22495/cocv15i2art6

Calderon, T. G., & Gao, L. (2020). Cybersecurity risks disclosure and implied audit risks: Evidence from audit fees. *International Journal of Auditing*, *25*(1), 24–39. doi:10.1111/ijau.12209

Companies Are Satisfied with Business Outcomes from Big Data and Recognize Big Data as Very Important to Their Digital Transformation, Accenture Study Shows | Accenture. (2014, September 10). *Newsroom | Accenture*. Retrieved on June 2, 2022, from: https://newsroom.accenture.com/industries/systems-integration-technology/companies-are-satisfied-with-business-outcomes-from-big-data-and-recognize-big-data-as-very-important-to-their-digital-transformation-accenture-study-shows.htm

Cyber security: The changing role of the Board and the Audit Committee. (2016). Deloitte.

DHS. (2014). *A Glossary of Common Cybersecurity Terminology. National Initiative for Cybersecurity Careers and Studies: Department of Homeland Security*. https://www.fortunebusinessinsights.com/digital-transformation-market-104878

Economic Impact of Cybercrime. (n.d.). *Center for Strategic and International Studies*. https://www.csis.org/analysis/economic-impact-cybercrime

Eijkelenboom, E., & Nieuwesteeg, B. (2021). An analysis of cybersecurity in Dutch annual reports of listed companies. *Computer Law & Security Report*, *40*, 105513. doi:10.1016/j.clsr.2020.105513

Freeze, D. (2021, April 27). Cybercrime To Cost The World $10.5 Trillion Annually By 2025. *Cybercrime Magazine*. Retrieved on December 3, 2021, from: https://cybersecurityventures.com/cybercrime-damages-6-trillion-by-2021/

Gao, L., Calderon, T. G., & Tang, F. (2020). Public companies' cybersecurity risk disclosures. *International Journal of Accounting Information Systems*, *38*, 100468. doi:10.1016/j.accinf.2020.100468

Gartner IT Glossary. (2019). Retrieved on August 14, 2019, from: https://www.gartner. com/it-glossary/?s=chatbot

Gordon, L., Loeb, & Sohail. (2010). Market Value of Voluntary Disclosures Concerning Information Security. *Management Information Systems Quarterly*, *34*(3), 567. doi:10.2307/25750692

Gurumurthy, R., Schatsky, D., & Camhi, J. (2020). *Uncovering the connection between digital maturity and financial performance.* Academic Press.

Hilary, G., Segal, B., & Zhang, M. H. (2016). Cyber-Risk Disclosure: Who Cares? SSRN *Electronic Journal*. Retrieved on November 11, 2020, from: http://niccs.us-cert.gov/glossary#letter_c https://www.publicsafety.gc.ca/cnt/rsrcs/pblctns/cbr-scrt-strtgy/index-en… doi:10.2139/ssrn.2852519

James, L. (2018). Making cyber-security a strategic business priority. *Network Security*, *2018*(5), 6–8. doi:10.1016/S1353-4858(18)30042-4

Lindsey, N. (2020, April 13). Voluntary Disclosure of Cybersecurity Risks Mitigates Contagion Effect With Investors. *CPO Magazine*. Retrieved on August 4, 2021, from: https://www.cpomagazine.com/cyber-security/voluntary-disclosure-of-cybersecurity-risks-mitigates-contagion-effect-with-investors/

Mazumder, M. M. M., & Hossain, D. M. (2022). Voluntary cybersecurity disclosure in the banking industry of Bangladesh: does board composition matter? *Journal of Accounting in Emerging Economies*. doi:10.1108/JAEE-07-2021-0237

Public Safety Canada. (2010). *Canada's Cyber Security Strategy*. Public Safety Canada, Government of Canada.

Radu, C., & Smaili, N. (2021). Board Gender Diversity and Corporate Response to Cyber Risk: Evidence from Cybersecurity Related Disclosure. *Journal of Business Ethics*, *177*(2), 351–374. doi:10.100710551-020-04717-9

Ramírez, M., Rodríguez Ariza, L., Gómez Miranda, M. E., & Vartika. (2022). The Disclosures of Information on Cybersecurity in Listed Companies in Latin America—Proposal for a Cybersecurity Disclosure Index. *Sustainability (Basel)*, *14*(3), 1390. doi:10.3390u14031390

Seets, C., & Niemann, P. (2022, September 7). *How cyber governance and disclosures are closing the gaps in 2022*. EY - US. Retrieved on December 3, 2022, from: https://www.ey.com/en_us/board-matters/how-cyber-governance-and-disclosures-are-closing-the-gaps-in-2022

Soni, S. (2021, September 27). 2 in 3 Indian SMBs suffered over Rs 3.5 crore business loss in post-pandemic cyber attacks: Survey. *Financial Express*. https://www.financialexpress.com/industry/sme/msme-tech-2-in-3-indian-smbs-suffered-over-rs-3-5-crore-business-loss-in-post-pandemic-cyber-attacks-survey/2338676/

Spanos, G., & Angelis, L. (2016). The impact of information security events to the stock market: A systematic literature review. *Computers & Security*, *58*, 216–229. doi:10.1016/j.cose.2015.12.006

Williams, C. M., Chaturvedi, R., & Chakravarthy, K. (2020). Cybersecurity Risks in a Pandemic. *Journal of Medical Internet Research*, *22*(9), e23692. doi:10.2196/23692 PMID:32897869

KEY TERMS AND DEFINITIONS

Bombay Stock Exchange: The Bombay Stock Exchange (BSE), is an Indian stock exchange which is located on Dalal Street in Mumbai, India.

Corporate Reputation: A collective perception, view and belief about a company held by others.

Cybercrime: A criminal activity carried out in order to damage or disable a networked device or network in order to derive monetary gains for cyber criminals, or harm an entity's ability to earn further.

Financial Loss: Loss measured in terms of money and decrease in monetary value.

Information Security: The practice of protecting information against unauthorised use and by mitigation of information risk.

Malware: Malware is any software that is purposefully created to disrupt a computer, server, client, or computer network, leak confidential information, obtain unauthorised access to data or systems, prevent access to data, or inadvertently compromise a user's privacy and security online.

Market Value: It refers to how much a company or asset is valued by market players on the financial market.

National Stock Exchange: According to the World Federation of Exchanges(WFE), the National Stock Market (NSE) is the largest stock exchange in India and the fourth largest in the world by volume of equities trading in 2015. The NSE was the first exchange in India to introduce screen-based or electronic trading. It started in 1994.

Reputational Loss: Damage in opinion or belief about an entity through loss suffered in terms of social identity, financial loss or loss in market share.

Chapter 9
Equifinality in Cybersecurity Research:
Opportunities and Future Research

Brett J. L. Landry
https://orcid.org/0000-0002-0408-2408
University of Dallas, USA

Renita Murimi
University of Dallas, USA

Greg Bell
University of Dallas, USA

ABSTRACT

Cybersecurity is inherently uncertain due to the evolving threat vectors. Indeed, the constant battle between attackers and defenders in cyberspace is compounded by the multiplicity of causes, environments, threat vectors, motives, and attack outcomes. The role of improvisation and equifinality are investigated in understanding cyber incidents as incident bundles that may include both the presence and/or absence of factors that can contribute to a single outcome. Equifinality in cybersecurity operations is discussed along five dimensions: stakeholders, cyber operation bundles, end users, networks, and the threat environment for future research. For each of these dimensions, a set of themes and an associated portfolio of examples of cybersecurity activities at three levels—individual, firm, and community—is provided. Qualitative case analysis (QCA) can be employed to understand incident bundles better to understand that incidents vulnerabilities and solutions use equifinality in their paths to a given outcome.

DOI: 10.4018/978-1-6684-9018-1.ch009

INTRODUCTION

Among the many characterizations of the complex cybersecurity landscape in our environments, none is more apt than that of a high-uncertainty environment (Anant et al., 2019). The high uncertainty inherent in cyberspace is a direct outcome of the evolving threat vectors that seek to disrupt the many digital networks we inhabit. These threat vectors differ considerably in how they are manifested. For example, the failure of a particular cybersecurity control in a network supporting healthcare applications has different ramifications compared to the failure of the same control in a supply chain application. Further, the causes that lead to a cyber incident in a particular environment might be different from the causes that lead to a similar cyber incident in another environment. The same can be said about the solutions that are adopted to counter the threat vectors.

While modern cybersecurity tools are continuously evolving their mechanisms to scan the attack surface for clues about potential cyber incidents, the complexity of the networks and their attack surfaces present limitations on how we can effectively secure digital environments. For example, in the aftermath of a cyber incident, root cause analysis usually points to a set of factors that were responsible for the incident. However, the challenge posed here is that the contributing factors are only a few of the hundreds or thousands of possible points on an attack surface that threat agents could have leveraged to attack a network. Indeed, the constant battle between attackers and defenders in cyberspace is compounded by the multiplicity of causes, environments, threat vectors, motives, and attack outcomes.

The uncertainty of cyberspace has led organizations to leverage an anchor-and-adjust heuristic to mitigate the adverse effects of our bounded rationality in cybersecurity. The anchor-and-adjust heuristic, first studied in behavioral economics (Furnham & Boo, 2011), is used in situations with high uncertainty and involves choosing an anchor and then systematically moving higher or lower until any future gains in uncertainty reduction cannot be achieved with other movements. Cybersecurity measures adopted by firms over the past decades have been anchored to best practices recommended by the industry, such as the choice of solutions to protect different applications, network components, data, and systems (Tirumala et al., 2019). These solutions are then adjusted over time to reflect changes in recommendations for best practices, compliance and regulatory frameworks, threat vectors, and technology advances. For example, the NIST SP 800 (SP: special publication) guidelines on cybersecurity are provided as industry standards for best practices in various areas such as configuration, software development, vulnerability management, cryptographic key management, access controls, and dozens of other cybersecurity-related activities. These guidelines, far from prescriptive, provide recommendations for designing, developing, and maintaining secure networks and data. Their applicability to a wide range of domains and use cases makes them an apt example of an anchor, which organizations then use and adjust for their unique environments. At the same time, these guidelines offer room for improvisation or equifinality in cybersecurity operations.

The efficacy of such an anchor-and-adjust approach is rooted in the versatility of choice. Organizations can assess their own unique digital environments and evaluate their risk profile. The cybersecurity risk profile of an organization is a dynamic attribute as vulnerabilities and zero-day attacks continue to proliferate. Such a risk profile requires that organizations be equipped with a range of solutions to protect their different assets and that these solutions should be improvisable to meet their stakeholders' critical needs. One such example is the development of business continuity plans and disaster recovery plans. These plans encompass a range of threat scenarios and related recovery activities.

This chapter contributes to theory and practice by introducing equifinality, a widely recognized approach in the social sciences, to cybersecurity. While this is not unfamiliar, the chapter will define and explain equifinality, configurational logic, and Qualitative Comparative Analysis (QCA). The chapter emphasizes the importance of adopting this approach into cybersecurity practice and discusses various research possibilities. Equifinality and improvisation have the potential for improving the efficiency of cybersecurity operations. Specifically, the optimal cybersecurity solution space design should be both improvisable and configurable to face the uncertainty inherent in global cybersecurity operations. The concept of equifinality, which refers to the ability to achieve a given outcome using multiple paths, is leveraged to support this argument. Specifically, a recommendation for equifinality is a significant factor in improvising and configuring cybersecurity operations.

The chapter also makes the following contributions. First, the concepts of improvisation, bricolage, and the notion that improvisation is a form of discontinuous innovation are introduced. Such a discontinuous approach to innovation in cybersecurity offers multiple ways to respond to cybersecurity threats. Next, an interdisciplinary perspective to incorporating existing research from the areas of conjunctions, equifinality, and causal complexity into cybersecurity operations is offered. With the help of cyber incident examples from three different domains (critical infrastructure, gaming, and fintech), the use of equifinality in cyber incidents is illustrated. Likewise, the chapter highlights critical research questions for future examination of analyzing cyber resilience at the individual, community, and firm levels of cybersecurity operations. Finally, the chapter gives implications for scholars and security professionals.

IMPROVISATION, BRICOLAGE, AND DISCONTINUOUS INNOVATION

The notion of improvisation crosses disciplines and domains. At a foundational level, improvisation deals with the unknown or the unplanned. The best example of improvisation is jazz music, where the musician has to play spontaneously on the spot (Barrett, 1998). Although the musicians have played the same songs with each other before, the music is dynamically changing. In a business sense, improvisation can be defined as "the ability to use time and resources to advantage in response to the unexpected and unplanned" (Meyer, 2002, p. 17).

Another term for this improvisation is the French word *bricolage*. Baker and Nelson (2005), relying on Levi-Strauss's 1967 work, define bricolage as "making do by applying combinations of the resources at hand to new problems and opportunities (p.333)." Verjans (2005) describes Ciborra's definition of bricolage in English as "tinkering" and suggests that this is possibly not the best definition of bricolage and offers a more common definition of 'do-it-yourself' as a better fit. Tinkering has a negative connotation, whereas the concept of bricolage has a positive connotation for contingency theory and improvisation. The do-it-yourself concept can be extended to situations where the problem is encountered and fixed simultaneously.

Nevertheless, there is a different lens through which to view improvisation and bricolage: innovation. Both bricolage and improvisation can be seen as discontinuous innovations rather than incremental innovations. Buffington and McCubbrey (2011) found that discontinuous innovations are developed by the creativity of experts in the area and require gaps in the existing methodologies. Whether called improvisation, bricolage, or discontinuous innovation, it is not a planned event and sometimes can only be recognized by reviewing previous activities (Fuglsang & Sørensen, 2011). The high uncertainty environments that are characteristic of cybersecurity operations require a high degree of improvisation and innovation. This is not to say that the established disaster recovery or incident response plans should be ignored or discontinued. However, it is essential to understand that the severity and scope of an incident call for multiple ways to respond to the incident.

CONJUNCTIONS, EQUIFINALITY, AND CAUSAL COMPLEXITY

Cybersecurity research has been dominated by correlational or variance theorizing, which is characterized by "the linking together of concepts expressed as dependent, independent, mediating and moderating variables, usually accompanied by formal propositions, and with a focus principally on explaining variance in outcomes" (Cloutier & Langley, 2020, pp. 1-2). However, correlational or variance theorizing is limited in its ability to develop explanations of phenomena that are marked by causal complexity (Furnari et al., 2021).

There is a growing recognition among organizational researchers that not only do many factors contribute to organizational outcomes, but they also should not be evaluated in isolation from each other. Instead, they should be examined as 'bundles,' or combinations, that may mutually enhance the ability of each to achieve critical organizational outcomes. A vital dimension of this research identifies interdependencies among multiple explanatory factors that combine to bring about an outcome of interest (Bell et al., 2014; Furnari et al., 2021). This line of research also demonstrates that understanding the simultaneous operation of multiple factors is essential for decision-makers.

Causal complexity is defined as "a situation in which a given outcome may follow from several different combinations of causal conditions" (Ragin, 2008, p. 124). This suggests that configurations are comprised of multiple explanatory factors rather than singular factors bringing about outcomes. In addition, more than one configuration could lead to the same outcome under investigation. Scholars suggest that "conjunction" focuses on how or why explanatory factors jointly bring about an outcome (Furnari et al., 2021; Mackie, 1973). Secondly, "equifinality" refers to the condition where "a system can reach the same final state, from different initial conditions and by a variety of different paths" (Katz & Kahn, 1978, p. 30).

Configurational theorizing enables researchers to transition attention from evaluations of the "net effects" of causal variables to a more contextual understanding of the multiple possible ways in which causal conditions may combine to produce a given effect (Ragin, 2008). As Iannacci and Kraus (2022) point out, configurational theorizing revolves around three tenets: 1) Conjunctural causation: the effect of a single condition unfolds in combination with other conditions; 2) Equifinality: multiple configurations (or combinations) of conditions may lead to the same outcome; 3) Causal asymmetry: the causes leading to the presence of an outcome of interest may be quite different from those leading to the absence of the outcome.

Configurational approaches are particularly appropriate when researchers argue that a combination or bundle of factors work in concert with one another to be a sufficient cause for an outcome (Mahoney & Goertz, 2006). Configurational theory provides a lens through which scholars can argue that multiple factors could produce an outcome. In addition, the theoretical lens enables scholars to argue that multiple factors can combine to lead to the outcome under investigation. This is particularly important as cybersecurity scholars increasingly recognize that outcomes under investigation are often best explained by a combination, or bundle, of factors working in concert with one another.

Fiss (2007, 2011) suggests that configurational approaches allow for the study of "multi-dimensional constellations of conceptually distinct characteristics that commonly occur together" (Fiss, 2007, p. 1180). He argues that this approach allows researchers to move beyond the singular causality and linear relationships of the linear paradigm that dominates organizational research. Instead, the configurational lens assumes a more complex and non-linear causality where factors theorized to be causally related in one configuration may be unrelated in other configurations (Fiss, 2007). In addition, this approach emphasizes the concept of equifinality, which assumes that a system can reach the same final state from various initial conditions and along a variety of paths.

Configurational theorizing benefits from thinking about linkages among the attributes combined in a configuration both in terms of the presence of specific attributes and the absence of other attributes may combine in a variety of ways to create a range of 'recipes' that lead to an outcome under investigation. The absence of attributes is an essential feature of configurational theorizing and points to opportunities for cybersecurity scholars. Indeed, scholars, as well as security professionals, should move beyond considering the absence of an attribute as unimportant and consider how the absence of attributes contributes to the overall impact of various bundle combinations.

While scholars are increasingly taking a configurational approach to explore organizational phenomena, much of this research has been limited to the fields of strategic management and international business (Fiss, 2007; Fiss, 2011; Furnari et al., 2021). In the following section, how equifinality can extend to cybersecurity, especially in the area of improvisation, is discussed.

DEPLOYING EQUIFINALITY FOR CYBER RESILIENCE

For organizations to succeed, they must pivot and be agile to face global opportunities and challenges. Specifically, for organizations to have agile cybersecurity operations, they must maintain an environment where it is safe to improvise (within boundaries) and go beyond established procedures. The management literature has considered equifinality due to the presence of items or activities. That is, there are many ways to achieve the same outcome, and bundles of items should be considered in reaching that outcome. Specifically, in the cybersecurity context, configurational theory enables scholars to argue that the combination of factors that lead to a cyber incident may result from the presence and the absence of different conditions or factors. Indeed, conjunctural causation is particularly useful when it is likely that there can be multiple reasons to bring about an outcome and when causal conditions could combine in unique and multiple ways to bring about an outcome.

In cybersecurity, equifinality offers the foundational construct that outcomes are the results of bundles of things, and the bundles include things that were both present and absent. To begin, there needs to be a precise definition of a cyber incident. NIST defines an incident as "an occurrence that actually or potentially jeopardizes the confidentiality, integrity, or availability of an information system or the information the system processes, stores, or transmits or that constitutes a violation or imminent threat of violation of security policies, security procedures, or acceptable use policies" (National Institute of Standards and Technology, 2006, p. 7). A common method for determining the causes of incidents is root cause analysis (RCA). However, sometimes the bundles of events contain too many possibilities to fit cleanly into an RCA. Moreover, just because an outcome was reached by one path does not mean it is the only path to that outcome.

Conger and Landry (2009) encountered this phenomenon while conducting an action-based research project with a global logistics company in the United Kingdom. The client's leadership team was convinced that their problems were due to technology, not a result of their people and processes. The researchers found that the traditional analysis tools of Ishikawa diagrams, maturity models, RCA, and 2x2 matrices did not address the client's needs due to the immaturity of IT infrastructure. The reality was that most problems were based on people and processes, not directly on technology. The researchers took an improvisation approach, understanding that the tools in their toolbox did not fit and that there were more complicated relationships at work causing the issues. The firm's low IT maturity significantly contributed to its high-entropy network. The researchers developed a new model for the client that captured the relationships and presented the items in a new way.

To illustrate how equifinality is pervasive in cybersecurity operations, cybersecurity incidents from diverse domains will be examined. The first three cases involve financial incentives for threat actors with ransomware at Colonial Pipeline, theft of intellectual property at EA Games, and identity theft and extortion at Robinhood. The fourth case at the Oldsmar water treatment plant highlights the fragility of digitized critical infrastructure, where the threat actor intended to harm the public.

Colonial Pipeline

Consider the May 2021 Colonial Pipeline ransomware attack that led to a six-day production outage (U. S. Department of Energy, 2021). While there are a variety of bundles of ways to perform this attack, there was a specific bundle of activities that took place. First, a Colonial Pipeline VPN password was used on another system that had been compromised (Culafi, 2021). It is unknown what system was compromised, but the password was part of a group found on the dark web (Fung & Sands, 2021). Once inside the network, the threat actor stole 100 gigabytes of data and encrypted Colonial's internal IT systems using ransomware as a service software (Kerner, 2022). It was reported that the ransomware did not impact their operational technologies (OT) because Colonial quickly shut down the enterprise systems.

These activities can be included in an incident bundle. First, password reuse is the mechanism through which threat actors entered the network via the VPN. Secondly, it was wrongly assumed that this legacy account profile was not active on the VPN but in fact, was still active. Thirdly, the legacy VPN account did not require multi-factor authentication (MFA) (Kelly & Resnick-ault, 2021). Fourth, while VPNs are designed to protect crucial network resources from threat actors, it allowed direct encrypted access into the Colonial network in this case. Fifth, although the compromised password used complexity in both length and special characters, this measure failed to stop the attack because the password was already breached and used on multiple systems. Lastly, although Colonial Pipeline invested over $200 million in IT systems during the previous five years (Kelly & Resnick-ault, 2021), this investment did not block the attack.

The incident bundle for Colonial Pipeline is included in Table 1. It is important to note that viewing this cyber incident through the lens of equifinality is one way to analyze the causes of this incident, but it is not the only way. The variability of attack methods and tools is the biggest challenge for cyber defenders. The defenders must get it right every time; the threat actors only need to get it right once.

Table 1. Colonial pipeline incident bundle

Item	Issue
Reused password	• Once one system is compromised, all systems are compromised that use shared passwords
Passwords breached and leaked to the dark web	• Password breach may be unknown • If known, passwords should be changed
Legacy VPN account	• VPN is an open door into the network
VPN authentication	• VPN used SFA only. If MFA had been employed, the incident could have been prevented
Password complexity	• Password complexity does not stop compromised password usage
$200 million IT investment	• IT investment did not prevent the incident

EA Games

Similar to how cybersecurity defense employs equifinality, threat actors also improvise and employ equifinality in their approaches to attack networks and systems. The EA cyber incident is an excellent example of how equifinality was employed by both the attackers and defenders. Threat actors were able to steal 780 GB of data from the EA Games network. Stolen session cookies were bought on the dark web for $10 to gain access to the firm's Slack channel (Fung, 2021; Spadafora, 2021). With a small amount of social engineering, the threat actor was able to use Slack to message and convince IT to send them an MFA token. This allowed the threat actor to bypass MFA controls and successfully enter the network. The threat actor then built persistence into the network and created a virtual machine to explore the network and exfiltrate 780 GB of data, including source code, software development kits, and proprietary tools. The EA Games incident bundle is discussed in Table 2.

Table 2. EA Games incident bundle

Item	Issue
Stolen session cookies	• A threat actor masqueraded as a valid user to connect to Slack
Social engineering	• IT was tricked into issuing a MFA token to the threat actor based on a Slack connection
Network persistence	• A threat actor was able to build a stable connection to enumerate the network
Rogue virtual machine	• A threat actor was able to build a platform to exfiltrate data

Robinhood

If a threat actor wanted to get into an enterprise network, why not just ask for remote access? In November of 2021, Robinhood, a stock trading app, reported a data breach on approximately seven million customer accounts (Brown, 2021; O'Brien, 2021). Robinhood stated that a threat actor was able to social engineer a customer support employee over the telephone to install remote access software on his PC (Abrams, 2021; Barry, 2021). The threat actor then attempted to extort Robinhood for money (Egan, 2021). Robinhood said they contacted law enforcement when asked to pay the extortion fee. A few days after the attack, the threat actor was selling the data on hacking forums (Abrams, 2021). As a result, approximately 40,000 Robinhood customer accounts have been victims of cyber-attacks after the original breach (Avery, 2022). The Robinhood incident bundle is discussed in Table 3.

Table 3. Robinhood incident bundle

Item	Issue
Social engineering	• IT staff member was tricked into installing remote access software
Network persistence	• A threat actor was able to build a stable connection to enumerate the network

Oldsmar Water Treatment Plant

The Oldsmar water treatment plant in Florida was hacked in February 2021 due to a collection of problems. First, the targeted computer was running Microsoft Windows 7, which is no longer supported. Second, this PC allowed remote access with a program called TeamViewer with a password that was shared among users and used on all computers at the plant. Third, the PC was directly connected to the Internet without a firewall (Matthews, 2021). The attack was discovered when an operator noticed the mouse cursor moving independently (Bergal, 2021). By gaining remote access to the PC controlling the water chemicals, the threat actor increased the sodium hydroxide (lye) level in the water supply to 100 times the standard amount. The action was reversed before harm could be done.

In this case, there were several vulnerabilities: an old operating system, shared passwords among users, shared passwords among PCs, single-factor authentication, and the lack of a firewall. However, only two of these items contributed to the incident bundle, the shared passwords among users and PCs and single-factor authentication, as shown in Table 4. The end-of-life Windows 7 computer is a vulnerability for the operating system and, most likely, the hardware. The incident could have occurred on a Windows 11, a Mac, or a Linux device if they had remote access software installed with a shared password. The lack of a firewall is a definite concern, but like the operating system, it did not directly contribute to this incident bundle. If remote access was needed to this PC, then there would be firewall exceptions to allow connectivity. So, the legacy PC and the lack of a firewall are components of an alternative incident bundle, as shown in Table 5.

Table 4. Oldsmar Water Treatment Plant incident bundle

Item	Issue
Shared passwords among users and machines	• Easy-to-use password scheme • One password allows access for everyone and everywhere
Single-factor authentication for remote access	• Password is the only factor used

Table 5. Alternate hypothetical Oldsmar Water Treatment Plant incident bundle

Item	Issue
Windows 7 Computer	• Legacy hardware and operating systems • Lack of hardware refresh cycles • Possible legacy software/hardware compatibility issues
No firewall	• A firewall did not protect the PC

Deploying Incident Bundles and Equifinality

This list of data breaches illustrates how incident bundles and equifinality can play a role for the threat actor to compromise cyber targets. Additionally, for each of these incidents mentioned, many alternate attack methods and tools could be used and exploited. Cyber defenders can use equifinality in their network monitoring and change the existing mindset in cybersecurity to emphasize that cybersecurity is everyone's job. This could be something as simple as deploying honeypots on every subnet to generate early warnings of network reconnaissance (Landry & Koger, 2023b).

Defense in depth, while widely studied and implemented, has been a protection strategy that has not adequately protected networks and data repositories. As a result, organizations should transition towards zero trust network architectures (ZTNA). ZTNA is not a technology but a new way to examine protection using security by design (Landry & Koger, 2023a). ZTNA requires an understanding of every device on the network and understanding how it could be used for both good and bad activities. This dual purpose of devices fits well into equifinality and bundles in cybersecurity operations. For example, while a legacy device can provide a connection to historical data, the same legacy infrastructure can also be used by threat actors to launch attacks across the network. So, if the organization had a legitimate need for a Windows 7 computer, the configuration bundle would need other protection mechanisms, such as external firewalls or isolation from the network. It is the combination of these items that creates the security bundle for the Windows 7 computer.

Newer technologies such as cloud computing, infrastructure as code, blockchain, and IoT must also be considered in a security bundle before a breach or in an incident bundle post-event. A primary consideration is that poor network architecture, weak access controls, and undocumented processes are absolute problems in an on-premise environment. Migrating these problems to hybrid or full cloud implementations does not fix the issue; it only transfers where the problem is located. It does, however, change the incident bundle with new and different concerns than when these items were on premise.

DIRECTIONS FOR FUTURE RESEARCH

There are many opportunities for research investigating equifinality and configurations in cybersecurity. Below, the focus of the discussion of equifinality in cybersecurity operations is expanded along five dimensions: stakeholders, cyber operation bundles, end users, networks, and the threat environment (see Table 6 for a summary of these dimensions). For each of these dimensions, a set of themes and an associated portfolio of examples of cybersecurity activities at three levels – individual, firm, and community is provided. The individual level comprises cyber-related decisions and activities that people perform when dealing with systems, networks, and data. A top-down approach to designing and implementing cybersecurity policies and controls characterizes firm-level decisions and activities. An example of a firm-level set of actions would be adopting a specific firewall or migrating to a cloud service provider.

On the other hand, the community level encompasses a grassroots, bottom-up approach to decision-making, exemplified by open-source communities, hacker communities, and even the communities that make up our living and working environments. The concerns of each of these entities (individual, firm, community) differ regarding cybersecurity, and so do their approaches toward adopting bundles that achieve equifinality in cybersecurity operations. Each of these dimensions are discussed in detail below.

Stakeholders

The concept of motives, opportunities, and means (Grabosky, 2001) has been used widely in cybersecurity literature as a way to analyze the growing trend of cybercrime. The same concept of motives, opportunities, and means to analyze how individuals, firms, and communities can adopt equifinality in configuring their cybersecurity solution space. Consider the role of stakeholder motives, which can be leveraged to maximize the effectiveness of an equifinal configuration of cybersecurity solutions. At the individual level, consider a user who is unable to login into their work account for a brief period of time. In an attempt to maximize efficiency, the user emails work files to their personal email account and works on those files despite the lack of access to the work account. The motives for this lapse are undoubtedly justified, and the work still gets completed, but there is a lapse in the network perimeter.

At the firm level, organizations are equipped with different sets of resources, which provides them with an unequal footing to maintain and improve the security of their systems and networks. Organizations that lack in-house cybersecurity expertise and resources use managed security service providers (MSSP) or cloud solutions services, thus obtaining external resources for equifinal cybersecurity solutions. At the community level, consider an open-source software code community that uses code reviews, bug bounties, hackathons, and other mechanisms to improve the efficiency of the codebase in a distributed manner. In each of these cases, the motives for adopting cybersecurity solutions differ, thus leading to the equifinality of cybersecurity operations.

Table 6. Directions for future research

Critical Research Questions for Future Study	Individual Level	firm Level	Community level
Stakeholder (motives-opportunity-means)			
How can stakeholders' motives be leveraged to maximize the effectiveness of an equifinal configuration of cybersecurity solutions?	How can we create solutions for users to avoid sending work data to a personal account?	How can organizations that lack in-house cybersecurity resources use external services for equifinal cybersecurity solutions?	How can open-source communities that use code reviews, bug bounties, and hackathons to improve the efficiency of the codebase in a distributed manner?
How can stakeholders use desire path opportunities to improve, rather than, hinder the effectiveness of cybersecurity solutions?	How can users refrain from password sharing with an understanding why a certain password policy dictates frequent change, complexity, and uniqueness?	How could firm-level restructuring present opportunities for desire paths?	How can we increase the understanding of the relationship between good cybersecurity posture and cyber resilience?
How can stakeholders efficiently indicate their commitment and adoption of equifinal approaches to cybersecurity without oversharing or under-sharing?	How can users be encouraged to be mindful of data-sharing to limit potential malicious OSINT/HUMINT activities?	How can firms use phishing campaigns to identify the baseline of phishing awareness and improve these baselines?	How can community discovery of bug bounty programs be used prudently to improve cybersecurity posture?
Bundle (bundle overload – dynamicity – sociotechnical perspectives)			
How does the dynamicity of cybersecurity solutions affect the ability to create equifinal paths?	How can we simplify the credential management process for users, who are typically faced with multiple accounts?	How can organizations make informed decisions about changes to their network architecture to avoid crucial components from going offline for extended periods?	How can communities manage equifinal cybersecurity operations with an understanding that the culture informs the technology design and implementation?
For a given equifinal configuration, what is the process of updating individual paths and discovering their impact on other paths?	How can users make informed decisions about equifinality in secure operations for everyday computing and connectivity?	How might organizations benefit from the expertise and vision of boards with cybersecurity-minded individuals?	How does a smart city's equifinal cyber configuration differ from that of a rural community?
How do the attributes of a bundle impact the efficiency of the equifinal configuration?	Is there a tipping point beyond which usability concerns override security concerns among users?	How is the valuation of companies impacted in the wake of cyber incidents?	How are the social dynamics of communities factored into the development of information-sharing platforms?
End-user (biases – limitations – strengths)			
How can end users recognize their limitations in navigating equifinal cybersecurity outcomes?	How can we nudge users toward voluntary adoption of best practices in equifinal cybersecurity operations?	How can firms move toward adopting a holistic approach to cybersecurity?	How can communities rely on the security of technologies that power these environments?
How can firms create cybersecurity solutions that are mindful of users' biases while still navigating equifinality in solutions?	How can users entrust the security of their accounts to the service providers?	How can companies build risk profiles considering biases that affect the adoption of equifinality in cybersecurity operations?	How can collective biases which lead to collective circumvention of security controls be avoided?
How can the cognitive strengths of users be leveraged alongside emerging technologies to create adaptable solutions spaces?	How can our multiple intelligences be leveraged alongside the narrow intelligence of AI-enabled tools for cybersecurity operations?	How can firms' choice of security controls be informed by equifinality?	How can communities bundle cyber security technologies for their needs?
Network (centrality – assortativity – tie strengths)			

Continued on following page

Table 6. Continued

Critical Research Questions for Future Study	Individual Level	firm Level	Community level
How does the centrality of nodes impact the decisions about equifinality in cybersecurity operations?	How do people share information about their security controls of choice?	How do highly competitive environments cause firms to sacrifice security in favor of agility?	How do communities determine the elements of critical infrastructure that are central to their functioning?
How do the assortativity tendencies in security control adoption impact the decisions about equifinality in cybersecurity operations?	How do users overestimate their tendencies to be security-conscious and underestimate their proneness to breaches?	How do failures of security controls lead to lawsuits and personnel termination at firms?	How does vendor monopoly and herd mentality cause similar security controls to be used throughout an industry vertical?
How might adoption of security controls (nodes) in well-resourced environments differ from those in low-resourced environments?	How efficient are users' mental models in the understanding the complexity of the networks they inhabit?	How can we create equifinality in cybersecurity operations for differently-resourced environments?	How do communities respond to the pressure to consider investment in equifinal cybersecurity controls?
Environment (Threat landscape – technology complexity - regulation)			
How do perceptions of the cybersecurity threat landscape vary?	Do individuals adopt mostly free technologies, ignore threats, or respond with the minimum possible effort?	Do organizations participate in knowledge sharing initiatives such as cves to disseminate information?	Do communities provide forums for regular inventory of security controls of critical infrastructure?
How does the black-box-like nature of emerging technologies like AI, ML, blockchain, and IoT impact equifinality of cybersecurity operations?	What factors cause individuals to rush to adopt newer technologies without fully understanding security implications?	How does cyber insurance fit into an equifinal bundle for cybersecurity operations?	What factors cause communities to ban certain technologies?
How is the regulatory landscape affected by the environment?	How do users understand the implications of violating the terms of use in their varied computing and networked environments?	How do firms' actions protect or render it liable to unprecedented legal rulings?	How can equifinality of IoT operations help communities mitigate disastrous outcomes from IoT compromise?

A similar case can be made for opportunities that leverage instead of attempting to eliminate desire paths. Desire paths, commonly used in architecture, refer to people's shortcuts to navigate the physical space around them (Smith & Walters, 2018). For example, people would rather trample upon grass instead of taking the longer paved path to quickly reach a particular building entrance. Similar instances can be found in cybersecurity behaviors such as shadow IT. While desire paths in architecture, human-computer interaction, or cybersecurity cannot be eliminated, they can be leveraged to rethink the design of a bundle of equifinal cybersecurity operations. At the individual level, consider the problem of a password policy that dictates frequent change, complexity, and uniqueness to encourage users to refrain from password sharing across sites and accounts, which represents a desire path (Singer et al., 2013). Firms that undergo restructuring due to internal or external factors also present a prime opportunity for employees and administration to take desire paths instead of dealing with the challenges of developing secure networks (Lohrke et al., 2016). At the community level, consider a rapidly changing set of critical infrastructure components that are being connected to cloud services via the Internet. This increases convenience, efficiency, and ease of access but also presents a large attack surface (Foreman & Gurugubelli, 2015). Communities should be mindful of the desired path in rapid digitization and find ways to improve their cybersecurity and cyber resilience.

How equifinality in cybersecurity operations is achieved is equally important. The structure of a stakeholder's bundle of equifinal cyber solutions may or may not be as helpful in informing the structure of another's stakeholder's equifinal bundle. Sharing resources or information about resources is helpful but also expands the attack surface. For example, given the wide variety of social networking platforms for work and leisure, individuals need to be mindful about how much data they share in limiting potential malicious open-source intelligence/human intelligence activities that could correlate between databases and extract crucial inferences (Kelleher et al., 2020). An organization's findings about the baseline of phishing awareness can be used positively or negatively by external stakeholders. Similarly, communities of independent stakeholders, such as those who participate in bug bounty programs, may discover items of varying importance to the cybersecurity posture, and companies need to be prudent in managing the scope of discovered bugs by third parties (Kuehn & Mueller, 2014).

Bundles of Solutions

The bundle of solutions adopted to address cybersecurity challenges varies according to the needs being met. Due to the rapidly changing nature of technologies and the threat environment, bundles are not static and must be frequently revisited to update the bundle's components. While having a choice of potential solutions to incorporate in a bundle is helpful, this bundle overload also leads to decision fatigue when it comes to adoption. This is especially true due to the dynamic nature of the solutions and the need to adapt these bundles to meet the needs of communities in their distinct environments. Directions regarding the bundle in terms of its dynamicity, attributes, and codependencies between bundle elements that affect the design and implementation of equifinal bundles for cybersecurity operations are provided here.

The dynamicity of bundles impacts individuals, firms, and communities differently. For example, at the individual level, users are faced with a plethora of login credential requirements for different accounts and find it challenging to keep up with account change and management. Here, a bundle of login credentials for access to different kinds of accounts makes it challenging for users to find services for credential management. Similarly, due to the highly embedded nature of technology within every industry vertical, organizations must make informed decisions about changes to their network architecture to avoid crucial components from going offline for extended periods. Finally, within communities, the adoption of certain kinds of technology for a given need does not translate to equivalent performance or security guarantees. For example, the choice of a water utility online bill pay system for a community of 50,000 people differs from that of a rural community using residential water sources (Malecki, 2003).

Bundles are also inherently dynamic. For example, the botnets that were heavily leveraged to spread spam have now found utility in ransomware command and control operations (Jarjoui et al., 2021; Murimi, 2020). Since threats constantly evolve, a bundle's individual elements must be updated, replaced, or modified. Entities must find resources for updating individual paths and discovering their impact on other paths. One such instance is users' decisions regarding products for everyday computing and connectivity usage. Organizations face such decision-making challenges on a much larger scale, such as choosing individuals to serve on the boards. While in the past, boards have traditionally been comprised of individuals representing essential business functions; it is becoming increasingly important for boards to have representation of cybersecurity-minded individuals (Rothrock et al., 2018). At the community level, digital connectivity defines the adoption of many technology-dependent solutions (Salemink et al., 2017).

As illustrated earlier in this chapter, a cyber incident may have different causes in different environments. Consequently, the incident bundles need adaptable solution bundles, which also define the concept of equifinality in cybersecurity operations. The attributes of a bundle, as measured by the types of resources in the bundles, the challenges that these resources are designed to meet, and the significance of each of these resources for other elements in the bundle and for the entire bundle itself, impact the efficiency of the equifinal configuration. For individual users, there exists a tipping point beyond which users will value usability more than security (Nurse et al., 2011). The same is also true for privacy, where users will adopt technology, especially newer IoT technologies such as voice-based assistants, because of usability and not because of the security controls provided (Awojobi & Landry, 2023).

Regarding this discussion on equifinal bundles of solutions, beyond the tipping point, solutions prioritizing usability will be weighted higher than those focusing on security. Furthermore, regulation and compliance, along with the power of social media, have created complex post-breach environments that can have lasting consequences for both the organization and the affected individuals. Finally, the social dynamics of communities also factor heavily in how information is exchanged on social media platforms, which have turned into veritable information-sharing platforms (Cyr & Wei Choo, 2010).

End-User

End users have been famously, but not always accurately, portrayed as the weakest link in our networks. Our cognitive biases and limitations in understanding the scope and granularity of the complex networks that we inhabit inform the ways in which we interact with computing technology (Caraban et al., 2019). The equifinality of solutions for cybersecurity operations is one of the mechanisms in which our biases and limitations can be viewed as strengths in terms of choosing solutions that best address our security needs in the digital space.

The limitations of end users affect our personal, professional, and social lives. Like the nudging mechanisms enabling responsible stewardship, such as double-sided printing the default (Thaler, 2018), users can also be nudged toward default security operations (Acquisti et al., 2017). Within organizations, cybersecurity has traditionally been the purview of the IT departments. However, this approach is flawed since it causes cybersecurity to be approached as a siloed business function. In contrast, cybersecurity is best addressed when firms move forward, adopting a holistic approach to cybersecurity by integrating it into business functions across the community (Jarjoui & Murimi, 2021). At the community level, the efficient operation of our everyday work, home, and leisure environments is dependent on the security of technologies that power these environments, making it all the more imperative to be mindful of our limited understanding of the security of these technologies.

Kahneman and Tversky (2012) famously refuted the notion of the rational human and showed how heuristics and biases govern our decision-making processes. Knowing that our biases inform our interactions with our computing environments, individuals cannot be lax in entrusting the security of their accounts to the companies that provide services. Organizations, too, must build risk profiles with an understanding of their data and system assets, which will aid in understanding how biases affect the adoption of equifinality in cybersecurity operations. Existing literature abounds in identifying how the wisdom of the crowds sometimes is not really wisdom, but conformity to social thought, even if it is flawed (Lorenz et al., 2011). Thus, collective decision-making suffers from the amplification of individual biases due to pressures of the herd mentality (Loxton et al., 2020), leading to collective circumvention of security controls, and communities have to be mindful of these biases when adopting equifinal bundles of security solutions (Wu et al., 2022).

However, despite biases and limitations, leveraging multiple intelligences and rapidly adapting to new circumstances confers a unique advantage. A recent wave of generative predictive AI tools have shown that these tools, while intelligent, are still only good at one or a few tasks (Fox, 2017). When aided by these tools, our cognitive strengths offer individuals, firms, and companies a wide range of possibilities in achieving equifinality in cybersecurity operations as well.

Network

Graph-theoretic models of networks have been used extensively in uncovering patterns of flows within networks. This section examines applications of network effects (centrality, assortativity, and tie strengths) to cybersecurity solutions by considering the nodes in a network as security controls and the edges between nodes as codependencies between security controls. By notating security controls and their codependencies in this manner, network science offers tools to uncover the most influential nodes in a network, the most valuable links between nodes, and uncover patterns of clustering. One such pattern is denoted as assortativity, which refers to the rich-get-richer effect, also known as the Matthew effect, where nodes with more extensive networks keep getting larger (Cheng et al., 2019). Another pattern is centrality, which denotes the importance of a node in information flows through the network. In our context, a node with a high centrality index indicates a widely adopted solution. Similarly, tie strengths, first studied by Granovetter (1973) to describe strong and weak social ties in human networks, can be used to analyze the codependency links between security solutions in an equifinal approach to cyber solutions.

From the perspective of security controls as nodes in a network that represents the cybersecurity operations spaces, it is interesting to analyze how the centrality of nodes impacts the decisions about equifinality in cybersecurity operations. At the individual level, users share information about their cyber solutions, such as the choice of a password vault application or anti-virus software, with their family, friends, and acquaintances. This word-of-mouth endorsement creates conditions that enable the adoption of certain controls more than others. A similar effect can be found in organizations, where word-of-mouth information about the activities of peer and rival firms in competitive environments causes firms to adopt similar cybersecurity processes, which may result in a tradeoff between security and agility of product launches (Winterrose et al., 2016). Communities, too, are prone to such behavior where similar cyber solutions are adopted due to their usage in similar communities (Arce, 2020). While these approaches might signal the efficiency of a particular solution, they also hinder the consideration of equifinality in cyber operation solutions as individuals, firms, and communities fail to consider their own distinct cybersecurity environments.

This reluctance or inability to consider equifinal operations that are customized for one's own needs results in assortativity in terms of solution adoption. This is true for individual users in networks, who have been shown to overestimate their tendencies to be security-conscious and underestimate their proneness to breaches. At the firm level, the tendency toward assortativity of solution adoption might lead to cyber incidents, leaving companies with lawsuits and the termination of key employees. The herd mentality similarly causes vendor monopoly and the adoption of similar security controls to be used throughout multiple industry domains.

Individuals, firms, and communities are endowed with different kinds of resources for cybersecurity, where some entities possess disproportionate levels of resources in dealing with cyber threats compared to others. This gives such well-resourced entities an upper hand in managing and responding to cyber incidents. It is important to note that equifinality presents a promising option to deal with this problem since organizations and communities can adopt solution bundles that fit their needs. This is helpful for individual users, who rarely understand the complexity of the networks they inhabit and instead rely on mental models to guide their decisions regarding bundle formation (Brase et al., 2017).

Environment (Threat Landscape – Technology Complexity – Regulation)

The environment within which cybersecurity operates is constantly under change. This change comes from three broad factors – the changing threat landscape, the increasing complexity of existing and emerging technologies, and the evolving regulatory domain. Newer forms of malware, applications, and regulatory requirements present unique challenges in cybersecurity operations, and equifinality is poised to be an efficient mechanism for dealing with the environmental challenges posed by these three factors.

Individuals, firms, and communities are faced with a multitude of options, ranging from free to freemium and paid subscription models, to manage their cybersecurity solutions. At the individual level, it is interesting to analyze the factors that contribute to people's decisions to choose a particular cybersecurity solution. These factors could be the cost, ease of access and usage, popularity, or other behavioral factors (Pfleeger & Caputo, 2012). At the firm level, the vast array of available options and the lack of information about the vulnerabilities in these options has given rise to several knowledge-sharing platforms, such as the Common Vulnerability Enumeration (CVE) list, which serves as a dynamic catalog of vulnerabilities in platforms and applications. First proposed by MITRE and now managed by a partnership of industry, academic, and government institutions, the CVE is a widely used platform for gaining information about vulnerabilities (MITRE Corporation, 2023). The CVE is also community-led, and its success depends on the participation of organizations in reporting and disseminating information about vulnerabilities. Open-source and bug bounty communities have similarly responded with community-led initiatives for information sharing about vulnerabilities and flaws, creating an ecosystem of flaw discovery and remediation (Ponta et al., 2019).

With newer technologies, the attack surface increases because of the tendency toward abstraction. The rise of applications powered by artificial intelligence (AI) and machine learning, as well as the demands of newer technologies such as blockchain and Internet of Things, all pose massive demands on our networks and our cognitive capacity for understanding the operation, complexity, and implications for our everyday life. As individuals rush to adopt newer technologies, such as mining of cryptocurrencies, using generative predictive AI tools, and adopting smart home technologies without fully understanding security implications, the attack surface rises proportionately (Ayinala & Murimi, 2022; Bécue et al., 2021; Edu et al., 2020; He et al., 2020; Saad et al., 2020). Firms have responded to this crisis in various ways, including using cyber insurance to protect against the unintended outcomes of cyber incidents (Marotta et al., 2017). Similarly, the decision of specific communities to ban applications of certain technologies represents another mechanism to deal with the uncertainty of the adoption of new technologies (Conger, K. et al., 2019; Gadzheva, 2007; Meckling & Nahm, 2019; Taylor, 2016). Such decisions, although myopic, serve to provide stopgap solutions while other solutions of deeper scope are being formulated.

Governments and institutions have attempted to regulate various aspects of technology, but the gap between law and technology is increasing faster with the strides in technology advances. This has significantly affected the regulatory landscape. For example, individuals routinely use work computers to conduct personal activities while unaware of the scope of the terms of use (D'Arcy et al., 2014). At the organizational level, companies have to rethink their technologies' broader implications, as seen in the Gonzalez v Google case (2023). In this case, the Gonzalez family brought a lawsuit against Google accusing its YouTube recommender algorithms of providing training for jihadist organizations such as ISIS, whose Paris attack was responsible for the death of Nohemi Gonzalez. At the community level, the equifinality of IoT cybersecurity operations must also be considered with a granular lens since IoT compromises can result in disastrous outcomes (Kimani et al., 2019).

DISCUSSION

Cybersecurity scholars and security professionals should look to methodologies geared to understanding configurations that lead to incidences as well as those associated with recoveries. One worthwhile methodology is Qualitative Comparative Analysis (QCA) which is grounded in a set-theoretic approach that develops causal claims utilizing supersets and subsets (Ragin, 2008). QCA is especially helpful because the methodology allows for an outcome to be produced by multiple conditions. In addition, the methodology helps to identify how multiple factors can combine to lead to the outcome under investigation. Finally, QCA allows for outcomes to occur due to either the presence of variables or their absence. The number of scholars investigating economic and organizational phenomena with set-theoretic methods has risen considerably in the last few years (Fiss, 2007; Fiss, 2011; Grandori & Furnari, 2008; Pajunen, 2008).

QCA's approach to causality, referred to as multiple conjunctural causation, has three important implications. First, an outcome can be produced by multiple conditions. Second, QCA recognizes that multiple conditions can lead to the outcome under investigation. This is known as equifinality, and it is a central element of QCA. Third, QCA allows for outcomes to occur as a result of the presence or absence of a condition. Conjunctural causation is particularly useful when it is likely that there can be multiple reasons to bring about an outcome and when causal conditions could combine in unique and multiple ways to bring about an outcome. The methodology is not centered on variable distributions and the search for patterns of covariation, difference, or frequency clustering.

Moreover, QCA relaxes some of the assumptions often associated with quantitative techniques, such as permanent causality, additivity, and causal symmetry (Ragin, 2008). Instead, the technique is quite helpful in evaluating both the number and complexity of alternative paths leading to a desired outcome. QCA can be deployed in investigating cyber incident bundles using either crisp (binary membership) or fuzzy (membership percentages) sets to explore multiple cases at the same time to example what factors were present, absent, or did not contribute.

Implications for Educators

Educators need to create scenarios that develop and reinforce the concepts of equifinality, improvisation, and bricolage. This goes beyond examining previous breaches where the causes can be obtained through an online search. Such a scenario-focused analysis involves developing Kobayashi Maru scenarios where learners are presented with the choice between two options, both of which are bad decisions (Stemwedel, 2015). Learners can then choose one of the bad decisions or use the new tools to develop an entirely new solution. It involves reframing the problem and understanding which constraints are fixed and which ones are variable and can be changed to develop new solutions.

Implications for Security Professionals

The cyber landscape is not going to flatten or get simpler. The number of critical vulnerabilities, data breaches, ransomware, and attacks not conceived yet will only continue to increase. With every asset, every protection mechanism, and every vulnerability, security professionals should take the equifinality approach and consider them in related bundles and not in isolation. There are various ways to make this change, from isolated items and events to related bundles. The first is brainstorming and tabletop exercises so that more people are involved in developing solutions providing a difference in thought as well as abilities. Participants can then examine and explore multiple alternative paths for every process, solution, or threat using improvisation for totally new solutions. During this examination, it is essential to focus not only on policy and procedures but on the desire paths of how processes are actually done. Finally, it is critical to examine solutions from different stakeholder levels (individual, firm, community). By employing equifinality and improvisation, security professionals can be more agile and better prepared for the threats around the corner.

REFERENCES

Abrams, L. (2021). *7 million Robinhood user email addresses for sale on hacker forum*. BleepingComputer. Retrieved on June 2, 2022, from: https://www.bleepingcomputer.com/news/security/7-million-robinhood-user-email-addresses-for-sale-on-hacker-forum/

Acquisti, A., Adjerid, I., Balebako, R., Brandimarte, L., Cranor, L., Komanduri, S., Leon, P., Sadeh, N., Schaub, F., Sleeper, M., Wang, Y., & Wilson, S. (2017). Nudges for privacy and security. *ACM Computing Surveys*, *50*(3), 1–41. doi:10.1145/3054926

Anant, V., Bailey, T., Cracknell, R., Kaplan, J., & Schwartz, A. (2019). *Understanding the uncertainties of cybersecurity: Questions for chief information-security officers*. McKinsey & Company. Retrieved on September 4, 2022, from: https://www.mckinsey.com/capabilities/mckinsey-digital/our-insights/digital-blog/understanding-the-uncertainties-of-cybersecurity-questions-for-chief-information-security-officers

Arce, D. G. (2020). Cybersecurity and platform competition in the cloud. *Computers & Security*, *93*, 1–9. doi:10.1016/j.cose.2020.101774

Avery, D. (2022). *Robinhood app's $20 million data breach settlement: Who is eligible for money?* CNET. Retrieved on October 19, 2022, from: https://www.cnet.com/personal-finance/banking/robinhood-20-million-settlement-who-is-eligible-for-money/

Awojobi, B., & Landry, B. J. L. (2023). An examination of factors determining user privacy perceptions of voice-based assistants. *International Journal of Management, Knowledge and Learning*, *12*, 53–62. doi:10.53615/2232-5697.12.53-62

Ayinala, S., & Murimi, R. (2022). On a territorial notion of a smart home. In *Proceedings of the 1st Workshop on Cybersecurity and Social Sciences* (pp. 33–37). Association for Computing Machinery. 10.1145/3494108.3522766

Baker, T., & Nelson, R. E. (2005). Creating something from nothing: Resource construction through entrepreneurial bricolage. *Administrative Science Quarterly*, *50*(3), 329–366. doi:10.2189/asqu.2005.50.3.329

Barrett, F. J. (1998). Creativity and improvisation in jazz and organizations: Implications for organizational learning. *Organization Science*, *9*(5), 605–622. doi:10.1287/orsc.9.5.605

Barry, C. (2021). *Robinhood breach illustrates the impact of social engineering attacks.* Retrieved on March 22, 2022, from: https://blog.barracuda.com/2021/11/19/robinhood-breach-illustrates-the-impact-of-social-engineering-attacks/

Bécue, A., Praça, I., & Gama, J. (2021). Artificial intelligence, cyber-threats and Industry 4.0: Challenges and opportunities. *Artificial Intelligence Review*, *54*(5), 3849–3886. doi:10.100710462-020-09942-2

Bell, R. G., Filatotchev, I., & Aguilera, R. V. (2014). Corporate governance and investors' perceptions of foreign IPO value: An institutional perspective. *Academy of Management Journal*, *57*(1), 301–320. doi:10.5465/amj.2011.0146

Bergal, J. (2021). *Florida hack exposes danger to water systems.* https://pew.org/3btxWBc

Brase, G. L., Vasserman, E. Y., & Hsu, W. (2017). Do different mental models influence cybersecurity behavior? Evaluations via statistical reasoning performance. *Frontiers in Psychology*, *8*, 1929. doi:10.3389/fpsyg.2017.01929 PMID:29163304

Brown, S. (2021). *Robinhood data breach is bad, but we've seen much worse.* CNET. Retrieved on June 2, 2022, from: https://www.cnet.com/news/privacy/robinhood-data-breach-is-bad-but-weve-seen-much-worse/

Buffington, J., & McCubbrey, D. (2011). A conceptual framework of generative customization as an approach to product innovation and fulfillment. *European Journal of Innovation Management*, *14*(3), 388–403. doi:10.1108/14601061111148852

Caraban, A., Karapanos, E., Gonçalves, D., & Campos, P. (2019). 23 ways to nudge. In *Proceedings of the 2019 CHI Conference on Human Factors in Computing Systems* (pp. 1-15). https://doi.org/10.1145/3290605.3300733

Cheng, C., Wang, H., Sigerson, L., & Chau, C. (2019). Do the socially rich get richer? A nuanced perspective on social network site use and online social capital accrual. *Psychological Bulletin*, *145*(7), 734–764. doi:10.1037/bul0000198 PMID:31094537

Cloutier, C., & Langley, A. (2020). What makes a process theoretical contribution? *Organization Theory*, *1*(1), 1–32. doi:10.1177/2631787720902473

Conger, F. R., & Kovaleski, S. F. (2019, May 14,). San Francisco bans facial recognition technology. *The New York Times.* https://www.nytimes.com/2019/05/14/us/facial-recognition-ban-san-francisco.html

Conger, S., & Landry, B. J. L. (2009). Problem analysis: When established techniques don't work. In *Proceedings of the Conf-IRM Conference* (pp. 1-8). Academic Press.

Culafi, A. (2021). *Mandiant: Compromised Colonial Pipeline password was reused.* Retrieved on July 14, 2022, from: https://www.techtarget.com/searchsecurity/news/252502216/Mandiant-Compromised-Colonial-Pipeline-password-was-reused

Cyr, S., & Wei Choo, C. (2010). The individual and social dynamics of knowledge sharing: An exploratory study. *The Journal of Documentation*, *66*(6), 824–846. doi:10.1108/00220411011087832

D'Arcy, J., Herath, T., & Shoss, M. K. (2014). Understanding employee responses to stressful information security requirements: A coping perspective. *Journal of Management Information Systems*, *31*(2), 285–318. doi:10.2753/MIS0742-1222310210

Edu, J. S., Such, J. M., & Suarez-Tangil, G. (2020). Smart home personal assistants. *ACM Computing Surveys*, *53*(6), 1–36. doi:10.1145/3412383

Egan, M. (2021). *Robinhood discloses breach that exposed information of millions of customers.* CNN. Retrieved on August 4, 2022, from: https://www.cnn.com/2021/11/08/tech/robinhood-data-breach/index.html

Fiss, P. C. (2007). A set-theoretic approach to organizational configurations. *Academy of Management Review*, *32*(4), 1180–1198. doi:10.5465/amr.2007.26586092

Fiss, P. C. (2011). Building better causal theories: A fuzzy set approach to typologies in organization research. *Academy of Management Journal*, *54*(2), 393–420. doi:10.5465/amj.2011.60263120

Foreman, C. J., & Gurugubelli, D. (2015). Identifying the cyber attack surface of the advanced metering infrastructure. *The Electricity Journal*, *28*(1), 94–103. doi:10.1016/j.tej.2014.12.007

Fox, S. (2017). Beyond AI: Multi-Intelligence (MI) combining natural and artificial intelligences in hybrid beings and systems. *Technologies*, *5*(3), 1–14. doi:10.3390/technologies5030038

Fuglsang, L., & Sørensen, F. (2011). The balance between bricolage and innovation: Management dilemmas in sustainable public innovation. *Service Industries Journal*, *31*(4), 581–595. doi:10.1080/02642069.2010.504302

Fung, B. (2021). *Hackers breach Electronic Arts, stealing game source code and tools.* CNN. https://www.cnn.com/2021/06/10/tech/electronic-arts-hack/index.html

Fung, B., & Sands, G. (2021). *Ransomware attackers used compromised password to access Colonial Pipeline network.* CNN. https://www.cnn.com/2021/06/04/politics/colonial-pipeline-ransomware-attack-password/index.html

Furnari, S., Crilly, D., Misangyi, V. F., Greckhamer, T., Fiss, P. C., & Aguilera, R. (2021). Capturing causal complexity: Heuristics for configurational theorizing. *Academy of Management Review*, *46*(4), 778–799. doi:10.5465/amr.2019.0298

Furnham, A., & Boo, H. C. (2011). A literature review of the anchoring effect. *Journal of Socio-Economics*, *40*(1), 35–42. doi:10.1016/j.socec.2010.10.008

Gadzheva, M. (2007). Getting chipped: To ban or not to ban. *Information & Communications Technology Law*, *16*(3), 217–231. doi:10.1080/13600830701680537

Gonzalez, R., et al. v. Google LLC, (United States Court of Appeals for the Ninth Circuit. Docket Number. 18-16700. 2023).

Grabosky, P. N. (2001). Virtual criminality: Old wine in new bottles? *Social & Legal Studies*, *10*(2), 243–249. doi:10.1177/a017405

Grandori, A., & Furnari, S. (2008). A chemistry of organization: Combinatory analysis and design. *Organization Studies*, *29*(3), 459–485. doi:10.1177/0170840607088023

Granovetter, M. S. (1973). The strength of weak ties. *American Journal of Sociology*, *78*(6), 1360–1380. doi:10.1086/225469

He, D., Li, S., Li, C., Zhu, S., Chan, S., Min, W., & Guizani, N. (2020). Security analysis of cryptocurrency wallets in android-based applications. *IEEE Network*, *34*(6), 114–119. doi:10.1109/MNET.011.2000025

Iannacci, F., & Kraus, S. (2022). *Configurational theory: A review* (S. Papagiannidis, Ed.). Springer International Publishing. doi:10.1007/978-3-319-09450-2_23

Jarjoui, S., & Murimi, R. (2021). A framework for enterprise cybersecurity risk management. In K. Daimi & C. Peoples (Eds.), *Advances in Cybersecurity Management* (pp. 139–161). Springer International Publishing., doi:10.1007/978-3-030-71381-2_8

Jarjoui, S., Murimi, R., & Murimi, R. (2021). Hold my beer: A case study of how ransomware affected an Australian beverage company. In *2021 International Conference on Cyber Situational Awareness, Data Analytics and Assessment (CyberSA)* (pp. 1-6). https://doi.org/10.1109/CyberSA52016.2021.9478239

Kahneman, D., & Tversky, A. (2012). Prospect theory: An analysis of decision under risk. In *Handbook of the Fundamentals of Financial Decision Making* (pp. 99–127). World Scientific. doi:10.1142/9789814417358_0006

Katz, D., & Kahn, R. L. (1978). *The social psychology of organizations*. Wiley.

Kelleher, J. D., Mac Namee, B., & D'arcy, A. (2020). *Fundamentals of machine learning for predictive data analytics: Algorithms, worked examples, and case studies*. MIT Press.

Kelly, S., & Resnick-ault, J. (2021). *One password allowed hackers to disrupt Colonial Pipeline, CEO tells senators*. Retrieved on August 1, 2022, from: https://www.reuters.com/business/colonial-pipeline-ceo-tells-senate-cyber-defenses-were-compromised-ahead-hack-2021-06-08/

Kerner, S. M. (2022). *Colonial Pipeline hack explained: Everything you need to know*. https://www.techtarget.com/whatis/feature/Colonial-Pipeline-hack-explained-Everything-you-need-to-know

Kimani, K., Oduol, V., & Langat, K. (2019). Cyber security challenges for IoT-based smart grid networks. *International Journal of Critical Infrastructure Protection*, *25*, 36–49. doi:10.1016/j.ijcip.2019.01.001

Kuehn, A., & Mueller, M. (2014). Analyzing bug bounty programs: An institutional perspective on the economics of software vulnerabilities. SSRN *Electronic Journal,* https://doi.org/ doi:10.2139/ssrn.2418812

Landry, B. J. L., & Koger, M. S. (2023a). Exploring zero trust network architectures for building secure networks. In *Proceedings of the Decision Sciences Institute Southwest Region* (pp. 47261-47266). Academic Press.

Landry, B. J. L., & Koger, M. S. (2023b). Leveraging unified threat management based honeypots in small and midsized businesses and educational environments. In *Proceedings of the Decision Sciences Institute Southwest Region* (pp. 98301-98306). Academic Press.

Lohrke, F. T., Frownfelter-Lohrke, C., & Ketchen, D. J. Jr. (2016). The role of information technology systems in the performance of mergers and acquisitions. *Business Horizons*, *59*(1), 7–12. doi:10.1016/j.bushor.2015.09.006

Lorenz, J., Rauhut, H., Schweitzer, F., & Helbing, D. (2011). How social influence can undermine the wisdom of crowd effect. In *Proceedings of the National Academy of Sciences - PNAS* (pp. 9020-9025). National Academy of Sciences. 10.1073/pnas.1008636108

Loxton, M., Truskett, R., Scarf, B., Sindone, L., Baldry, G., & Zhao, Y. (2020). Consumer behaviour during crises: Preliminary research on how coronavirus has manifested consumer panic buying, herd mentality, changing discretionary spending and the role of the media in influencing behaviour. *Journal of Risk and Financial Management, 13*(8/166), 1-21. https://doi.org/ doi:10.3390/jrfm13080166

Mackie, J. L. (1973). *Truth, probability and paradox: Studies in philosophical logic*. Oxford University Press.

Mahoney, J., & Goertz, G. (2006). A tale of two cultures: Contrasting quantitative and qualitative research. *Political Analysis*, *14*(3), 227–249. doi:10.1093/pan/mpj017

Malecki, E. J. (2003). Digital development in rural areas: Potentials and pitfalls. *Journal of Rural Studies*, *19*(2), 201–214. doi:10.1016/S0743-0167(02)00068-2

Marotta, A., Martinelli, F., Nanni, S., Orlando, A., & Yautsiukhin, A. (2017). Cyber-insurance survey. *Computer Science Review*, *24*, 35–61. doi:10.1016/j.cosrev.2017.01.001

Matthews, L. (2021, Feb 15). *Florida water plant hackers exploited old software and poor password habits*. Retrieved on April 22, 2021, from: https://www.forbes.com/sites/leemathews/2021/02/15/florida-water-plant-hackers-exploited-old-software-and-poor-password-habits/?sh=6b0c16ca334e

Meckling, J., & Nahm, J. (2019). The politics of technology bans: Industrial policy competition and green goals for the auto industry. *Energy Policy*, *126*, 470–479. doi:10.1016/j.enpol.2018.11.031

Meyer, P. (2002). Improvisation power. *Executive Excellence,* 17-18.

MITRE Corporation. (2023). *CVE – MITRE.* https://www.cve.mitre.org

Murimi, R. (2020). Use of botnets for mining cryptocurrencies. In *Botnets* (1st ed., pp. 359–386). Routledge. doi:10.1201/9780429329913-11

National Institute of Standards and Technology. (2006). Minimum security requirements for federal information and information systems. Federal Information Processing Standards Publications (FIPS PUBS) 200. doi:10.1016/0378-7206(89)90025-6

Nurse, J. R. C., Creese, S., Goldsmith, M., & Lamberts, K. (2011). Guidelines for usable cybersecurity: Past and present. In *2011 Third International Workshop on Cyberspace Safety and Security (CSS)* (pp. 21-26). IEEE. 10.1109/CSS.2011.6058566

O'Brien, S. (2021). *Robinhood's data breach involved about 7 million customers. Here's how to protect your credit from fraudsters.* CNBC. https://www.cnbc.com/2021/11/09/robinhood-data-breach-involved-7-million-clients-protect-your-credit.html

Pajunen, K. (2008). Institutions and inflows of foreign direct investment: A fuzzy-set analysis. *Journal of International Business Studies*, *39*(4), 652–669. doi:10.1057/palgrave.jibs.8400371

Pfleeger, S. L., & Caputo, D. D. (2012). Leveraging behavioral science to mitigate cyber security risk. *Computers & Security*, *31*(4), 597–611. doi:10.1016/j.cose.2011.12.010

Ponta, S., Plate, H., Sabetta, A., Bezzi, M., & Dangremont, C. (2019). A manually-curated dataset of fixes to vulnerabilities of open-source software. In *2019 IEEE/ACM 16th International Conference on Mining Software Repositories (MSR)* (pp. 383-387). IEEE Press. 10.1109/MSR.2019.00064

Ragin, C. (2008). *Redesigning social inquiry: Fuzzy sets and beyond*. University of Chicago. doi:10.7208/chicago/9780226702797.001.0001

Rothrock, R. A., Kaplan, J., & Van Der Oord, F. (2018). Board role in cybersecurity risks. *MIT Sloan Management Review*, *59*(2), 12–15.

Saad, M., Spaulding, J., Njilla, L., Kamhoua, C., Shetty, S., Nyang, D., & Mohaisen, D. (2020). Exploring the attack surface of blockchain: A comprehensive survey. *IEEE Communications Surveys and Tutorials*, *22*(3), 1977–2008. doi:10.1109/COMST.2020.2975999

Salemink, K., Strijker, D., & Bosworth, G. (2017). Rural development in the digital age: A systematic literature review on unequal ICT availability, adoption, and use in rural areas. *Journal of Rural Studies*, *54*, 360–371. doi:10.1016/j.jrurstud.2015.09.001

Singer, A., Anderson, W., & Farrow, R. (2013). Rethinking password policies. *Login—. The USENIX Magazine*, *38*, 14–18.

Smith, N., & Walters, P. (2018). Desire lines and defensive architecture in modern urban environments. *Urban Studies (Edinburgh, Scotland)*, *55*(13), 2980–2995. doi:10.1177/0042098017732690

Spadafora, A. (2021). *EA hack reportedly used stolen cookies and Slack to target gaming giant.* TechRadar. Retrieved on September 3, 2022, from: https://www.techradar.com/news/ea-hack-reportedly-used-stolen-cookies-and-slack-to-hack-gaming-giant

Stemwedel, J. D. (2015). *The philosophy of Star Trek: The Kobayashi Maru, no-win scenarios, and ethical leadership.* Retrieved on November 19, 2021, from: https://www.forbes.com/sites/janetstemwedel/2015/08/23/the-philosophy-of-star-trek-the-kobayashi-maru-no-win-scenarios-and-ethical-leadership/?sh=7a1285be5f48

Taylor, S. B. (2016). Can you keep a secret: Some wish to ban encryption technology for fears of data going dark. *SMU Science and Technology Law Review*, *19*(2), 216–248.

Thaler, R. H. (2018). From cashews to nudges. *The American Economic Review*, *108*(6), 1265–1287. doi:10.1257/aer.108.6.1265

Tirumala, S. S., Valluri, M. R., & Babu, G. (2019). A survey on cybersecurity awareness concerns, practices and conceptual measures. In *2019 International Conference on Computer Communication and Informatics (ICCCI)* (pp. 1-6). 10.1109/ICCCI.2019.8821951

U. S. Department of Energy. (2021). *Colonial Pipeline cyber incident.* Energy.gov. https://www.energy.gov/ceser/colonial-pipeline-cyber-incident

Verjans, S. (2005). Bricolage as a way of life - improvisation and irony in information systems. *European Journal of Information Systems*, *14*(5), 504–506. doi:10.1057/palgrave.ejis.3000559

Winterrose, M. L., Carter, K. M., Wagner, N., & Streilein, W. W. (2016). Balancing security and performance for agility in dynamic threat environments. In *2016 46th Annual IEEE/IFIP International Conference on Dependable Systems and Networks (DSN)* (pp. 607-617). 10.1109/DSN.2016.61

Wu, Y., Edwards, W. K., & Das, S. (2022). SoK: Social cybersecurity. In *2022 IEEE Symposium on Security and Privacy (SP)* (pp. 1863-1879). IEEE. 10.1109/SP46214.2022.9833757

Chapter 10 Information Security Threats of Automation in the Water Industry: An Exploratory Study of England and Wales

James Taylor
Bournemouth University, UK

Festus Adedoyin
https://orcid.org/0000-0002-3586-2570
Bournemouth University, UK

ABSTRACT

Critical infrastructure is reliant on automation to efficiently deliver services. Supervisory control and data acquisition (SCADA) systems monitor and control the operational network and these devices can be compromised with a cyber attack. This report evaluates the significance of such threats, the economic impact, reviews foreign ownership of critical infrastructure and the current legislation as it relates to the water industry. The report concludes with potential recommendations the United Kingdom might consider protecting this vital service.

INTRODUCTION

Cyber warfare is being actively waged, and the opportunity to disrupt another nation-state is being fought over the internet. As was witnessed in 2010 when Stuxnet delivered a worm that disrupted Iranian nuclear enrichment research in Natanz. Specifically infecting Siemens controllers within Iran and preventing them from doing anything useful (Langner 2011). More recently, in 2015, BlackEnergy notoriously infected the Ukrainian power grid causing power outages for more than 6 hours. The US Department of Homeland Security has discovered BlackEnergy malware within their national critical infrastructure,

DOI: 10.4018/978-1-6684-9018-1.ch010

including nuclear power plants, oil and gas pipelines as well as water filtration systems (Khan et al. 2016). Both attacks were focused on digitally connected automation controls.

SCADA is part of the wider Industrial Control Systems (ICS) or Operational Technology (OT), and many industries use SCADA controls to automate the delivery of their services. Critical National Infrastructure (CNI) such as the electricity grid, rail services, telecommunications and water services all make use of SCADA controls. A deliberate attack on these services in times of conflict amounts to cyber warfare (Nicholson et al., 2012) and as such, the nation must be assured of minimal disruption. This chapter explores SCADA deployment within water authorities in England and Wales, the implications of a cyber-attack, the economic impact such an attack may have as well as the current legislation to encourage cyber resilience. The chapter concludes with recommendations the industry could consider assuring the nation, vital services are delivered as expected.

Within the water utility sector, SCADA provides automation for a wide variety of uses. Monitoring and controlling pumps, valves and filters used in the treatment of water, with similar controls in the management of sewage. SCADA can also be used in monitoring the physical security (e.g., CCTV, alarm systems, and so forth) of remote locations as part of the overall security considerations, protecting plant equipment from tampering, theft, or damage. With the advancement of the industrial internet, more automation is possible. OT needs to be rigorously managed as the potential for actual physical harm is possible; if the attackers compromised water purification processes and produce false readings on water testing devices, this could prove fatal to consumers.

IT and OT share similarities and both teams should share resources (Desai 2016). This convergence of technologies will present security vulnerabilities requiring both disciplines to proactively work together. IT still has many responsibilities securing the privacy of their customers and whilst this paper is focused on protecting OT, it has been known for attacks on consumer data to be launched via vulnerabilities in OT, such as the data breach with Target whereby access was gained through the heating and ventilation systems (Committee on Commerce, Science, and Transportation 2014). Unfortunately, SCADA lacks basic security controls and therefore is exposed to threats and vulnerabilities (Singh, 2022). This was recently highlighted at the Pwn2Own Championships, where the hackers noted the SCADA challenges were the easiest yet (O'Neil, 2022).

To understand the threat, it is worth considering the likely threat actors. Nation states committing cyber warfare, socio-political groups furthering their cause through cyber terrorism or even possibly a disgruntled employee looking to disrupt operations. Or in the case of an Irish water treatment facility, crypto miners leverage computing power to mine cryptocurrency (Thomson, 2018). In reality, due to the anonymity of the internet, "cyberspace is unknowable" (Barnard-Wills & Ashenden, 2012). It is possible to assume who the likely threat actors are, in the case of Stuxnet and the Ukrainian BlackEnergy attacks, one could conjecture nation states were responsible; however, this is not proven. Whilst it is virtually impossible to regulate the internet or pursue e-criminals, the only course of action is to ensure a robust and resilient approach to all potential threat actors.

Threats and vulnerabilities and the associated risk of SCADA usage are considered below alongside possible mitigation strategies: Internet Exposure: Does the control need to be internet enabled? Just because it can, does not mean it should; Poor Network Segregation: Segregation of duty is a well-founded cyber principle, as was the case with Target the IT systems were compromised via OT; Default configuration: Thousands of controllers are deployed across a SCADA network, whilst it may benefit the operator to keep access simple, the default options must be changed, for example, Admin / Admin;

ICS protocol weakness: Attackers can easily eavesdrop on communications; for instance, the MODBUS protocol is in plain text.

Additonally, poor authorisation controls could allow an attacker to modify the program; ICS applications vulnerabilities: No different to other applications, the software that is used to manage ICS networks could be vulnerable. With a poor relationship to cyber security, the patch management regime must be continuously tested; and Lack of security awareness: OT has not had the same emphasis as IT on security awareness, although awareness is required, risk assessment with associated policies, procedures and controls require implementation. The significance of the threat is of the highest level, and the threat to human life is possible (Anderson & Fuloria, 2010).

METHOD

This review is literature based and focuses on the economics of information security. The report reviews the market conditions for water and sewerage companies and those economic factors to motivate cyber hygiene. The report is qualitative in its presentation, there is an opportunity to research the economic costs to the water industry to provide cyber resilience and that could be considered as an enhancement.

The literature reviewed is from a variety of sources including academic papers, industry articles, government legislation, cyber sources, news articles as well as studies from the water regulator. The reading list was extensive, however, simple searches like "Cyber" "Security" and "SCADA" quickly guide the research to the relevant (or lack of content) documentation.

The scope of the report does not include organisations' appetite towards cyber security. There is little evidence from the literature reviewed that this has a high priority, although this might change after the recent South Staffs Water incident (BBC 2022). Equally the report does not evaluate the competencies of the water authorities to sufficiently protect digital resources. OT and IT departments, while having similar disciplines are distinct functions. Cyber resilience must be deployed with OT as rigorously (if not to a higher degree) as within IT. Further research in these two critical areas (attitude and ability) is essential in assisting the economic considerations to enable the appropriate investments to secure the nation's water supply.

ECONOMIC ANALYSIS

Margaret Thatcher's government sold off the water industry through privatisation with all existing debts written off in 1989. Today, water companies operate as regional monopolies in the United Kingdom (Willis & Sheldon, 2022). Unlike gas, telecoms and electricity that have national grids, allowing local competition, the consumer has no choice for the supply of water or removal of sewage. In England and Wales, a total of 11 local authorities provide both water and sewage services. Figure 1 shows both water and sewage companies as well as those companies that only supply water.

Figure 1. Map showing both water/water and sewage authorities
Source: Ofwat (2018)

Table 1 shows the owners of water and sewage authorities in England and Wales

Table 1. Water and sewage authority ownership

Water and Sewage Authority	Owner Company	Geolocation
Anglian Water Services Limited	Osprey Consortiul	Australia, Canada, UK, Luxembourg
Dwr Cymru Cyfyngedig	Clas Cymru	Private Company - UK
Hafren Dyfrdwy Cyfyngedig	Hafren Dyfrdwy Cyfyngedig	Private Company - UK
Northumbrian Water Limited	Cheung Kong Infrastructure Holdings	China, Hong Kong
Severn Trent Water Limited	Severn Trent PLC	UK - Listed on LSE
Southern Water Services Limited	Greensands Holding Limited	UK, US, Australia
South West Water Limited	Pennon Group	UK - Listed on LSE
Thames Water Utilities Limited	Investment Companies	50% Foreign ownership
United Utilities Water Limited	United Utlities	UK - Listed on LSE
Wessex Water Services Limited	YTL Corporation	Malaysia
Yorkshire Water Services Limited	Kelda Holdings	Jersey

The Water Services Regulation Authority (Ofwat) is the economic regulator that sets the price water companies can charge. The normal laws of supply and demand of perfect competition do not apply to this sector. Ofwat seeks to allow water companies to make a reasonable return on their investment of about 6%. Prices are reviewed every 5 years and the next review date is in 2024 (Ofwat, 2017). The price to the consumer is a complex calculation; it considers the Retail Price Index (RPI) plus a K factor, which is the ongoing incentive charge to fund the improvement of services offered. Water demand will fluctuate, and agriculture needs as well as household consumption will increase during long periods of hot weather.

Consumption-based on stated preference has been suggested as a measure of reduced water usage (Willis & Sheldon, 2022). Consumers prefer to drink bottled water instead of water from a tap. However, at the current rate of 45.8 litres of bottled water consumed per capita per annum (Statista, 2021), drinking water from a bottle is a minimal consideration when the average person consumes approximately 152 litres per day (Consumer Council for Water, 2021).

Today any new account will be supplied with a water meter, the opportunity for consumers to control their consumption is their responsibility (Bohanna, 1998). Fewer baths, water hippos in the cistern or a drought-resistant garden enable consumers to conserve water and make savings instead of the original flat charge based on the property's council tax. Likewise, the supply of water can change, during drought conditions, and water restrictions are enforced with either rationing or hosepipe bans (Taylor et al., 2009). Potentially in severe incidents, water tankers may need to supply residents, standpipes erected or even bottled water provided. These additional considerations will come at an additional cost to the water company.

Theory of Demand and Consumer Behaviour

As can be seen from Figure 2, if this was perfect competition, we might anticipate a demand curve that slopes – the higher the price, the demand reduction and conversely the lower the price the increase in demand. However, with no competition and a fixed price set by Ofwat, the demand curve is flat. The average cost per litre[1], supplying water under normal conditions suggests that provided demand stays below B, the average cost per litre is lower than the price charged.

Figure 2. Economics of water supply

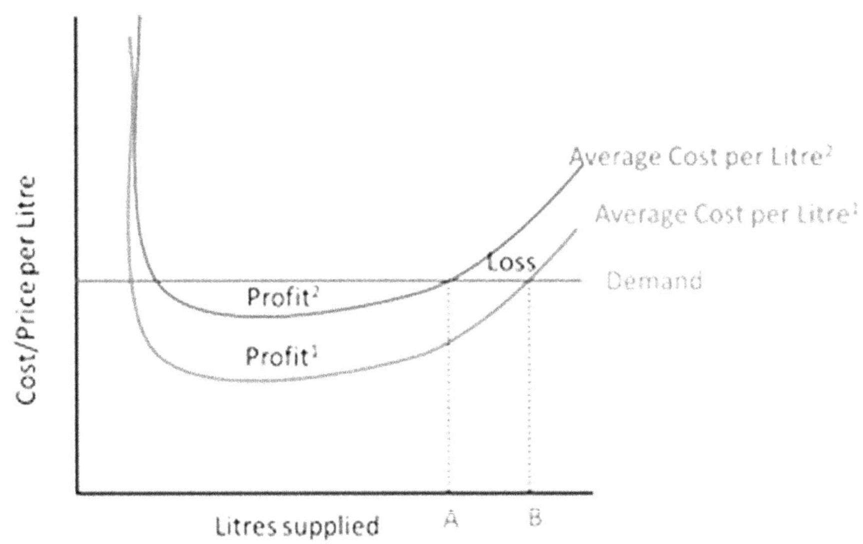

Should the water supply be interrupted due to a cyber incident, depending on the attack, there are a couple of potential outcomes that may be considered. Water supply is prevented from being delivered by an attack on pumping stations, reducing capacity or water treatment plants are compromised, making the water unusable due to the risk to human health. In the first instance, whilst demand may still be normal, the water authority is unable to deliver; in the second incident, demand will reduce as consumers stop using water, in fear of potential contamination. With approximately 50% of all households on a water meter (Water UK, 2021), billing receipts are significantly impacted and costs to the water authority are increased to supply fresh water, either with water tankers or supplying bottled water to drink.

Following a cyber incident, there will be further costs to the water authority, firstly in the rectification of the incident and then secondly in implementing the controls needed to prevent further attacks. Undoubtedly the regulator and government will be involved, and the subsequent litigation costs and penalty fines will also factor as a cost to the authority. These increases in costs are represented by the average cost per litre^2 in Figure 2 and show a squeeze on profitability (as shown in the area marked Profit^2). Point A on the demand curve now shows the level of supply at which the cost to supply water per litre, results in a loss. Due to a captive market, consumers are not able to change suppliers, so reputational damage is limited to public indignation.

Overseeing infrastructure improvement is part of the regulator's role and it has been argued since privatisation, water is more affordable (in real terms), our beaches are cleaner, and water quality and pressure have improved (Edwards, 2017). Conversely, it has been suggested, England and Wales do not receive value for money. Potentially a perverse incentive of £55Bn being paid in dividends to shareholders while incurring £44 Billion of debt to fund infrastructure projects (Yearwood, 2018).

The cost of servicing this debt is estimated at £1.3 Billion per year (Laville and correspondent, 2020). The expectation of the government was infrastructure improvements would be paid for by profits not borrowing. Such is the concern, the shadow chancellor of the exchequer cites 83% of the population is in favour of re-nationalising this service (CIWEM, 2019). The decision to make the appropriate levels of expenditure to safeguard critical national infrastructure versus maximising the return on shareholder investment places the UK and the water authorities into conflicting interests. Ultimately, it is only through policy and legislation, the UK can seek to control sufficient protection, and this is explored further in the final section.

Foreign Ownership of Critical Infrastructure

Beyond the economic arguments of private investment serving the public good, national security concerns are a factor in protecting national interests. The potential for cyber warfare has already been highlighted, but when your infrastructure is owned by an un-friendly state, the potential for insider threats presents itself. With this perceived threat, the debate for regulation of deals that could damage technology and security interests continues (Rabe & Gippner, 2017).

With the current political climate in China, there are shared concerns between MI5 and the Federal Bureau of Investigation (FBI). MI5 has more than doubled efforts concerning Chinese activity. In a speech in July 2022, national resilience was mentioned, specifically highlighting investments and acquisitions amongst other concerns such as espionage and political interference (MI5, 2022). China holds more than £143 Billion of UK assets, including shares in Hinkley Point C nuclear power station (33% stake), Northumbrian Water, Heathrow Airport (10%), Neptune Energy (49%) and Thames Water (9%). Even AstraZeneca has over £1Bn Chinese investment (Stubley 2021).

The concerns regarding national security prompted Theresa May's government in 2016 to temporarily place the Hinkley Point project on hold, with a senior advisor warning that China General Nuclear (CGN) could leave backdoors in the computer systems to shut-down power (Bulman, 2016). Despite wanting stronger trading ties with China, their involvement in funding nuclear development has been called into question and CGN could be blocked from investing in both the Sizewell B and Bradwell projects. In the case of the Sizewell investment, a minority stake hold might be tolerable, however, the investment in Bradwell is not politically palatable' (Ambrose, 2021).

The National Security and Investment Act that came into force on 4/01/2022 grants the government the ability to intervene and scrutinise business transactions in the interests of national security (Gov. UK 2022). Currently, there are 17 sensitive areas within the economy called "notifiable acquisitions", water supply is not included in this list. Should water be included in this list alongside other nationally distributed utilities such as communications and energy? Given the recent disruptions in the Ukraine conflict with Russia (Harding et al., 2022), maybe a potential oversight

Beyond foreign ownership, certain foreign companies are no longer approved for UK deployment. Within the telecommunication industry, Huawei is no longer an approved supplier of 5G equipment (Department for Digital, Culture, Media & Sport, 2020). No new equipment could be purchased from 31 December 2020 and all existing Huawei equipment has to be removed from 5G networks by 2027. The decision to ban was in part following similar US sanctions against Huawei and updated technical advice from UK cyber experts. The economics of this decision are expensive, with initial estimates of between 14% and 42% in deploying 5G networks (Baird, 2019).

Similarly, Kaspersky was banned from the US and whilst the UK did not follow suit, the National Cyber Security Centre (NCSC) warned the government department against using Kaspersky products for those systems related to national security (Corera, 2022). Germany is taking a harder line against Kaspersky despite the Federal Office for Information Security finding no evidence of any issues. It should also be noted, even friendly nations have backdoors, following Shadow Brokers' hack into Equation Group (linked to the NSA) – ExtraBacon, described in CVE-2016-6366, allowed a potential attacker to take full control of a Cisco ASA firewall (Paganini, 2016).

Intriguingly, Bruce Schneier presents an equities issue, do you declare a vulnerability to spy on the bad guys, or do you declare the vulnerability to protect the good guys (Schneier 2013)? It is a fine balancing act to secure UK infrastructure as well as enjoy the economics of trading between countries, trade agreements and investment opportunities are influenced by politics and as such, consequences of UK policy are felt economically.

POLICIES AND LEGISLATION

Many public bodies within England and Wales are involved with water, including Ofwat, DEFRA, Environment Agency, Consumer Council for Water (CCW) and many others. The regulations that control the economics of water authorities are briefly outlined below (Ofwat, 2022):

- **The Water Act 1989:** Privatisation of the former water authorities.
- **Water Industry Act 1991:** Appointment of Ofwat as a regulator.
- **Competition and Service (Utilities) Act 1992:** Increased Ofwat's powers concerning competition.
- **Competition Act 1998:** Prohibiting any abuse, due to dominant market position.

- **Water Industry Act 1999:** Consumer protection to assure the supply of water.
- **Water Act 2003:** Changes in economic regulation allowing large users access to competitors.
- **Enterprise Act 2002:** Certain mergers must be referred to the Competition Commission.
- **Water Act 2014:** Greater competition for non-household users.

However, in terms of cyber (and physical) resilience, Network, and Information Systems Regulations 2018 (NIS) gives appropriate guidance. The accompanying guidance from the Centre for the Protection of National Infrastructure (CPNI) and NCSC set out expectations for critical infrastructure. Cybersecurity maturity models have been criticised for not addressing specific market needs (Miron & Muita, 2014), especially within critical infrastructure. The Cyber Assurance of Physical Security Systems (CAPSS) helps address this concern, to gain confidence in the security of the components deployed having effective cyber mitigation controls (CPNI, 2022). Not dissimilar from other frameworks in its structure, CAPSS goes beyond the framework and certifies products for their security controls. The supply chain of SCADA controls is competitive; therefore, manufacturers of these devices are now proactively encouraged to ensure their devices meet the CAPSS standards.

Other legislation such as the Serious Crimes Act (legislation.gov.uk) helps support prosecution. From a cyber-warfare perspective that provides little discouragement to the attacking nation, despite calls that civilian operations be afforded similar protection as provided by the Geneva convention (Sutherland et al., 2012). Whilst other legislation is applicable (should OT be used to attack IT), such as the Data Protection Act or General Data Protection Regulation (GDPR) to preserve consumer privacy.

Within utility OT networks, a compromised smart meter may impact the right to private life, however, the link is tenuous. At present, smart water meters are only just being introduced to UK households. Whilst the meter is linked to a property and not a person, they are susceptible to compromise (Khattak et al., 2019), however, it will be within IT that any privacy concerns are experienced as that is where the meter will be linked to a person responsible for paying the bill.

DISCUSSIONS

The water innovation strategy published in 2021 (Water Innovation 2050, 2021) is not aware of its role as part of the UK's critical infrastructure. The report recognises resilience as a requirement (in terms of continued supply); however, it is not specific enough in terms of cyber. There is an opportunity to affect change, the strategy mentions a Centre of Excellence, if cyber can be baked into that initiative there is a potential opportunity to improve awareness. Recommending potential next steps to a sector that is seemingly blind to its responsibilities will prove frustrating. The report considers recommendations from both economic theory and legislation.

It is difficult from an economic theory to encourage any organisation to invest in cyber security, let alone water authorities that have a unique privilege in the market. Lack of board awareness of their responsibility for cyber-attacks is a part of the issue (Hartmann & Carmenate, 2021). There are guidelines on what an organisation should spend on cyber security (Gordon et al., 2020), and whilst this assists most organisations with a budget to consider, for critical infrastructure the investment formula from Gordon and Loeb is insufficient. Ofwat does have powers to remove the water extraction licence from a water authority, and despite the many failings in this sector (sewage spills, water loss etc.), this power has yet to be used.

Corporate and social responsibility programmes within the water authorities have little to no focus on cyber issues, nor do they seem to acknowledge their role within critical infrastructure. This lack of awareness coupled with 5 of the 11 water authorities under foreign ownership (see Table 1), suggests that shared values to national security will not be as determined as they could be. There is a possible incentive scheme, whereby a water authority that is fully compliant with the CAPSS and NIS programmes, enjoys a VAT rebate (corporate tax receipts may vary based on foreign ownership).

If profitability is the primary concern for the board, this could motivate the board into action. Whilst the consumer is concerned about their privacy from an IT perspective, it is doubtful they are demanding a secure supply of water or removal of sewage. Even in the event of an incident, they are unable to change suppliers as they suffer the consequences of a disruption. It is only the nation that can impose a requirement, and this can only be achieved through legislation.

Fining an organisation for any breach or lack of sufficient controls may control behaviour (Herath & Rao, 2009). These fines ultimately are borne by the consumer and potentially reduced dividends to shareholders. In an industry where £2 Billion is paid in dividends the £17 Million in potential fines awarded in 2018 across all of the critical infrastructure (Hall, 2018), the use of monetary fines barely impacts decision-making. NIS legislation is clear in its intent, while the consequences of non-compliance are monetary today, vicarious liability (Laski, 1916) or corporate negligence of board members should be considered. The law should be made abundantly clear that board members are personally held liable for the actions or lack of action of their organisations.

Organisations do not like fines, and often the employee to whom a cyber incident can be blamed is relieved of their employment. This however does not impact the board who were responsible for ensuring cyber security is properly applied. The penalties for not protecting critical infrastructure (and possibly privacy under GDPR) should include jail sentences; only when a board member is held personally liable for cyber incidents, will the incentive to implement sufficient controls to protect an organisation be fully realised.

The regulator is in favor of jail sentences and recently proposed this course of action should be followed (Plimmer, 2022), this was in reaction to the excessive sewage pollution witnessed in 2021. Given the levels of public health at risk of these spills, similar public health issues are exposed if the supply of water is tampered with.

Further legislation to prevent the payment of dividends if an organisation does not meet CPNI standards could also be considered. The nation's interests must take precedence over shareholders, no matter where they are resident in the world. Audits are performed routinely on water authorities for water quality, reducing leaks and sewage spillover (amongst other measures). Cyber resilience needs to be part of this review ultimately with Ofwat but also in partnership with CPNI and NCSC.

CONCLUSION

Critical infrastructure cannot be left alone to defend the services they offer. However, the impetus to do so must be within, starting with the board of directors. Without a strong cyber security culture, any external attempts to help, encourage, audit or punish will be viewed as an interruption to normal operations and will continue to fail. Some areas of national infrastructure already have a high-risk awareness for the services they provide, and air traffic control has a high cyber awareness program, although they too suffered a resilience incident in 2014 (Civil Aviation Authority, 2018). This expertise needs to be shared amongst all organisations that provide critical services. This does not suggest a homogenised approach to cyber, as one vulnerability will affect many, but rather the collective capability of the wider cyber community to realise the ambitions NIS and CPNI have.

REFERENCES

legislation.gov.uk. (2015). *Serious Crime Act 2015*. Retrieved on April 12, 2022, from: https://www.legislation.gov.uk/ukpga/2015/9/contents/enacted

Ambrose, J. (2021). China's nuclear power firm could be blocked from UK projects. *The Guardian*. Retrieved on November 3, 2022, from: https://www.theguardian.com/environment/2021/jul/26/chinas-nuclear-power-firm-could-be-blocked-from-uk-projects

Anderson, R., & Fuloria, S. (2010). Security Economics and Critical National Infrastructure. In T. Moore, D. Pym, & C. Ioannidis (Eds.), *Economics of Information Security and Privacy* (pp. 55–66). Springer US. doi:10.1007/978-1-4419-6967-5_4

Baird, W. (2019). Counting the International Costs of Huawei Exclusion. *American Enterprise Institute - AEI*. Retrieved on November 3, 2022, from: https://www.aei.org/technology-and-innovation/telecommunications/counting-the-international-costs-of-huawei-exclusion/

Barnard-Wills, D., & Ashenden, D. (2012). *Securing Virtual Space*. Retrieved on April 12, 2022, from: https://journals.sagepub.com/doi/epub/10.1177/1206331211430016

BBC. (2022). 'Worrying precedent' as hackers target South Staffs Water. *BBC News*. Retrieved on October 13, 2022, from: https://www.bbc.com/news/uk-england-stoke-staffordshire-62565937

Bohanna, D. (1998). Water meters: An incentive to conserve and a signal to the market. *Economic Affairs*, *18*(2), 10–13. doi:10.1111/1468-0270.00085

Bulman, M. (2016). *Hinkley Point: Overwhelming majority of British public oppose Theresa May's decision to approve nuclear plant*. The Independent. Retrieved on November 3, 2022, from: https://www.independent.co.uk/news/uk/home-news/hinkley-point-theresa-may-nuclear-power-poll-majority-uk-opposes-plant-edf-china-a7308701.html

Civil Aviation Authority. (2018). *CAP1480: Implementation of the recommendations from the Independent Enquiry into the NATS Systems Failure on 12th December 2014*. Retrieved on April 15, 2022, from: https://publicapps.caa.co.uk/modalapplication.aspx?appid=11&mode=detail&id=7614&filter=2

CIWEM. (2019). *Thirty years on, what has water privatisation achieved?* CIWEM. Retrieved on April 12, 2022, from: https://www.ciwem.org/the-environment/how-should-water-and-environmental-management-firms-tap,-retain-and-promote-female-talent

Committee on Commerce, Science, and Transportation. (2014). *'Kill Chain' Analysis of the 2013 Target Data Breach*. Retrieved on April 12, 2022, from: https://www.hsdl.org/?abstract&did=751170

Consumer Council for Water. (2021). *How much water do you use?* CCW. Retrieved on April 12, 2022, from: https://www.ccwater.org.uk/households/using-water-wisely/averagewateruse/

Corera, G. (2022, March 29). More must reconsider Russian anti-virus software use, UK warns. *BBC News*. Retrieved on November 3, 2022, from: https://www.bbc.com/news/technology-60854882

CPNI. (2022). *Cyber Assurance of Physical Security Systems*. Retrieved on April 13, 2022, from: https://www.cpni.gov.uk/cyber-assurance-physical-security-systems-capss

Department for Digital, Culture, Media & Sport (2020). *Huawei to be removed from UK 5G networks by 2027*. Retrieved on November 3, 2022, from: https://www.gov.uk/government/news/huawei-to-be-removed-from-uk-5g-networks-by-2027

Desai, N. (2016). *IT vs. OT for the Industrial Internet*. GlobalSign GMO Internet, Inc. Retrieved on February 28, 2022, from: https://www.globalsign.com/en/blog/it-vs-ot-industrial-internet

Edwards, C. (2017). *Thatcher's golden legacy of privatisation*. CapX. Retrieved on March 2, 2022, from: https://capx.co/thatchers-golden-legacy-of-privatisation/

Gordon, L. A., Loeb, M. P., & Zhou, L. (2020). Integrating cost–benefit analysis into the NIST Cybersecurity Framework via the Gordon–Loeb Model. *Journal of Cybersecurity*, *6*(1), tyaa005. doi:10.1093/cybsec/tyaa005

Gov.UK. (2022). *National Security and Investment Act 2021*. Retrieved on November 3, 2022, from: https://www.gov.uk/government/collections/national-security-and-investment-act

Hall, K. (2018). *Brit water firms, power plants with crap cyber security will pay up to £17m, peers told*. Retrieved on February 1, 2022, from: https://www.theregister.com/2018/05/22/house_of_lords_new_cybersecurity_regulations/

Harding, L., Sabbagh, D., & Koshiw, I. (2022, October 31. Russia targets Ukraine energy and water infrastructure in missile attacks. *The Guardian*. Retrieved on November 3, 2022, from: https://www.theguardian.com/world/2022/oct/31/russian-missiles-kyiv-ukraine-cities

Hartmann, C. C., & Carmenate, J. (2021). Academic Research on the Role of Corporate Governance and IT Expertise in Addressing Cybersecurity Breaches: Implications for Practice, Policy, and Research. *Current Issues in Auditing*, *15*(2), A9–A23. doi:10.2308/CIIA-2020-034

Herath, T., & Rao, H. R. (2009). Encouraging information security behaviors in organizations: Role of penalties, pressures and perceived effectiveness. *Decision Support Systems*, *47*(2), 154–165. doi:10.1016/j.dss.2009.02.005

Khan, R., Maynard, P., McLaughlin, K., Laverty, D. M., & Sezer, S. (2016). *Threat Analysis of BlackEnergy Malware for Synchrophasor based Real-time Control and Monitoring in Smart Grid*. Retrieved on April 11, 2022, from: https://www.scienceopen.com/hosted-document?doi=10.14236/ewic/ICS2016.7

Khattak, A., Khanji, S., & Khan, W. (2019). Smart Meter Security: Vulnerabilities, Threat Impacts, and Countermeasures. In, 554–562.

Langner, R. (2011). Stuxnet: Dissecting a Cyberwarfare Weapon. *IEEE Security and Privacy*, *9*(3), 49–51. doi:10.1109/MSP.2011.67

Laski, H. J. (1916). Basis of Vicarious Liability. *The Yale Law Journal*, *26*(2), 105. doi:10.2307/786314

Laville, S. (2020, July 1). England's privatised water firms paid £57bn in dividends since 1991. *The Guardian*. Retrieved on February 28, 2022, from: https://www.theguardian.com/environment/2020/jul/01/england-privatised-water-firms-dividends-shareholders

MI5. (2022). *Joint address by MI5 and FBI Heads*. Retrieved on November 3, 2022, from: https://www.mi5.gov.uk/news/speech-by-mi5-and-fbi

Miron, W., & Muita, K. (2014). Cybersecurity Capability Maturity Models for Providers of Critical Infrastructure. *Technology Innovation Management Review*, *4*(10), 33–39. doi:10.22215/timreview/837

Nicholson, A., Webber, S., Dyer, S., Patel, T., & Janicke, H. (2012). SCADA security in the light of Cyber-Warfare. *Computers & Security*, *31*(4), 418–436. doi:10.1016/j.cose.2012.02.009

O'Neil, P. (2022). *These hackers just showed how easy it is to target critical infrastructure*. Retrieved on May 2, 2022, from: https://www-technologyreview-com.cdn.ampproject.org/c/s/www.technologyreview.com/2022/04/21/1050815/hackers-target-critical-infrastructure-pwn2own/amp/

Ofwat. (2017). *Delivering Water 2020: Our final methodology for the 2019 price review*. Ofwat. Retrieved on April 13, 2022, from: https://www.ofwat.gov.uk/publication/delivering-water-2020-final-methodology-2019-price-review/

Ofwat. (2018). *Your water company*. Ofwat. Retrieved on October 13, 2022, from: https://www.ofwat.gov.uk/households/your-water-company/

Ofwat. (2022). *Legislation*. Ofwat. Retrieved on May 2, 2022, from: https://www.ofwat.gov.uk/regulated-companies/ofwat-industry-overview/legislation/

Paganini, P. (2016). *NSA EXTRABACON exploit still threatens tens of thousands of CISCO ASA boxes*. Security Affairs. Retrieved on November 3, 2022, from: https://securityaffairs.co/wordpress/50971/hacking/nsa-extrabacon.html

Plimmer, G. (2022, July 14). English water company bosses threatened with jail for sewage pollution. *Financial Times*.

Rabe, W., & Gippner, O. (2017). Perceptions of China's outward foreign direct investment in European critical infrastructure and strategic industries. *International Politics*, *54*(4), 468–486. doi:10.105741311-017-0044-x

Schneier, B. (2013). *Carry On: Sound Advice from Schneier on Security*. John Wiley & Sons, Inc. Retrieved on February 1, 2022, from: https://ebookcentral.proquest.com/lib/bournemouth-ebooks/detail.action?docID=1568423

Singh, S. (2022). *Biggest threats to ICS/SCADA systems*. Infosec Resources. Retrieved on February 28, 2022, from: https://resources.infosecinstitute.com/topic/biggest-threats-to-ics-scada-systems/

Statista. (2021). *Bottled water consumption per capita UK 2013-2026*. Statista. Retrieved on April 11, 2022, from: https://www.statista.com/forecasts/1186840/uk-average-volume-bottled-water-per-capita

Stubley, P. (2021). *China now owns £143bn in UK assets, from nuclear power to pubs and schools*. The Independent. Retrieved on November 3, 2022, from: https://www.independent.co.uk/news/uk/home-news/china-now-owns-ps143bn-in-uk-assets-from-nuclear-power-to-pubs-and-schools-b1841056.html

Sutherland, I., Xynos, K., Jones, A., & Blyth, A. (2012). Protective Emblems in Cyber Warfare. *Australian Information Warfare and Security Conference*. Available from: https://ro.ecu.edu.au/isw/49

Taylor, V., Chappells, H., Medd, W., & Trentmann, F. (2009). Drought is normal: The socio-technical evolution of drought and water demand in England and Wales, 1893–2006. *Journal of Historical Geography*, *35*(3), 568–591. doi:10.1016/j.jhg.2008.09.004

Thomson, I. (2018). *Now that's taking the p... Sewage plant 'hacked' to craft crypto-coins*. Retrieved on February 1, 2022, from: https://www.theregister.com/2018/02/08/scada_hackers_cryptocurrencies/

Water UK. (2021). *Water meters*. Retrieved on April 13, 2022, from: https://www.water.org.uk/advice-for-customers/water-meters/

Water Innovation 2050. (2021). *UK Water Innovation Strategy 2050*. Water Innovation 2050. Retrieved on April 14, 2022, from: http://waterinnovation2050.org.uk/

Willis, K., & Sheldon, R. (2022). Research on customers' willingness-to-pay for service changes in UK water company price reviews 1994–2019. *Journal of Environmental Economics and Policy*, *11*(1), 4–20. doi:10.1080/21606544.2021.1927850

Yearwood, K. (2018). *The privatised water Industry in the UK. An ATM for investors*. Public Services International Research Unit (PSIRU) University of Greenwich. Working Paper. Retrieved on April 12, 2022, from: https://gala.gre.ac.uk/id/eprint/21097/

Chapter 11
Exploring Cybersecurity, Misinformation, and Interference in Voting and Elections Through Cyberspace

S. Raschid Muller
https://orcid.org/0000-0002-1742-7575
Arizona State University, USA

Darrell Norman Burrell
https://orcid.org/0000-0002-4675-9544
Marymount University, USA

Calvin Nobles
https://orcid.org/0000-0003-4002-1108
Illinois Institute of Technology, USA

Horace C. Mingo
https://orcid.org/0000-0002-2395-2990
Marymount University, USA

Andreas Vassilakos
Illinois Institute of Technology, USA

ABSTRACT

Interference in the election process from both abroad and within the United States has produced chaos and confusion in business markets, communities, and among voters. Elections have become less reliable as a result of misleading statements. Election deniers are actively working to undermine confidence in our elections and suppress turnout, particularly among voters of color and other communities that have historically been marginalized. The false information spread, which includes lies about the voting process and election workers, has the potential to have significant repercussions for people's abilities to vote and their faith in our elections. Election misinformation poses a threat to democratic processes in the United States. Sixty-four percent of election officials reported in 2022 that spreading false information had made their jobs more dangerous. This chapter uses emerging content from extant literature to discuss cyberpsychology and the complex dynamics of these issues with a primary focus on finding solutions to these problems.

DOI: 10.4018/978-1-6684-9018-1.ch011

INTRODUCTION

The United States elections officials faced extreme pressure in 2020 to safeguard the presidential election process (Vanderwalker, 2020). According to a Collaborative Multi-Racial Political Study, Sanchez et al. (2022) found that 64% of the American public feels that U.S. democracy is in crisis and at risk of crumbling. In a Quinnipiac University study, Sanchez found that more than half of Americans anticipate that political tensions will worsen rather than improve throughout their lifetime. Tenove, Bffie, McKay, and Moscrop (2018) suggested profound threats to fair political participation and that these threats may affect some groups disproportionately.

Vladimir Putin's administration has waged an unrelenting campaign to undermine the democratic process and the rule of law in Europe and the United States for many years. Military incursions, cyberattacks, disinformation, support for extreme political factions, the weaponization of natural resources, organized crime, and corruption are all part of the Kremlin's arsenal (Taylor, 2019). Digital communication technologies are being used to interfere in democracy and elections unprecedentedly (Anderson & Raine, 2020).

Cybersecurity risks and misinformation have become significant threats in the U.S. and globally (Anderson & Raine, 2020; Vanderwalker, 2020). Government interference in cyberspace can raise concerns about privacy, freedom of expression, and the potential for abuse of power. Government interference in cyberspace refers to actions taken by governments to regulate, control, or otherwise influence the use of the Internet and other digital technologies within their borders. This interference can take many forms, such as censorship, surveillance, and implementing laws and regulations related to online activity. Governments may engage in these activities for various reasons, including protecting national security, enforcing laws and regulations, and promoting particular political or ideological agendas. Klepper (2022) posits that political misinformation often focuses on immigration, crime, public health, geopolitics, disasters, education, or mass shootings. Klepper fund that claims about the security of mail ballots has increased, as have baseless rumors about noncitizens voting. That is in addition to claims about dead people casting ballots, moving ballot drop boxes, or wild stories about voting machines (Klepper, 2022).

Disinformation can take many forms, including false or misleading claims about candidates, voter suppression tactics, and attempts to manipulate the outcome of elections. Republican candidate Donald Trump assailed the election's validity even before he lost. He then refused to accept, disseminating falsehoods about the election that spurred the deadly attack on the U.S. Capitol on January 6, 2021. His attorney general, William Barr, denied his claim in over 60 court decisions (Klepper, 2022). The proliferation of intentionally misleading material intended to disrupt the democratic process has contributed to the erosion of public faith in the political system (Sanchez et al., 2022). President Trump reaffirmed that the deception of the 2020 election results enhanced Russian efforts and had long-lasting consequences on voter faith in election outcomes (Sanchez et al., 2022).

State and municipal election officials are concerned about electoral fraud claims, which include misleading assertions about the 2020 presidential election and this month's California recall process (Vasilogambros, 2021). The commonwealth is increasingly alleging voter fraud. Some election officials worry about verbal and physical attacks due to electoral system misinformation. This summer, the Justice Department launched a law enforcement task force to address election officials and volunteer threats (Vasilogambros, 2021).

The COVID-19 pandemic created new challenges for election officials who were forced to make emergency changes to the voting process, typically with rapidly scarce resources (Vanderwalker, 2020).

Pandemic-related voting changes were an election issue, with political actors propagating confusion concerning candidates, voting locations, and policies. The pandemic has caused significant disruptions to America's election system. It risks those other real crises, such as natural disasters, mail-in ballots, machine breakdown, and foreign interference that caused significant disruptions to the U.S. election in 2020 (Feldman, 2020).

METHODOLOGY

The method employed in this project was a content analysis review of the literature. Key search terms included: Election interference, cyber-defense, misinformation, geopolitics, mail-in voting, social media propaganda, social media manipulation, psychological operations, nation-state actors, and cyber-warfare. The databases and their hosts (shown in parentheses) included PEW Research, ABI Inform Complete (ProQuest), ResearchGate, Academia.edu, Business Source Premier (EBSCO), Google Scholar, ACM Digital Library, European Reference Index for the Humanities and Social Sciences (ERIH), Baidu Scholar, and DOAJ (Directory of Open Access Journals).

AIM OF THIS RESEARCH

Social media sites have now surpassed print newspapers as a news source for Americans; twenty percent of U.S. adults surveyed say that they often get their news via social media, as opposed to the sixteen percent who obtain their news from print newspapers (Stuart, 2019). Russia, its government Internet Research Agency, uses misleading website names to suggest its stories are coming from the U.S. rather than Russia (Stuart, 2019). This research aims to advance dialog and build literature related to 2020 election interference, misinformation campaigns, and social media manipulation through psychological operations of foreign advisories by taking a limited amount of dispersed research on the topic and combining it for future research.

CONTEXTS

Nation-state actors (i.e., Russia, Iran, China, and North Korea) circulated falsehoods to deceive certain groups from voting. Social media rapidly proliferated deceptive practices that instantly reached enormous numbers of people (Pew Research Center, 2019). Experts warned that foreign powers learned from Russia's 2016 election interference efforts and attempted to clandestinely influence the American electorate this year (Vanderwalker, 2020). State and local election officials played a crucial role in defending the 2020 presidential elections against these threats and protecting American voters from marginalization due to disinformation. Internet companies and public members also acted against deceptive practices, voter intimidation, and other digital vote suppression (Vanderwalker, 2020).

Before and during the presidential election, the Internet was under attack by hackers, thieves, and spies (Aftergood, 2017). Klimburg, director of cyber policy at the Hague Centre for Strategic Studies in the Netherlands, reported in The Darkening Web that governments that insisted on superiority were increasingly assaulting the idea of a digitized landscape as a global common. Cyberspace is a war zone in a new era of ideological combat. Members of the United States Navy Cyber Defense Operations Command monitored unauthorized network activity. Klimburg predicted that the soldiers belonged to two groups. The Free internet forces favored the unconstrained flow of information, independent of national borders or cultural barriers. The Cyber Sovereignty Camp, led by Russia and China, demanded greater government control of the Internet and information. To sustain its massive censorship operation, China's Great Firewall employed more people than served in the country's armed forces (Aftergood, 2017).

The Darkening Web barely indicated any Russian intervention in the presidential election since the Darken Web did not mention the hacking group. In 2016, the Shadow Brokers acquired stolen intelligence tools from the United States National Security Agency, the global WannaCry ransomware episode in May 2020. The new Chinese cybersecurity law vaguely aimed to regulate the cross-border data movement. The cybersecurity law provided a framework for assessing developments in this swiftly moving area.

An informed public is essential for democracy to survive. "Today and every day, the American people must make decisions on which their whole survival may depend. To make s und decisions, the people must be informed" (Brydon, 1958). Access to credible information and being well-informed is crucial for citizens to understand issues. They must rely on media when they do not have confidential sources or direct access to the news (Davies, 2009).

Trusting that the information obtained from media is credible is vital, especially when the media is the sole provider of data (Jackob, 2010). Social media usage intensifies, and so does reliance and dependence on media. A critical question is whether this dependence on media can impact the individual's perception of the credibility of the information. The issue of dependency and credibility is critical in times of change and uncertainty, such as during elections. Media use intensifies during electoral transitions of power (Loveless, 2008). This situation is compounded by the growing use of social media–platforms that lack traditional news gatekeeping and editorial functions. Shearer & Grieco (2019) found that sixty-two percent of Americans acquire news from social media platforms. Foreign actors have used these platforms to interfere with the U.S. elections in 2016 and 2020.

Social media needs more traditional gatekeepers and, as a result, needs more fact-checking and filtered content. With no g gatekeepers, there is no control over potential danger. Those dangers can include misinformation, including deliberate attempts to misinform. These election security risks can consist of foreign intervention. These interventions can generally reinforce policies and the political system or be hostile. During the 2016 U.S. Presidential election, Russian operatives known as the Internet Research Agency (IRA) spread false information through social media on issues that had already divided Americans (U.S. Senate Select Committee on Intelligence, 2018). The "information warfare campaign" on social media aimed to weaken U.S. democracy by spreading misinformation (U.S. Senate Select Committee on Intelligence, 2019).

FOUNDATIONS

Malicious cyber-attacks evolved as Internet technology, and mobile applications increased in volume and intricacy (Li et al., 2019). Consequently, society faces more significant security risks in cyberspace than ever before. Li et al. extended the published literature on Cybersecurity by theoretically defining the ethereal sphere of influence of employees' security behavior. Li et al. also developed and tested operational measures to advance information security behavior research in the workplace. A conceptual framework was proposed and tested using survey results from 579 business managers and professionals.

Structural equation modeling and analysis of variance procedures were employed to test the proposed hypotheses. The results showed that when employees were aware of their company's information security policy and practices, they were more competent in managing cybersecurity tasks than those unaware of their cybersecurity policies (Li et al., 2019). Li et al. also found that an organizational information security environment positively influenced employees' threat appraisal and coping appraisal abilities, positively contributing to their cybersecurity compliance behavior.

Boisrond (2020) described how foreign actors attempted to influence the United States Presidential 2020 election outcome. Nation-state actors (i.e., Russia, Iran, China, and North Korea) are more antagonistic, and the cybersecurity institutions nations must determine new initiatives against those threat actors. To better understand how the election environments operate, Boisrond described how the local jurisdictions are responsible for the election in America's election system. Although the federal government sets the laws and regulations, the presidential election process is the complete responsibility of each state to enforce the laws and regulations (Boisrond, 2020).

RULES AND REGULATIONS FOR THE IMPLEMENTATION AND USE OF ELECTION TECHNOLOGIES

Each state nominates a Chief State Election Official based on federal law, establishing rules and regulations for implementing and using election technologies (Boisrond, 2020). Each state has its protocols for managing or controlling its voting process. However, the COVID-19 pandemic introduced another complexity in the 2020 presidential race. Nation-state actors used the COVID-19 pandemic to ransomware (i.e., Botnet, Digital Ware, and Darknet) on several institutions throughout the world, including government agencies, financial firms, healthcare organizations, and educational institutions (Akamai Technologies, 2020; Andrews, 2018; Henriquez, 2020; Herberger, 2016; New York Times, 2019, 2020).

FEDERAL ENTITIES ROLES AND RESPONSIBILITIES

The Government Accountability Office (GAO) found that Federal entities are responsible for supporting cybersecurity efforts (U.S. Government Accountability Office, 2020a). Twenty-three federal entities developed policies, monitored critical infrastructure protection efforts, shared information to enhance Cybersecurity across the nation, responded to cyber incidents, investigated cyberattacks, and conducted cybersecurity research (U.S. Government Accountability Office, 2020a).

CYBERSECURITY CHALLENGES FACING THE NATION: A HIGH-RISK ISSUE

The Federal government must protect the nation's infrastructure, individual privacy, and sensitive data from cyber threats (U.S. Government Accountability Office, 2020b). America's infrastructure includes energy, transportation systems, communications, and financial services. Information Technology (I.T.) systems should perform operations and processes to protect essential data (U.S. Government Accountability Office, 2020b). As seen in Figure 1, federal executive branch agencies reported more than 35,000 security incidents to the Department of Homeland Security in 2017.

Figure 1. GAO analysis of U.S. computer emergency readiness team and office of management and budget data for the fiscal year 2017

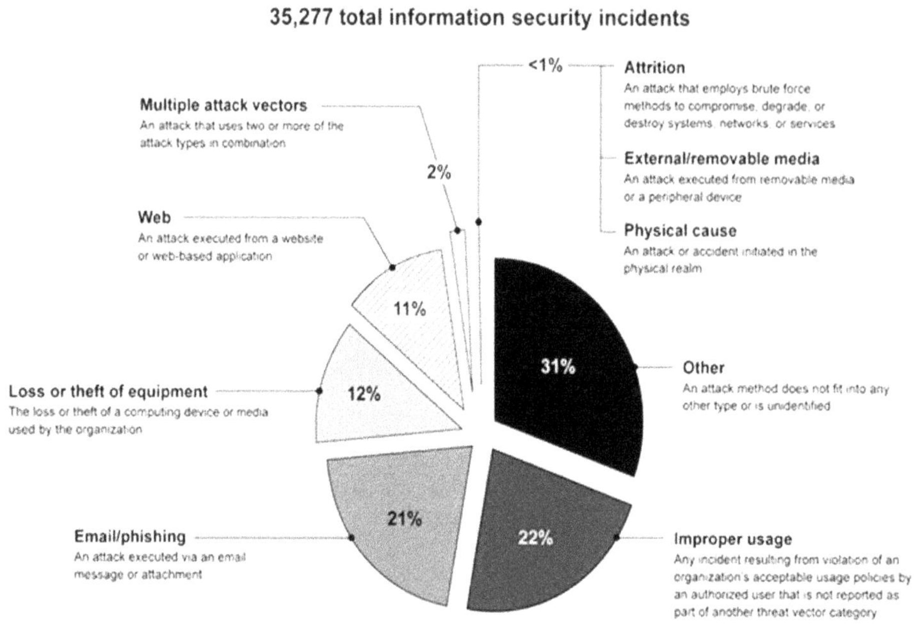

Source: GAO analysis of United States Computer Emergency Readiness Team and Office of Management and Budget data for fiscal year 2017 | GAO-18-622

Additionally, many government I.T. systems contain enormous amounts of personally identifiable information (PII). Federal agencies must protect this information's confidentiality and integrity and respond to data breaches and security incidents (U.S. Government Accountability Office, 2020b). Ten critical actions are needed to address four significant cybersecurity challenges, as depicted in Figure 2. GAO made over 3,000 recommendations to federal agencies to address cybersecurity shortcomings. GAO should have implemented approximately 700 recommendations. National.T. systems and data are increasingly susceptible to cyber threats (U.S. Government Accountability Office, 2020b).

Figure 2. Significant cybersecurity challenges and critical actions are needed

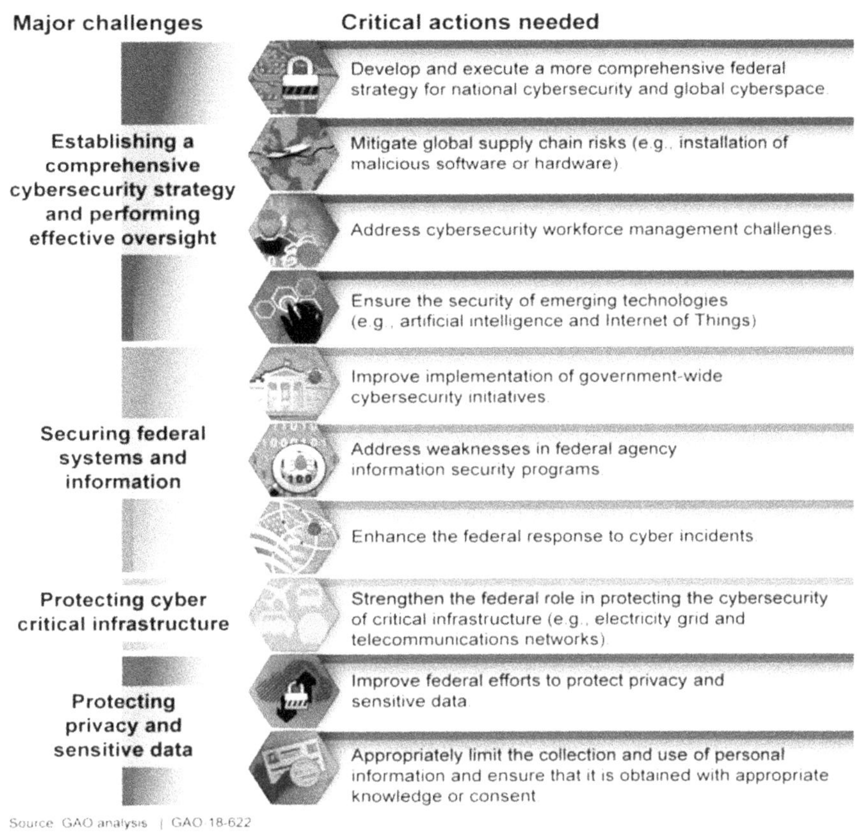

FINANCING ELECTION CAMPAIGNS

Federal agencies strengthen efforts to help secure election infrastructure, oversee accessibility of voting for individuals with disabilities, and enforce campaign finance laws (U.S. Government Accountability Office, 2020c). America's federal laws regulate election administration and voter registration and protect the voting rights of individuals with disabilities and minority groups. However, states and local election jurisdictions primarily administer federal elections (U.S. Government Accountability Office, 2020c). States regulate voting methods, periods for voting on or before Election Day, and voting equipment. Local jurisdictions, however, registered eligible voters, designed ballots, arranged for polling place locations, prepared voting equipment, and counted votes (U.S. Government Accountability Office, 2020c).

Federal law requires that states provide voter registration opportunities, such as when an individual obtains a driver's license, and provide infrastructure for online registration that requires time and money. However, federal laws generated savings to enhance accuracy by reducing the need for local election officials to manually process paper registration forms and maintain accurate voter registration lists (U.S. Government Accountability Office, 2020c).

States replaced antiquated voting equipment with up-to-date equipment to keep up with modern voting devices. Jurisdictions and states considered the equipment needs to meet federal, state, and local requirements, costs to obtain the new equipment, maintained equipment from timely vendors, and evaluated the equipment's overall performance and features (U.S. Government Accountability Office, 2020c).

Voter turnout was affected by election administration policies such as same-day registration, absentee voting, neutral polling places for voters regardless of assigned precincts, and text messages to increase voter turnout (U.S. Government Accountability Office, 2020c). The changes to increase voter turnout benefited African American voters and other ethnic groups, due to a 2014 review (U.S. Government Accountability Office, 2020c). Since 2014, numerous cyberattacks have occurred on U.S. companies (Walters, 2014).

State and local election officials secured voting machines, election infrastructure, and online voter registration with the Department of Homeland Security's CISA (U.S. Government Accountability Office, 2020c). Figure 3 shows examples of election assets subject to physical or cyber threats (U.S. Government Accountability Office, 2020c).

Figure 3. Examples of election assets are subject to physical or cyber threats
Note. The Harvard University John F. Kennedy School of Government's Better Center for Science and International Affairs and the Center for Internet Security.

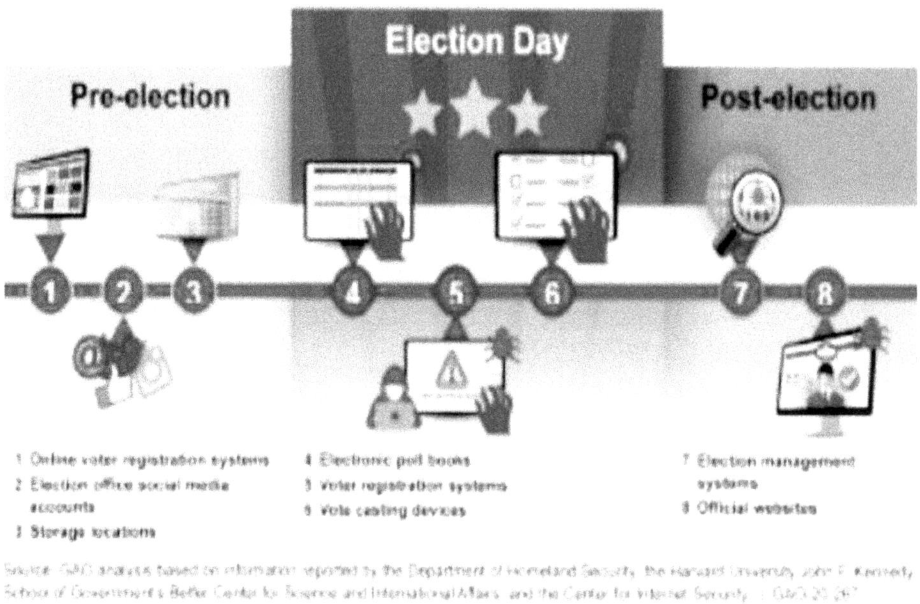

Election polling locations were accessible to voters with disabilities. According to Federal law, every polling place in every state in America was accessible to individuals with disabilities. Some regulations included parking spaces, ramps, and voting booths that accommodated wheelchairs, crutches, walkers, and canes, permitting individuals with disabilities to vote ahead of others. These accessibilities resulted from voting locations during the 2000, 2008, and 2016 general elections to help individuals with disabilities enter and move through polling places, access voting systems, and cast a private and independent vote (U.S. Government Accountability Office, 2020c).

THE 2016 PRESIDENTIAL ELECTION

In 2016, the Russian government caused a cybersecurity breach during the presidential election, so Hillary Clinton would not win the nomination (Ewing, 2020). Although election officials eventually identified the cybersecurity breach, they responded to the attacks that never stopped. The 2020 election was met with vigorous and robust practices to circumvent election fraud with tighter security measures in place with the assistance of the Federal Bureau of Investigation (FBI), CISA, and the Department of Homeland Security (Ewing, 2020).

The 2020 election could have been better, but it was the most well-planned and protected election ever, with some electronic polling booth problems in a few places. Still, county officials used paper records and ledgers as a backup to maintain voting despite electronic polling booth failures (Ewing, 2020). In the 20 6 elections, Russian actors attempted to compromise the Democratic National Convention (Meyler & Kaneko, 2020). Russia's attempt to steal passwords was a growing concern about the replay of the 2016 election interference (Andrews, 2018).

Russian cybercriminals focused on division in the United States as the preferred tactic in 2020. While this tactic was part of Russian strategies in 2016, political divisions have surpassed those of 2016 (Meyler & Kaneko, 2020). Trolls are people who deceive people into believing in the information that is not true. Disinformation campaigns attempt to establish truthfulness by creating blogs, news stories, social media accounts, and groups that unsuspecting users might lean toward (Meyler & Kaneko, 2020).

FOREIGN THREATS TO THE 2020 U.S. PRESIDENTIAL ELECTION

Russian actors also used cognitive hacking for propaganda effects. Cognitive hacking is a strategic cyberattack to manipulate people's perceptions by exploiting their psychological vulnerabilities. The attack aims to change users' behavior by exposing them to misinformation (Rouse, 2017). Cognitive hacking differs from cybersecurity because cybersecurity focuses on security vulnerabilities of technical features like intellectual property theft. Waltzman stated two "examples of cognitive hacking" (1) "the unprecedented speed and extent of disinformation distribution" and (2) "the intended audience's cognitive vulnerability—a premise that the audience is already predisposed to accept [misinformation] because it appeals to existing fears or anxieties" (Waltzman, 2017, p. 3)

An Internet "troll" is a person who posts deceptive messages online to incite a response from social media users. Users were not the only ones spreading information; according to the Badawy et al. study (2019), out of the 40 thousand users who spread information, 34 thousand were bots. Fifty-six percent of Americans have not heard much about social media bots (Stocking & Sumida, 2018). Social media bots are algorithmically controlled accounts that operate independently by emulating real users' activity. The bots host information and interact with social media users; nevertheless, users can aid bots by tweeting, resharing, and interacting with them. Through algorithms, bots operate faster than human users (Bessi & Ferrara, 2016). Bessi and Ferrara's findings suggest that social media bots' presence can negatively affect democratic political discussion (Bessi & Ferrara, 2016).

One mechanism to spread this fabricated information was the troll farm. A troll f rm is a systematized operation that consists of multiple users who work together on social media platforms by generating misinformation and disinformation to affect public opinion (U. S House of Representatives Permanent Select Committee on Intelligence, 2019). The Internet Research Agency (IRA), a Russian troll farm in

St. Petersburg, Russia, in 2015, had around 400 employees working 12-hour shifts filling 40 rooms (U. S House of Representatives Permanent Select Committee on Intelligence, 2018).

Digital Shadows, the leader in external threat intelligence, revealed research findings that there were currently 550 fake domains set up against the 19 Democrats and four Republican presidential candidates and Republican Party funding sites (Henriquez, 2020). Digital shadows explored counterfeit Internet domains registered that could increase confusion and spread misinformation among American voters. Digital shadows released its latest research examining foreign threats to the 2020 U.S. presidential election. After compromised elements of the 2016 Election, connected to malevolent actors linked to the Russian state, Digital Shadows uncovered further evidence of similar efforts in 2020 (Henriquez, 2020).

ELECTION ACTIVITIES ACROSS THE ELECTORAL CYCLE

A view of the International Institute's election cycle for responding to challenges discovered during electoral processes and encompassing international best practices (Brown, Marsden, Lee, & Veal, 2020). Some activities within this cycle were vulnerable to cybersecurity threats before, during, and after voting (see Table 1).

Table 1. Aspects of the electoral cycle are vulnerable to cybersecurity risks

Categories	Pre-Polling	Polling	Post-Polling
Planning and logistics: training and education	Boundary delimitation. Polling station placement. Recruitment of polling station staff. Candidate/party/registration/education. Procurement.	Disseminating logistical information. Disseminating electoral materials.	Retrieving results and electoral materials. Analyzing delays and other issues in specific polling locations. Preparing election teams for the future.
Electoral rolls and registration	Compiling rolls. Checking for ineligibility or duplication. Adding/verifying voters. Setting dates for final pre-election registration. Coordinating with local authorities where necessary.	Verification of voters. Electronic voter roll systems. Providing unverified voters with appeal mechanisms/process information.	Domestic and overseas turnout calculation. Assessment of issues in vulnerable communities based on surveys (e.g., disabled, minority, indigenous, rural groups. Response to individual voter concerns and complaints.
Campaign regulation	Enforcement of campaigning rules online. Oversight of electoral rolls provided to candidates and parties. Monitoring for fake electoral information.	Monitoring inappropriate restrictions of information such as Internet switch off. Monitoring and reporting of electoral incidents at polling stations.	Reporting of all electoral competencies, such as campaign spending
Vote counting, verification, and reporting	Postal vote tallies, summary data, and verification. Registration of proxy voters or special arrangements. Standards for results feed to media and individuals.	Ensuring secure voting machines and infrastructure. Ensuring functional verification. Tabulation and transmission. Ensuring the integrity of backup procedures.	Investigation of electoral abnormalities. Maintaining secrecy of ballots such as Internet voting. Securely aggregating votes by district. Using results for future planning.
Audit and challenge, legal reform, and best practice adoption	Citizen/candidate facing verification of registration	Compromise of observers, monitoring, and observation systems. Counteracting disinformation about logistics.	Case management system for electoral irregularities. The electoral court, recall of candidates.

Source: Brown et al. (2020)

FOREIGN CYBER THREATS TO THE 2020 U.S. PRESIDENTIAL ELECTION

Like the 2016 presidential election, Russia or some other foreign actors' attempt to sabotage the 2020 election met strong, vigorous, and robust force from the United States due to preparedness. Notwithstanding the advent of the COVID-19 pandemic, foreign actors undermined the American election process in 2020, as they did in 2016 (Meyler & Kaneko, 2020). With the election surpassed on November 3, 2020, undermining the American democracy emerged from different corners of the world, and intelligence officials warned there could be more in the future (Meyler & Kaneko, 2020). Intelligence officials warned that foreign actors' attacks favored the presidential candidate who could better serve their national interests or foreign policy. Threat actors attempted to further their agenda by conducting cyberattacks, and while not all attempts were successful, they demonstrated the intent to disrupt and influence the election (Meyler & Kaneko, 2020).

Misinformation includes all wrong information attributed to errors, rumors, and false and misleading information that causes confusion and fear (Meyler & Kaneko, 2020). Organized crime groups, traditional media, reporters, bots, hack and leak operations, and foreign government agencies cause misinformation leaks. In contrast to misinformation, disinformation campaigns orchestrated operations without rules and boundaries to subvert American democracy (Meyler & Kaneko, 2020).

DIGITAL INTERFERENCE IN ELECTIONS

Foreign actors use digital interference in presidential elections that breach and violate campaign laws and voting systems and create a sense of mistrust and fear among women and minority voters (Tenove et al., 2018). Before 20 6, digital interference in elections was recognized as a severe problem. However, recently, more severe attention focused on digital interference from foreign actors. As a result, Tenove et al. concluded a need for significant research findings on short-term or long-term damage from digital techniques. Also, little clarity on the policy measures those democratic countries should take to address digital threats to elections effectively. Research and policy experimentation is much needed (Tenove et al., 2018).

AMERICAN OPERATIVES ON THE OFFENSE TO PROTECT THE ELECTION

Before November 3, 2020, American operatives went on the offense. Under the Defense Department, the cyber-troopers of U.S. Cyber Command could investigate by identifying targets within the United States (Ewing, 2020). Before election day, officials in the Defense Department identified Russian, Iranian, and other foreign actors' practices and knew the type of malware used (Ewing, 2020). Election workers checked the voting machines' tapes to verify correct voter signatures from polling stations after the polls closed on November 3, 2020, in Detroit, Michigan. When American election officials discovered a possible breach from Iranian intimidation attacks, the time frame was over a day, exactly 27 hours. Whether voters cast ballots in person or by mail, the chances of fraud with an individual's vote were improbable (Ng, 2020).

ELECTION DAY, NOVEMBER 3, 2020

On November 3, 2020, early voters numbered over 150 million as one of the most significant voters in any presidential election. Voters cast ballots that were counted repeatedly (Ewing, 2020). As 150 million Americans headed to the polls for the U.S. Presidential Election, security officials worked 24/7 to ensure that cyberattacks, disinformation, and misinformation campaigns did not interfere with citizens' votes and right to vote. Russia, Iran, and China hackers launched attacks to influence the election (Ng, 2020). Voters cast ballots in person, absentee ballots, and by mail; however, there were unlikely occurrences of fraud. Mail-in votes were discounted as fraud, as claimed by the Trump administration.

Moreover, Trump found no evidence supporting the charge of mail-in voting fraud (Ng, 2020). Election officials protected American voters' votes and disinformation from Iran and Russia's attempt to keep people from voting (Ng, 2020). Foreign actors made several attempts to disrupt the election in a logistically complicated election. Federal authorities were cautiously optimistic about having made it through voting without significant disruption by cyberattacks or other destructive activity. However, sources cautioned that it could still happen in the coming days (Ewing, 2020). As evidence, United States officials were declarative about the large turnout recorded nationwide, as evidence of the agency leaders and how confident Americans were in securing their votes and the election's validity (Ewing, 2020).

On November 3, 2020, early voters numbered over 150 million, one of the largest in any presidential election (Ewing, 2020). Voters cast ballots, and election officials repeatedly counted votes. Foreign a actors made several attempts to disrupt the election in a logistically complicated election (Ewing, 2020). As evidence, United States officials were declarative about the colossal turnout recorded across the nation, as evidence of the agency leaders and how confident Americans were in securing their votes and the election's validity (Ewing, 2020).

On November 17, 2020, Chris Krebs, head of CISA, was terminated by President Trump because he said that the election was secure and well done and refused to shut down the election fraud claim. As Trump claimed, Krebs reported no evidence of voter fraud in Michigan (Ng, 2020). Krebs pushed early on Russia to avoid interference, refuting baseless voter fraud claims, and Trump fired Krebs because he found no fraud during the presidential election (Ng, 2020).

The members of Election Infrastructure Government Coordinating Council (GCC) Executive Committee – Cybersecurity and Infrastructure Security Agency (CISA) Assistant Director Bob Kolasky, U.S. Election Assistance Commission Chair Benjamin Hovland, National Association of Secretaries of State (NASS) President Maggie Toulouse Oliver, National Association of State Election Directors (NASED) President Lori Augino, and Escambia County (Florida) Supervisor of Elections David Stafford, and the members of the Election Infrastructure Sector Coordinating Council (SCC), Chair Brian Hancock (Unisyn Voting Solutions), Vice-Chair Sam Derheimer (Hart InterCivic), Chris Wlaschin (Election Systems & Software), Ericka Haas (Electronic Registration Information Center), and Maria Bianchi (Democracy Works) released the following statement:

The November 3rd election was the most secure in American history. Electoral officials reviewed and double-checked the entire election process across the country before finalizing the result. When states have close elections, many will recount ballots. All conditions with immediate results in the 2020 presidential race have paper records of each vote, allowing them to go back and count each franchise, if necessary, which was an added benefit for security and resilience. This process allows for the identification and correction of any mistakes or errors. There is evidence that any voting system deleted or lost votes, changed votes, or was compromised. Other security measures like pre-election testing, state certification of voting equipment, and the U.S. Election Assistance Commission's (EAC) certification of voting equipment help build additional confidence in the voting systems used in 2020. Simultaneously, there are many unfounded claims and opportunities for misinformation about the elections process, most assuredly the utmost confidence in the security and integrity of elections. When you have questions, turn to elections officials as trusted voices as they administer elections. (Cybersecurity and Infrastructure Security Agency, 2020, p. 1)

ELECTORAL VOTES DETERMINED WHO WON THE PRESIDENTIAL ELECTION

Among the States based on the Census on allocated electoral votes. Every state gave several ballots equal to the number of senators and representatives in its U.S. Congressional delegation—two options for its senators in the U.S. Senate plus many votes similar to its number of Congressional districts (Chowdhury, 2020). The Electoral College consists of 538 electors. A majority of 270 electoral votes is required to elect the President. The state has the same electors as its members in its Congressional delegation: one for each member of the House of Representatives plus two Senators. As of December 2020, states voted for a popular vote adopted by 15 states and Columbia. These states have 196 electoral votes, 36% of the Electoral College, and 73% of the 270 votes needed to give the compact legal force (Chowdhury, 2020). President-elect Joe Biden spoke after the Electoral College affirmed his election win, saying, "The will of the people prevailed. Once again, the rule of law, our Constitution, and the people's will prevailed in America. Our democracy pushed, tested, threatened, proved resilient, true, and strong." Biden noted that he and Vice President-elect Kamala Harris received more votes than any ticket in America's history (Chowdhury, 2020).

CERTIFICATION OF ELECTORAL COLLEGE RESULTS

According to CNN's tally in Honolulu, Hawaii, all 50 states and the District of Columbia have certified their presidential results as the Electoral College process moves forward with electors' meetings (Stark & Cohen, 2020). West Virginia was one of the final states to certify its presidential election results, formally declaring that President Donald Trump was entitled to the state's five electoral votes (Montellaro, 2020). In Honolulu, Hawaii's electors cast four votes for President-elect Joe Biden during their meeting. Hawaii was the last state to cast its electoral votes, concluding the esoteric process in the United States Constitution. The final Electoral College results were 306 for Biden and 232 for Trump. Biden defeated Trump in Hawaii, about 64% to 34% (Cohen & Cohen, 2020).

To win the election, the presidential candidate needed 270 electoral votes of the 538 available to become President (Stark & Cohen, 2020). The state's certifications came as Trump, without evidence, claimed that the election was "rigged" and spread doubt about the presidential race's outcome. Barr disputed Trump and said there was no widespread election fraud (Balsamo, 2020). Numerous lawsuits challenged the election, and the courts dismissed the results at the state and federal levels nationwide since November 3, 2020, election (Stark & Cohen, 2020). The judge rejected the Trump campaign lawsuit seeking to block states' election results because there was no evidence that the election was affected by fraud (Snyder, 2020).

Each state has different certifying results, and some states certified their slate of presidential electors separately from state and local election results. The next major step in the Electoral College process was the electors' meeting, required by law to convene on the first Monday after the second Wednesday in December, December 14, 2020. The electors' votes were later transmitted to officials and counted in Congress's joint session on January 6, 2021 (Stark & Cohen, 2020).

Some states' laws sought to bind their electors to the winning candidate and, in some instances, stipulate that faithless electors may be subject to penalties or replaced by another elector. The Supreme Court ruled that laws punishing the Electoral College members for breaking a pledge to vote for the state's popular vote winner were conditional (Stark & Cohen, 2020).

CONCLUSION

Imagine a campaign for the presidency of the United States in 2020 in which Russia, Saudi Arabia, and North Korea engage in activities designed to help re-elect Donald Trump while China, Iran, and other countries work to bring him down. The United States of America may wake up the day after the election without knowing whether or not they were influenced to vote a certain way by either direct or indirect foreign activity. Considering that something like that might occur should make all Americans uneasy (West, 2019).

The most widely disseminated false information frequently causes readers to feel anger or fear, which prompts them to share the information before they have had a chance to investigate the underlying claim (Klepper, 2022). Before the election in 2020, advertisements on Facebook written in Spanish made the false claim that Biden, a Democrat, was a communist (Klepper, 2022). On other online forums, users cautioned Latinos living in the United States to abstain from the electoral process altogether. The issue is deeper and more systemic than social media (Klepper, 2022). Recently, there has been an increase in the number of false claims communicated via text and email (Klepper, 2022).

Theories of fraud surrounding the use of mail-in ballots. Anonymous text messages advising voters to abstain from casting their ballots—platforms on the margins of social media where false information about elections is freely disseminated. State and local election officials are concerned about the future as a result of the lies that have been spread about election fraud. These lies range from false claims about who will win the presidential race in 2020 to accusations about who will win the midterm elections in 2022. (Vasilogambros, 2021).

Although it is beneficial to make an effort to educate voters by holding community events and maintaining active social media accounts, a sizeable portion of the electorate will not listen to election officials (Vasilogambros, 2021). The issue is not one of voter fraud and extends further than what can be explained by what a candidate says. There are ripple effects caused by the effects of people living in separate silos, different worlds, and different facts for years and years (Vasilogambros, 2021).

As a result of the desire of many nations, including the United States, to streamline the voting process, balloting systems are increasingly focused on voter convenience at the expense of election integrity (West, 2019). At the same time, companies specializing in information technology have developed social media platforms that can be easily manipulated by spreading misinformation, fabricated news, and fabricated videos (West, 2019). The proliferation of internet applications and other digital communications has made interference efforts more affordable and difficult to detect. This is because there are now multiple low-cost avenues through which large numbers of people can be directly reached and influenced (West,

2019). False information is spread organically on Facebook through users' shared posts and commercially through advertisements. Twitter is highly susceptible to the spread of false information because user accounts are not verified, and it is simple to create and disseminate false content (West, 2019). In addition, using this technology to sabotage campaigns is inexpensive and difficult to track (West, 2019).

Officials in charge of elections require assistance in combating misleading information and ensuring the safety of voters' ballots (Vasilogambros, 2021). The vast majority of voters' misconceptions about the voting process can be cleared up by inviting them into the office and demonstrating how the vote tallying process works and the various security measures the county has in place (Vasilogambros, 2021).

It is recommended that counties set up advisory committees so that voters can provide input on issues relating to voter education and outreach, as well as accessibility and language assistance. To ensure that voting results are accurate, state law requires a manual audit of one percent of ballots (Vasilogambros, 2021). New voting machines that use paper ballots and are not connected to the Internet are one example of an innovative approach. Officials verify the machines' reliability before and after elections (Vasilogambros, 2021). Because every ballot is scanned digitally, candidates in particularly close races can go back and verify the results by looking at individual ballots. These are the means that can be used to verify that the systems in question are accurate and do not contain any fraudulent activity (Vasilogambros, 2021).

A ballot marking device is a voting machine that is less common than other types. With these machines, voters select their options on a screen. Instead of storing the selections electronically, the machine prints them out on a paper ballot, which can then be counted by hand or scanned into a computer (Gambhir & Karsten, 2019).

Direct-recording electronic (DRE) machines are the only widely utilized machines that do not require the use of paper as an essential component of their design (Gambhir & Karsten, 2019). When utilizing DREs, voters select their preferences onscreen, and the information is then transmitted directly into the voting machine's memory. However, R.E.s can record voters' selections onto paper, but many still need to (Gambhir & Karsten, 2019). These DRE, which dispense entirely with paper ballots, are among the most vulnerable aspects of the election infrastructure in the United States (Gambhir & Karsten, 2019).

As the government (U.S. House of Representatives Permanent Select Committee on Intelligence, 2018) already found, Russia used Facebook in the 2016 election to spread false information to influence the U.S. election. In September 2019, Facebook announced a corporate policy change, which included a new authorization process for running ads about social issues, elections, or politics (Romm, 2019). Changes in laws and corporate policies may impact future interference attempts and their perception. With the growth and spread of technology, the potential for interference can also grow.

One of the primary challenges in the fight against it is locating and combating misinformation, particularly when it is spread via social media platforms. This is one of the main obstacles (Vasilogambros, 2021). It may be challenging to determine the reasons behind its distribution because it could be spread to gain political power or financial gain, or it could be spread to create disorder and confusion (West, 2019). People need to be more skeptical of the information they find online and check to make sure it is accurate before they spread it if they want to solve the problem of misinformation. It is also highly essential for social media platforms and other online platforms to take measures to prevent the spread of misinformation. These measures include providing users with tools to report false information and collaborating with fact-checking organizations to identify and remove inaccurate content. Legislation or other regulatory actions could be necessary for governments to take in order to combat the spread of misinformation. These actions would involve the promotion of fact-checking, media literacy, and responsible reporting practices (West, 2019).

Taylor (2019) claims that foreign interference in Swedish elections aims to lower public confidence in the electoral process and divide Swedes on the most critical social and political issues. Sweden has invested significant resources into developing an all-encompassing strategy to combat foreign interference in their democracy. Their efforts have, for the most part, been successful (Taylor, 2019). Sweden developed a comprehensive strategy based on a clear understanding of the threat, learned lessons from other targeted elections (including the United States), and developed a whole-of-society defense strategy that includes its media and citizens. This strategy successfully protected Sweden's elections (Taylor, 2019).

Sweden uses a collaborative national platform to plan, prepare, and protect elections. The forum of choice is a high-level interagency coordination forum (Taylor, 2019). Workers in local elections were given the training to recognize and combat this kind of influence. The most prominent media outlets joined forces to combat fake news (Taylor, 2019). In the run-up to the election, a group of college journalism students, international journalists, and fact-checkers tracked sources of disinformation. It published a daily newsletter sent to news organizations (Taylor, 2019). To help citizens become more resistant to the misinformation, propaganda, and hate speech found online, efforts to improve media literacy initially aimed at school children have been expanded to include the general population (Taylor, 2019). Literacy on the use of digital technologies is, in fact, a component of Sweden's National Strategy for a robust democracy (Taylor, 2019).

RECOMMENDATIONS FOR FUTURE RESEARCH

More research is needed to specify the downstream effects of digital interference (Tenove et al., 2018). Whether foreign actors using digital techniques have flipped elections (Merritt, 2020). However, there is clear evidence that digital strategies can undermine participation and do so in ways that may significantly affect groups that already struggle for equal political participation (Tenove et al., 2018). As a result, Tenove et al. concluded a need for robust research findings on short-term or long-term damage from digital techniques. Also, little clarity on the policy measures those democratic countries should address digital threats to elections effectively. Research and policy experimentation is much needed (Tenove et al., 2018). Future research can examine the impact of changing technologies, explore the effectiveness of various safeguards to prevent unwanted interference, and inform and educate people about the forms and potential for misuse.

CONFLICT OF INTEREST STATEMENT

This article/paper does not represent the views of a specific university, the U.S. Government, the Department of State, or any other U.S. Government agency. The views and work presented within this item strictly represent the authors' academic work.

REFERENCES

Aftergood, S. (2017). Cybersecurity: The cold war online. *Nature, 57*, 30–31. https://doi.org/10.1038/547030a

Akamai Technologies. (2020). *W at is a botnet attack?* https://www.akamai.com/us/en/resources/what-is-a-botnet.jsp

Anderson, A., & Raine, L. (2020). *Concerns about democracy in the digital age*. Pew Research. https://www.pewresearch.org/internet/2020/02/21/concerns-about-democracy-in-the-digital-age/

Andrews, N. (2018). McCaskill says Senate Office was target of phishing scam. *Wall Street Journal*. https://www.wsj.com/articles/mccaskill-says-senate-office-was-target-of-phishing-scam1532656049

Badawy, A., Addawood, A., Lerman, K., & Ferrara, E. (2019). Characterizing the 2016 Russian IRA influence campaign. *Social Network Analysis and Mining, 9*(1), 31. https://doi.org/10.1007/s13278-019-0578-6

Balsamo, M. (2020). Disputing Trump: Barr says no widespread election fraud. *Associate Press News*. https://apnews.com/article/barr-no-widespread-election-fraud-b1f1488796c9a98c4b1a9061a6c7f49d

Bessi, A., & Ferrara, E. (2016). Social bots distort the 2016 U.S. Presidential election online discussion. *First Monday*. https://doi.org/10.5210/fm.v21i11.7090

Boisrond, P. D. (2020). *Cybersecurity and the 2020 United States presidential elections: Beware of nation-state actors*. Research state. https://www.researchgate.net/publication/344135067_Cybersecurity_and_the_2020_United_States_Presidential_Election_Beware _of_Nation-State_Actors

BrownI.MarsdenC. T.LeeJ.VealeM. (2020). *Cybersecurity for elections: A commonwealth guide on best practice*. doi:10.31228/osf.io/tsdfb

Brydon, L. (1958). *The Press and the People (No. 2). In Washington and the Press*. WGBH-TV. https://openvault.wgbh.org/catalog/V_F3669EDCE0044D9C97FD3661EF031D9 5

Chowdhury, M. (2020). Biden praises local and state officials who showed unwavering faith in the law. *CNN*. https://www.cnn.com/politics/live-news/electoral-college-vote-2020-biden-trump/index.html

CNN. (2021, Oct 13). *2016 Presidential Campaign Hacking Fast Facts*. Retrieved from: https://www.cnn.com/2016/12/26/us/2016-presidential-campaign-hacking-fast-facts

Cohen, E., & Cohen, M. (2020). Hawaii casts its 4 electoral votes for Biden, concluding Electoral College process. *CNN*. https://www.cnn.com/politics/live-news/electoral-college-vote-2020-biden-trump/index.html

Cybersecurity and Infrastructure Security Agency. (2020). *Jint statement from elections infrastructure government coordinating council and the election infrastructure sector coordinating executive committees*. https://ww.cisa.gov/news/2020/11/12/joint-statement-elections-infrastructure-government-coordinating-council-election

Davies, J. (2009). The effect of media dependency on voting decisions. *Journal of Media Sociology, 1*(3/4), 160–181.

Ewing, E. (2020). *The 2020 election was attacked, but not severely disrupted. Here's how*. https://www.npr.org/2020/11/04/931090626/the-2020-election-was-attacked-but-not-severely-disrupted-heres-how

Feldman, M. (2020). *Dirty tricks: 9 falsehoods that could undermine the 2020 election*. https://www.brennancenter.org/our-work/research-reports/dirty-tricks-9-falsehoods-could-undermine-2020-election

Gambhir, R., & Karsten, J. (2019, August 14). *Why paper is considered state-of-the-art voting technology*. Brookings. Retrieved from: https://www.brookings.edu/blog/techtank/2019/08/14/why-paper-is-considered-state-of-the-art-voting-technology/

Henriquez, M. (2020). *Domestic and foreign cybersecurity threats surrounding the 2020 election*. https://www.securitymagazine.com/articles/93744-domestic-and-foreign-threats-surrounding-the-2020-election

Herberger, C. (2016). *The 3 biggest cybersecurity risks posed in the 2016 presidential election*. https://www.helpnetsecurity.com/2016/05/17/cybersecurity-presidential-election/

Jackob, N. G. E. (2010). The relationship between perceived media dependency, use of alternative information sources, and general trust in mass media. *International Journal of Communication*, *4*, 18.

Klepper, D. (2022, November 3). *Misinformation and the midterm elections: What to expect*. AP News. https://apnews.com/article/2022-midterm-elections-misinformation-219762637bacf49bf7ec723546b46fb3

Li, L., He, W., Xu, L., Ash, I., Anwar, M., & Yuan, X. (2019). Investigating the impact of cybersecurity policy awareness on employees' cybersecurity behavior. *International Journal of Information Management, 45*, 13–24. https://doi.org/10.1016/j.ijinfomgt.2018.10.017

Loveless, M. (2008). Media dependency: Mass media as sources of information in the democratizing countries of central and eastern Europe. *Democratization, 15*(1), 162–183. https://doi.org/10.1080/13510340701770030

Merritt, A. (2020). *Foreign cyber threats to the 2020 U.S. presidential election*. https://www.digitalshadows.com/blog-and-research/foreign-cyber-threats-to-the-2020-us-presidential-election/

Meyler, J., & Kaneko, J. (2020). *Netenrich introduces a threat and attack surface intelligence solution for faster detection, insight, and response to immediate threats*. https://netenrich.com/newsroom/netenrich-introduces-a-threat-and-attack-surface-intelligence-solution-for-faster-detection-insight-and-response-to-immediate-threats/

Montellaro, Z. (2020). *What you need to know about when states finalize their election results*. https://www.politico.com/news/2020/11/11/swing-states-recounts-certify-election-results-435889

New York Times. (2019). *Iranian hackers target Trump campaign as threats to 2020 mount*. https://www.nytimes.com/2019/10/04/technology/iranian-campaign-hackers microsoft.html

Ng, A. (2020). A primer on how hackers are targeting the election and what officials are doing to protect it. *CNET Dail News*. https://www.cnet.com/news/election-2020-your-cybersecurity-questions-answered/

Perlroth, N., Scott, M., & Frenkel, S. (2017). *Cyberattack hits Ukraine and then spreads internationally*. https://www.nytimes.com/2017/06/27/technology/ransomware-hackers.html

Pew Research Center. (2019). *Social Media Fact Sheet*. https://www.pewresearch.org/internet/fact-sheet/social-media/

Romm, T. (2019, August 28). Facebook to require buyers of political ads to provide more information about who paid for them. *The Washington Post*. https://www.washingtonpost.com/technology/2019/08/28/facebook-requirepolitical-campaigns-say-who-paid-their-ads-new-transparency-push/

Rouse, M. (2017). *Tech target. Cognitive Hacking*. https://watis.techtarget.com/definition/cognitive-hacking

Sanchez, G. R., Middlemass, K., & Rodriguez, A. (2022, July 26). *Misinformation is eroding the public's confidence in democracy*. Brookings https://www.brookings.edu/blog/fixgov/2022/07/26/misinformation-is-eroding-the-publics-confidence-in-democracy/

Shearer, E., & Greico, E. (2019). *Americans Are Wary of the Role Social Media Sites Play in Delivering the News*. Pew Research Center.

Snyder, R. (2020). Judge rejects Trump campaign lawsuit seeking to block states election results, says no evidence election was affected by fraud. *The Nevada Independent*. https://tenevadaindependent.com/article/judge-rejects-trump-campaign-lawsuit-seeking-to-block-states-presidential-election-results

Stark, L., & Cohen, E. (2020). *All 50 states and D.C. have now certified their presidential election results*. Cable New Network.

Stocking, G., & Sumida, N. (2018). *Social Media Bots Draw Public's Attention and Concern*. Pew Research.

Stuart, A. H. (2019). Social Media, Manipulation, and Violence. *South Carolina Journal of International Law and Business, 15*(2).

Taylor, M. L. (2022, March 8). *Combating disinformation and foreign interference in democracies: Lessons from Europe*. Brookings. https://ww.brookings.edu/blog/techtank/2019/07/31/combating-disinformation-and-foreign-interference-in-democracies-lesso ns-from-europe/

TenoveC.BuffieJ.McKayS.MoscropD. (2018). *Digital threats to democratic elections: How foreign actors use digital techniques to undermine democracy*. Center for the Study of Democratic Institutions, The University of British Columbia. doi:10.2139/ssrn.3235819

The United States Senate Republican Policy Committee. (2021, October 5). *Social media and mental health*. Senate Republican Policy Committee. https://ww.rpc.senate.gov/policy-papers/social-media-and-men tal-health

U.S. Government Accountability Office. (2020a). *Clarity on leadership urgently needed to implement the national strategy* fully. https://ww.gao.gov/assets/710/709555.pdf

U.S. Government Accountability Office. (2020b). *Ensuring the security of federal information systems*. https://www.gao.gov/key_issues/ensuring_security_federal_inf ormation_systems/issue_summary

U.S. Government Accountability Office. (2020c). *Elections and cyber security*. https://www.gao.gov/key_issues/elections_campaign_finance/is sue_summary

U.S. House of Representatives Permanent Select Committee on Intelligence. (2018). *E posing Russia's effort to sow discord online: The Internet Research Agency and advertisements*. https://intelligence.house.gov/social-media-content/

U.S. Senate Select Committee on Intelligence. (2019). *Russian Active Measures Campaigns and Interference in the 2016 U.S. Election Volume 2: Russia's use of social media with additional views*. Author.

Vandewalker, I. (2020). *Digital disinformation and vote suppression*. Brennan Center. https://www.brennancenter.org/our-work/research-reports/digital-disinf ormation-and-vote-suppression

Vasilogambros, M. (2021, September 21). *Disinformation may be the new normal, election officials fear.* The Pew Charitable Trusts. https://ww.pewtrusts.org/en/research-and-analysis/blogs/stat eline/2021/09/21/disinformation-may-be-the-new-normal-electi on-officials-fear

Walters, R. (2014). *Cyber-attacks on U.S. companies since November 2014*. http://ww.heritage.org/cybersecurity/report/cyber-attacks-us -companies-november-2014

Waltzman, R. (2017). *The weaponizing of information*. Senate Armed Services Committee. RAND Corporation. https://www.armedservices.senate.gov/imo/media/doc/Waltzman_ 04-27-17.pdf

West, D. (2019, August 9). *Foreign campaign intervention may go way beyond Russia to China, Iran, North Korea, and Saudi Arabia*. Brookings. Retrieved from: https://www.brookings.edu/blog/fixgov/2019/08/09/foreign-campaign-intervention-may-go-way-beyond-russia-to-china-iran-north-korea-and-saudi-arabia/

Chapter 12
A Human-Centric Cybersecurity Framework for Ensuring Cybersecurity Readiness in Universities

Blessing Gavaza
Africa University, Zimbabwe

Agripah Kandiero
https://orcid.org/0000-0001-8201-864X
Africa University, Zimbabwe

Chipo Katsande
Manicaland State University of Applied Sciences, Zimbabwe

ABSTRACT

The escalating number of cyberattacks on universities worldwide resulted in universities losing valuable information assets leading to disruption of operations and loss of reputation. The research sought to explore a framework for human-factor vulnerabilities related to cybersecurity knowledge and skills, which enabled cybercriminals to manipulate human elements into inadvertently conveying access to critical information assets through social engineering attacks. Descriptive and inferential statistics were used to test the data, and Pearson's correlation statistics were used to measure the statistical relationships and association of variables. The results revealed that students and staff are vulnerable to social engineering attacks and their ability to protect themselves and other information assets is limited mainly due to poor cybersecurity knowledge and skills resulting from poor cybersecurity awareness and education.

DOI: 10.4018/978-1-6684-9018-1.ch012

INTRODUCTION

For all organisations that are committed to the fourth industrial revolution paradigm, Cybersecurity risks pose a complex challenge. (Lezzi, Lazoi, & Corallo, 2018). It is therefore important for Universities and academic institutions around the world to be diligent against these cyber-risks as they have been lucrative victims of cyber-attacks in recent years with several high-profile incidents. Cybercriminals can manipulate unaware humans by exploiting human factored vulnerabilities and involving them to contribute to such offenses.

Universities manage large amounts of valuable research and sensitive personal data, financial information and manage infrastructure resources such as servers, bandwidth capacity, and hosting making up a rich network of critical information assets (Ulven & Wangen, 2021) making universities an attractive target for cybercriminals, espionage, and hacktivists. These critical assets are available to both students and staff to facilitate teaching, learning, and administrative work. The free flow of the workforce and annual rotations of new students, employees, and guests creates security challenges in protecting the information assets and their different users whilst balancing these security measures with the academic openness and free flow of information that universities are trying to promote.

These cybercrime statistics and examples of cyber-attacks on universities around the world are the basis for this research and the development of a human-centric cybersecurity framework to deter potential cybercriminals from successfully attacking universities by exploiting the human vulnerabilities of students and staff. Cybersecurity frameworks help minimise the danger of harmful cyberattacks on applications, computers, and infrastructure, cybersecurity protects computer networks and the information they contain from intrusion and malicious harm or interruption (Craigen, Diakun-thibault, & Purse, 2014).

However, this research also adds humans as an asset that also needs to be protected from intruders with malicious intent. This research proposes a human-centric cybersecurity framework which is a collection of the necessary knowledge and skills required to create a capable workforce that can provide security safeguards, and develop, implement and enforce policies, standard operating procedures, tools, technologies and guidelines for best practices.

BACKGROUND TO THE STUDY

In Zimbabwe, the Cyber-Security and Data Protection Act [Chapter 11:22] draft specifies in Clause 5 that the Postal and Telecommunications Regulatory Authority of Zimbabwe (POTRAZ) is designated as the Cyber Security Centre in Zimbabwe (Channon, 2019) and one of several functions of the Cyber Security Centre which this study is focusing on is providing guidelines to public and private sector interested parties on matters relating to awareness, training, enhancement, investigation, prosecution and combating cybercrime, and managing cyber security threats.

As a result, there is a demand for well-trained cybersecurity workers, and these specialists are developed in universities. Universities must invest in establishing cyber security expertise, which may be assessed by the number of initiatives, training and certification programs, and certified professionals of teams. This is also necessary to close the education-to-workforce gaps that are hindering efforts to fill cybersecurity jobs with qualified workers. These include gaps in competency, professional experience, and education speed-to-market (Milller & Molina-Ray, 2014).

There is a need to investigate existing cybersecurity knowledge and skills of students and staff members in universities to come up with recommendations on how universities can improve human analytical abilities through knowledge and skill capabilities development to mitigate common cyber-attacks like social engineering attacks common in all industries thereby producing graduates with adequate cybersecurity knowledge and skills as workforce (Ani et al., 2019; Muniandy, Muniandy, & Samsudin, 2017). As a result, a human-centric cybersecurity framework is being developed to equip the human constituents in universities (students and staff) with the necessary cybersecurity knowledge and skills to assist them with identification, protection, detection, response, and recovery in the event of a cyber-attack.

According to Garwe & Thondhlana (2020), Zimbabwe has a robust higher education system, which consists of 24 registered universities, 14 public, and 10 private and there has been an increase in cybersecurity related attacks in Zimbabwe which was attested by the government of Zimbabwe with their "Think b4 Click" awareness program meant to educate the general public about the consequences of their actions online. Most universities leave their systems available to facilitate academic accessibility and the free flow of information between staff and students, universities and colleges are popular targets for cyberattacks (Garwe & Thondhlana, 2020; Matyokurehwa, Rudhumbu, Gombiro, & Mlambo, 2021; Ulven & Wangen, 2021).

On the other hand, Matyokurehwa et al., (2021) noted that, due to poor cybersecurity awareness (CSA), students and staff in higher education spend the majority of their time online and are careless with their personal information, such as passwords. Furthermore, they save their passwords in browsers like Firefox and Chrome as cookies. Most students share workstations with their colleagues, and they frequently leave private accounts on social networking accounts opened on public computers without fear of fraudulent activity, as well as visiting non-secure websites.

Many university students and staff have become easy targets for cyberattacks because of their lack of understanding of cybersecurity concepts (Bada, Sasse, & Nurse, 2019). It is therefore evident that there is a need for CSA in higher education to curb cyberattacks on students and staff and protect them from unknowingly exposing university information assets to cyber threats (Ani et al., 2019; Gratian, Bandi, Cukier, Dykstra, & Ginther, 2018; Matyokurehwa et al., 2021).

STATEMENT OF THE PROBLEM

The escalating number of cyberattacks on universities worldwide has resulted in universities losing valuable information assets leading to disruption of operations and loss of reputation (VMWare, 2016). However, cyber-attacks have successfully circumvented human-factor vulnerabilities related to cybersecurity knowledge and competencies/skills, enabling cyber criminals to manipulate human elements into inadvertently conveying access to critical information assets through social engineering attacks (Ani et al., 2019; Fatokun Faith et al., 2020). Several research projects have established that humans are the weakest link with regard to enforcing cybersecurity measures hence there is a need to first recognise humans as an asset and also outline the measures that can be taken to ensure that they are not vulnerable to cyberattacks or unknowingly participate in cyberattacks (Fatokun Faith et al., 2020; Muniandy et al., 2017; Von Solms & Van Niekerk, 2013).

Therefore, this research investigates the human-factored cybersecurity framework required to identify the capabilities of the human constituents in universities (students and staff) to recognise and respond appropriately to cyber intrusion events as the first and most important line of defence in protecting critical assets.

LITERATURE REVIEW

The extant literature on the various facets of implementing a cybersecurity program and the vast amount of information is found in the following areas. The literature needs to be condensed in order to create and carry out a cybersecurity plan. A major problem of the program discussed in this study is the impact of humans on cybersecurity (Coffey, Haveard, & Golding 2018) and is well coveed in this section.

Implementing Cybersecurity Programs

Garbars' (2002) work in Coffey, Haveard & Golding 2018 provides insight into how daunting a task it is to create a comprehensive cybersecurity program. He describes guidelines developed at the SANS Institute that integrate a wide variety of federal and state law, federal regulations and guidelines. He lists the National Institute of Standards and Technology (NIST), the Office of Management and Budget (OMB) the National Security Agency (NSA) and the General Accounting Office (GAO) as just a few of the federal agencies who weigh in on how to implement cybersecurity programs. It is likely that, if he had written the article a few years later, he would have included the Department of Homeland Security (DHS) on the list as well. To take one example from Garbars' list, the NIST Cybersecurity Framework (2014) in (Coffey, Haveard & Golding 2018) provides guidelines for the implementation of a cybersecurity program.

The overarching approach in the framework is to identify assets and risks, protect critical assets, detect intrusions, respond to intrusions and recover from incidents, a very broad-stroke framework in which each aspect is complex. Their seven-step process for cybersecurity program implementation includes prioritizing and scoping the undertaking, determining critical assets, determining current organizational cybersecurity strengths and weaknesses, assessing risks, determining cybersecurity goals for the organization, performing gap analysis, and creating and implementing an action plan.

Baker Tilly (2014) provide many broad guidelines regarding the implementation of cybersecurity programs. They describe the need for the classification of data by criticality, implementation of security control management and periodic assessment, breach planning, and decisions either to accept risks associated with data breaches or to transfer risk through a cyberliability insurance policy. Their recommendations are comprehensive with the exception of a relative lack of focus on preventing end user errors. Howarth (2014) concludes that organizations that implement strong technological security procedures still often pay insufficient attention to human sources of vulnerability, and strongly advocates for enhanced security training (Coffey, Haveard, & Golding 2018). Armerding (2014) cites a report that indicates that 56% of workers who use the Internet on their jobs receive no security training at all.

The NIST Cybersecurity Framework (2014) offers principles for the execution of a cybersecurity program, to use one example from Garbars' list. The framework's primary strategy is to identify assets and hazards, safeguard crucial assets, find and stop intrusions, and recover from accidents. This is a fairly general framework, and each component is intricate (Coffey, Haveard, & Golding 2018). Prioritizing and scoping the project, identifying critical assets, identifying organizational cybersecurity strengths and weaknesses, assessing risks, deciding on cybersecurity goals for the organization, performing gap analysis, and developing and implementing an action plan are all part of their seven-step process for implementing cybersecurity programs. Regarding the development of cybersecurity initiatives, Baker Tilly (2014) offers a number of general principles. They discuss the necessity of managing security controls and classifying data according to criticality.

Regarding the development of cybersecurity initiatives, Baker Tilly (2014) offers a number of general principles. They go on to discuss the necessity of categorizing data according to its criticality, the adoption of security control management and periodic assessment, breach preparation, and choices over whether to accept the risks connected with data breaches or transfer risk via a cyberliability insurance policy. Except for a relative lack of attention to preventing end user errors, their advice are thorough (Coffey, Haveard, & Golding 2018).

Howarth (2014) draws the conclusion that businesses with robust technological security procedures frequently overlook human sources of vulnerability and is a strong proponent of improved security training. According to a study cited by Armerding (2014), 56% of employees who use the Internet for work receive no security training at all.

The Payment Card Industry (PCI) Security Standards Council's (2014) recommendations offer some information on how training programs should be implemented. Instead of a one-size-fits-all training strategy, their methodology offers role-based security training decisions. The standards list three main function categories: management positions with continuous duties to encourage strong security practices, specialized roles specified by the company, and all staff for baseline security training. What the specialized roles might be is not specified in these recommendations (Coffey, Haveard, & Golding 2018).

The recommendations indicate a number of ways that training might be delivered, such as traditional face-to-face programs, online training, social media use, sporadic emails, memos, posters, and bulletins, among others. For messages pertaining to security, numerous communication channels are stressed. Separate training for new workers and those who switch jobs within an organization is another PCI recommendation (Coffey, Haveard, & Golding 2018).

Human Factors in Cybersecurity Breaches

IBM's 2016 Cyber Security Intelligence Index (IBM Security Services, 2016) contained many interesting statistics on sources of cybersecurity attacks. The report cited a 5% increase in attacks coming from inside organizations (from 55% to 60%). Of the 55% in 2014, 31.5% were deliberate and 23.5% involved human error. In 2016, the percentage of error-mediated attacks decreased, but still accounted for 15.5% of all security breaches. IBM's 2014 report (IBM Security Services, 2014) provides some evolutionary perspective. It was based upon nearly 1000 clients in 133 countries and literally billions of events per year.

IBM reported that human errors included those made by IT professionals such as improper system security configurations and poor patch management, and those made by end-users such as weak or shared Passwords, lost gadgets that contained sensitive data, and—by far—the most frequent—opening a risky attachment or visiting a risky URL. Current IBM research amply demonstrates the importance of end-user error in cybersecurity (Coffey, Haveard, & Golding, 2018).

Breach is seriously important, and its influence as a primary cause is obviously not waning. Verizon (2013) provides information that supports IBM's report. In Verison's analysis, it is said that weak or default passwords, or the theft of passwords, had a significant part in 63% of confirmed data breaches. According to that report, 93% of data breaches happen shortly after the password is compromised, yet more than 80% of them are not found for several weeks. The issue is still very much present in 2017 saw an increase in password theft due to increasingly sophisticated phishing assaults (Coffey, Haveard, & Golding 2018).

According to Woodhouse (2007), organizations require much more than yearly awareness training to change end user behavior. He claims that fostering an information security culture through active engagement in sound security procedures is essential. Woodhouse's post, like so many others on the issue, is rich on generalizations but short on specifics about how to foster such a culture (Coffey, Haveard, & Golding 2018).

Furman, Theofanos, Choong, and Stanton (2011) discovered that although end users are frequently aware of and concerned about cybersecurity, they lack a thorough awareness of the threats that are currently present and how to protect themselves. Defining terminology related to security risks including key loggers, spoofing, and viruses Participants in Furman's study who used phrases like "botnet" and "etc." claimed to be familiar with them, but frequently gave incorrect definitions.

The participants clearly lacked the information necessary to mitigate these hazards because they were unaware of what they were. The report made absolutely no mention of participant understanding about prevention, despite this being quite intriguing (Coffey, Haveard, & Golding 2018). The fact that the Federal Information Processing rules (FIPS, 2015), US government rules for civilian employee computer use, address three security concerns, as stated by Furman et al., is quite intriguing.

- **Availability:** Ensuring that data can be accessed when necessary;
- **Integrity:** Preventing data from being corrupted or deleted; and
- **Confidentiality:** Ensuring that sensitive data is protected from unauthorized individuals.

According to poll results, secrecy was the study's top worry out of these three crucial issues, people, and that the majority of participants were not aware of the problems with data access and integrity (Coffey, Haveard, & Golding 2018).

CONCEPTUAL FRAMEWORK

Many theoretical cybersecurity frameworks can be applied to different cybersecurity environments because cyber threats are considered challenges at a national and institutional level. This study makes use of the variable in the (1) National Institute of Standards and Technology (NIST) Framework and (2) NICE Framework building blocks Approach.

National Institute of Standards and Technology (NIST)

The National Institute of Standards and Technology (NIST) is key in defining and discussing cybersecurity issues it has developed a highly referenced cybersecurity framework. NIST in collaboration with several public and private organisations developed a cybersecurity framework represented in Figure 1 that emphasises the use of business drivers to steer cybersecurity operations and the inclusion of cybersecurity risks in risk management processes.

Figure 1. Cybersecurity framework
Source: National Institute of Standards and Technology (2018, p. 288)

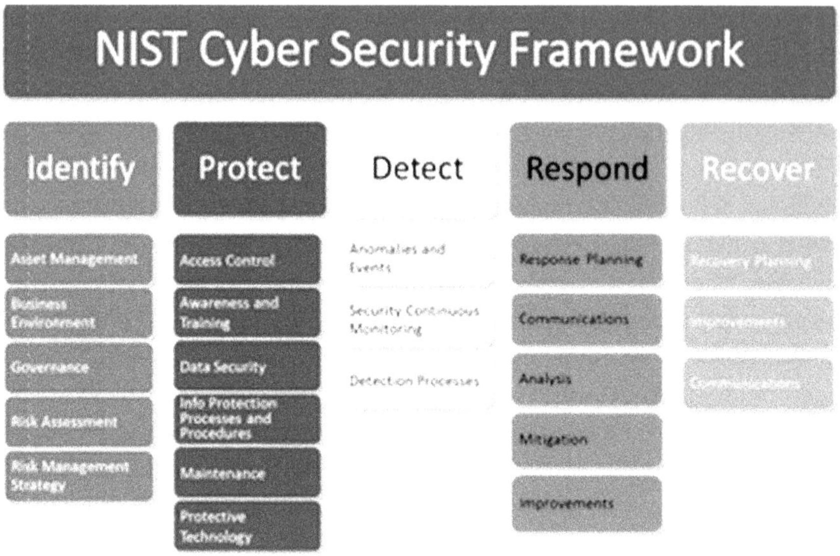

Cybersecurity Workforce Framework

This framework contends that organisations have expressed worry that their asset owners and operators lack general cybersecurity awareness, which could be attributed to a lack of education and training.

Figure 2. NICE framework building blocks approach
Source: NIST (2020, p. 178)

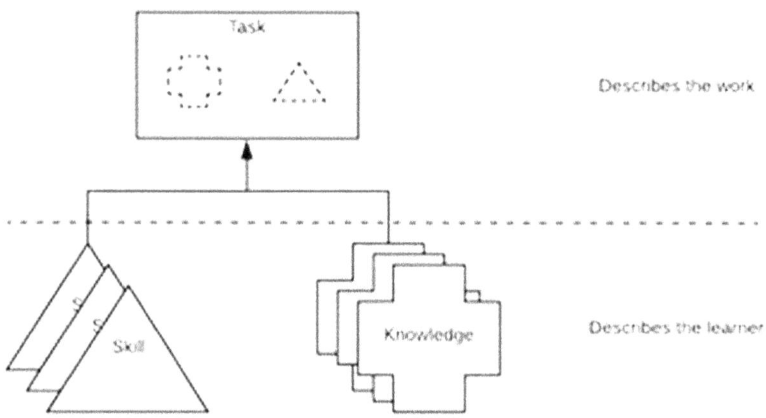

By relating knowledge and skill assertions to an individual or group, the NICE Framework allows organisations to describe learners. Learners can perform tasks to meet organisational goals by applying their knowledge and skills. While not every organisation will employ every learner-related notion, the

NICE Framework gives organisations a modular collection of building pieces to employ as their circumstances dictate. The NICE Framework's applicability to education and training providers is further enhanced by the acknowledgement of the learner's role in acquiring competencies to execute cybersecurity activities (Nilsen, 2017; NIST, 2020; Schmeelk & Dragos, 2021).

Initial Framework

The initial conceptual framework was arrived at after a thorough review of literature in light of the research problem and research objectives and was conceptualized using two already existing frameworks which are the NIST Cybersecurity framework which emphasises five core cybersecurity functions which are to identify, protect, detect, recover and respond; and the NICE Framework which identifies the job tasks, knowledge, skills, and abilities that individuals must demonstrate to successfully perform the five core cybersecurity functions of the NIST framework effectively as illustrated.

Figure 3. Initial conceptual framework
Source: Author compilation

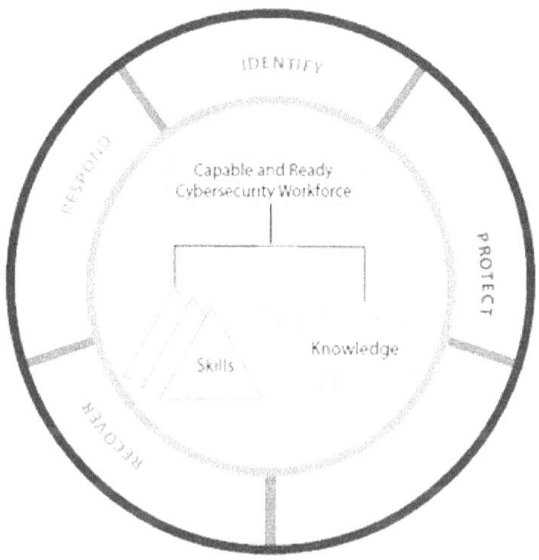

From the two candidate conceptual frameworks Job tasks, knowledge, skills, and abilities that individuals must demonstrate to perform effectively were presented in seven categories namely:

1. **Secure Provision:** Specialty areas responsible for conceptualizing, designing, and building secure IT systems are also responsible for systems development. These skills are specifically for IT staff members and students working towards such professions as these skills are necessary for programmers/developers, network engineers and system engineers/administrators.
2. **Operate and Maintain:** Specialty areas responsible for providing support, administration, and maintenance necessary to ensure effective and efficient IT system performance and security. These specialities are necessary for giving user support, awareness and education as they constantly interact with users with critical information assets

3. **Protect and Defend:** Specialty areas responsible for the identification, analysis, and mitigation of threats internal to critical information assets like the network and IT systems. These skills are necessary for both staff and students as it is their mandate to safeguard their cyberspace. Both students and staff must have the knowledge and skills of detecting social engineering attacks which are the most common problem in universities hence they have to be educated about the Social Engineering detection Model (SEADM) to improve their human analytical abilities in detecting social engineering attacks to improve their ability to protect and defend their university cyberspaces.
    - **Investigate:** Specialty areas responsible for the investigation of cyber events and/or crimes of IT systems, networks, and digital evidence. These skills are crucial in recovery and responding to cyber-attacks. These are the skills necessary for emergency response teams and crisis management in the event of a cyber-attack.
4. **Collect and Operate:** Specialty areas responsible for specialised denial and deception operations and collection of cybersecurity information that may be used to develop intelligence. These skills are very crucial in updating already existing cybersecurity educational material to improve knowledge and skills relating to trending cyber threats and help in the identification and detection of new threats and also prepare crisis management teams with close to reality simulations of cyber-attacks.
5. **Analyze:** Specialty areas responsible for highly specialized review and evaluation of incoming cybersecurity information to determine its usefulness for intelligence.
6. **Oversight and Development:** Specialty areas providing leadership, management, direction, and/or development and advocacy so that individuals and organisations may effectively conduct cybersecurity work. Management has to invest in cybersecurity knowledge and skills development which should be supported by organisational policies and be part of the organisation's strategy.

With these cybersecurity skills and knowledge, it is then possible for the human assets to perform the following functions:

Identify: This core function's efforts are aimed at increasing organisational understanding and awareness of cybersecurity risk to organisational systems, assets, data, and capabilities. Understanding business contexts, critical function resources, and related cybersecurity risks allow an organisation to focus and prioritize actions following its risk management strategy and business objectives. This function aligns with the first objective of the study which is to identify the major human factored cybersecurity challenges faced by universities.

Protect: The basic responsibility of designing and executing suitable protections to ensure that critical information assets are functioning. The Protect feature aids in limiting or containing the consequences of a potential cybersecurity event or incident. This function aligns with the second objective which is to outline the key factors to consider to eliminate human factored cyber-attacks.

Detect: The third core function focuses on establishing and implementing the required and necessary organizational processes to detect and recognize the occurrence of a cybersecurity event or incident in a timely and proactive manner. The third object is to assess the contribution of poor cybersecurity knowledge and skills gaps to social engineering attacks in universities.

Respond: The Respond function addresses the identification of the activities to take action regarding a detected cybersecurity event or incident. It is a post-event function, focusing on reactive activities, and supporting the ability of impact containment.

Recover: A recovery is a post event or incident reactive function. It focuses mainly on developing and putting to practice the appropriate set of activities to maintain plans for resilience and to restore any capabilities or services that were impaired due to a cybersecurity event or incident, supporting timely recovery to a normal operation state, thus reducing the overall impact of the event. Both the response and recovery function address the fourth objective which is to outline the measures required to reduce social engineering attacks through improved cybersecurity knowledge and skills development of students and staff.

From the results of the study, it is evident that the cybersecurity knowledge and skills of students and staff are required to reduce human factored vulnerabilities that can be exploited by cybercriminals to launch social engineering attacks that could damage the cyberspace of the university. The results also show that as much as students and staff claim to have an understanding of cybersecurity, they have limited access to cybersecurity educative materials and information which limits their cybersecurity knowledge and skills and leads them to behave in a certain way only because they are forced to do so by organisational policies set in place to help protect them and other information assets. Inadequate knowledge and skills to protect themselves from common social engineering attacks like phishing, pharming, and malware, exposes the overall cyberspace of the university. The conceptual framework is therefore a guide as to how universities can develop cybersecurity knowledge and skills through awareness, training, and policies and produce a capable workforce of professionals who are well aware of their role and responsibility towards safeguarding their organisational cyberspace.

MAIN RESEARCH OBJECTIVE

To identify the cybersecurity framework required by universities to safeguard their human assets from human factored cyber-attacks.

Research Objectives

1. To identify the major human factored cybersecurity challenges faced by universities.
2. To outline the key factors to consider to eliminate human factored cyber-attacks
3. To assess the contribution of poor cybersecurity knowledge and skills gap to social engineering attacks in universities.
4. Outline the measures required to reduce social engineering attacks through improved cybersecurity knowledge and skills development of students and staff.

METHODOLOGY AND METHODS

Pragmatic research philosophy was adopted in this study. According to Mitchell (2018), a pragmatic philosophical position allows the researcher to view the research through windows that consider the role of social actors and also create a practical research approach. For pragmatists, the reality is true as far as it helps us to get into satisfactory relations with other parts of our experiences (Wahyuni, 2012). Truth is whatever proves itself good or what has stood the scrutiny of individual users over time (Baker & Schaltegger, 2015). The study used a mixed method as the methodology where both the qualitative and quantitative approaches will be used. This type of approach gave the researcher more than one type of data that can be collected.

Kaushik and Walsh (2019) mentioned that a combination of the two approaches will provide a holistic analysis of the research. They also went on to say that the two approaches although different in their implementation, complement each other well. In this study, a case study of Africa University was used where. A case study is an empirical in-depth inquiry or comprehensive study of a social unit where the subject of the study is a person, group, or social institution (Strang & James, 2007).

The sample was drawn from a target population of 2,875 currently active and registered students for the January – July 2021 semester and 329 active staff members at Africa University according to the Africa University Registry department. The researcher used a questionnaire because it provided a low cost way of acquiring data since the sample was a large one which consisted of 320 participants. Another reason for using a questionnaire was that less influence would be subjected to the participants as they could decide to complete the questionnaire when the researcher was not around thereby eliminating ethical issues like cohesion and bias.

The researcher used semi-structured interviews which allowed the researcher to determine the interviewee's knowledge to provide qualitative data to enrich the evaluation. Semi-structured interviews were conducted with key informant interviewees such as the Director of the ICT department, the Systems Administrator, the Head of Department of the Computer Science Department, The Registrar, and a student representative member of the Student Representative Committee (SRC). Semi-structured interviews enabled the use of open and closed-ended questions to understand the common perception of cybersecurity, and their understanding of the knowledge and skills necessary. An expert review technique was used to validate the initial conception framework in Figure 4.

PARAMETERS FOR FRAMEWORK VALIDATION

The expert review technique was utilized by Beecham, Hall, Britton, Cottee, & Rainer (2005) to validate their model creation when they wanted independent feedback on how well their model fulfilled their study objectives. This research will use the Expert Review technique to validate the applicability and relevance of the developed framework for universities and its adoptability by other higher and tertiary institutions even other organisations in a different industry. Figure 4 shows a framework developed by (Hevner, March, Park, & Ram, 2004) for understanding, executing, and evaluating Information system research.

Figure 4. Information systems research framework
Source: Hevner et al. (2004, p. 88)

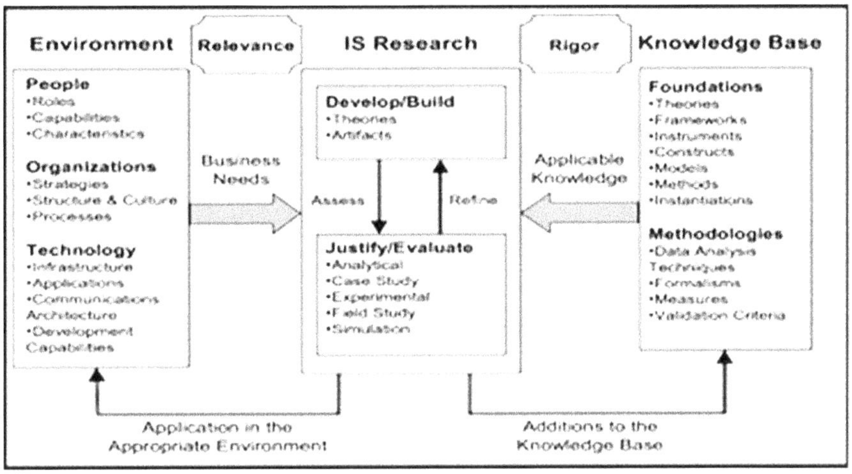

The environment defines the problem space, in this research we are looking at universities as the problem space, where a phenomenon of an interest which is cybersecurity resides in this research. For this research, the environment is composed of people, (business) organisations, and their existing or planned technologies. The focus of this research is on the people or human assets and the correlation between human factor vulnerabilities caused by poor cybersecurity knowledge and skills, and common cybersecurity challenges that universities face.

Therefore, there is indeed a problem, and opportunities that define business needs as they are perceived by people within the organisation in this case, universities require a cybersecurity framework that is focused on the human element instead of technology to change these perceptions which are shaped by the roles, capabilities, and characteristics of people within the organisation (Hevner et al., 2004), there is a critical dependence upon human cognitive abilities to produce effective solutions which are the cybersecurity knowledge and skills.

There is also a critical dependence upon human social abilities to produce effective solutions like communication in the case of cyber threat detection, mitigating the threat, and recovering from an attack therefore the cybersecurity framework is being applied in an appropriate environment meaning the proposed research is relevant. The research is developing a framework by assessing a case study and refining already existing theories and frameworks. A conceptual framework developed by the researcher from reviewing literature shows that there has been a gap in the knowledgebase and by combining two well developed frameworks, this research aims to add applicable knowledge to the existing knowledgebase; therefore, the research has rigor (Hevner et al., 2004).

FRAMEWORK VALIDATION

This research will use the Expert Review technique to validate the Sufficiency, Relevance, Comprehensiveness, Understandability, and Ease of use of the proposed conceptual framework through independent feedback as to how well the framework meets the research objectives.

Table 1. Expert review validation template

Conceptual Framework Validation	Yes	No
The proposed human-centric cybersecurity framework is sufficient to create a capable cybersecurity workforce that has minimized human-factored vulnerabilities that expose universities to cyber threats (Sufficiency)		
Training cybersecurity professionals and introduction of new curricula with cybersecurity content to enhance study programs, and courses to improve cybersecurity knowledge and skills is relevant to the cybersecurity domain (Relevance)		
Training in cybersecurity knowledge and skills covers all human factored vulnerabilities impacting cybersecurity readiness? (Comprehensiveness)		
The components and levels of the proposed framework are understandable		
The framework is useful for cybersecurity knowledge and skills development		
The framework is practical for use in the industry		

Follow Up Questions

1. Would you add any components or levels to the proposed conceptual framework? If so please explain what and why?
2. Would you update the conceptual framework description? If so please explain what and why?
3. Would you add any processes or practices? If so please explain what and why?
4. Would you remove any of the processes or practices? If so please explain what and why? Q5. Would you redefine/update any of the processes or practices? If so please explain what and why?
5. Could the framework be made more useful? How?
6. Could the framework be made more practical? How?

RESEARCH ETHICS

Research ethics is important in research since it requires that researchers should protect the dignity of their subjects and publish well-articulated information (Fleming & Zegwaard, 2018). After Chapter 3, a proposal was sent to Africa University Research and Ethics Committee (AUREC) for reviewing before being approved and cleared to enable the investigation to take place. Permission to enter the study area, in this case, Africa University was sought from AUREC and the Registrar through a research application letter. The application letter clearly stated the objectives of the study and made it clear that the results of this research are purely for academic purposes and will not prejudice any informant. Participants were also fully informed about the research, how the data would be used, and what consequences there could be.

Informed Consent

Participants were also fully informed about the research, how the data would be used, and what consequences there could be. The participants were provided with an explicit, active, signed consent to taking part in the research, including understanding their rights to access their information and the right to withdraw at any point. Before the study began, the researcher explained all of the study's requirements in detail, and if there were any ambiguous questions, the researcher provided contact details to clarify them. All of the information gathered was used for academic purposes only. An informed consent message appended to the questionnaire (Appendix B) was used to this effect.

Confidentiality, Privacy, and Anonymity

The ethical considerations oblige researchers to treat privacy, confidentiality, and anonymity with extreme caution (Reid, Brown, Smith, Cope, & Jamieson, 2018). The privacy, anonymity, and confidentiality of the participants and data were given due consideration and highlighted in the informed consent message on the questionnaire. Embedding the informed consent was a process rather than just an event on the questionnaire (Kanyangale, 2019). The researcher emphasized on maintain confidentiality throughout the study processes and after the research has been completed by maintaining the anonymity of the supplier of information to the researcher. The research did not require participants to provide their identities during data collection.

PRESENTATION, INTERPRETATION, AND DISCUSSION OF RESULTS

The response rate was 91% which is a satisfactory response rate according to Sekaran Uma (2016) as only 290 responses were recorded and returned for analysis. The researcher also conducted interviews with four key informants. From the staff interviewed by the researcher, most of them showed a positive response towards the research questions and they were free to open up on how they perceive cybersecurity issues and expressed their views on cybersecurity knowledge and skills.

PRESENTATION AND INTERPRETATION OF RESULTS

Analysis of the Major Human-Factored Cybersecurity Challenges Faced by Universities

Table 2. Understanding of cybersecurity roles and responsibilities

	Strongly Agree	Agree	Neutral	Disagree	Strongly Disagree
I have a role to play in safeguarding the information assets and the cyberspace of africa university.	130	94	36	30	0
	45%	32%	12%	10%	0%
My behaviour whilst using shared computers, my browsing behaviour, and password usage can expose AU information assets to cyber-attacks.	66	154	15	20	35
	23%	53%	5%	7%	12%
I have the necessary knowledge and skills to safeguard the information assets and the cyberspace of Africa University.	66	137	50	31	6
	23%	47%	17%	11%	2%

From the analysis of the responses presented in Table 2, we see that 77% of the respondents agree that they have a role to play in safeguarding the information assets and cyberspace of Africa University. However, a total of 76% of the respondents also agree that their behaviour whilst using these resources can expose critical information assets to cyber-attacks even after 70% of the respondents agree to have the necessary knowledge and skills to safeguard cyberspace at AU.

Table 3. Analysis of the perception of cybersecurity roles and responsibilities and ability to safeguard information assets

Statistics			
	I have a role to play in safeguarding the cyberspace of Africa University.	My behaviour whilst using computers, my browsing behaviour and password usage can expose AU information asserts to cyber attackers.	I have necessary knowledge and skills to safe guard the information assets and the cyberspace of AU.
N Valid	290	290	290
Missing	0	0	0
Mean	1.88	2.32	2.23
Mode	1	2	2
Std. Deviation	.982	1.244	.991

From Table 3, we observe mode Figures 1 and 2 which signifies that there is a consensus amongst research participants in acknowledging having a role to play in safe guarding the cyberspace of Africa University and also admitting that their behaviour when using shared computers, their browsing behaviour and password usage can expose Africa University to cyber-attacks despite claiming to have necessary knowledge and skills to safe guard the information assets and the cyberspace of Africa University. The high figures of the standard deviation which are above 0.5 indicate that they are some respondents who were neutral or did not necessarily agree with the cybersecurity role and responsibilities they are supposed to play in safeguarding the university's cyberspace.

This is evident that unclear roles and responsibilities towards safeguarding university assets and cyberspace brings forth issues related to poor cybersecurity awareness and the risk of having people without an appreciation of cybersecurity using critical information systems which increases the risk of human factored vulnerabilities that expose critical information assets to cyber-attacks.

Table 4. Understanding of cyber security versus having antivirus software, firewall or antispyware installed

How would you rate your understanding of cybersecurity? Do you have any antivirus software, firewall or antispyware installed?				
Crosstabulation Count				
		Do you have any antivirus software, firewall or antispyware installed?		
		yes	**no**	**Total**
How would you rate your understanding of cybersecurity	**Excellent**	4	6	10
	Above Average	13	17	30
	Average	238	2	240
	Below Average	8	2	10
Total		263	27	290

Chi Square Tests			
	Value	**df**	**Asymp.Sig.(2-sided)**
Pearson Chi-Square	1.319E2[a]	3	.000
Likelihood Ratio	91.947	3	.000
Linear-by-linear Association	85.848	1	.000
N of Valid Cases	290		

Consistent with information found within the literature review, the results in Table 4 show that research participants unanimously perceived to have an average understanding of cybersecurity (87%) and have a technical appreciation of protecting their information assets by having antivirus software, firewall or antispyware installed on their machines (91%). This shows that they know how important it is to safeguard their devices against malware. The perceptions support previous research found within the scholarly literature indicating that most university students and staff have some meaningful understanding of cybersecurity concepts that have been implemented through policy however they are misguided in believing that installing an antivirus is sufficient to protect information assets from cyber-attacks.

The Pearson chi-square figure of 0.0 signifies a very strong association between understanding cybersecurity and having some form of protection through the installation of antivirus software, firewall or antispyware however this is only a technical solution that is effective in protecting against known viruses,

Trojan horses, worms, adware, spyware and ransomware if the antivirus software is always updated and when users scan shared or downloaded files to detect malware before opening them on their devices.

Table 5. Analysis of behaviours which expose university information assets to cyber attacks

Statictics								
	Updating the antivirus software on your personal computer	Open email from unknown sources	Download freeware on the internet	Scan removable drives prior to using it on your personal computer	Change your password	Click hyperlinks in email messages	Use the remember my password option	Share your username and password to get assistance from friends
N Valid	290	290	290	290	290	290	290	290
Missing	0	0	0	0	0	0	0	0
Mode	2	4	2	2	3	1	1	3

An analysis of the behaviour of the participants unanimously perceived that the respondents frequently engage in risky behaviour which exposes the university's cyberspace to cyberattacks. According to the results showing the mode values that resemble frequency, respondents confirmed that they do not frequently update their antivirus software, download freeware, and scan removable drives before using them. Moreover, they also acknowledged frequently opening emails from unknown sources and sharing their credentials to get assistance from colleagues. Clicking on hyperlinks in email messages and using the "Remember password option" had a low mode showing that few participants frequently engaged in these activities.

According to the literature, the behaviour of the participants is a reflection of the behaviours that expose them to downloading infected files which come as freeware or cracked software. By clicking on hyperlinks that are in emails, users are susceptible to social engineering attacks like phishing and pharming. Moreover, some respondents admitted to frequently sharing their credentials and saving their credentials through the "Remember password" option which is a vulnerability that can be exploited by cybercriminals who seek to steal credentials and commit crimes like CEO fraud (Maranga & Nelson, 2019).

Analysis of the Challenges Being Faced by Universities That Are Caused by Human-Factored Vulnerabilities

Figure 5. Time spent online

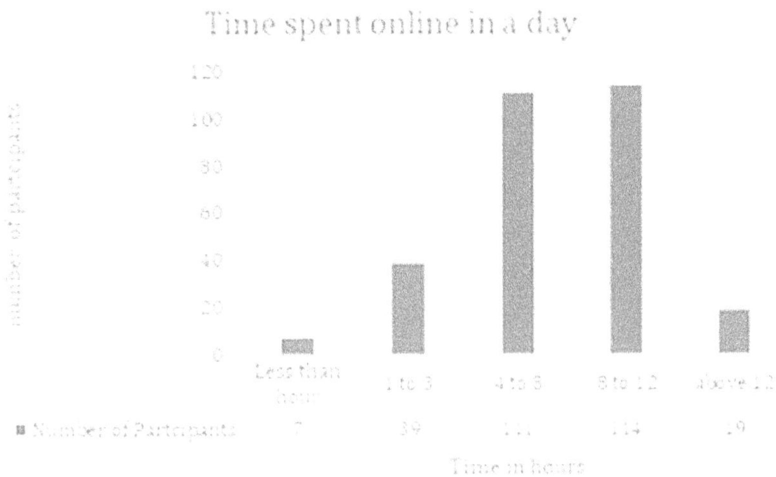

From the analysis of the time spent online by the participants (Figure 5), 77% of the respondents admitted to spending between 4-12 hours online. From these figures, it can be seen that students and staff are heavy internet users for a diverse range of reasons however this also increases the level of vulnerability to social engineers who are always actively seeking ways to reach out to unaware users through malware, spyware or adware that is designed to deceive and trick recipients into taking an action such as clicking a malicious link, or opening an attachment with a virus (Bullée & Junger, 2020; Zwilling et al., 2020) which has been established earlier that participants are indeed vulnerable and are highly likely to fall for these tricks.

Table 6. Analysis of infrequent important security measures placed by the university to protect its human assets

Statistics							
	How important do you think websites and online services using 2-step aunthentication or 2-step verification	How important do you think using password consisting of lowercase, uppercase, numbers and special characters	How important do you think using different passwords for different applications	How important do you think blocking freeware sites and torrent sites	How important is the stance bring your own device	How important do you think marking emails from unknown sources as SPAM	How important do you think using VPNto access restricted sites
N Valid	290	290	290	290	290	290	290
Missing	0	0	0	0	0	0	0
Mode	5	5	2	5	1	5	1

The researcher analysed the behaviour of participants towards some common measures that are put in place by universities to protect their human assets from being susceptible to social engineering attacks by enforcing security measures like implementing strong password policies, blocking freeware sites, encouraging students and staff to enrol in two-step verification and having different passwords for different applications. However, from the analysis of data presented in Table 6, most participants found these measures placed by the university as unnecessary or of little importance which is shown by the high mode value of 5 showing that most participants found these measures unnecessary.

Assessment of the Contribution of Poor Cybersecurity Knowledge and Skills Gap to Social Engineering Attacks in Universities

Table 7. Assessment of some basic knowledge

	Yes	No
Are you exposed to cybersecurity educational materials	**93**	**197**
Do you suspect something is wrong when your computer runs extremely slow	**263**	**27**
Do you know where to report if you suspect a cyber incident	**115**	**175**

Table 7 shows that 68% of the respondents are not exposed to cybersecurity educational materials. This is an indication that there is poor cybersecurity education and awareness. The majority of respondents (91%) often suspect that something is wrong when their computers run extremely slow; however, 60% of the respondents do not know where to report if they suspect a cyber incident.

Table 8. Analysis of various reactions to some social engineering vulnerabilities

Descriptive Statistics				
	N	**Sum**	**Mean**	**Std. Deviation**
URL must be "https" if I'm transmitting confidential information	290	903	3.11	1.471
The padlock symbol is a must to transmit sensitive information	290	826	2.85	1.533
I prefer to type URL in a new browser rather than clicking it on hyperlinks	290	934	3.22	1.283
Receiving a suspicious email will prompt me to contact the relevant party for verification	290	475	1.64	.678
Not a target of social engineering attacks due to student status	290	520	1.79	.895
I should check the authorization or identity of someone sharing any confidential details	290	495	1.71	.711
Valid N (listwise)	290			

From Table 8 it can be deduced that the majority of respondents are not aware of browser security which is very crucial when dealing with social engineering attacks. From the results presented earlier, we can see that there is a knowledge gap in browser security, password management, malware use, incident reporting systems, and clear cybersecurity roles and responsibilities.mainly due to poor education and awareness which in turn affects the ability of staff and students to detect, respond and recover appropriately in the event of a cyber-attack.

Analysis of Measures Required to Reduce Social Engineering Attacks Through Improved Cybersecurity Knowledge and Skills Development of Students and Staff

Table 9. Perceptions on the measures that can be adopted to improve cybersecurity knowledge and skills development

Statistics					
		Does enhancing cybersecurity knowledge and skills capabilities through training and awareness increase a person's ability to identify, protect, respond and recover from a cyber threat?	Does giving awareness and training of cybersecurity concepts improve cybersecurity knowledge and skills and in turn reduce human factored vulnerabilities	Does improved cybersecurity knowledge and skills help in the creation of a capable workforce	Does age play a role in the ability to learn new cybersecurity concepts
N	Valid	290	290	290	290
	Missing	0	0	0	0
Mean		2.03	1.97	1.92	1.99
Mode		2	1	2	2
Std. Deviation		1.042	1.188	.960	1.039

Table 9 shows the results after analyzing the responses from the participants regarding how the university could improve their cybersecurity knowledge and skills we see that the mean value is ranging between 1 and 2 showing that most participants strongly agreed to the proposed measures that were presented in this section. They agreed that training and awareness could increase their ability to identify, protect, detect, respond and recover from cyber-attacks. They also agreed that human factored vulnerabilities that result from poor cybersecurity knowledge and skills would be reduced through training in cybersecurity concepts and awareness.

The participants also strongly believe that with the right education, they can be equipped with the necessary cybersecurity knowledge and skills to create a capable workforce that can safeguard its university cyberspace. It is also important to note that participants also strongly agreed that age plays a role in the ability to learn new cybersecurity concepts hence it is necessary to bring awareness and educate users on cybersecurity matters as early as they start interacting with cyberspaces so that they develop these skills from an early age and understand how their behaviour plays an important role in safeguarding other critical assets around them.

Table 10. Inclusion of cybersecurity knowledge and skills into existing practice and policies

Statistics						
		Cybersecurity knowledge and skills should be a requirement assessed when employers are recruiting	The inclusion of cybersecurity content in introductory campus wide computer courses may help leaners understand and retain cybersecurity concepts more easily	A person's willingness or ability to adopt new cybersecurity knowledge may be affected by his/her behaviour or attitude to protect themselves from cyber-attacks	Prior knowledge provided by introductory computer skills courses or workplace processes and policies affects the ease with which a person can comprehend new cybersecurity concepts	Educating people on how to protect their cyberspace will reduce the risk of them being exposed to cyber attacks
N	Valid	290	290	290	290	290
	Missing	0	0	0	0	0
Mean		2.14	1.89	1.95	2.06	1.71
Mode		1	2	2	1	1
Std. Deviation		1.365	.907	1.019	1.282	.709

Table 10 shows the results of how participants responded regarding measures that universities can take to improve the development of cybersecurity knowledge and skills. By observing the mean value between 1 and 2, we can conclude that most respondents strongly agreed with the ideas of assessing cybersecurity knowledge and skills at the recruitment stage, the inclusion of cybersecurity content in introductory computer courses that are mandatory for all students to take and they also agree that the cybersecurity knowledge and skills gained will assist in reducing human factored vulnerabilities, therefore, reducing the chances of them in exposing critical information systems to cyberattacks and unknowingly engaging in or taking part in cybercrime.

RESULTS FROM THE INTERVIEW

The interviews also yielded responses that supported the results yielded from the questionnaire. All four interviews agreed that human is an asset that requires protection from cyber threats. The interview informants also agreed that human factored vulnerabilities do expose organisational information systems to cyber threats and a greater extend, sharing or leaking of passwords, and clicking on harmful links or suspicious emails. The systems administrator admitted to having mechanisms currently in place to protect human assets from cyber threats such as limited user account and network access (firewall and VLANs) privileges; restricted workstation privileges where users cannot install or modify programs or applications; the university has antivirus security software; makes use of strong passwords and two-factor authentication and spotting of reported spam and phishing scams.

These mechanisms are integrated with policies to protect human assets from cyber-attacks through enforcing password policy, network usage and access policy, internet use policy, physical security of office equipment, and email use policy that prohibits the use of personal email accounts for business matters. Additional measures like prohibiting opening email attachments from unknown sources (as they may contain malicious software), prohibiting accessing email accounts of other individuals, prohibiting sharing email account passwords and prohibiting excessive personal use of the organization's email are measures that have been put in place to try and protect users from exposure to cyber-attacks.

When interviewed about their perspective regarding the extent of cybersecurity knowledge and skills needed to protect students and staff from cyber threats, The ICT Director confirmed that indeed, users know of the imminent threat of cyber-attacks; however, there is a need for students and staff to be constantly educated and reminded of the old and current threat trends. The Registrar suggested that current organisational strategies to protect human assets from cyber threats can be communicated to students and staff in a better and much improved manner like the opening of broadcasting channels for circulating cybersecurity awareness materials, opening a cybersecurity hotline for reporting suspected cyber incidents and developing cybersecurity workshops, presentations and course material that are endorsed by management and taken by both students and staff to improve their cybersecurity knowledge and skills.

Currently, the university has tailored its cybersecurity knowledge and skills to protect human assets from internal cyber threats by configuring firewall and domain policies in advance to stop cyber threats, on the spot investigation when a user raises concern and email use policy that acts as guidance on the proper use of the email platform. When asked about any added information that the interviewees could offer about measures that can be used to protect human assets from cyber threats, the suggestions that stood out were:

1. There should be cybersecurity processes that maintain the integrity of information and protection of all assets including human assets. These processes should include establishing and maintaining cybersecurity roles and responsibilities, polices, standards, and procedures.
2. Proper IT governance procedures are crucial in implementing a formal risk assessment process and developing policies that critical information assets are not misused and that cybersecurity policies are continually reviewed and updated to reflect the most current risks thus developing incident response policies and procedures to properly respond to, account for and help mitigate the cost of a successful cyber-attack or breach.
3. Establish a resilient recovery plan to mitigate the risk of key people being unavailable in the event of a system failure resulting in a breach. Documenting the configuration of hardware and software applications and keeping these up to date so that the crisis management and recovery team can quickly rebuild the affected systems.

FEEDBACK FROM EXPERT REVIEW

The initial framework was reviewed by an expert with extensive knowledge of cybersecurity, education and policy formulation. Their feedback revealed that the proposed human-centric cybersecurity framework is indeed sufficient to create a capable cybersecurity workforce with minimized human-factored vulnerabilities that expose universities to cyber threats. They also agreed that training cybersecurity professionals and introduction of new curricula with cybersecurity content to enhance study programs, and courses to improve cybersecurity knowledge and skills are relevant to the cybersecurity domain. However, they expressed that the training in cybersecurity knowledge and skills would not cover all human factored vulnerabilities as an element of human behaviour and attitudes will always play a role in how well they apply the cybersecurity knowledge and skills taught in pieces of training. The expert also agreed that the proposed framework is useful for cybersecurity knowledge and skills development and framework is practical for use in the industry however they argued that additional components and levels are required for the framework to be understandable saying:

The framework covers all technical aspects and issues relating to the sociology of technology however I feel context or environmental factors are well represented for the framework to be universally applicable across different environments or contexts. I would add another outer ring with Institutional policy, National cybersecurity regulation framework, and Industry practice. These components are equally important and complementary. This framework should inform policymakers and industry practice. These are major weaknesses in this environment that stand in the relevance and application of your good framework.

The expert also went on to add that the proposed framework could be made more practical if it is supported by a relevant act of law, specific institutional policies, and active industry cybersecurity associations to share and promote best practices.

JUSTIFICATION FOR MODIFYING THE FRAMEWORK

The expert raised critical issues pertaining to the environmental factors which the researcher had overlooked whilst designing the conceptual framework. To improve its practicality and usefulness, the expert added some components to the proposed framework.

FRAMEWORK REDESIGN: CYBERSECURITY WORKFORCE FRAMEWORK FOR UNIVERSITIES

After factoring the considerations from the expert review, the proposed framework can indeed be enhanced if it exists in an environment that supports the development of a capable and ready cybersecurity workforce which are: a national cybersecurity regulatory framework with a relevant act of law specifically for cybersecurity issues, institutional cybersecurity policies, and active industry cybersecurity associations to share and promote best practices and industry practice that promotes and values the development of cybersecurity knowledge and skills.

Figure 6. Cybersecurity workforce framework for universities

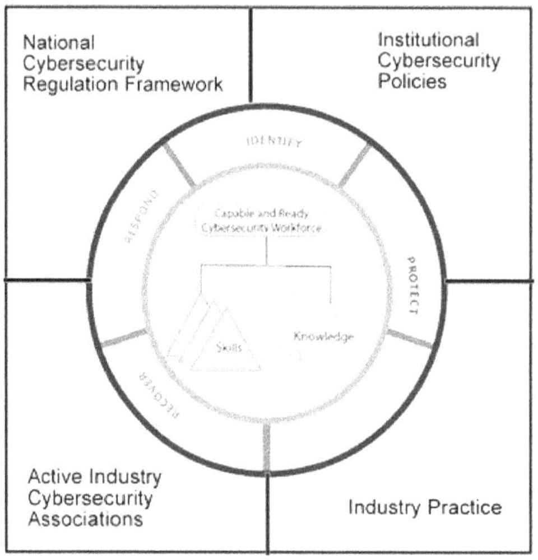

The redesigned framework has the following four additional elements that will make it understandable and improve its usefulness and practicality.

National Cybersecurity Regulation Framework

A national regulatory body that effectively fights cybercrime through promoting coordinated tactics and planning, as well as creating a cybersecurity capable workforce with necessary cybersecurity knowledge, skills and infrastructure. The regulator has to have the ability to successfully coordinate institutional resources to achieve common Cybersecurity safety and security goals (including planning, response coordination, monitoring, and evaluation). In the case of Zimbabwe, POTRAZ is the regulator that has been tasked with this mandate in the draft Cyber Bill however, the implementation and coordination of this mandate to the educational institutions, especially universities. It is also possible to begin imparting cybersecurity knowledge as early as primary and high school when the introduction to computers begins.

Institutional Policies

The cybersecurity roles and responsibilities should be clearly articulated in institutional policies to an individual level in standard operating procedures and job descriptions. Cybersecurity crisis management, emergency response plans and recovery plans should be properly communicated to all stakeholders and users should also be educated on the importance of adhering to these policies instead of them just being documents.

Active Industry Cybersecurity Association

This is necessary to provide an education and networking platform for cybersecurity professionals and senior IT security leaders in different industries for peer learning and knowledge sharing in the form of workshops, presentations, and lectures on trending cybersecurity challenges and updating of required knowledge and skills to be considered by higher education institutions like universities when developing cybersecurity course content and programs so that they always produce professionals with valid cybersecurity knowledge and skills.

Industry Practice

The industry must make it a standard to assess cybersecurity knowledge and skills during the recruitment stage. As much as universities can setup training, best practice policies and standard operating procedures, it is necessary that they also recruit staff members who have adequate cybersecurity knowledge and skills and an attitude of stewardship and an understanding of their roles and responsibilities in safeguarding institutional assets from cyberattacks.

DISCUSSION OF RESULTS

It can be summarized that students and staff in universities have an appreciation of cybersecurity and can do better in safeguarding cyberspace. However, due to limited cybersecurity skills and knowledge emanating from a lack of exposure to cybersecurity education material. These findings are similar to the findings of the study conducted by Matyokurehwa et al. (2021) which found that there was poor cybersecurity awareness (CSA) in Zimbabwean universities and there was a need for decision-makers to come up with policies concerning CSA in the higher education sector.

Universities are responsible for producing professionals with the necessary skills and capabilities; however, from the findings of the study we observed that there is a gap between cybersecurity skills and knowledge necessary for a capable workforce of professionals that have the specialities to handle cybersecurity matters and this is in line with observations made by Milller and Molina-Ray (2014) that with the growing demand for competent cybersecurity professionals, industry leaders are increasingly advocating for a unified definition of cybersecurity's scope of work and agreed-upon competencies that cybersecurity professionals must exhibit. Defining a set of industry-aligned professional competences can aid in educating, hiring, developing, and retaining high-quality employees.

The findings of the study linked student and staff cybersecurity behaviour with common cybersecurity challenges that universities face caused by human factored vulnerabilities which were poor familiarity with cyber threats especially social engineering attacks which are the most common in universities, lack of exposure to cybersecurity education materials, poor cybersecurity self-efficacy, poor cues to action in the event of a detected cyber-attack, poor computer and internet skills and lack of prior experience with computers. These findings were similar to the findings of the study conducted by Fatokun Faith et al. (2020) which instigates the need for more cybersecurity training and practices in tertiary institutions.

Exploring the relationship between these factors and the cybersecurity behaviour of staff and students highlighted the cybersecurity knowledge and skills gap that is existent in universities. Regular updating of content in mandatory introductory computer courses with cybersecurity material, taken by new students and staff will go a long way in cultivating a cybersecurity culture in universities that is reinforced by follow up training and workshops so that students and staff are always up to date with trending threats and will always have valid skills to tackle them. This is an initiative that needs to be driven by a national cybersecurity education authority which advocates for cybersecurity education from as early as primary when students are introduced to using computers.

It is of outermost importance now more than ever to have a cybersecurity culture and development of cybersecurity knowledge and skills as most businesses including universities have shifted most of their processes online to facilitate learning and working from home due to the COVID-19 pandemic. This means that universities are relaxing most security measures to cater for academic openness and freedom, however, exposing these systems to students and staff without the necessary knowledge and skills to safeguard the extended cyberspace.

An interesting finding about this research is that universities are bodies of knowledge however it is evident from the findings that students and staff are not exposed to cybersecurity educational materials. These findings support the conclusion of other studies that decision-makers and management need to support and come up with policies concerning cybersecurity education in universities (Matyokurehwa et al., 2021) and engage in cybersecurity capacity building instead of it just being a function of IT.

SUMMARY OF RESULTS OR FINDINGS

From the findings of the interviews that were carried out, major themes like the behaviour of students and staff towards matters of cybersecurity, their understanding of cybersecurity and the mechanisms currently in place to protect them and other information assets from cyber threats were explored. It was established that measures such as limited user account and network access (firewall and VLANs) privileges; restricted workstation privileges where users cannot install or modify programs or applications; availability of university antivirus security software; use of strong passwords and two-factor authentication and spotting of reported spam and phishing scams have been enforced by the university however most students and staff do not have an appreciation of these measures and, hence, do not see their importance and necessity which is mainly attributed to poor awareness and education.

The other findings of the study also showed that these cybersecurity mechanisms are integrated with policies to protect human assets from cyber-attacks through enforcement of password policy, network usage and access policy, internet use policy, physical security of office equipment, email use policy however the effectiveness of these measures is still dependent on the behaviour of the staff and students when they are in the cyberspace. It is also evident from the results that there is room for improvement, especially in the communication strategies that the university can use to raise awareness like updating content for mandatory introductory computer courses as interview findings showed that the university curriculum is not being adjusted fast enough to ensure an adequate pipeline of qualified individuals for cybersecurity roles in the industry.

CONCLUSION

The following conclusions are observed from the study:

University students and staff acknowledged that they were interested in safeguarding the cyber space of the university. Despite measures and efforts taken by universities in protecting their human assets, they were limitations including poor exposure to cybersecurity educational materials which has affected the understanding and appreciation of cybersecurity issues and contributed to poor cybersecurity behaviour that exposes university assets to cyber-attacks.

Exploring and identifying the key cybersecurity challenges affecting universities and the factors causing these challenges at Africa University allowed a greater understanding of the current state of affairs before implementing the suggested human-centric cybersecurity framework to facilitate the development of cybersecurity knowledge and skills, empowerment and strengthening of human analytical abilities of students and staff to identify, protect, detect, respond and recover from cyber-attacks and overall improving the quality of education and professionals going in the industry.

The key participants in this study identified the following as barriers to the development of cybersecurity knowledge and skills: a lack of sufficient and relevant cybersecurity educational materials, poor understanding of measures and policies already in place, poor knowledge of common cyber threats like social engineering attacks and invalid course material in computer introductory courses.

Results from this research align with findings of other studies supporting that cybercriminals target people and not computers and also humans are the weakest link in cybersecurity solutions hence it is critical to protect the human asset. However, human asset has to be aware of their role and responsibility in safeguarding their cyberspace and this is only possible if they have the right cybersecurity knowledge and skills, tools and resources to do so. Results also revealed that there is a misconception that having an antivirus installed on a computer solves all cybersecurity challenges and that individuals are not targets of cybercrime when in fact their cyber behaviour is what social engineers target and exploit when carrying out cyber-attacks.

Although the results from this study cannot be generalised to larger universities, they resound with findings submitted by other studies conducted around Zimbabwe and the world that there is a need for the development and improvement of cybersecurity knowledge and skills to produce a cybersecurity capable workforce to deal with looming cybersecurity challenges in all industries.

The implementation of the developed human-centric framework is a step in a good direction in protecting universities from the imminent problem of cyber-attacks that are currently plaguing the higher education sector at a global level. The development of cybersecurity knowledge and skills in universities as a preventive measure will also help protect national cyberspace and improve cybersecurity readiness as the result of this framework is having a cybersecurity capable workforce. By addressing human factored vulnerabilities through the development of cybersecurity knowledge and skills, universities can contribute to solving a pertinent problem in the field of cybersecurity which is the human element being the weakest link in cybersecurity solutions. The effectiveness of technical solutions improves if the human element plays its part which is not being vulnerable due to lack of knowledge.

Overall , the body of knowledge for cybersecurity needs to be driven by universities and they need to inform cybersecurity education initiatives about trending cybersecurity issues whilst practising what they discover through research and feeding the industry with seasoned cybersecurity professionals.

RECOMMENDATIONS FOR FUTURE PRACTICE

Cybersecurity is a fast growing field that is in dire need of qualified professionals who can address complex cybersecurity challenges in different industries across a variety of existing and emerging technologies and digital environments. This demand for cybersecurity professionals means there are job opportunities in different industries with high incomes for those with cybersecurity specialities. This is an opportunity for universities to fill in this education to workforce gap. There is an opportunity for universities to tailor make cybersecurity programs that align with this need.

Cyberattacks and successful breaches are costly in terms of reputation and financially. Human asset is frequently the weak link in an organization's security therefore organisations need to invest in cybersecurity policy development. A cybersecurity policy establishes the rules of engagement for all operations hence individual duties for protecting critical information assets must be outlined in a cybersecurity policy. These policies also need to be guided by a national regulatory framework that interacts with the government, universities and industry and gives guidelines on cybersecurity concerns regarding emerging technologies and the technical knowledge and skills required to adopt such technologies.

RECOMMENDATIONS FOR FUTURE RESEARCH

Human development involves a wide range of changes and patterns. Individual differences in the abilities that are developed and those that stay underdeveloped are significant as a result of diversity in social practices. Future research could delve into the social cognitive theory by Bandura (1989) in the development of cybersecurity knowledge and skills, which could examine students' and staff's unique cybersecurity capacities and human analytical abilities. Knowledge and thinking skills provide the substance and tools for cognitive problem solving. Further studies could investigate cognitive functioning which involves knowledge and cognitive skills for operating on the knowledge. Cognitive achievements necessitate the learning of domain-relevant knowledge as well as the applicable judgement criteria.

REFERENCES

Addae, J., Radenkovic, X. S., & Towey, D. (2016). An Extended Perspective on Cybersecurity Education. *2016 IEEE International Conference on Teaching, Assessment, and Learning for Engineering (TALE)*, 367-369. 10.1109/TALE.2016.7851822

Airehrour, D., Nair, N. V., & Madanian, S. (2018). Social engineering attacks and countermeasures in the New Zealand Banking System: Advancing a user-reflective mitigation model. *Information (Basel)*, *9*(5), 110. Advance online publication. doi:10.3390/info9050110

Alharbi, T., & Tassaddiq, A. (2021). Assessment of cybersecurity awareness among students of Majmaah University. *Big Data and Cognitive Computing*, *5*(2), 23. Advance online publication. doi:10.3390/bdcc5020023

Alshenqeeti, H. (2014). Interviewing as a Data Collection Method: A Critical Review. *English Linguistics Research*, *3*(1). Advance online publication. doi:10.5430/elr.v3n1p39

Ani, U. D., He, H., & Tiwari, A. (2019). Human factor security: Evaluating the cybersecurity capacity of the industrial workforce. *Journal of Systems and Information Technology*, *21*(1), 2–35. doi:10.1108/JSIT-02-2018-0028

APWG. (2017). *APWG: Unifying the Global Response to Cybercrime*. Retrieved on September 22, 2022, from: http://www.antiphishing.org/

Armerdeing, T. (2014). *Security training is lacking: Here are tips on how to do it better*. Retrieved on August 2, 2022, from: https://www.csoonline.com/article/2362793/security-leadership/security-training-islacking-here-are-tips-on-how-to-do-it-better.html

Bada, M., Sasse, A. M., & Nurse, J. R. C. (2019, January 9). *Cyber Security Awareness Campaigns: Why do they fail to change behaviour?* arXiv.

Baker, M., & Schaltegger, S. (2015). Pragmatism and new directions in social and environmental accountability research. *Accounting, Auditing & Accountability Journal*, *28*(2), 263–294. doi:10.1108/AAAJ-08-2012-01079

Beecham, S., Hall, T., Britton, C., Cottee, M., & Rainer, A. (2005). Using an expert panel to validate a requirements process improvement model. *Journal of Systems and Software*, *76*(3), 251–275. doi:10.1016/j.jss.2004.06.004

Bezuidenhout, M., Mouton, F., & Venter, H. S. (2010). Social engineering attack detection model: SEADM. *Proceedings of the 2010 Information Security for South Africa Conference, ISSA 2010*. 10.1109/ISSA.2010.5588500

Bullée, J., & Junger, M. (2020). The Palgrave Handbook of International Cybercrime and Cyberdeviance. The Palgrave Handbook of International Cybercrime and Cyberdeviance. doi:10.1007/978-3-319-90307-1

Channon, M. (2019). Cyber security and data protection. *The Law and Autonomous Vehicles*, 47–63. doi:10.4324/9781315268187-5

Coffey, J. W., Haveard, M., & Golding, G. (2018). A case study in the implementation of a human-centric higher education cybersecurity program. *Journal of Cybersecurity Education, Research and Practice*, *2018*(1), 4.

Cojocariu, A.-C., Verzea, I., & Chaib, R. (2020). Aspects of Cyber-Security in Higher Education Institutions. *Aspects of Cyber-Security in Higher Education Institutions*, (August), 3–11. doi:10.1007/978-3-030-44711-3_1

Craigen, D., Diakun-Thibault, N., & Purse, R. (2014). Defining Cybersecurity. *Technology Innovation Management Review*, *4*(10), 13–21. doi:10.22215/timreview/835

Creswell, J. (2013). Steps in Conducting a Scholarly Mixed Methods Study Abstract for DBER Group Discussion on 2013 - 11 - 14. *Steps in Conducting a Scholarly Mixed Methods Study*, 1–54. Retrieved from https://digitalcommons.unl.edu/cgi/viewcontent.cgi?article=1047&context=dberspeakers

Crowe. (2011). The case study approach. *Business Communication Quarterly*, 1. PMID:21707982

Dell. (2017). Recovering from a Destructive Cyber-attack. *Dell EMC*. Retrieved on November 2, 2021, from: https://www.emc.com/collateral/whitepaper/recovering-business-destructive-cyber-attack.pdf?isKoreaPage=false&domainUrlForCanonical=https%3A%2F%2Fwww.emc.com

Deloitte. (2016). *Readiness, response, and recovery*. Retrieved on May 9, 2021, from: https://www2.deloitte.com/content/dam/Deloitte/global/Documents/Risk/gx-cm-cyber-pov.pdf

Dhillon, G. (2015). What To Do Before And After A Cybersecurity Breach? *The Changing Faces of Cybersecurity Governance*, 1–16.

Fàbregues, S., & Molina-Azorín, J. F. (2017). Addressing quality in mixed methods research: A review and recommendations for a future agenda. *Quality & Quantity*, *51*(6), 2847–2863. doi:10.100711135-016-0449-4

Fatokun Faith, B., Hamid, S., Norman, A., Fatokun Johnson, O., & Eke, C. I. (2020). Relating Factors of Tertiary Institution Students' Cybersecurity Behavior. *2020 International Conference in Mathematics, Computer Engineering and Computer Science, ICMCECS 2020*. 10.1109/ICMCECS47690.2020.246990

FERPA. (1974). *Family Educational Rights and Privacy Act (FERPA)*. Available on https://ed.gov/policy/gen/guid/fpco/ferpa/index.html

FIPS. (2015). *Federal Information Processing Standateds Publications*. Available on: https://csrc.nist.gov/publications/PubsFIPS.html

Fleming, J., & Zegwaard, K. E. (2018). Methodologies, methods and ethical considerations for conducting research in work-integrated learning. *International Journal of Work-Integrated Learning*, *19*(3), 205–213.

Furman, S., Theofanos, M. F., Choong, Y. Y., & Stanton, B. (2011). Basing cybersecurity training on user perceptions. *IEEE Security and Privacy*, *10*(2), 40–49. doi:10.1109/MSP.2011.180

Gallegos-Segovia, P. L., Vintimilla-Tapia, P. E., Bravo-Torres, J. F., Yuquilima-Albarado, I. F., Larios-Rosillo, V. M., & Jara-Saltos, J. D. (2017). Social engineering as an attack vector for ransomware. *2017 CHILEAN Conference on Electrical, Electronics Engineering, Information and Communication Technologies, CHILECON 2017 - Proceedings*, 1–6. 10.1109/CHILECON.2017.8229528

Garcia-Alis, A. N. C. (2020). *'Lessons learnt' from the Maastricht University cyber attack*. Academic Press.

Garwe, E. C., & Thondhlana, J. (2020). Encyclopedia of International Higher Education Systems and Institutions. Encyclopedia of International Higher Education Systems and Institutions. doi:10.1007/978-94-017-9553-1

Gastellier-Prevost, S., Granadillo, G. G., & Laurent, M. (2011). A dual approach to detect pharming attacks at the client-side. *2011 4th IFIP International Conference on New Technologies, Mobility and Security, NTMS 2011 - Proceedings*. 10.1109/NTMS.2011.5721063

Goldkhul, G. (2012). Pragmatism vs interpretivism in qualitative information systems research. *European Journal of Information Systems*, *21*(2), 135–146. doi:10.1057/ejis.2011.54

Gratian, M., Bandi, S., Cukier, M., Dykstra, J., & Ginther, A. (2018). Correlating human traits and cyber security behaviour intentions. *Computers & Security*, *73*(December), 345–358. doi:10.1016/j.cose.2017.11.015

Hadnagy, C. (2015). *Phishing Dark Waters*. Retrieved on November 11, 2020, from: http://www.wiley.com/go/permissions

Hevner, A. R., March, S. T., Park, J., & Ram, S. (2004). Design science in information systems research. *Management Information Systems Quarterly*, *28*(1), 75–105. doi:10.2307/25148625

Howarth, F. (2014). *The Role of Human Error in Successful Security Attacks. Online*. Available: https://securityintelligence.com/the-role-of-human-error-in-successful-security-attacks/

Hummer, L. (2016). *Security Starts with People: Three Steps to Build a Strong Insider Threat Protection Program Online*. Available: https://securityintelligence.com/security-starts-withpeople-three-steps-to-build-a-strong-insider-threat-protection-prog
ram

ITU. (2012). *Cybercrime Understanding Cybercrime : Understanding Cybercrime: Phenomena, Challenges and Legal Response*. ITU.

Joint Technology Committee. (2016). *Responding to a Cyberattack*. Retrieved on October 7, 2021, from: https://www.ncsc.org/~/media/Files/PDF/About Us/Committees/JTC/JTC Resource Bulletins/RespondingtoCyberAttack2-26-2016FINAL.ashx

Kanyangale, M. (2019). Seven Snags of Research Ethics on the Qualitative Research Voyage. *International Business Research*, *12*(6), 1. doi:10.5539/ibr.v12n6p1

Kaushik, V., & Walsh, C. A. (2019). Pragmatism as a research paradigm and its implications for Social Work research. *Social Sciences, 8*(9). doi:10.3390/socsci8090255.h

Kinyongo, T. (2020, February). *Data presentation, analysis and interpretation 4.0 introduction*. Academic Press.

KPMG. (2014). *Cyber Security: It's not Just about Technology The Five Most Common Mistakes*. Retrieved on June 2, 2020, from: http://www.kpmg.com/US/informationprotection

Krombholz, K., Hobel, H., Huber, M., & Weippl, E. (2015). Advanced social engineering attacks. *Journal of Information Security and Applications*, *22*(October), 113–122. doi:10.1016/j.jisa.2014.09.005

Kubai, E. (2019). *Reliability and Validity of Research Instruments*. UNICAF University. Retrieved on January 28, 2021, from: https://www.researchgate.net/publication/335827941_Reliability_and_Validity_of_Research_Instruments_Correspondence_to_ku
baiedwinyahoocom

Lansley, M., Polatidis, N., Kapetanakis, S., Amin, K., Samakovitis, G., & Petridis, M. (2019). Seen the villains: Detecting social engineering attacks using case-based reasoning and deep learning. *CEUR Workshop Proceedings*, *2567*, 39–48.

Lehto, M. (2020). Cyber security capacity building: Cyber security education in finnish universities. *European Conference on Information Warfare and Security, ECCWS,* 221–231. 10.34190/EWS.20.112

Maranga, M. J., & Nelson, M. (2019). Emerging Issues in Cyber Security for Institutions of Higher Education. *International Journal of Computer Science and Network, 8*(4), 371–379. Retrieved from www.IJCSN.org

Matyokurehwa, K., Rudhumbu, N., Gombiro, C., & Mlambo, C. (2021). Cybersecurity awareness in Zimbabwean universities: Perspectives from the students. *Security and Privacy*, *4*(2). Advance online publication. doi:10.1002py2.141

Milller, L., & Molina-Ray, C. (2014). *Cybersecurity workforce competencies: Preparing tomorrow's risk-ready professionals*. Retrieved on August 3, 2019, from: https://securityexpo.asisonline.org/Pages/default.aspx

Mitchell, A. J. (2018). (PDF) "A Review of Mixed Methods, Pragmatism and Abduction Techniques" has now been published in The Electronic Journal of Business Research Methods, Volume 16 Issue 3. *Electronic Journal of Business Research Methods*, *16*(3), 103–116. Retrieved March 30, 2019, from https://www.researchgate.net/publication/328343822_A_Review_of_Mixed_Methods_Pragmatism_and_Abduction_Techniques_has_now_been_published_in_The_Electronic_Journal_of_Business_Research_Methods_Volume_16_Issue_3

Mohajan, H. K. (2017). Two Criteria for Good Measurements in Research: Validity and Reliability. *Annals of Spiru Haret University. Economic Series*, *17*(4), 59–82. doi:10.26458/1746

Muniandy, L., Muniandy, B., & Samsudin, Z. (2017). Cyber Security Behaviour among Higher Education Students in Malaysia. *Journal of Information Assurance & Cybersecurity*, 1–13. doi:10.5171/2017.800299

National Institute of Standards And Technology. (2018). *Framework for Improving Critical Infrastructure Cybersecurity*. Retrieved from https://nvlpubs.nist.gov/nistpubs/CSWP/NIST.CSWP.04162018.pdf%0Ahttps://doi.org/10.6028/NIST.CSWP.04162018

Navarro-Rivera, J., & Kosmin, B. A. (2013). Surveys and questionnaires. The Routledge Handbook of Research Methods in the Study of Religion, 395–420. https://doi.org/ doi:10.4324/9780203154281-35

Nguyen, H. V. (2019). Cybersecurity Strategies for Universities with Bring Your Own Device Programs. *ProQuest Dissertations and Theses*, 150. Retrieved on September 4, 2020, from: https://search.proquest.com/docview/2329729362?accountid=17242

Nilsen, R. K. (2017). Measuring cybersecurity competency: An exploratory investigation of the cybersecurity knowledge, skills, and abilities necessary for organizational network access privileges. *ProQuest Dissertations and Theses UMI Number*, *10641545*(1017), i–292.

NIST. (2020). *NICE Framework*. NIST.

Nohlberg, M. (2008). Securing Information Assets: Understanding, Measuring and Protecting against Social Engineering Attacks. *Engineering*. Retrieved from https://www.mendeley.com/research/securing-information-assets-understanding-measuring-protecting-against-social-engineering-attacks/

Oblinger, D. (2003). *Higher Education IT Security and Academic Values*. Academic Press.

Podsakoff, P. M., MacKenzie, S. B., Lee, J. Y., & Podsakoff, N. P. (2003). Common Method Biases in Behavioral Research: A Critical Review of the Literature and Recommended Remedies. *The Journal of Applied Psychology*, *88*(5), 879–903. doi:10.1037/0021-9010.88.5.879 PMID:14516251

PWC. (2016). *Global Economic Crime Survey 2016: US Results*. PwC. Retrieved from https://www.pwc.com/us/en/forensic-services/economic-crime-survey-us-supplement.html

Reid, A. M., Brown, J. M., Smith, J. M., Cope, A. C., & Jamieson, S. (2018). Ethical dilemmas and reflexivity in qualitative research. *Perspectives on Medical Education*, *7*(2), 69–75. doi:10.1007/S40037-018-0412-2 PMID:29536374

Richardson, M. D., Lemoine, P. A., & Waller, R. E. (2020). Planning for cyber security in schools. *The Human Factor*, *27*(2), 23–39.

Rogers, G., & Ashford, T. (2015). Mitigating Higher Ed Cyber Attacks. *Association Supporting Computer Users in Education*, 48. Retrieved from https://liverpool.idm.oclc.org/login?url=https://search.ebscohost.com/login.aspx?direct=true&db=eric&AN=ED571277&site=eds-live&scope=site

Ryan, F., Coughlan, M., & Cronin, P. (2009). Interviewing in qualitative research: The one-to-one interview. *International Journal of Therapy and Rehabilitation*, *16*(6), 309–314. doi:10.12968/ijtr.2009.16.6.42433

Saunders, M. N. K., Lewis, P., & Thornhill, A. (2019). Research Methods for Business Students. In *Understanding research philosophy and approaches to theory development*. Retrieved from www.pearson.com/uk

Schmeelk, S., & Dragos, D. (2021). *2020 CSJ NICE Special Issue Online*. Academic Press.

Sekaran Uma, B. R. (2016). *Research Methode for Business: a skill-building approach* (7th ed.). John Wiley & Sons Ltd.

Shedden, P., Ahmad, A., Smith, W., Tscherning, H., & Scheepers, R. (2016). Asset identification in information security risk assessment: A business practice approach. *Communications of the Association for Information Systems*, *39*(1), 297–320. doi:10.17705/1CAIS.03915

Showkat, N., & Parveen, H. (2017). *Quadrant-I (e-Text)*. Academic Press.

Srinivasan, J. (2017). Disaster Recovery, an Element of Cyber Security-a Flick Through. *Researchgate.Net*. Retrieved from https://www.researchgate.net/profile/J_Srinivasan/publication/320244744_DISASTER_RECOVERY_AN_ELEMENT_OF_CYBER_SECURITY-A_FLICK_THROUGH/links/59d74e74a6fdcc52acae4816/DISASTER-RECOVERY-AN-ELEMENT-OF-CYBER-SECURITY-A-FLICK-THROUGH.pdf

Strang, M., & James, W. (2007). *Research Onion*. Academic Press.

Taherdoost, H. (2016). Sampling Methods in Research Methodology; How to Choose a Sampling Technique for Research. *International Journal of Academic Research in Management*, *5*(2), 18–27.

Taherdoost, H. (2018). Validity and Reliability of the Research Instrument; How to Test the Validation of a Questionnaire/Survey in a Research. SSRN *Electronic Journal*. doi:10.2139/ssrn.3205040

Teodoro, N., Gonçalves, L., & Serrão, C. (2015). NIST cybersecurity framework compliance: A generic model for dynamic assessment and predictive requirements. *Proceedings - 14th IEEE International Conference on Trust, Security and Privacy in Computing and Communications, TrustCom 2015, 1*, 418–425. 10.1109/Trustcom.2015.402

Tilly, B. (2014). *Implementing an effective cybersecurity management program*. Retrieved on July 4, 2022, from: https://bakertilly.com/insights/implementing-an-effective-cybersecuritymanagement-program/

Tongco, M. D. C. (2007). Purposive sampling as a tool for informant selection. *Ethnobotany Research and Applications*, *5*, 147–158. doi:10.17348/era.5.0.147-158

Turner, S. L., Karahalios, A., Forbes, A. B., Taljaard, M., Grimshaw, J. M., Cheng, A. C., Bero, L., & McKenzie, J. E. (2020). Design characteristics and statistical methods used in interrupted time series studies evaluating public health interventions: A review. *Journal of Clinical Epidemiology*, *122*, 1–11. doi:10.1016/j.jclinepi.2020.02.006 PMID:32109503

Ulven, J. B., & Wangen, G. (2021). A systematic review of cybersecurity risks in higher education. *Future Internet*, *13*(2), 1–40. doi:10.3390/fi13020039

Vishik, C., Matsubara, M., & Plonk, A. (2016). Key Concepts in Cyber Security: Towards a Common Policy and Technology Context for Cyber Security Norms. *International Cyber Norms: Legal, Policy & Industry Perspective*, 221–242.

VMWare. (2016). *University Challenge : Cyber Attacks in Higher Education A report by VMware exploring the*. Author.

Von Solms, R., & Van Niekerk, J. (2013). From information security to cyber security. *Computers & Security*, *38*, 97–102. doi:10.1016/j.cose.2013.04.004

Wahyuni, D. (2012). The research design maze: Understanding paradigms, cases, methods and methodologies. *Journal of Applied Management Accounting Research*, *10*(1), 69–80.

Wedawatta, G., Ingirige, B., & Amaratunga, D. (2011). Case study as a research strategy : Investigating extreme weather resilience of construction SMEs in the. *7th Annual International Conference of International Institute for Infrastructure*, 1–9.

Zwilling, M., Klien, G., Lesjak, D., Wiechetek, Ł., Cetin, F., & Basim, H. N. (2020). Cyber Security Awareness, Knowledge and Behavior: A Comparative Study. *Journal of Computer Information Systems*, 1–16. doi:10.1080/08874417.2020.1712269

Compilation of References

Abrams, L. (2021). *7 million Robinhood user email addresses for sale on hacker forum.* BleepingComputer. Retrieved on June 2, 2022, from: https://www.bleepingcomputer.com/news/security/7-million-robinhood-user-email-addresses-for-sale-on-hacker-forum/

Abri, F., Siami-Namini, S., Khanghah, M. A., Soltani, F. M., & Namin, A. S. (2019, December). Can machine/deep learning classifiers detect zero-day malware with high accuracy? In 2019 IEEE international conference on big data (Big Data) (pp. 3252-3259). IEEE.

Acquisti, A., Adjerid, I., Balebako, R., Brandimarte, L., Cranor, L., Komanduri, S., Leon, P., Sadeh, N., Schaub, F., Sleeper, M., Wang, Y., & Wilson, S. (2017). Nudges for privacy and security. *ACM Computing Surveys*, *50*(3), 1–41. doi:10.1145/3054926

Addae, J., Radenkovic, X. S., & Towey, D. (2016). An Extended Perspective on Cybersecurity Education. *2016 IEEE International Conference on Teaching, Assessment, and Learning for Engineering (TALE),* 367-369. 10.1109/TALE.2016.7851822

Afianian, A., Niksefat, S., Sadeghiyan, B., & Baptiste, D. (2019). Malware dynamic analysis evasion techniques: A survey. *ACM Computing Surveys*, *52*(6), 1–28. doi:10.1145/3365001

Aftergood, S. (2017). Cybersecurity: The cold war online. *Nature, 57*, 30–31. https://doi.org/10.1038/547030a

Agrawal, A., Khan, R. A., & Ansari, M. T. J. (2023). Empowering Indian citizens through the secure e-governance: The digital India initiative context. In *Emerging Technologies in Data Mining and Information Security* (pp. 3–11). Springer. doi:10.1007/978-981-19-4676-9_1

Ahmed, O. (2022). *Behaviour Anomaly on Linux Systems to Detect Zero-day Malware Attacks* [Doctoral dissertation]. Auckland University of Technology.

Ahmed, N., Ahmed, N., & Nafees, A. (2020). Cybersecurity challenges in healthcare: A systematic review. *International Journal of Healthcare Management*, *13*(1), 33–41.

AICPA. (2022). *SOC Service Organizations: Information for Service Organizations.* AICPA. https://us.aicpa.org/interestareas/frc/assuranceadvisoryservices/serviceorganization-smanagement

Airehrour, D., Nair, N. V., & Madanian, S. (2018). Social engineering attacks and countermeasures in the New Zealand Banking System: Advancing a user-reflective mitigation model. *Information (Basel)*, *9*(5), 110. Advance online publication. doi:10.3390/info9050110

Aivazpour, Z. (2019). *Impulsivity and Risky Cybersecurity Behaviors: A Replication Impulsivity View project.* Academic Press.

Akamai Technologies. (2020). *W at is a botnet attack?* https://www.akamai.com/us/en/resources/what-is-a-botnet.jsp

Alharbi, T., & Tassaddiq, A. (2021). Assessment of cybersecurity awareness among students of Majmaah University. *Big Data and Cognitive Computing*, *5*(2), 23. Advance online publication. doi:10.3390/bdcc5020023

Alismail, A., Altulaihan, E., Rahman, M. M., & Sufian, A. (2023). *A Systematic Literature Review on Cybersecurity Threats of Virtual Reality (VR) and Augmented Reality*. Data Intelligence and Cognitive Informatics.

AlKalbani, A., AlBusaidi, H., & Deng, H. (2023). Using a Q-Methodology in Demystifying Typologies for Cybersecurity Practitioners: A Case Study. In *Intelligent Sustainable Systems* (pp. 291–303). Springer. doi:10.1007/978-981-19-7660-5_26

Almalki, M., & Giannicchi, A. (2021). Health Apps for Combating COVID-19: Descriptive Review and Taxonomy. *JMIR mHealth and uHealth*, *9*(3), e24322. Advance online publication. doi:10.2196/24322 PMID:33626017

Almatari, O., Wang, X., Zhang, W., & Khan, M. K. (2023). *VTAIM: Volatile Transaction Authentication Insurance Method for Cyber Security Risk Insurance of Banking Services*. Academic Press.

Aloul, F. A. (2012). The Need for Effective Information Security Awareness. *Journal of Advances in Information Technology*, *3*(3). Advance online publication. doi:10.4304/jait.3.3.176-183

Alshenqeeti, H. (2014). Interviewing as a Data Collection Method: A Critical Review. *English Linguistics Research*, *3*(1). Advance online publication. doi:10.5430/elr.v3n1p39

Altmann, S., Milsom, L., Zillessen, H., Blasone, R., Gerdon, F., Bach, R., Kreuter, F., Nosenzo, D., Toussaert, S., & Abeler, J. (2020). Acceptability of app-based contact tracing for COVID-19: Cross-country survey study. *JMIR mHealth and uHealth*, *8*(8), e19857. Advance online publication. doi:10.2196/19857 PMID:32759102

Amann, J., Sleigh, J., & Vayena, E. (2021). Digital contact-tracing during the Covid-19 pandemic: An analysis of newspaper coverage in Germany, Austria, and Switzerland. *PLoS One*, *16*(2), e0246524. Advance online publication. doi:10.1371/journal.pone.0246524 PMID:33534839

Ambrose, J. (2021). China's nuclear power firm could be blocked from UK projects. *The Guardian*. Retrieved on November 3, 2022, from: https://www.theguardian.com/environment/2021/jul/26/chinas-n uclear-power-firm-could-be-blocked-from-uk-projects

Amir, E., Levi, S., & Livne, T. (2018). Do firms underreport information on cyber-attacks? Evidence from capital markets. *Review of Accounting Studies*, *23*(3), 1177–1206. doi:10.100711142-018-9452-4

Anand, P., Singh, Y., & Selwal, A. (2022). Learning-Based Techniques for Assessing Zero-Day Attacks and Vulnerabilities in IoT. In *Recent Innovations in Computing* (pp. 497–504). Springer. doi:10.1007/978-981-16-8248-3_41

Anant, V., Bailey, T., Cracknell, R., Kaplan, J., & Schwartz, A. (2019). *Understanding the uncertainties of cybersecurity: Questions for chief information-security officers*. McKinsey & Company. Retrieved on September 4, 2022, from: https://www.mckinsey.com/capabilities/mckinsey-digital/our-i nsights/digital-blog/understanding-the-uncertainties-of-cybe rsecurity-questions-for-chief-information-security-officers

Anderson, A., & Raine, L. (2020). *Concerns about democracy in the digital age*. Pew Research. https://www.pewresearch.org/internet/2020/02/21/concerns-about-democra cy-in-the-digital-age/

Anderson, R., Barton, C., Böhme, R., Clayton, R., Gañán, C., Grasso, T., Levi, M., Moore, T., & Vasek, M. (2019). *Measuring the Changing Cost of Cybercrime*. Available from: https://www.paccsresearch.org.uk/wp content/uploads/2019/06/ WEIS_2019_paper_25.pdf

Anderson, A. J., Kaplan, S. A., & Vega, R. P. (2014). The impact of telework on emotional experience: When, and for whom, does telework improve daily affective well-being? *European Journal of Work and Organizational Psychology*, *24*(6), 882–897. doi:10.1080/1359432X.2014.966086

Anderson, R., & Fuloria, S. (2010). Security Economics and Critical National Infrastructure. In T. Moore, D. Pym, & C. Ioannidis (Eds.), *Economics of Information Security and Privacy* (pp. 55–66). Springer US. doi:10.1007/978-1-4419-6967-5_4

Andreassen, C. S., Griffiths, M. D., Gjertsen, S. R., Krossbakken, E., Kvam, S., & Pallesen, S. (2013). The relationships between behavioral addictions and the five-factor model of personality. *Journal of Behavioral Addictions*, *2*(2), 90–99. doi:10.1556/JBA.2.2013.003 PMID:26165928

Andrews, N. (2018). McCaskill says Senate Office was target of phishing scam. *Wall Street Journal*. https://www.wsj.com/articles/mccaskill-says-senate-office-was-target-of-phishing-scam1532656049

Ani, U. D., He, H., & Tiwari, A. (2019). Human factor security: Evaluating the cybersecurity capacity of the industrial workforce. *Journal of Systems and Information Technology*, *21*(1), 2–35. doi:10.1108/JSIT-02-2018-0028

Aoudni, Y., Donald, C., Farouk, A., Sahay, K. B., Babu, D. V., Tripathi, V., & Dhabliya, D. (2022). Cloud security based attack detection using transductive learning integrated with Hidden Markov Model. *Pattern Recognition Letters*, *157*, 16–26. doi:10.1016/j.patrec.2022.02.012

Apollo Technical. (2021). *Statistics On Remote Workers That Will Surprise You (2021)*. Apollo Technical LLC. Available from: https://www.apollotechnical.com/statistics-on-remote-workers/

APWG. (2017). *APWG: Unifying the Global Response to Cybercrime*. Retrieved on September 22, 2022, from: http://www.antiphishing.org/

Arce, D. G. (2020). Cybersecurity and platform competition in the cloud. *Computers & Security*, *93*, 1–9. doi:10.1016/j.cose.2020.101774

Armerdeing, T. (2014). *Security training is lacking: Here are tips on how to do it better*. Retrieved on August 2, 2022, from: https://www.csoonline.com/article/2362793/security-leadership/security-training-islacking-here-are-tips-on-how-to-do-it-better.html

Aryal, K., Gupta, M., & Abdelsalam, M. (2023). *Analysis of Label-Flip Poisoning Attack on Machine Learning Based Malware Detector*. arXiv preprint arXiv:2301.01044.

Augustine, N., & Millstein, I. (2023). *Governing for Enterprise Security*. SEI Digital Library. https://resources.sei.cmu.edu/asset_files/technicalnote/2005_004_001_14513.pdf

Avery, D. (2022). *Robinhood app's $20 million data breach settlement: Who is eligible for money?* CNET. Retrieved on October 19, 2022, from: https://www.cnet.com/personal-finance/banking/robinhood-20-million-settlement-who-is-eligible-for-money/

Awojobi, B., & Landry, B. J. L. (2023). An examination of factors determining user privacy perceptions of voice-based assistants. *International Journal of Management, Knowledge and Learning*, *12*, 53–62. doi:10.53615/2232-5697.12.53-62

Aybar, C. A. M., Speranza, M., Armstrong, L., Ames, J., Phillips, G., & Saling, L. (2000). Potential determinants of heavier internet usage Related papers Psychological predictors of problem mobile phone use margigretel An Investigation of Goodman's Addictive Disorder Criteria in Eating Disorders Potential determinants of heavier internet usage. *International Journal of Human-Computer Studies*, *53*, 537–550.

Ayinala, S., & Murimi, R. (2022). On a territorial notion of a smart home. In *Proceedings of the 1st Workshop on Cybersecurity and Social Sciences* (pp. 33–37). Association for Computing Machinery. 10.1145/3494108.3522766

Bada, M., Sasse, A. M., & Nurse, J. R. C. (2019, January 9). *Cyber Security Awareness Campaigns: Why do they fail to change behaviour?* arXiv.

Bada, M., & von Solms, B. (2023). A cybersecurity guide for using fitness devices. *The Fifth International Conference on Safety and Security with IoT*, 35–45. 10.1007/978-3-030-94285-4_3

Badawy, A., Addawood, A., Lerman, K., & Ferrara, E. (2019). Characterizing the 2016 Russian IRA influence campaign. *Social Network Analysis and Mining, 9*(1), 31. https://doi.org/10.1007/s13278-019-0578-6

Baehr, P. (2001). The "Iron Cage" and the "Shell as Hard as Steel": Parsons, Weber, and the Stahlhartes Gehäuse Metaphor in the Protestant Ethic and the Spirit of Capitalism. *History and Theory*, *40*(2), 153–169. doi:10.1111/0018-2656.00160

Baird, W. (2019). Counting the International Costs of Huawei Exclusion. *American Enterprise Institute - AEI*. Retrieved on November 3, 2022, from: https://www.aei.org/technology-and-innovation/telecommunications/counting-the-international-costs-of-huawei-exclusion/

Baker, M., & Schaltegger, S. (2015). Pragmatism and new directions in social and environmental accountability research. *Accounting, Auditing & Accountability Journal*, *28*(2), 263–294. doi:10.1108/AAAJ-08-2012-01079

Baker, T., & Nelson, R. E. (2005). Creating something from nothing: Resource construction through entrepreneurial bricolage. *Administrative Science Quarterly*, *50*(3), 329–366. doi:10.2189/asqu.2005.50.3.329

Ball, K., & Webster, F. (2003). *The Intensification of Surveillance: Crime, Terrorism and Warfare in the Information Age* (K. Ball & F. Webster, Eds.). Pluto Press.

Balsamo, M. (2020). Disputing Trump: Barr says no widespread election fraud. *Associate Press News*. https://apnews.com/article/barr-no-widespread-election-fraud-b1f1488796c9a98c4b1a9061a6c7f49d

Baptista, E. (2022). *Hacker offers to sell data of 48.5 million users of Shanghai's COVID app*. https://www.reuters.com/world/china/hacker-offers-sell-data-485-mln-users-shanghais-covid-app-2022-08-12/

Barnard-Wills, D., & Ashenden, D. (2012). *Securing Virtual Space*. Retrieved on April 12, 2022, from: https://journals.sagepub.com/doi/epub/10.1177/1206331211430016

Barrett, F. J. (1998). Creativity and improvisation in jazz and organizations: Implications for organizational learning. *Organization Science*, *9*(5), 605–622. doi:10.1287/orsc.9.5.605

Barry, C. (2021). *Robinhood breach illustrates the impact of social engineering attacks*. Retrieved on March 22, 2022, from: https://blog.barracuda.com/2021/11/19/robinhood-breach-illustrates-the-impact-of-social-engineering-attacks/

Bauman, Z. (2000). *Liquid Modernity*. Polity Press.

BBC News. (2020). *Aarogya Setu: Why India's Covid-19 contact tracing app is controversial.* https://www.bbc.com/news/world-asia-india-52659520

BBC. (2022). 'Worrying precedent' as hackers target South Staffs Water. *BBC News*. Retrieved on October 13, 2022, from: https://www.bbc.com/news/uk-england-stoke-staffordshire-6256 5937

Bécue, A., Praça, I., & Gama, J. (2021). Artificial intelligence, cyber-threats and Industry 4.0: Challenges and opportunities. *Artificial Intelligence Review*, *54*(5), 3849–3886. doi:10.100710462-020-09942-2

Beecham, S., Hall, T., Britton, C., Cottee, M., & Rainer, A. (2005). Using an expert panel to validate a requirements process improvement model. *Journal of Systems and Software*, *76*(3), 251–275. doi:10.1016/j.jss.2004.06.004

Bellekens, X. (2021). Cyber security in the age of COVID-19: A timeline and analysis of cyber-crime and cyber-attacks during the pandemic. *Computers & Security*, *105*, 102248. doi:10.1016/j.cose.2021.102248 PMID:36540648

Bell, R. G., Filatotchev, I., & Aguilera, R. V. (2014). Corporate governance and investors' perceptions of foreign IPO value: An institutional perspective. *Academy of Management Journal*, *57*(1), 301–320. doi:10.5465/amj.2011.0146

Bergal, J. (2021). *Florida hack exposes danger to water systems.* https://pew.org/3btxWBc

Berkman, H., Jona, J., Lee, G., & Soderstrom, N. (2018). Cybersecurity awareness and market valuations. *Journal of Accounting and Public Policy*, *37*(6), 508–526. doi:10.1016/j.jaccpubpol.2018.10.003

Bessi, A., & Ferrara, E. (2016). Social bots distort the 2016 U.S. Presidential election online discussion. *First Monday*. https://doi.org/10.5210/fm.v21i11.7090

Bezuidenhout, M., Mouton, F., & Venter, H. S. (2010). Social engineering attack detection model: SEADM. *Proceedings of the 2010 Information Security for South Africa Conference, ISSA 2010.* 10.1109/ISSA.2010.5588500

Bick, A., Blandin, A., & Mertens, K. (2021). *Work from Home Before and After the COVID-19 Outbreak.* Federal Reserve Bank of Dallas, Working Papers.

Bilge, L., & Dumitraş, T. (2012, October). Before we knew it: an empirical study of zero-day attacks in the real world. In *Proceedings of the 2012 ACM conference on Computer and communications security* (pp. 833-844). 10.1145/2382196.2382284

Bilodeau, A., & Potvin, L. (2018). Unpacking complexity in public health interventions with the Actor–Network Theory. *Health Promotion International*, *33*(1), 173–181. PMID:27492825

Bischoff, P. (2021, February 9). How data breaches affect stock market share prices. *Comparitech*. Retrieved on May 22, 2022, from: https://www.comparitech.com/blog/information-security/data-breach-share-price-analysis/

Błachnio, A., Przepiorka, A., Senol-Durak, E., Durak, M., & Sherstyuk, L. (2017). The role of personality traits in Facebook and Internet addictions: A study on Polish, Turkish, and Ukrainian samples. *Computers in Human Behavior*, *68*, 269–275. doi:10.1016/j.chb.2016.11.037

Blaise, A., Bouet, M., Conan, V., & Secci, S. (2020). Detection of zero-day attacks: An unsupervised port-based approach. *Computer Networks*, *180*, 107391. doi:10.1016/j.comnet.2020.107391

Blieberger, J., Klasek, J., Redlein, A., & Schildt, G.-H. (1996). *Informartik 3. Auflage*. Springer Verlag.

Blumbergs, B., Dobelis, E., & Paikens, P. (2023). WearSec: Towards Automated Security Evaluation of Wireless Wearable Devices. *Secure IT Systems: 27th Nordic Conference, NordSec 2022, Reykjavic, Iceland, November 30–December 2, 2022 Proceedings*, *13700*, 311.

Boeckl, K., Fagan, M., Fisher, W., Lefkovitz, N., Megas, K., Nadeau, E., Piccarreta, B., O'Rourke, D. G., & Scarfone, K. (2019). *Considerations for managing internet of things (IoT) cybersecurity and privacy risks.* National Institute of Standards and Technology, NISTIR 8228.

Bohanna, D. (1998). Water meters: An incentive to conserve and a signal to the market. *Economic Affairs*, *18*(2), 10–13. doi:10.1111/1468-0270.00085

Boisrond, P. D. (2020). *Cybersecurity and the 2020 United States presidential elections: Beware of nation-state actors.* Research state. https://www.researchgate.net/publication/344135067_Cybersecurity_and_the_2020_United_States_Presidential_Election_Beware_of_Nation-State_Actors

Bonenberger, A. (2020). *Falling Through the Cracks in Quarantine.* Available from: https://medicine.yale.edu/news-article/falling-through-the-cracks-in-quarantine/

Borlovich, D., & Skovira, R. (2020). Working from home: Cybersecurity in the age of COVID-19. *Issues In Information Systems.*

Boyce, M. W., Duma, K. M., Hettinger, L. J., Malone, T. B., Wilson, D. P., & Lockett-Reynolds, J. (2011). Human Performance in Cybersecurity: A Research Agenda. *Proceedings of the Human Factors and Ergonomics Society Annual Meeting*, *55*(1), 1115–1119. doi:10.1177/1071181311551233

Brase, G. L., Vasserman, E. Y., & Hsu, W. (2017). Do different mental models influence cybersecurity behavior? Evaluations via statistical reasoning performance. *Frontiers in Psychology*, *8*, 1929. doi:10.3389/fpsyg.2017.01929 PMID:29163304

Brenner, V. (1997). Psychology of Computer Use: XLVII. Parameters of Internet Use, Abuse and Addiction: The First 90 Days of the Internet Usage Survey. *Psychological Reports*, *80*(3), 879–882. doi:10.2466/pr0.1997.80.3.879 PMID:9198388

Brogi, M., Arcuri, M. C., & Gandolfi, G. (2018). The effect of cyber-attacks on stock returns. *Corporate Ownership and Control*, *15*(2), 70–83. doi:10.22495/cocv15i2art6

Brooks, S. K., Webster, R. K., Smith, L. E., Woodland, L., Wessely, S., Greenberg, N., & Rubin, G. J. (2020). The psychological impact of quarantine and how to reduce it: Rapid review of the evidence. [online]. *Lancet*, *395*(10227), 912–920. doi:10.1016/S0140-6736(20)30460-8 PMID:32112714

Brown, S. (2019). *Most Americans don't think it's possible to keep their data private, report says.* https://www.msn.com/en-us/news/technology/most-in-us-don-t-think-it-s-possible-to-keep-data-private/ar-BBWUn0z?ocid=anaheimntp

Brown, S. (2021). *Robinhood data breach is bad, but we've seen much worse.* CNET. Retrieved on June 2, 2022, from: https://www.cnet.com/news/privacy/robinhood-data-breach-is-bad-but-weve-seen-much-worse/

BrownI.MarsdenC. T.LeeJ.VealeM. (2020). *Cybersecurity for elections: A commonwealth guide on best practice.* doi:10.31228/osf.io/tsdfb

Bryan, K. (2020). *Fraudsters impersonate airlines and Tesco in coronavirus scams.* https://www.thetimes.co.uk/article/fraudsters-impersonate-airlines-and-tesco-in-coronavirus-scams-5wdwhxq7p

Brydon, L. (1958). *The Press and the People (No. 2). In Washington and the Press.* WGBH-TV. https://openvault.wgbh.org/catalog/V_F3669EDCE0044D9C97FD3661EF031D9 5

Buchanan, J., & Kronk, H. (2023). *The Slow Adjustment in Tech Labor: Why Do High-Paying Tech Jobs Go Unfilled?* The Center for Growth and Opportunity.

Budd, J., Miller, B. S., Manning, E. M., Lampos, V., Zhuang, M., Edelstein, M., Rees, G., Emery, V. C., Stevens, M. M., Keegan, N., Short, M. J., Pillay, D., Manley, E., Cox, I. J., Heymann, D., Johnson, A. M., & McKendry, R. A. (2020). Digital technologies in the public-health response to COVID-19. *Nature Medicine*, *26*(8), 1183–1192. doi:10.103841591-020-1011-4 PMID:32770165

Buffington, J., & McCubbrey, D. (2011). A conceptual framework of generative customization as an approach to product innovation and fulfillment. *European Journal of Innovation Management*, *14*(3), 388–403. doi:10.1108/14601061111148852

Bukauskas, L., Brilingaitė, A., Juozapavičius, A., Lepaitė, D., Ikamas, K., & Andrijauskaitė, R. (2023). Remapping cybersecurity competences in a small nation state. *Heliyon*, *9*(1), 12808. doi:10.1016/j.heliyon.2023.e12808 PMID:36685367

Bullée, J., & Junger, M. (2020). The Palgrave Handbook of International Cybercrime and Cyberdeviance. The Palgrave Handbook of International Cybercrime and Cyberdeviance. doi:10.1007/978-3-319-90307-1

Bulman, M. (2016). *Hinkley Point: Overwhelming majority of British public oppose Theresa May's decision to approve nuclear plant.* The Independent. Retrieved on November 3, 2022, from: https://www.independent.co.uk/news/uk/home-news/hinkley-point-theresa-may-nuclear-power-poll-majority-uk-opposes-plant-edf-china-a7308701.html

Bulur, S. (2020). *İçişleri Bakanlığı: 22 Ağustos'tan bu yana 20 bin 94 kişinin izolasyon koşullarına uymadığı belirlendi* [Ministry of Interior: Since August 22, it has been determined that 20,094 people have not complied with the isolation conditions]. https://www.aa.com.tr/tr/turkiye/icisleri-bakanligi-22-agustostan-bu-yana-20-bin-94-kisinin-izolasyon-kosullarina-uymadigi-belirlendi/1974931

Burgess, M. (2022, July 16). Amazon handed Ring videos to cops without warrants. *Wired.* https://www.wired.com/story/amazon-ring-police-videos-security-roundup/

Calderon, T. G., & Gao, L. (2020). Cybersecurity risks disclosure and implied audit risks: Evidence from audit fees. *International Journal of Auditing*, *25*(1), 24–39. doi:10.1111/ijau.12209

Calic, D., Pattinson, M., Parsons, K., Butavicius, M., & Mccormac, A. (2016). *Naïve and Accidental Behaviors that Compromise Information Security: What the Experts Think.* Academic Press.

Camgöz Akdağ, H., & Menekşe, A. (2023). Cybersecurity Framework Prioritization for Healthcare Organizations Using a Novel Interval-Valued Pythagorean Fuzzy CRITIC. In *Intelligent Systems in Digital Transformation* (pp. 241–266). Springer. doi:10.1007/978-3-031-16598-6_11

Caplan, S. E. (2002). Problematic Internet use and psychosocial well-being: Development of a theory-based cognitive–behavioral measurement instrument. *Computers in Human Behavior*, *18*(5), 553–575. doi:10.1016/S0747-5632(02)00004-3

Caplan, S. E. (2003). Preference for Online Social Interaction. *Communication Research*, *30*(6), 625–648. doi:10.1177/0093650203257842

Caplan, S., Williams, D., & Yee, N. (2009). Problematic Internet use and psychosocial well-being among MMO players. *Computers in Human Behavior*, *25*(6), 1312–1319. doi:10.1016/j.chb.2009.06.006

Caraban, A., Karapanos, E., Gonçalves, D., & Campos, P. (2019). 23 ways to nudge. In *Proceedings of the 2019 CHI Conference on Human Factors in Computing Systems* (pp. 1-15). https://doi.org/10.1145/3290605.3300733

Casey, E., Jocz, J., Peterson, K. A., Pfeif, D., & Soden, C. (2023). Motivating youth to learn STEM through a gender inclusive digital forensic science program. *Smart Learning Environments*, *10*(1), 1–24. doi:10.118640561-022-00213-x

Castro, D., Dascoli, L., & Diebold, G. (2022). *The looming cost of a patchwork of state privacy laws.* https://www2.itif.org/2022-state-privacy-laws.pdf

CCM. (2023). *CSA Cloud Controls Matrix (CCM).* https://cloudsecurityalliance.org/research/cloud-controls-matrix/

CDC. (2022). *Health Insurance Portability and Accountability Act of 1996 (HIPAA).* https://www.cdc.gov/phlp/publications/topic/hipaa.html

Cellini, N., Canale, N., Mioni, G., & Costa, S. (2020). Changes in sleep pattern, sense of time and digital media use during COVID-19 lockdown in Italy. *Journal of Sleep Research*, *29*(4). Advance online publication. doi:10.1111/jsr.13074 PMID:32410272

Channon, M. (2019). Cyber security and data protection. *The Law and Autonomous Vehicles*, 47–63. doi:10.4324/9781315268187-5

Chen, C., Cui, B., Ma, J., Wu, R., Guo, J., & Liu, W. (2018). A systematic review of fuzzing techniques. *Computers & Security*, *75*, 118–137. doi:10.1016/j.cose.2018.02.002

Cheng, C., Wang, H., Sigerson, L., & Chau, C. (2019). Do the socially rich get richer? A nuanced perspective on social network site use and online social capital accrual. *Psychological Bulletin*, *145*(7), 734–764. doi:10.1037/bul0000198 PMID:31094537

Chernyshev, M., Zeadally, S., & Baig, Z. (2019). Healthcare data breaches: Implications for digital forensic Readiness. *Journal of Medical Systems*, *43*(7), 7. Advance online publication. doi:10.100710916-018-1123-2 PMID:30488291

Childers, G., Linsky, C. L., Payne, B., Byers, J., & Baker, D. (2023). K-12 educators' self-confidence in designing and implementing cybersecurity lessons. *Computers and Education Open*, *4*, 100119. doi:10.1016/j.caeo.2022.100119

Chowdhury, M. (2020). Biden praises local and state officials who showed unwavering faith in the law. *CNN.* https://www.cnn.com/politics/live-news/electoral-college-vote-2020-biden-trump/index.html

Chung, H., Seo, H., Forbes, S., & Birkett, H. (2020). *Working from home during the COVID-19 lockdown: changing preferences and the future of work.* Available from: https://kar.kent.ac.uk/83896/

Ciotti, M., Ciccozzi, M., Terrinoni, A., Jiang, W.-C., Wang, C.-B., & Bernardini, S. (2020). The COVID-19 Pandemic. *Critical Reviews in Clinical Laboratory Sciences*, *57*(6), 365–388. doi:10.1080/10408363.2020.1783198 PMID:32645276

CIS. (2022). *Mapping and Compliance.* CIS Center for Internet Security. https://www.cisecurity.org/cybersecurity-tools/mapping-compliance

CIS. (2023). *CIS Center for Internet Security.* https://learn.cisecurity.org/cis-controls-download

CISA. (2021). *CISA Cybersecurity Awareness Program.* Available from: https://www.cisa.gov/cisa-cybersecurity-awareness-program

Civil Aviation Authority. (2018). *CAP1480: Implementation of the recommendations from the Independent Enquiry into the NATS Systems Failure on 12th December 2014.* Retrieved on April 15, 2022, from: https://publicapps.caa.co.uk/modalapplication.aspx?appid=11&mode=detail&id=7614&filter=2

CIWEM. (2019). *Thirty years on, what has water privatisation achieved?* CIWEM. Retrieved on April 12, 2022, from: https://www.ciwem.org/the-environment/how-should-water-and-environmental-management-firms-tap,-retain-and-promote-female-talent

Clinton, L. (2023). *Fixing American Cybersecurity: Creating a Strategic Public-private Partnership.* Georgetown University Press.

Cloutier, C., & Langley, A. (2020). What makes a process theoretical contribution? *Organization Theory, 1*(1), 1–32. doi:10.1177/2631787720902473

CMMC. (2022). *About CMMC.* DoD CIO. https://dodcio.defense.gov/CMMC/About/

CNN. (2020). *Africans in Guangzhou Are on Edge, After Many Are Left Homeless Amid Rising Xenophobia as China Fights a Second Wave of Coronavirus.* https://edition.cnn.com/2020/04/10/china/africans-guangzhou-china-coronavirus-hnk-intl/index.html

CNN. (2021, Oct 13). *2016 Presidential Campaign Hacking Fast Facts.* Retrieved from: https://www.cnn.com/2016/12/26/us/2016-presidential-campaign-hacking-fast-facts

COBIT. (2022). *Control Objectives for Information Technologies.* ISACA. https://www.isaca.org/resources/cobit

Coffey, J. W., Haveard, M., & Golding, G. (2018). A case study in the implementation of a human-centric higher education cybersecurity program. *Journal of Cybersecurity Education, Research and Practice, 2018*(1), 4.

Cohen, E., & Cohen, M. (2020). Hawaii casts its 4 electoral votes for Biden, concluding Electoral College process. *CNN.* https://www.cnn.com/politics/live-news/electoral-college-vote-2020-biden-trump/index.html

Cojocariu, A.-C., Verzea, I., & Chaib, R. (2020). Aspects of Cyber-Security in Higher Education Institutions. *Aspects of Cyber-Security in Higher Education Institutions,* (August), 3–11. doi:10.1007/978-3-030-44711-3_1

Colomb, Y., White, P., Islam, R., & Alsadoon, A. (2023). Applying Zero Trust Architecture and Probability-Based Authentication to Preserve Security and Privacy of Data in the Cloud. In *Emerging Trends in Cybersecurity Applications* (pp. 137–169). Springer. doi:10.1007/978-3-031-09640-2_7

Committee on Commerce, Science, and Transportation. (2014). *'Kill Chain' Analysis of the 2013 Target Data Breach.* Retrieved on April 12, 2022, from: https://www.hsdl.org/?abstract&did=751170

Companies Are Satisfied with Business Outcomes from Big Data and Recognize Big Data as Very Important to Their Digital Transformation, Accenture Study Shows | Accenture. (2014, September 10). *Newsroom | Accenture*. Retrieved on June 2, 2022, from: https://newsroom.accenture.com/industries/systems-integration-technology/companies-are-satisfied-with-business-outcomes-from-big-data-and-recognize-big-data-as-very-important-to-their-digital-transformation-accenture-study-shows.htm

Conchon, E. (2023). Cyber Security Strategies While Safeguarding Information Systems in Public/Private Sectors. *Electronic Governance with Emerging Technologies: First International Conference, EGETC 2022, Tampico, Mexico, September 12–14, 2022, Revised Selected Papers*, 49.

Conger, F. R., & Kovaleski, S. F. (2019, May 14,). San Francisco bans facial recognition technology. *The New York Times*. https://www.nytimes.com/2019/05/14/us/facial-recognition-ban-san-francisco.html

Conger, S., & Landry, B. J. L. (2008). The intersection of privacy and security. In *Sprouts: Working Papers on Information Systems* (pp. 1-7). Academic Press.

Conger, S., & Landry, B. J. L. (2009). Problem analysis: When established techniques don't work. In *Proceedings of the Conf-IRM Conference* (pp. 1-8). Academic Press.

Consumer Council for Water. (2021). *How much water do you use?* CCW. Retrieved on April 12, 2022, from: https://www.ccwater.org.uk/households/using-water-wisely/averagewateruse/

Copeland, R., & Needleman, S. (2019). Google's 'Project Nightingale' triggers federal inquiry. *The Wall Street Journal*. https://www.wsj.com/articles/behind-googles-project-nightingale-a-health-data-gold-mine-of-50-million-patients-115735718
67

Corera, G. (2022, March 29). More must reconsider Russian anti-virus software use, UK warns. *BBC News*. Retrieved on November 3, 2022, from: https://www.bbc.com/news/technology-60854882

CPNI. (2022). *Cyber Assurance of Physical Security Systems*. Retrieved on April 13, 2022, from: https://www.cpni.gov.uk/cyber-assurance-physical-security-systems-capss

Craigen, D., Diakun-Thibault, N., & Purse, R. (2014). Defining Cybersecurity. *Technology Innovation Management Review*, *4*(10), 13–21. doi:10.22215/timreview/835

Creswell, J. (2013). Steps in Conducting a Scholarly Mixed Methods Study Abstract for DBER Group Discussion on 2013 - 11 - 14. *Steps in Conducting a Scholarly Mixed Methods Study*, 1–54. Retrieved from https://digitalcommons.unl.edu/cgi/viewcontent.cgi?article=1047&context=dberspeakers

Crowe. (2011). The case study approach. *Business Communication Quarterly*, 1. PMID:21707982

Cryan, J. F., & Holmes, A. (2005). The ascent of mouse: Advances in modelling human depression and anxiety. *Nature Reviews. Drug Discovery*, *4*(9), 775–790. doi:10.1038/nrd1825 PMID:16138108

Çubuk, E. B. S., Zeren, H. E., & Demirdöven, B. (2023). The role of data governance in cybersecurity for E-municipal services: Implications from the case of Turkey. In *Handbook of Research on Cybersecurity Issues and Challenges for Business and FinTech Applications* (pp. 410–425). IGI Global.

Culafi, A. (2021). *Mandiant: Compromised Colonial Pipeline password was reused.* Retrieved on July 14, 2022, from: https://www.techtarget.com/searchsecurity/news/252502216/Mandiant-Compromised-Colonial-Pipeline-password-was-reused

Cullen, W., Gulati, G., & Kelly, B. D. (2020). Mental health in the Covid-19 pandemic. *QJM: An International Journal of Medicine, 113*(5). Available from: https://academic.oup.com/qjmed/article/113/5/311/5813733?login=true

Cuthbertson, A. (2019). *Facebook deal makes it impossible to delete app from Android smartphones.* https://www.independent.co.uk/tech/facebook-app-delete-android-smartphones-samsung-galaxy-a8719081.html

Cyber Ark. (2018). *Survey: 46 Percent of Organizations Fail to Change Security Strategy After a Cyber Attack.* CyberArk. Retrieved on May 6, 2022, from: https://www.cyberark.com/press/global-advanced-threat-landscape-report-2018/

Cyber security: The changing role of the Board and the Audit Committee. (2016). Deloitte.

Cybersecurity and Infrastructure Security Agency. (2020). *Jint statement from elections infrastructure government coordinating council and the election infrastructure sector coordinating executive committees.* https://ww.cisa.gov/news/2020/11/12/joint-statement-elections-infrastructure-government-coordinating-council-election

Cyr, S., & Wei Choo, C. (2010). The individual and social dynamics of knowledge sharing: An exploratory study. *The Journal of Documentation, 66*(6), 824–846. doi:10.1108/00220411011087832

D'Arcy, J., Herath, T., & Shoss, M. K. (2014). Understanding employee responses to stressful information security requirements: A coping perspective. *Journal of Management Information Systems, 31*(2), 285–318. doi:10.2753/MIS0742-1222310210

Dave, P. (2020). *Apple-Google contact tracing tech draws interest in 23 countries, some hedge bets.* https://www.reuters.com/article/us-health-coronavirus-apps-tracing-idUSKBN22W2NW

Davies, J. (2009). The effect of media dependency on voting decisions. *Journal of Media Sociology, 1*(3/4), 160–181.

Davillas, A., & Jones, A. M. (2020). *The COVID-19 Pandemic and its Impact on Inequality of Opportunity in Psychological Distress in the UK.* Available from: https://papers.ssrn.com/sol3/papers.cfm?abstract_id=3614940

Davis, S. L. M. (2020). Contact Tracing Apps: Extra Risks for Women and Marginalized Groups. *Health and Human Right Journal.* https://www.hhrjournal.org/2020/04/contact-tracing-apps-extra-risks-for-women-and-marginalized-groups/#_edn17

Davis, R. A. (2001). A cognitive-behavioral model of pathological Internet use. *Computers in Human Behavior, 17*(2), 187–195. doi:10.1016/S0747-5632(00)00041-8

Dawson, J., & Thomson, R. (2018). The Future Cybersecurity Workforce: Going Beyond Technical Skills for Successful Cyber Performance. *Frontiers in Psychology, 9*, 9. doi:10.3389/fpsyg.2018.00744 PMID:29946276

De Arroyabe, I. F., Arranz, C. F., Arroyabe, M. F., & de Arroyabe, J. C. F. (2023). Cybersecurity capabilities and cyberattacks as drivers of investment in cybersecurity systems: A UK survey for 2018 and 2019. *Computers & Security, 124*, 102954. doi:10.1016/j.cose.2022.102954

Dedrick, J., Perrin, K. A., Sabaghian, E., & Wilcoxen, P. J. (2023). Assessing cyber attacks on local electricity markets using simulation analysis: Impacts and possible mitigations. *Sustainable Energy, Grids and Networks*, 100993.

Deflem, M. (2000). Bureaucratization and Social Control: Historical Foundations of International Police Cooperation. *Law & Society Review*, *34*(3), 601–640. doi:10.2307/3115142

Deleuze G., (1992). Postscript on the societies of control. *October, 59*, 3–7.

Dell. (2017). Recovering from a Destructive Cyber-attack. *Dell EMC*. Retrieved on November 2, 2021, from: https://www.emc.com/collateral/whitepaper/recovering-business-destructive-cyber-attack.pdf?isKoreaPage=false&domainUrlForCanonical=https%3A%2F%2Fwww.emc.com

Deloitte. (2016). *Readiness, response, and recovery*. Retrieved on May 9, 2021, from: https://www2.deloitte.com/content/dam/Deloitte/global/Documents/Risk/gx-cm-cyber-pov.pdf

Demetrovics, Z., Király, O., Koronczai, B., Griffiths, M. D., Nagygyörgy, K., Elekes, Z., Tamás, D., Kun, B., Kökönyei, G., & Urbán, R. (2016). Psychometric Properties of the Problematic Internet Use Questionnaire Short-Form (PIUQ-SF-6) in a Nationally Representative Sample of Adolescents. *PLoS One*, *11*(8), e0159409. doi:10.1371/journal.pone.0159409 PMID:27504915

Department for Digital, Culture, Media & Sport (2020). *Huawei to be removed from UK 5G networks by 2027*. Retrieved on November 3, 2022, from: https://www.gov.uk/government/news/huawei-to-be-removed-from-uk-5g-networks-by-2027

Desai, N. (2016). *IT vs. OT for the Industrial Internet*. GlobalSign GMO Internet, Inc. Retrieved on February 28, 2022, from: https://www.globalsign.com/en/blog/it-vs-ot-industrial-internet

Deutrom, J., Katos, V., & Ali, R. (2021). Loneliness, life satisfaction, problematic internet use and security behaviors: Re-examining the relationships when working from home during COVID-19. *Behaviour & Information Technology*, 1–15.

Deutrom, J., Katos, V., Al-Mourad, M. B., & Ali, R. (2022). The Relationships between Gender, Life Satisfaction, Loneliness and Problematic Internet Use during COVID-19: Does the Lockdown Matter? *International Journal of Environmental Research and Public Health*, *19*(3), 1325. doi:10.3390/ijerph19031325 PMID:35162348

Dhillon, G. (2015). What To Do Before And After A Cybersecurity Breach? *The Changing Faces of Cybersecurity Governance*, 1–16.

DHS. (2014). *A Glossary of Common Cybersecurity Terminology. National Initiative for Cybersecurity Careers and Studies: Department of Homeland Security*. https://www.fortunebusinessinsights.com/digital-transformation-market-104878

Dionísio, N., Alves, F., Ferreira, P. M., & Bessani, A. (2019, July). Cyberthreat detection from twitter using deep neural networks. In 2019 international joint conference on neural networks (IJCNN) (pp. 1-8). IEEE. doi:10.1109/IJCNN.2019.8852475

Dixit, P. (2020). *India's Contact Tracing App Is All But Mandatory. So This Programmer Hacked It So That He Always Appears Safe*. https://www.buzzfeednews.com/article/pranavdixit/india-aarogya-setu-hacked

Dolan, P., Hallsworth, M., Halpern, D., King, D., Metcalfe, R., & Vlaev, I. (2012). Influencing behaviour: The mindspace way. *Journal of Economic Psychology*, *33*(1), 264–277. doi:10.1016/j.joep.2011.10.009

Donaldson, S. I., & Grant-Vallone, E. J. (2002). Understanding Self-Report Bias in Organizational Behavior Research. *Journal of Business and Psychology*, *17*(2), 245–260. doi:10.1023/A:1019637632584

Dougherty, C., Sayre, K., Seacord, R. C., Svoboda, D., & Togashi, K. (2009). *Secure design patterns*. Carnegie-Mellon Univ.

Dowthwaite, L., Fischer, J., Perez Vallejos, E., Portillo, V., Nichele, E., Goulden, M., & McAuley, D. (2021). Public Adoption of and Trust in the NHS COVID-19 Contact Tracing App in the United Kingdom: Quantitative Online Survey Study. *Journal of Medical Internet Research*, *23*(9), e29085. Advance online publication. doi:10.2196/29085 PMID:34406960

Drozdiak, N., & Turner, G. (2019). *Tech giants risk privacy probes over Alexa, Siri reviewers*. https://www.bloomberg.com/news/articles/2019-08-05/tech-giants-risk-privacy-probes-over-alexa-siri-eavesdropping

Dufour, M., Brunelle, N., Tremblay, J., Leclerc, D., Cousineau, M.-M., Khazaal, Y., Légaré, A.-A., Rousseau, M., & Berbiche, D. (2016). Gender Difference in Internet Use and Internet Problems among Quebec High School Students. *Canadian Journal of Psychiatry*, *61*(10), 663–668. doi:10.1177/0706743716640755 PMID:27310231

Durak, M., & Senol-Durak, E. (2014). Which personality traits are associated with cognitions related to problematic Internet use? *Asian Journal of Social Psychology*, *17*(3), 206–218. doi:10.1111/ajsp.12056

Dykstra, J. (2023). *The Slippery Slope of Cybersecurity Analogies*. Academic Press.

EC. (2020). *Coronavirus: Guidance to ensure full data protection standards of apps fighting the pandemic*. https://ec.europa.eu/commission/presscorner/detail/en/ip_20_669

EC. (n.d.). *Mobile contact tracing apps in EU Member States*. https://commission.europa.eu/strategy-and-policy/coronavirus-response/travel-during-coronavirus-pandemic/mobile-contact-tracing-apps-eu-member-states_en

Economic Impact of Cybercrime. (n.d.). *Center for Strategic and International Studies*. https://www.csis.org/analysis/economic-impact-cybercrime

EDPB. (2020a). *Statement on the processing of personal data in the context of the COVID-19 outbreak*. https://edpb.europa.eu/sites/default/files/files/news/edpb_statement_2020_processingpersonaldataandcovid-19_en.pdf

EDPB. (2020b). *Guidelines 04/2020 on the use of location data and contact tracing tools in the context of the COVID-19 outbreak*. https://edpb.europa.eu/sites/default/files/files/file1/edpb_guidelines_20200420_contact_tracing_covid_with_annex_en.pdf

Edu, J. S., Such, J. M., & Suarez-Tangil, G. (2020). Smart home personal assistants. *ACM Computing Surveys*, *53*(6), 1–36. doi:10.1145/3412383

Edwards, C. (2017). *Thatcher's golden legacy of privatisation*. CapX. Retrieved on March 2, 2022, from: https://capx.co/thatchers-golden-legacy-of-privatisation/

Efstathopoulos, G., Grammatikis, P. R., Sarigiannidis, P., Argyriou, V., Sarigiannidis, A., Stamatakis, K., . . . Athanasopoulos, S. K. (2019, September). Operational data based intrusion detection system for smart grid. In *2019 IEEE 24th International Workshop on Computer Aided Modeling and Design of Communication Links and Networks (CAMAD)* (pp. 1-6). IEEE. 10.1109/CAMAD.2019.8858503

Egan, M. (2021). *Robinhood discloses breach that exposed information of millions of customers.* CNN. Retrieved on August 4, 2022, from: https://www.cnn.com/2021/11/08/tech/robinhood-data-breach/index.html

Egelman, S., Harbach, M., & Peer, E. (2016). Behavior Ever Follows Intention? *Proceedings of the 2016 CHI Conference on Human Factors in Computing Systems.* 10.1145/2858036.2858265

Egelman, S., & Peer, E. (2015). Predicting privacy and security attitudes. *Computers & Society*, *45*(1), 22–28. doi:10.1145/2738210.2738215

Eijkelenboom, E., & Nieuwesteeg, B. (2021). An analysis of cybersecurity in Dutch annual reports of listed companies. *Computer Law & Security Report*, *40*, 105513. doi:10.1016/j.clsr.2020.105513

Eltahir, M. E., & Ahmed, O. S. (2023). *Cybersecurity Awareness in African Higher Education Institutions: A Case Study of Sudan.* Academic Press.

English, R., & Maguire, J. (2023). Exploring Student Perceptions and Expectations of Cyber Security. In Computing Education Practice (pp. 25–28). doi:10.1145/3573260.3573267

ENISA. (2015). *ENISA Threat Landscape.* ENISA.

ENISA. (2019). *Cybersecurity Culture Guidelines: Behavioural Aspects of Cybersecurity.* https://www.enisa.europa.eu/publications/cybersecurity-culture-guidelines-behavioural-aspects-of-cybersecurity

ENISA. (2020). *Threat Landscape Report: From January 2019 to April 2020.* https://www.enisa.europa.eu/publications/enisa-threat-landscape-2020-main-incidents/at_download/fullReport

Ericson, R., & Haggerty, K. (1997). *Policing the Risk Society.* University of Toronto Press. doi:10.3138/9781442678590

Erwin, B. A., Turk, C. L., Heimberg, R. G., Fresco, D. M., & Hantula, D. A. (2004). The Internet: Home to a severe population of individuals with social anxiety disorder? *Journal of Anxiety Disorders*, *18*(5), 629–646. doi:10.1016/j.janxdis.2003.08.002 PMID:15275943

Estrada, S., & Reyes Álvarez, J. (2023). Conclusions: The Challenge Towards the Future Is Digital and Sustainable Transformations from a Systemic Perspective in a Changing COVID World. In *Digital and Sustainable Transformations in a Post-COVID World* (pp. 475–502). Springer. doi:10.1007/978-3-031-16677-8_18

Ewing, E. (2020). *The 2020 election was attacked, but not severely disrupted. Here's how.* https://www.npr.org/2020/11/04/931090626/the-2020-election-was-attacked-but-not-severely-disrupted-heres-how

Fàbregues, S., & Molina-Azorín, J. F. (2017). Addressing quality in mixed methods research: A review and recommendations for a future agenda. *Quality & Quantity*, *51*(6), 2847–2863. doi:10.100711135-016-0449-4

Faltermaier, S., Strunk, K., Obermeier, M., & Fiedler, M. (2023). *Managing Organizational Cyber Security–The Distinct Role of Internalized Responsibility.* Academic Press.

Fatokun Faith, B., Hamid, S., Norman, A., Fatokun Johnson, O., & Eke, C. I. (2020). Relating Factors of Tertiary Institution Students' Cybersecurity Behavior. *2020 International Conference in Mathematics, Computer Engineering and Computer Science, ICMCECS 2020.* 10.1109/ICMCECS47690.2020.246990

Feldman, M. (2020). *Dirty tricks: 9 falsehoods that could undermine the 2020 election.* https://www.brennancenter.org/our-work/research-reports/dirty-tricks-9-falsehoods-could-undermine-2020-election

Feldman, J. M. (2016). Technology, Power and Social Change: Comparing Three Marx-Inspired Views. *Socialism and Democracy*, *30*(2), 28–72. doi:10.1080/08854300.2016.1184913

Feldmann, A., Gasser, O., Lichtblau, F., Poese, I., Christoph, B., De-Cix, D., Wagner, D., De-Cix, M., Tapiador, J., Vallina-Rodriguez, N., Hohlfeld, O., Smaragdakis, G., & Berlin, T. (2020). The Lockdown Effect: Implications of the COVID-19 Pandemic on Internet Traffic. *Enric Pujol BENOCS, 20.*

FERPA. (1974). *Family Educational Rights and Privacy Act (FERPA).* Available on https://ed.gov/policy/gen/guid/fpco/ferpa/index.html

FIPS. (2015). *Federal Information Processing Standateds Publications.* Available on: https://csrc.nist.gov/publications/PubsFIPS.html

Fiske, D. W. (1949). Consistency of the factorial structures of personality ratings from different sources. *Journal of Abnormal and Social Psychology*, *44*(3), 329–344. doi:10.1037/h0057198 PMID:18146776

Fiss, P. C. (2007). A set-theoretic approach to organizational configurations. *Academy of Management Review*, *32*(4), 1180–1198. doi:10.5465/amr.2007.26586092

Fiss, P. C. (2011). Building better causal theories: A fuzzy set approach to typologies in organization research. *Academy of Management Journal*, *54*(2), 393–420. doi:10.5465/amj.2011.60263120

Fleming, J., & Zegwaard, K. E. (2018). Methodologies, methods and ethical considerations for conducting research in work-integrated learning. *International Journal of Work-Integrated Learning*, *19*(3), 205–213.

Florackis, C., Louca, C., Michaely, R., & Weber, M. (2023). Cybersecurity risk. *Review of Financial Studies*, *36*(1), 351–407. doi:10.1093/rfs/hhac024

Fogg, B. (2009). *A Behavior Model for Persuasive Design.* Academic Press.

Foreman, C. J., & Gurugubelli, D. (2015). Identifying the cyber attack surface of the advanced metering infrastructure. *The Electricity Journal*, *28*(1), 94–103. doi:10.1016/j.tej.2014.12.007

Forsyth, D. R. (2008). *International Encyclopedia of the Social Sciences.* Available from: https://scholarship.richmond.edu/cgi/viewcontent.cgi?article=1164&context=jepson-faculty-publications

Fox, S. (2017). Beyond AI: Multi-Intelligence (MI) combining natural and artificial intelligences in hybrid beings and systems. *Technologies*, *5*(3), 1–14. doi:10.3390/technologies5030038

Freeze, D. (2021, April 27). Cybercrime To Cost The World $10.5 Trillion Annually By 2025. *Cybercrime Magazine.* Retrieved on December 3, 2021, from: https://cybersecurityventures.com/cybercrime-damages-6-trillion-by-2021/

French, A. (2017, Jan 5). *Q&A: Alexa may be listening, but will she tell on you?* https://www.latimes.com/business/technology/la-fi-tn-amazon-echo-privacy-qa-20170105-story.html

FTC. (2023). *Children's Online Privacy Protection Rule (COPPA).* FTC. https://www.ftc.gov/legal-library/browse/rules/childrens-online-privacy-protection-rule-coppay-protection-rule

Fuglsang, L., & Sørensen, F. (2011). The balance between bricolage and innovation: Management dilemmas in sustainable public innovation. *Service Industries Journal*, *31*(4), 581–595. doi:10.1080/02642069.2010.504302

Fung, B. (2021). *Hackers breach Electronic Arts, stealing game source code and tools.* CNN. https://www.cnn.com/2021/06/10/tech/electronic-arts-hack/index.html

Fung, B., & Sands, G. (2021). *Ransomware attackers used compromised password to access Colonial Pipeline network.* CNN. https://www.cnn.com/2021/06/04/politics/colonial-pipeline-ransomware-attack-password/index.html

Furman, S., Theofanos, M. F., Choong, Y. Y., & Stanton, B. (2011). Basing cybersecurity training on user perceptions. *IEEE Security and Privacy*, *10*(2), 40–49. doi:10.1109/MSP.2011.180

Furnari, S., Crilly, D., Misangyi, V. F., Greckhamer, T., Fiss, P. C., & Aguilera, R. (2021). Capturing causal complexity: Heuristics for configurational theorizing. *Academy of Management Review*, *46*(4), 778–799. doi:10.5465/amr.2019.0298

Furnell, S., & Clarke, N. (2012). Power to the people? The evolving recognition of human aspects of security. *Computers & Security*, *31*(8), 983–988. doi:10.1016/j.cose.2012.08.004

Furnham, A., & Boo, H. C. (2011). A literature review of the anchoring effect. *Journal of Socio-Economics*, *40*(1), 35–42. doi:10.1016/j.socec.2010.10.008

Gadzheva, M. (2007). Getting chipped: To ban or not to ban. *Information & Communications Technology Law*, *16*(3), 217–231. doi:10.1080/13600830701680537

Gallegos-Segovia, P. L., Vintimilla-Tapia, P. E., Bravo-Torres, J. F., Yuquilima-Albarado, I. F., Larios-Rosillo, V. M., & Jara-Saltos, J. D. (2017). Social engineering as an attack vector for ransomware. *2017 CHILEAN Conference on Electrical, Electronics Engineering, Information and Communication Technologies, CHILECON 2017 - Proceedings*, 1–6. 10.1109/CHILECON.2017.8229528

Gambhir, R., & Karsten, J. (2019, August 14). *Why paper is considered state-of-the-art voting technology*. Brookings. Retrieved from: https://www.brookings.edu/blog/techtank/2019/08/14/why-paper-is-considered-state-of-the-art-voting-technology/

GAO. (2018). *Reports Challenges and Successes in Cybersecurity Framework Adoption*. Van Ness Feldman LLP. https://www.vnf.com/gao-reports-challenges-and-successes-in-cybersecurity-framework

Gao, L., Calderon, T. G., & Tang, F. (2020). Public companies' cybersecurity risk disclosures. *International Journal of Accounting Information Systems*, *38*, 100468. doi:10.1016/j.accinf.2020.100468

Garcia-Alis, A. N. C. (2020). *'Lessons learnt' from the Maastricht University cyber attack.* Academic Press.

Garfin, D. R. (2020). Technology as a Coping Tool during the COVID-19 Pandemic: Implications and Recommendations. *Stress and Health*, *36*(4). PMID:32762116

Garg, S., & Baliyan, N. (2019). A novel parallel classifier scheme for vulnerability detection in android. *Computers & Electrical Engineering*, *77*, 12–26. doi:10.1016/j.compeleceng.2019.04.019

Garre, J. T. M., Pérez, M. G., & Ruiz-Martínez, A. (2021). A novel Machine Learning-based approach for the detection of SSH botnet infection. *Future Generation Computer Systems*, *115*, 387–396. doi:10.1016/j.future.2020.09.004

Gartner IT Glossary. (2019). Retrieved on August 14, 2019, from: https://www.gartner. com/it-glossary/?s=chatbot

Gartner. (2014). *Gartner's 2014 Hype Cycle for Emerging Technologies Maps the Journey to Digital Business.* https://www.gartner.com/newsroom/id/2819918

Garwe, E. C., & Thondhlana, J. (2020). Encyclopedia of International Higher Education Systems and Institutions. Encyclopedia of International Higher Education Systems and Institutions. doi:10.1007/978-94-017-9553-1

Gastellier-Prevost, S., Granadillo, G. G., & Laurent, M. (2011). A dual approach to detect pharming attacks at the client-side. *2011 4th IFIP International Conference on New Technologies, Mobility and Security, NTMS 2011 - Proceedings.* 10.1109/NTMS.2011.5721063

GDPR.EU. (2023). *Everything you need to know about the "Right to be forgotten".* https://gdpr.eu/right-to-be-forgotten/

Gerke, S., Minssen, T., & Cohen, I. G. (2020). Ethical and legal challenges of artificial intelligence-driven healthcare. In A. Bohr & K. Memarzadeh (Eds.), *Artificial Intelligence in Healthcare* (pp. 21–36). Academic Press., doi:10.1016/B978-0-12-818438-7.00012-5

Ghiasi, M., Niknam, T., Wang, Z., Mehrandezh, M., Dehghani, M., & Ghadimi, N. (2023). A comprehensive review of cyber-attacks and defense mechanisms for improving security in smart grid energy systems: Past, present and future. *Electric Power Systems Research*, *215*, 108975. doi:10.1016/j.epsr.2022.108975

Gierveld, J. D. J., & Tilburg, T. V. (2006). A 6-Item Scale for Overall, Emotional, and Social Loneliness. *Research on Aging*, *28*(5), 582–598. doi:10.1177/0164027506289723

Girasa, R. (2023). Taxation of Virtual Currencies; Environmental, Social and Governance Considerations; Protection of Intellectual Property Rights; Antitrust; and Cybersecurity. In *Regulation of Cryptocurrencies and Blockchain Technologies* (pp. 261–311). Springer. doi:10.1007/978-3-031-21812-5_7

Girdhar, R., Srivastava, V., & Sethi, S. (2020). Managing mental health issues among elderly during COVID-19 pandemic. *Journal of Geriatric Care and Research*, *7*(1). http://pu.edu.pk/MHH-COVID-19/Articles/Article22.pdf

Gjerde, L. E. L. (2021). Governing humans and 'things': Power and rule in Norway during the Covid-19 pandemic. *Journal of Political Power*, *14*(3), 472–492. doi:10.1080/2158379X.2020.1870264

Goffman, E. (1956). *The Presentation of Self in Everyday Life.* Available from: https://monoskop.org/images/1/19/Goffman_Erving_The_Presentation_of_Self_in_Everyday_Life.pdf

Goldberg, L. R. (1992). The development of markers for the Big-Five factor structure. *Psychological Assessment*, *4*(1), 26–42. doi:10.1037/1040-3590.4.1.26

Goldkhul, G. (2012). Pragmatism vs interpretivism in qualitative information systems research. *European Journal of Information Systems*, *21*(2), 135–146. doi:10.1057/ejis.2011.54

Gonzalez, R., et al. v. Google LLC, (United States Court of Appeals for the Ninth Circuit. Docket Number. 18-16700. 2023).

Gordon, L. A., Loeb, M. P., & Zhou, L. (2020). Integrating cost–benefit analysis into the NIST Cybersecurity Framework via the Gordon–Loeb Model. *Journal of Cybersecurity*, *6*(1), tyaa005. doi:10.1093/cybsec/tyaa005

Gordon, L., Loeb, & Sohail. (2010). Market Value of Voluntary Disclosures Concerning Information Security. *Management Information Systems Quarterly*, *34*(3), 567. doi:10.2307/25750692

gov.uk. (2020). *Next phase of NHS coronavirus (COVID-19) app announced. Department of Health and Social Care.* https://www.gov.uk/government/news/next-phase-of-nhs-coronavirus-covid-19-app-announced

Gov.UK. (2022). *National Security and Investment Act 2021.* Retrieved on November 3, 2022, from: https://www.gov.uk/government/collections/national-security-and-investment-act

Grabosky, P. N. (2001). Virtual criminality: Old wine in new bottles? *Social & Legal Studies*, *10*(2), 243–249. doi:10.1177/a017405

Grandori, A., & Furnari, S. (2008). A chemistry of organization: Combinatory analysis and design. *Organization Studies*, *29*(3), 459–485. doi:10.1177/0170840607088023

Granovetter, M. S. (1973). The strength of weak ties. *American Journal of Sociology*, *78*(6), 1360–1380. doi:10.1086/225469

Gratian, M., Bandi, S., Cukier, M., Dykstra, J., & Ginther, A. (2018). Correlating human traits and cyber security behaviour intentions. *Computers & Security*, *73*(December), 345–358. doi:10.1016/j.cose.2017.11.015

Greenfield, D. N., & Davis, R. A. (2002). Lost in Cyberspace: The Web @ Work. *Cyberpsychology & Behavior*, *5*(4), 347–353. doi:10.1089/109493102760275590 PMID:12216699

Greenhalgh, T., Koh, G. C. H., & Car, J. (2020). Covid-19: A remote assessment in primary care. *British Medical Journal*, 368. PMID:32213507

Griffiths, M. (2010). Internet abuse and internet addiction in the workplace. *Journal of Workplace Learning*, *22*(7), 463–472. doi:10.1108/13665621011071127

Gurman, M., & Burnson, R. (2019). *Apple sued over Siri's unauthorized recording of users.* https://www.msn.com/en-us/news/technology/apple-sued-over-siris-unauthorized-recording-of-users/ar-AAFu9gi

Gurumurthy, R., Schatsky, D., & Camhi, J. (2020). *Uncovering the connection between digital maturity and financial performance.* Academic Press.

Hadlington, L. (2017). Human factors in cybersecurity; examining the link between Internet addiction, impulsivity, attitudes towards cybersecurity, and risky cybersecurity behaviors. *Heliyon*, *3*(7), e00346. doi:10.1016/j.heliyon.2017.e00346 PMID:28725870

Hadlington, L., & Murphy, K. (2018). Is Media Multitasking Good for Cybersecurity? Exploring the Relationship Between Media Multitasking and Everyday Cognitive Failures on Self-Reported Risky Cybersecurity Behaviors. *Cyberpsychology, Behavior, and Social Networking*, *21*(3), 168–172. doi:10.1089/cyber.2017.0524 PMID:29638157

Hadlington, L., & Parsons, K. (2017). Can Cyberloafing and Internet Addiction Affect Organizational Information Security? *Cyberpsychology, Behavior, and Social Networking*, *20*(9), 567–571. doi:10.1089/cyber.2017.0239 PMID:28872364

Hadnagy, C. (2015). *Phishing Dark Waters.* Retrieved on November 11, 2020, from: http://www.wiley.com/go/permissions

Hall, K. (2018). *Brit water firms, power plants with crap cyber security will pay up to £17m, peers told.* Retrieved on February 1, 2022, from: https://www.theregister.com/2018/05/22/house_of_lords_new_cybersecurity_regulations/

Harbert, T. (2021). *The weakest link in cybersecurity*. SHRM. https://www.shrm.org/hr-today/news/all-things-work/pages/the-weakest-link-in-cybersecurity.aspx

Harding, L., Sabbagh, D., & Koshiw, I. (2022, October 31. Russia targets Ukraine energy and water infrastructure in missile attacks. *The Guardian*. Retrieved on November 3, 2022, from: https://www.theguardian.com/world/2022/oct/31/russian-missiles-kyiv-ukraine-cities

Hartmann, C. C., & Carmenate, J. (2021). Academic Research on the Role of Corporate Governance and IT Expertise in Addressing Cybersecurity Breaches: Implications for Practice, Policy, and Research. *Current Issues in Auditing*, *15*(2), A9–A23. doi:10.2308/CIIA-2020-034

Hayat Eve Sigar. (n.d.). *Republic of Turkey Ministry of Health Hayat Eve Sığar (HES) Application*. https://hayatevesigar.saglik.gov.tr/gizlilik_politikasi_eng_index_V2.html

He, D., Li, S., Li, C., Zhu, S., Chan, S., Min, W., & Guizani, N. (2020). Security analysis of cryptocurrency wallets in android-based applications. *IEEE Network*, *34*(6), 114–119. doi:10.1109/MNET.011.2000025

Henriquez, M. (2020). *Domestic and foreign cybersecurity threats surrounding the 2020 election*. https://www.securitymagazine.com/articles/93744-domestic-and-foreign-threats-surrounding-the-2020-election

Henshel, D., Cains, M. G., Hoffman, B., & Kelley, T. (2015). Trust as a Human Factor in Holistic Cyber Security Risk Assessment. *Procedia Manufacturing*, *3*, 1117–1124. doi:10.1016/j.promfg.2015.07.186

Herath, T., & Rao, H. R. (2009). Encouraging information security behaviors in organizations: Role of penalties, pressures and perceived effectiveness. *Decision Support Systems*, *47*(2), 154–165. doi:10.1016/j.dss.2009.02.005

Herberger, C. (2016). *The 3 biggest cybersecurity risks posed in the 2016 presidential election*. https://www.helpnetsecurity.com/2016/05/17/cybersecurity-presidential-election/

Hern, A. (2020). *Qatari contact-tracing app 'put 1m people's sensitive data at risk'*. https://www.theguardian.com/world/2020/may/27/qatar-contact-tracing-app-1m-people-sensitive-data-at-risk-coronavirus-covid-19

Hevner, A. R., March, S. T., Park, J., & Ram, S. (2004). Design science in information systems research. *Management Information Systems Quarterly*, *28*(1), 75–105. doi:10.2307/25148625

HHS - Anthem. (2020). *Pays OCR $16 Million in Record HIPAA Settlement Following Largest U.S. Health Data Breach in History | Guidance Portal*. HHS.gov. https://www.hhs.gov/guidance/document/anthem-pays-ocr-16-million-record-hipaa-settlement-following-largest-us-health-data-breach

Higgins, E. T. (1998). Promotion and Prevention: Regulatory Focus as A Motivational Principle. *Advances in Experimental Social Psychology*, *30*, 1–46. Available from: https://www.sciencedirect.com/science/article/pii/S0065260108603810

Hilary, G., Segal, B., & Zhang, M. H. (2016). Cyber-Risk Disclosure: Who Cares? SSRN *Electronic Journal*. Retrieved on November 11, 2020, from: http://niccs.us-cert.gov/glossary#letter_c https://www.publicsafety.gc.ca/cnt/rsrcs/pblctns/cbr-scrt-strtgy/index-en... doi:10.2139/ssrn.2852519

Hill, C., James, B. I., & Sahyoun, N. (2023). *What is Missing in Data Governance? Regulation, Board Oversight, and a New Role for Accountants*. Academic Press.

HIPAA. (2022). *HIPAA for Professionals*. HHS.gov. https://www.hhs.gov/hipaa/for-professionals/index.html

HITRUST Alliance. (2023). *Information Risk Management and Compliance*. https://hitrustalliance.net/

Howarth, F. (2014). *The Role of Human Error in Successful Security Attacks. Online*. Available: https://securityintelligence.com/the-role-of-human-error-in-successful-security-attacks/

Hughes, M. E., Waite, L. J., Hawkley, L. C., & Cacioppo, J. T. (2004). A Short Scale for Measuring Loneliness in Large Surveys. *Research on Aging*, *26*(6), 655–672. doi:10.1177/0164027504268574 PMID:18504506

Hummer, L. (2016). *Security Starts with People: Three Steps to Build a Strong Insider Threat Protection Program Online*. Available: https://securityintelligence.com/security-starts-withpeople-three-steps-to-build-a-strong-insider-threat-protection-prog
ram

Hu, Q., West, R., & Smarandescu, L. (2015). The Role of Self-Control in Information Security Violations: Insights from a Cognitive Neuroscience Perspective. *Journal of Management Information Systems*, *31*(4), 6–48. doi:10.1080/07421222.2014.1001255

Iannacci, F., & Kraus, S. (2022). *Configurational theory: A review* (S. Papagiannidis, Ed.). Springer International Publishing. doi:10.1007/978-3-319-09450-2_23

IAPP. (2023a). *Opt-In*. https://iapp.org/resources/article/opt-in/

IAPP. (2023b). *Opt-Out*. https://iapp.org/resources/article/opt-out/

IAPP. (2023c). *U.S. state comprehensive privacy laws*. https://iapp.org/media/pdf/resource_center/us_state_privacy_laws_overview.pdf

IBM. (2020). *Cost of a Data Breach Report 2020 2 Contents*. Available from: https://www.capita.com/sites/g/files/nginej291/files/2020-08/Ponemon-Global-Cost-of-Data-Breach-Study-2020.pdf

IEC. (2022). *IEC 27001:2022 - Information security, cybersecurity and privacy protection — Information security management systems — Requirements*. https://www.iso27001security.com/html/27034.html

Institute for Government. (2021). *Timeline of UK Government Coronavirus Lockdowns*. Available from: https://www.instituteforgovernment.org.uk/charts/uk-government-coronavirus-lockdowns

Intersoft Consulting. (2023). *Art. 17 GDPR – Right to erasure ('right to be forgotten')*. General Data Protection Regulation (GDPR). https://gdpr-info.eu/art-17-gdpr/

Ipsen, C., van Veldhoven, M., Kirchner, K., & Hansen, J. P. (2021). Six Key Advantages and Disadvantages of Working from Home in Europe during COVID-19. *International Journal of Environmental Research and Public Health*, *18*(4), 1–17. doi:10.3390/ijerph18041826 PMID:33668505

ITU. (2012). *Cybercrime Understanding Cybercrime : Understanding Cybercrime: Phenomena, Challenges and Legal Response*. ITU.

Jaber, A., & Fritsch, L. (2023). Towards AI-powered Cybersecurity Attack Modeling with Simulation Tools: Review of Attack Simulators. In *International Conference on P2P, Parallel, Grid, Cloud and Internet Computing* (pp. 249-257). Springer.

Jaber, A., & Fritsch, L. (2023). Towards AI-powered Cybersecurity Attack Modeling with Simulation Tools: Review of Attack Simulators. *International Conference on P2P, Parallel, Grid, Cloud and Internet Computing*, 249–257.

Jackob, N. G. E. (2010). The relationship between perceived media dependency, use of alternative information sources, and general trust in mass media. *International Journal of Communication*, *4*, 18.

Jacobs, J., Romanosky, S., Adjerid, I., & Baker, W. (2020). Improving vulnerability remediation through better exploit prediction. *Journal of Cybersecurity*, *6*(1), tyaa015. doi:10.1093/cybsec/tyaa015

James, L. (2018). Making cyber-security a strategic business priority. *Network Security*, *2018*(5), 6–8. doi:10.1016/S1353-4858(18)30042-4

Jarjoui, S., & Murimi, R. (2021). A framework for enterprise cybersecurity risk management. In K. Daimi & C. Peoples (Eds.), *Advances in Cybersecurity Management* (pp. 139–161). Springer International Publishing., doi:10.1007/978-3-030-71381-2_8

Jarjoui, S., Murimi, R., & Murimi, R. (2021). Hold my beer: A case study of how ransomware affected an Australian beverage company. In *2021 International Conference on Cyber Situational Awareness, Data Analytics and Assessment (CyberSA)* (pp. 1-6). https://doi.org/10.1109/CyberSA52016.2021.9478239

Jessor, R. (1987). Problem-Behavior Theory, Psychosocial Development, and Adolescent Problem Drinking. *Addiction*, *82*(4), 331–342. Retrieved on June 2, 2021 from: https://onlinelibrary.wiley.com/doi/abs/10.1111/j.1360-0443.1987.tb01490.x

Johri, A., & Kumar, S. (2023). Exploring Customer Awareness towards Their Cyber Security in the Kingdom of Saudi Arabia: A Study in the Era of Banking Digital Transformation. *Human Behavior and Emerging Technologies*, *2023*, 2023. doi:10.1155/2023/2103442

Joint Security and Privacy Committee NEMA/COCIR/JIRA. (2003). *Defending Medical Information Systems Against Malicious Software*. https://www.medicalimaging.org/wp-content/uploads/2011/02/medical-defending.pdf

Joint Technology Committee. (2016). *Responding to a Cyberattack*. Retrieved on October 7, 2021, from: https://www.ncsc.org/~/media/Files/PDF/About Us/Committees/JTC/JTC Resource Bulletins/RespondingtoCyberAttack2-26-2016FINAL.ashx

Kahneman, D., & Tversky, A. (2012). Prospect theory: An analysis of decision under risk. In *Handbook of the Fundamentals of Financial Decision Making* (pp. 99–127). World Scientific. doi:10.1142/9789814417358_0006

Kamariotou, M., & Kitsios, F. (2023). Information Systems Strategy and Security Policy: A Conceptual Framework. *Electronics (Basel)*, *12*(2), 382. doi:10.3390/electronics12020382

Kanyangale, M. (2019). Seven Snags of Research Ethics on the Qualitative Research Voyage. *International Business Research*, *12*(6), 1. doi:10.5539/ibr.v12n6p1

Kassin, S. M., Dror, I. E., & Kukucka, J. (2013). The forensic confirmation bias: Problems, perspectives, and proposed solutions. *Journal of Applied Research in Memory and Cognition*, *2*(1), 42–52. doi:10.1016/j.jarmac.2013.01.001

Katz, D., & Kahn, R. L. (1978). *The social psychology of organizations*. Wiley.

Kaushik, B., Sharma, R., Dhama, K., Chadha, A., & Sharma, S. (2023). Performance evaluation of learning models for intrusion detection system using feature selection. *Journal of Computer Virology and Hacking Techniques*, 1-20.

Kaushik, V., & Walsh, C. A. (2019). Pragmatism as a research paradigm and its implications for Social Work research. *Social Sciences, 8*(9). doi:10.3390/socsci8090255.h

Kelleher, J. D., Mac Namee, B., & D'arcy, A. (2020). *Fundamentals of machine learning for predictive data analytics: Algorithms, worked examples, and case studies*. MIT Press.

Keller, C., Siegrist, M., & Gutscher, H. (2006). The Role of the Affect and Availability Heuristics in Risk Communication. *Risk Analysis*, *26*(3), 631–639. doi:10.1111/j.1539-6924.2006.00773.x PMID:16834623

Kelly, S., & Resnick-ault, J. (2021). *One password allowed hackers to disrupt Colonial Pipeline, CEO tells senators.* Retrieved on August 1, 2022, from: https://www.reuters.com/business/colonial-pipeline-ceo-tells-senate-cyber-defenses-were-compromised-ahead-hack-2021-06-08/

Kerner, S. M. (2022). *Colonial Pipeline hack explained: Everything you need to know.* https://www.techtarget.com/whatis/feature/Colonial-Pipeline-hack-explained-Everything-you-need-to-know

Khan, R., Maynard, P., McLaughlin, K., Laverty, D. M., & Sezer, S. (2016). *Threat Analysis of BlackEnergy Malware for Synchrophasor based Real-time Control and Monitoring in Smart Grid.* Retrieved on April 11, 2022, from: https://www.scienceopen.com/hosted-document?doi=10.14236/ewic/ICS2016.7

Khan, H. A., Sehatbakhsh, N., Nguyen, L. N., Prvulovic, M., & Zajić, A. (2019). Malware detection in embedded systems using neural network model for electromagnetic side-channel signals. *Journal of Hardware and Systems Security*, *3*(4), 305–318. doi:10.100741635-019-00074-w

Khan, N. F., Ikram, N., Murtaza, H., & Javed, M. (2023). Evaluating protection motivation based cybersecurity awareness training on Kirkpatrick's Model. *Computers & Security*, *125*, 103049. doi:10.1016/j.cose.2022.103049

Khan, S., & Mailewa, A. B. (2023). Discover Botnets in IoT Sensor Networks: A Lightweight Deep Learning Framework with Hybrid Self-Organizing Maps. *Microprocessors and Microsystems*, *97*, 104753. doi:10.1016/j.micpro.2022.104753

Khattak, A., Khanji, S., & Khan, W. (2019). Smart Meter Security: Vulnerabilities, Threat Impacts, and Countermeasures. In, 554–562.

Kim, T., Kim, C. H., Rhee, J., Fei, F., Tu, Z., Walkup, G., . . . Xu, D. (2019). {RVFuzzer}: Finding Input Validation Bugs in Robotic Vehicles through {Control-Guided} Testing. In *28th USENIX Security Symposium (USENIX Security 19)* (pp. 425-442). USENIX.

Kimani, K., Oduol, V., & Langat, K. (2019). Cyber security challenges for IoT-based smart grid networks. *International Journal of Critical Infrastructure Protection*, *25*, 36–49. doi:10.1016/j.ijcip.2019.01.001

Kim, J., LaRose, R., & Peng, W. (2009). Loneliness as the Cause and the Effect of Problematic Internet Use: The Relationship between Internet Use and Psychological Well-Being. *Cyberpsychology & Behavior*, *12*(4), 451–455. doi:10.1089/cpb.2008.0327 PMID:19514821

King P, D., Delfabbro, P., Billieux, J., & Potenza, M. (2020). *Problematic online gaming and the COVID-19 pandemic*. Academic Press.

Kinyongo, T. (2020, February). *Data presentation, analysis and interpretation 4.0 introduction*. Academic Press.

Király, O., Potenza, M. N., Stein, D. J., King, D. L., Hodgins, D. C., Saunders, J. B., Griffiths, M. D., Gjoneska, B., Billieux, J., Brand, M., Abbott, M. W., Chamberlain, S. R., Corazza, O., Burkauskas, J., Sales, C. M. D., Montag, C., Lochner, C., Grünblatt, E., Wegmann, E., ... Demetrovics, Z. (2020). Preventing problematic internet use during the COVID-19 pandemic: Consensus guidance. *Comprehensive Psychiatry*, *100*, 152180. doi:10.1016/j.comppsych.2020.152180 PMID:32422427

Klepper, D. (2022, November 3). *Misinformation and the midterm elections: What to expect.* AP News. https://apnews.com/article/2022-midterm-elections-misinformation-219762637bacf49bf7ec723546b46fb3

Kolar, M., Fernandez-Gago, C., & Lopez, J. (2023). Trust Negotiation and Its Applications. In *Collaborative Approaches for Cyber Security in Cyber-Physical Systems* (pp. 171–190). Springer. doi:10.1007/978-3-031-16088-2_8

KPMG. (2014). *Cyber Security: It's not Just about Technology The Five Most Common Mistakes.* Retrieved on June 2, 2020, from: http://www.kpmg.com/US/informationprotection

Krombholz, K., Hobel, H., Huber, M., & Weippl, E. (2015). Advanced social engineering attacks. *Journal of Information Security and Applications*, *22*(October), 113–122. doi:10.1016/j.jisa.2014.09.005

Kruse, C. S., Frederick, B., Jacobson, T., & Monticone, D. K. (2017). Cybersecurity in healthcare: A systematic review of modern threats and trends. *Technology and Health Care*, *25*(1), 1–10. doi:10.3233/THC-161263 PMID:27689562

Kubai, E. (2019). *Reliability and Validity of Research Instruments.* UNICAF University. Retrieved on January 28, 2021, from: https://www.researchgate.net/publication/335827941_Reliability_and_Validity_of_Research_Instruments_Correspondence_to_ku
baiedwinyahoocom

Kuehn, A., & Mueller, M. (2014). Analyzing bug bounty programs: An institutional perspective on the economics of software vulnerabilities. SSRN *Electronic Journal,* https://doi.org/ doi:10.2139/ssrn.2418812

Kumaraguru, P., Acquisti, A., Cranor, L. F., Hong, J., & Nunge, E. (2010). Privacy in mobile and social computing. Synthesis Lectures on Information Security. *Privacy and Trust*, *3*(1), 1–131.

Kumaran, N., & Lugani, S. (2020). *Protecting against cyber threats during COVID-19 and beyond.* Google Cloud Blog. Retrieved on August 14, 2021 from: https://cloud.google.com/blog/products/identity-security/protecting-against-cyber-threats-during-covid-19-and-beyond

Kumar, P., Kumar, N., Aggarwal, P., & Yeap, J. A. L. (2021). Working in lockdown: The relationship between COVID-19 induced work stressors, job performance, distress, and life satisfaction. *Current Psychology (New Brunswick, N.J.)*, *40*(12), 6308–6323. doi:10.100712144-021-01567-0 PMID:33746462

Kumar, R., & Subbiah, G. (2022). Zero-Day Malware Detection and Effective Malware Analysis Using Shapley Ensemble Boosting and Bagging Approach. *Sensors (Basel)*, *22*(7), 2798. doi:10.339022072798 PMID:35408413

Kuss, D. J., Griffiths, M. D., & Binder, J. F. (2013). Internet addiction in students: Prevalence and risk factors. *Computers in Human Behavior*, *29*(3), 959–966. doi:10.1016/j.chb.2012.12.024

KVKK. (2020). *Kamuoyu Duyurusu (Public Announcement).* https://www.kvkk.gov.tr/Icerik/6721/KAMUOYU-DUYURUSU-Covid-19-ile-Mucadele-Surecinde-Kisisel-Verilerin-Korunmasi-Kanunu-Kapsaminda-Bilinmesi-Gerekenler-

Kwet, M. (2019). *In stores, secret surveillance tracks your every move.* https://www.nytimes.com/interactive/2019/06/14/opinion/bluetooth-wireless-tracking-privacy.html

Lad, S. (2023). Creating a Security Culture. In *Azure Security For Critical Workloads* (pp. 201–207). Springer. doi:10.1007/978-1-4842-8936-5_8

Lamba, T., & Kandwal, S. (2023). Global Outlook of Cyber Security. *Proceedings of the Third International Conference on Information Management and Machine Intelligence*, 269–276.

Landry, B. J. L., & Blanke, S. J. (2011). Enumerating RFID networks. In *Proceedings of the Decision Sciences Institute Southwest Region* (pp. 201-209). Academic Press.

Landry, B. J. L., & Koger, M. S. (2023a). Exploring zero trust network architectures for building secure networks. In *Proceedings of the Decision Sciences Institute Southwest Region* (pp. 47261-47266). Academic Press.

Landry, B. J. L., & Koger, M. S. (2023b). Leveraging unified threat management based honeypots in small and midsized businesses and educational environments. In *Proceedings of the Decision Sciences Institute Southwest Region* (pp. 98301-98306). Academic Press.

Langner, R. (2011). Stuxnet: Dissecting a Cyberwarfare Weapon. *IEEE Security and Privacy*, *9*(3), 49–51. doi:10.1109/MSP.2011.67

Lansley, M., Polatidis, N., Kapetanakis, S., Amin, K., Samakovitis, G., & Petridis, M. (2019). Seen the villains: Detecting social engineering attacks using case-based reasoning and deep learning. *CEUR Workshop Proceedings*, *2567*, 39–48.

Laricchia, F. (2022). *Average number of connected devices in UK households 2020.* Statista. Retrieved on September 22, 2022 from: https://www.statista.com/statistics/1107269/average-number-connected-devices-uk-house/

LaRose, R., Lin, C. A., & Eastin, M. S. (2003). Unregulated Internet Usage: Addiction, Habit, or Deficient Self-Regulation? *Media Psychology*, *5*(3), 225–253. doi:10.1207/S1532785XMEP0503_01

Laski, H. J. (1916). Basis of Vicarious Liability. *The Yale Law Journal*, *26*(2), 105. doi:10.2307/786314

Lavie, N., Beck, D. M., & Konstantinou, N. (2014). Blinded by the load: Attention, awareness and the role of perceptual load. *Philosophical Transactions of the Royal Society of London. Series B, Biological Sciences*, *369*(1641), 20130205. doi:10.1098/rstb.2013.0205 PMID:24639578

Laville, S. (2020, July 1). England's privatised water firms paid £57bn in dividends since 1991. *The Guardian.* Retrieved on February 28, 2022, from: https://www.theguardian.com/environment/2020/jul/01/england-privatised-water-firms-dividends-shareholders

Lee, Y., & Tarabay, J. (2021). *Singapore Passes Law to Use Covid Tracing in Criminal Probes.* https://www.bloomberg.com/news/articles/2021-02-02/singapore-passes-law-to-use-covid-tracing-for-criminal-probes#xj4y7vz
kg?leadSource=uverify%20wall?leadSource=uverify%20wall

Lee, T., & Lee, H. (2020). Tracing surveillance and auto-regulation in Singapore: 'smart' responses to COVID-19. *Media International Australia, Incorporating Culture & Policy*, *177*(1), 47–60. doi:10.1177/1329878X20949545

legislation.gov.uk . (2015). *Serious Crime Act 2015.* Retrieved on April 12, 2022, from: https://www.legislation.gov.uk/ukpga/2015/9/contents/enacted

Lehto, M. (2020). Cyber security capacity building: Cyber security education in finnish universities. *European Conference on Information Warfare and Security, ECCWS*, 221–231. 10.34190/EWS.20.112

Le, T. H., Chen, H., & Babar, M. A. (2022). A survey on data-driven software vulnerability assessment and prioritization. *ACM Computing Surveys*, *55*(5), 1–39. doi:10.1145/3529757

Li, L., He, W., Xu, L., Ash, I., Anwar, M., & Yuan, X. (2019). Investigating the impact of cybersecurity policy awareness on employees' cybersecurity behavior. *International Journal of Information Management, 45*, 13–24. https://doi.org/10.1016/j.ijinfomgt.2018.10.017

Li, L., & Goodchild, M. F. (2013). Is privacy still an issue in the era of big data? - Location disclosure in spatial footprints. In *21st International Conference on Geoinformatics* (pp. 1-4). IEEE. 10.1109/Geoinformatics.2013.6626191

Lindsey, N. (2020, April 13). Voluntary Disclosure of Cybersecurity Risks Mitigates Contagion Effect With Investors. *CPO Magazine*. Retrieved on August 4, 2021, from: https://www.cpomagazine.com/cyber-security/voluntary-disclosure-of-cybersecurity-risks-mitigates-contagion-effect-with-i nvestors/

Liu, V., Musen, M. A., & Chou, T. (2015). Data breaches of protected health information in the United States. *Journal of the American Medical Association, 313*(14), 1471–1473. doi:10.1001/jama.2015.2252 PMID:25871675

Liu, X., Lin, Y., Li, H., & Zhang, J. (2020). A novel method for malware detection on ML-based visualization technique. *Computers & Security*, *89*, 101682. doi:10.1016/j.cose.2019.101682

Li, W., Yang, Y., Liu, Z.-H., Zhao, Y.-J., Zhang, Q., Zhang, L., Cheung, T., & Xiang, Y.-T. (2020). Progression of Mental Health Services during the COVID-19 Outbreak in China. *International Journal of Biological Sciences, 16*(10), 1732–1738. doi:10.7150/ijbs.45120 PMID:32226291

Lohrke, F. T., Frownfelter-Lohrke, C., & Ketchen, D. J. Jr. (2016). The role of information technology systems in the performance of mergers and acquisitions. *Business Horizons*, *59*(1), 7–12. doi:10.1016/j.bushor.2015.09.006

Lorenz, J., Rauhut, H., Schweitzer, F., & Helbing, D. (2011). How social influence can undermine the wisdom of crowd effect. In *Proceedings of the National Academy of Sciences - PNAS* (pp. 9020-9025). National Academy of Sciences. 10.1073/pnas.1008636108

Lourenço, J., Morais, J. C., Sá, S., Neves, N., Figueiredo, F., & Santos, M. C. (2023). Cybersecurity Concerns Under COVID-19: Representations on Increasing Digital Literacy in Higher Education. In *Perspectives and Trends in Education and Technology* (pp. 739–748). Springer. doi:10.1007/978-981-19-6585-2_65

Loveless, M. (2008). Media dependency: Mass media as sources of information in the democratizing countries of central and eastern Europe. *Democratization, 15*(1), 162–183. https://doi.org/10.1080/13510340701770030

Loxton, M., Truskett, R., Scarf, B., Sindone, L., Baldry, G., & Zhao, Y. (2020). Consumer behaviour during crises: Preliminary research on how coronavirus has manifested consumer panic buying, herd mentality, changing discretionary spending and the role of the media in influencing behaviour. *Journal of Risk and Financial Management, 13*(8/166), 1-21. https://doi.org/ doi:10.3390/jrfm13080166

Lyon, D. (1994). *The Electronic Eye*. The Polity Press.

Lyon, D. (2001). *Surveillance Society: Monitoring Everyday Life*. Open University Press.

Lyon, D. (2007). *Surveillance Studies: An Overview*. Polity Press.

Mackie, J. L. (1973). *Truth, probability and paradox: Studies in philosophical logic*. Oxford University Press.

Mahoney, J., & Goertz, G. (2006). A tale of two cultures: Contrasting quantitative and qualitative research. *Political Analysis*, *14*(3), 227–249. doi:10.1093/pan/mpj017

Malecki, E. J. (2003). Digital development in rural areas: Potentials and pitfalls. *Journal of Rural Studies*, *19*(2), 201–214. doi:10.1016/S0743-0167(02)00068-2

Malhotra, P., Singh, Y., Anand, P., Bangotra, D. K., Singh, P. K., & Hong, W. C. (2021). Internet of things: Evolution, concerns and security challenges. *Sensors (Basel)*, *21*(5), 1809. doi:10.339021051809 PMID:33807724

Malley, O. L., & Patterson, M. (1998). Vanishing point: The mix management paradigm re-viewed. *Journal of Marketing Management*, *14*(8), 829–851. doi:10.1362/026725798784867545

Maranga, M. J., & Nelson, M. (2019). Emerging Issues in Cyber Security for Institutions of Higher Education. *International Journal of Computer Science and Network, 8*(4), 371–379. Retrieved from www.IJCSN.org

Marotta, A., Martinelli, F., Nanni, S., Orlando, A., & Yautsiukhin, A. (2017). Cyber-insurance survey. *Computer Science Review*, *24*, 35–61. doi:10.1016/j.cosrev.2017.01.001

Martins, I., Resende, J. S., Sousa, P. R., Silva, S., Antunes, L., & Gama, J. (2022). Host-based IDS: A review and open issues of an anomaly detection system in IoT. *Future Generation Computer Systems*, *133*, 95–113. doi:10.1016/j.future.2022.03.001

Marx, G. T. (2016). *Windows into the Soul: Surveillance and Society in an Age of High Technology*. The University of Chicago Press. doi:10.7208/chicago/9780226286075.001.0001

Masmali, H. H., & Miah, S. J. (2023). Emergent Insight of the Cyber Security Management for Saudi Arabian Universities: A Content Analysis. *Proceedings of Seventh International Congress on Information and Communication Technology*, 153–171. 10.1007/978-981-19-1610-6_14

Mattelart, A. (2010). *The globalization of surveillance*. The Polity Press.

Matthews, L. (2021, Feb 15). *Florida water plant hackers exploited old software and poor password habits*. Retrieved on April 22, 2021, from: https://www.forbes.com/sites/leemathews/2021/02/15/florida-water-plant-hackers-exploited-old-software-and-poor-password-habits/?sh=6b0c16ca334e

Matyokurehwa, K., Rudhumbu, N., Gombiro, C., & Mlambo, C. (2021). Cybersecurity awareness in Zimbabwean universities: Perspectives from the students. *Security and Privacy*, *4*(2). Advance online publication. doi:10.1002py2.141

Mayhew, S. (2020). The COVID-19 vaccine development landscape. *Nature Reviews. Drug Discovery*, *19*(19). Retrieved October 14, 2022, from https://www.nature.com/articles/d41573-020-00073-5

Mazumder, M. M. M., & Hossain, D. M. (2022). Voluntary cybersecurity disclosure in the banking industry of Bangladesh: does board composition matter? *Journal of Accounting in Emerging Economies*. doi:10.1108/JAEE-07-2021-0237

McAfee. (2014). *Net losses: Estimating the global cost of cybercrime*. McAfee.

Mcalaney, J., & Benson, V. (2020). Cybersecurity as a social phenomenon. *Cyber Influence and Cognitive Threats*, 1–8. Retrieved on April 24, 2021 from: https://www.sciencedirect.com/science/article/pii/B9780128192047000014

McKenna, K. Y. A., & Bargh, J. A. (1999). Causes and Consequences of Social Interaction on the Internet: A Conceptual Framework. *Media Psychology*, *1*(3), 249–269. doi:10.12071532785xmep0103_4

McKenna, K. Y. A., Green, A. S., & Gleason, M. E. J. (2002). Relationship Formation on the Internet: What's the Big Attraction? *The Journal of Social Issues*, *58*(1), 9–31. doi:10.1111/1540-4560.00246

Meckling, J., & Nahm, J. (2019). The politics of technology bans: Industrial policy competition and green goals for the auto industry. *Energy Policy*, *126*, 470–479. doi:10.1016/j.enpol.2018.11.031

Meerkerk, G.-J., Van Den Eijnden, R. J. J. M., Vermulst, A. A., & Garretsen, H. F. L. (2009). The Compulsive Internet Use Scale (CIUS): Some Psychometric Properties. *Cyberpsychology & Behavior*, *12*(1), 1–6. doi:10.1089/cpb.2008.0181 PMID:19072079

Meira, J., Andrade, R., Praça, I., Carneiro, J., Bolón-Canedo, V., Alonso-Betanzos, A., & Marreiros, G. (2020). Performance evaluation of unsupervised techniques in cyber-attack anomaly detection. *Journal of Ambient Intelligence and Humanized Computing*, *11*(11), 4477–4489. doi:10.100712652-019-01417-9

Mercaldo, F., & Santone, A. (2020). Deep learning for image-based mobile malware detection. *Journal of Computer Virology and Hacking Techniques*, *16*(2), 157–171. doi:10.100711416-019-00346-7

Merritt, A. (2020). *Foreign cyber threats to the 2020 U.S. presidential election*. https://www.digitalshadows.com/blog-and-research/foreign-cyber-threats-to-the-2020-us-presidential-election/

Mestre-Bach, G., Blycker, G. R., & Potenza, M. N. (2020). Pornography use in the setting of the COVID-19 pandemic. *Journal of Behavioral Addictions*, *9*(2), 181–183. doi:10.1556/2006.2020.00015 PMID:32663384

Meyer, C. (2022). *COVID-19 Fraud Could Cost UK Government Billions*. Retrieved on May 5, 2022 from: https://www.asisonline.org/security-management-magazine/latest-news/today-in-security/2022/february/covid19-fraud-could-cost-UK-government-billions/

Meyer, P. (2002). Improvisation power. *Executive Excellence,* 17-18.

Meyler, J., & Kaneko, J. (2020). *Netenrich introduces a threat and attack surface intelligence solution for faster detection, insight, and response to immediate threats*. https://netenrich.com/newsroom/netenrich-introduces-a-threat-and-attack-surface-intelligence-solution-for-faster-detection-insight-and-response-to-immediate-threats/

MI5. (2022). *Joint address by MI5 and FBI Heads*. Retrieved on November 3, 2022, from: https://www.mi5.gov.uk/news/speech-by-mi5-and-fbi

Milller, L., & Molina-Ray, C. (2014). *Cybersecurity workforce competencies: Preparing tomorrow's risk-ready professionals*. Retrieved on August 3, 2019, from: https://securityexpo.asisonline.org/Pages/default.aspx

Milsom, L., Abeler, J., Altmann, S., Toussaert, S., Zillessen, H., & Blasone, R. (2020). *Survey of acceptability of app-based contact tracing in the UK, US, France, Germany, and Italy*. https://osf.io/7vgq9/

Miron, W., & Muita, K. (2014). Cybersecurity Capability Maturity Models for Providers of Critical Infrastructure. *Technology Innovation Management Review*, *4*(10), 33–39. doi:10.22215/timreview/837

Mitchell, A. J. (2018). (PDF) "A Review of Mixed Methods, Pragmatism and Abduction Techniques" has now been published in The Electronic Journal of Business Research Methods, Volume 16 Issue 3. *Electronic Journal of Business Research Methods*, *16*(3), 103–116. Retrieved March 30, 2019, from https://www.researchgate.net/publication/328343822_A_Review_of_Mixed_Methods_Pragmatism_and_Abduction_Techniques_has_now_been_published_in_The_Electronic_Journal_of_Business_Research_Methods_Volume_16_Issue_3

MITRE Corporation. (2023). *CVE – MITRE.* https://www.cve.mitre.org

Mohajan, H. K. (2017). Two Criteria for Good Measurements in Research: Validity and Reliability. *Annals of Spiru Haret University. Economic Series*, *17*(4), 59–82. doi:10.26458/1746

Mohamed, A. Y., & Kamau, S. K. (2023). A Continent-Wide Assessment of Cyber Vulnerability Across Africa. ArXiv Preprint ArXiv:2301.03008.

Mohammed, V. (2022). Automatic Static Vulnerability Detection Approaches and Tools: State of the Art. *Advances in Information, Communication and Cybersecurity: Proceedings of ICI2C'21, 357*, 449.

Montasari, R. (2023). Cyber Threats and the Security Risks They Pose to National Security: An Assessment of Cybersecurity Policy in the United Kingdom. *Countering Cyberterrorism*, 7–25.

Montellaro, Z. (2020). *What you need to know about when states finalize their election results.* https://www.politico.com/news/2020/11/11/swing-states-recounts-certify-election-results-435889

Morahan-Martin, J., & Schumacher, P. (2000). Incidence and correlates of pathological Internet use among college students. *Computers in Human Behavior*, *16*(1), 13–29. doi:10.1016/S0747-5632(99)00049-7

Moreta, N., Aragon, D., Oña, S., Jaramillo, A., Ibarra, J., & Jahankhani, H. (2023). Comparison of Cybersecurity Methodologies for the Implementing of a Secure IoT Architecture. In *Cybersecurity in the Age of Smart Societies* (pp. 9–29). Springer. doi:10.1007/978-3-031-20160-8_2

Morgan, S. (2020). Global Cybercrime Damages Predicted To Reach $6 Trillion Annually By 2021. *Cybercrime Magazine*. Retrieved on September 18, 2021, from: https://cybersecurityventures.com/cybercrime-damages-6-trillion-by-2021/

Moukaddam, N. (2020). Psychiatrists Beware! The Impact of COVID-19 and Pandemics on Mental Health. *Psychiatric Times*. Retrieved on May 21, 2022, from: https://www.psychiatrictimes.com/view/psychiatrists-beware-impact-coronavirus-pandemics-mental-health

Moustafa, A. A., Bello, A., & Maurushat, A. (2021). The Role of User Behaviour in Improving Cyber Security Management. *Frontiers in Psychology*, *12*, 12. doi:10.3389/fpsyg.2021.561011 PMID:34220596

Mubaiwa, T. G., & Mukosera, M. (2022). *A hybrid approach to detect security vulnerabilities in web applications.* Academic Press.

Mucci, F., Mucci, N., & Diolaiuti, F. (2020). Lockdown and Isolation: Psychological Aspects of Covid-19 Pandemic in the General Population. *Clinical Neuropsychiatry*, *17*(2), 63–64. Retrieved on April 4, 2022, from: https://www.ncbi.nlm.nih.gov/pmc/articles/PMC8629090/

Mudra Rakshasa, A., & Tong, M. T. (2020). Making 'Good' Choices: Social Isolation in Mice Exacerbates the Effects of Chronic Stress on Decision Making. *Frontiers in Behavioral Neuroscience*, *14*, 14. doi:10.3389/fnbeh.2020.00081 PMID:32523519

Mulligan, C. (2017). *Cybersecurity: Cornerstone of the digital economy*. Imperial College Business School.

Muniandy, L., Muniandy, B., & Samsudin, Z. (2017). Cyber Security Behaviour among Higher Education Students in Malaysia. *Journal of Information Assurance & Cybersecurity*, 1–13. doi:10.5171/2017.800299

Murgia, M. (2021). *England's NHS plans to share patient records with third parties*. https://www.ft.com/content/9fee812f-6975-49ce-915c-aeb25d3dd748

Murimi, R. (2020). Use of botnets for mining cryptocurrencies. In *Botnets* (1st ed., pp. 359–386). Routledge. doi:10.1201/9780429329913-11

Nafees, T., Coull, N., Ferguson, I., & Sampson, A. (2018, November). Vulnerability anti-patterns: a timeless way to capture poor software practices (vulnerabilities). In *24th Conference on Pattern Languages of Programs* (p. 23). The Hillside Group.

Nagendran, K., Adithyan, A., Chethana, R., Camillus, P., & Varshini, K. B. S. (2019). Web application penetration testing. *International Journal of Innovative Technology and Exploring Engineering*, *8*(10), 1029–1035. doi:10.35940/ijitee.J9173.0881019

National Institute of Standards and Technology. (2006). Minimum security requirements for federal information and information systems. Federal Information Processing Standards Publications (FIPS PUBS) 200. doi:10.1016/0378-7206(89)90025-6

National Institute of Standards And Technology. (2018). *Framework for Improving Critical Infrastructure Cybersecurity*. Retrieved from https://nvlpubs.nist.gov/nistpubs/CSWP/NIST.CSWP.04162018.pdf%0Ahttps://doi.org/10.6028/NIST.CSWP.04162018

Navarro-Rivera, J., & Kosmin, B. A. (2013). Surveys and questionnaires. The Routledge Handbook of Research Methods in the Study of Religion, 395–420. https://doi.org/ doi:10.4324/9780203154281-35

NCSC. (2020). *Advisory: COVID-19 exploited by malicious cyber actors*. Retrieved on January 30, 2022, from: https://www.ncsc.gov.uk/news/covid-19-exploited-by-cyber-actors-advisory

Netshakhuma, N. S. (2023). Cybersecurity Management in South African Universities. In *Cybersecurity Issues, Challenges, and Solutions in the Business World* (pp. 196–211). IGI Global.

New York Times. (2019). *Iranian hackers target Trump campaign as threats to 2020 mount*. https://www.nytimes.com/2019/10/04/technology/iranian-campaign-hackers microsoft.html

NewsH. H. S. (2023) https://public3.pagefreezer.com/content/HHS.gov/31-12-2020T08:51/https://www.hhs.gov/about/news/2020/09/21/orthopedic-clinic-pays-1.5-million-to-settle-systemic-noncompliance-with-hipaa-rules.html#:~:text=Athens%20Orthopedic%20Clinic%20PA%20

Ng, A. (2019). *Amazon Alexa transcripts live on, even after you delete voice records*. https://www.cnet.com/home/smart-home/amazon-alexa-transcripts-live-on-even-after-you-delete-voice-records/

Ng, A. (2020). A primer on how hackers are targeting the election and what officials are doing to protect it. *CNET Dail News*. https://www.cnet.com/news/election-2020-your-cybersecurity-questions-answered/

Nguyen, H. V. (2019). Cybersecurity Strategies for Universities with Bring Your Own Device Programs. *ProQuest Dissertations and Theses*, 150. Retrieved on September 4, 2020, from: https://search.proquest.com/docview/2329729362?accountid=17242

NICCS. (2021). *NICE Framework Mapping Tool | NICCS*. https://niccs.cisa.gov/workforce-development/nice-framework-mapping-tool

Nicholson, A., Webber, S., Dyer, S., Patel, T., & Janicke, H. (2012). SCADA security in the light of Cyber-Warfare. *Computers & Security*, *31*(4), 418–436. doi:10.1016/j.cose.2012.02.009

Nilsen, R. K. (2017). Measuring cybersecurity competency: An exploratory investigation of the cybersecurity knowledge, skills, and abilities necessary for organizational network access privileges. *ProQuest Dissertations and Theses UMI Number*, *10641545*(1017), i–292.

Nisbet, R. (1977). *Twilight of Authority*. Random House.

NIST. (2018). *Framework for Improving Critical Infrastructure Cybersecurity, Version 1.1*. NIST Technical Series Publications. https://nvlpubs.nist.gov/nistpubs/CSWP/NIST.CSWP.04162018.pdf

NIST. (2020). *NICE Framework*. NIST.

NIST. (2022). *Special Publication (SP) 800-53 Rev. 5, Security and Privacy Controls for Information Systems and Organizations*. NIST Computer Security Resource Center. https://csrc.nist.gov/publications/detail/sp/800-53/rev-5/final

Nobles, C. (2018). Botching Human Factors in Cybersecurity in Business Organizations. *HOLISTICA – Journal of Business and Public Administration*, *9*(3), 71–88.

Nohlberg, M. (2008). Securing Information Assets: Understanding, Measuring and Protecting against Social Engineering Attacks. *Engineering*. Retrieved from https://www.mendeley.com/research/securing-information-assets-understanding-measuring-protecting-against-social-engineering-attacks/

Norton Rose Fulbright. (2021). *Contact tracing apps: A new world for data privacy*. https://www.nortonrosefulbright.com/en-fr/knowledge/publications/d7a9a296/contact-tracing-apps-a-new-world-for-data-privacy#Germany

Nothias, T., Jasper, K., Vavrovsky, A. S., Beauvoir, S., & Bernholz, L. (2021). Digital Surveillance, Civil Society and The Media During The Covid-19 Pandemic. *Digital Civil Society Lab Stanford Center on Philanthropy and Civil Society*. https://pacscenter.stanford.edu/wp-content/uploads/2021/10/Digital-Surveillance-COVID-Report.pdf

NTV. (2022). *Pandemi cezaları nasıl silinecek?* [How will pandemic fines be deleted?]. https://www.ntv.com.tr/turkiye/ogrenim-kredisi-ve-covid-19-cezalarina-iliskin-tahsilat-genelgesi,OkYyOaRKdkOSBBpFifd6Zw

Nurse, J. R. C. (2018). Cybercrime and You: How Criminals Attack and the Human Factors That They Seek to Exploit. The Oxford Handbook of Cyberpsychology, 662–690.

Nurse, J. R. C., Creese, S., Goldsmith, M., & Lamberts, K. (2011). Guidelines for usable cybersecurity: Past and present. In *2011 Third International Workshop on Cyberspace Safety and Security (CSS)* (pp. 21-26). IEEE. 10.1109/CSS.2011.6058566

Nyarko, D. A., & Fong, R. C. (2023). Cyber Security Compliance Among Remote Workers. In *Cybersecurity in the Age of Smart Societies* (pp. 343–369). Springer. doi:10.1007/978-3-031-20160-8_18

O'Brien, S. (2021). *Robinhood's data breach involved about 7 million customers. Here's how to protect your credit from fraudsters.* CNBC. https://www.cnbc.com/2021/11/09/robinhood-data-breach-involved-7-million-clients-protect-your-credit.html

O'Neil, P. (2022). *These hackers just showed how easy it is to target critical infrastructure.* Retrieved on May 2, 2022, from: https://www-technologyreview-com.cdn.ampproject.org/c/s/www.technologyreview.com/2022/04/21/1050815/hackers-target-critical-infrastructure-pwn2own/amp/

Oblinger, D. (2003). *Higher Education IT Security and Academic Values.* Academic Press.

OCC. (2020). *Assesses $85 Million Civil Money Penalty Against USAA.* Office of the Comptroller of the Currency (OCC). https://www.occ.gov/news-issuances/news-releases/2020/nr-occ-2020-135.html

OECD. (2020). *OECD Policy Responses to Coronavirus (COVID-19). Ensuring data privacy as we battle COVID-19.* https://www.oecd.org/coronavirus/policy-responses/ensuring-data-privacy-as-we-battle-covid-19-36c2f31e/

Office for National Statistics. (2021). *Internet users, UK - Office for National Statistics.* Retrieved on January 22, 2022, from: https://www.ons.gov.uk/businessindustryandtrade/itandinternetindustry/bulletins/internetusers/2020

Ofwat. (2017). *Delivering Water 2020: Our final methodology for the 2019 price review.* Ofwat. Retrieved on April 13, 2022, from: https://www.ofwat.gov.uk/publication/delivering-water-2020-final-methodology-2019-price-review/

Ofwat. (2018). *Your water company.* Ofwat. Retrieved on October 13, 2022, from: https://www.ofwat.gov.uk/households/your-water-company/

Ofwat. (2022). *Legislation.* Ofwat. Retrieved on May 2, 2022, from: https://www.ofwat.gov.uk/regulated-companies/ofwat-industry-overview/legislation/

Okamoto, M., & Fujita, T. (2020). *A new data governance model for contact tracing: Authorized Public Purpose Access.* https://www.weforum.org/agenda/2020/08/contact-tracing-apps-privacy-framework-appa-data-governance/

Olenik-Shemesh, D., Heiman, T., & Eden, S. (2012). Cyberbullying victimisation in adolescence: Relationships with loneliness and depressive mood. *Emotional & Behavioural Difficulties, 17*(3-4), 361–374. doi:10.1080/13632752.2012.704227

Olteanu, C. & Olteanu, F. M. (2011). *Market portfolio and risk management of financial securities*. Publishing Foundation "Andrei Şaguna", Constanţa.

ONS. (2019). *Internet access—households and individuals*. https://www.ons.gov.uk/peoplepopulationandcommunity/householdcharacteristics/homeinternetandsocialmediausage/bulletins/internetaccesshouseholdsandindividuals/2019#main-points

ONS. (2021). *Business and individual attitudes towards the future of homeworking, UK - Office for National Statistics*. Retrieved on January 22, 2022, from: https://www.ons.gov.uk/employmentandlabourmarket/peopleinwork/employmentandemployeetypes/articles/businessandindividualattitudestowardsthefutureofhomeworkinguk/apriltomay2021

Orwell, G. (1987). *Nineteen Eighty-Four*. Penguin Books.

p, R. (2000). Examination of Psychological Processes Underlying Resistance to Persuasion. *Journal of Consumer Research*, *27*(2), 217–232.

Paganini, P. (2016). *NSA EXTRABACON exploit still threatens tens of thousands of CISCO ASA boxes*. Security Affairs. Retrieved on November 3, 2022, from: https://securityaffairs.co/wordpress/50971/hacking/nsa-extrabacon.html

Pajunen, K. (2008). Institutions and inflows of foreign direct investment: A fuzzy-set analysis. *Journal of International Business Studies*, *39*(4), 652–669. doi:10.1057/palgrave.jibs.8400371

Panda Security. (2020). *Is COVID-19 Making Cyberbullying Worse?* Panda Security Mediacenter. Retrieved on May 6, 2022, from: https://www.pandasecurity.com/en/mediacenter/mobile-news/covid-19-cyberbullying/

Papadatou, A. (2018). Workers are risking GDPR penalties by forwarding work emails to personal accounts. *HRreview*. Retrieved on August 4, 2020, from: https://www.hrreview.co.uk/hr-news/workers-are-risking-gdpr-penalties/114090#:~:text=Workers%20are%20risking%20GDPR%20penalties%20by%20forwarding%20work%20emails%20to%20personal%20accounts

Park, N. E., Lee, Y. R., Joo, S., Kim, S. Y., Kim, S. H., Park, J. Y., Kim, S.-Y., & Lee, I. G. (2023). Performance evaluation of a fast and efficient intrusion detection framework for advanced persistent threat-based cyberattacks. *Computers & Electrical Engineering*, *105*, 108548. doi:10.1016/j.compeleceng.2022.108548

Payne, D., Landry, B. J. L., & Dean, M. (2015). Data mining and privacy: An initial attempt at a comprehensive code of conduct for online business. *Communications of the Association for Information Systems*, *37*(34), 482–504. doi:10.17705/1CAIS.03734

PCI. (2022). *Official PCI Security Standards Council Site - Verify PCI Compliance, Download Data Security and Credit Card Security Standards*. PCI Security Standards Council. https://www.pcisecuritystandards.org/about_us/

Perakslis, E., & Knechtle, S. J. (2023). Information design to support growth, quality, and equity of the US transplant system. *American Journal of Transplantation*, *23*(1), 5–10. doi:10.1016/j.ajt.2022.10.005 PMID:36695621

Pérez-Díaz, N. W., Chinchay-Maldonado, J. O., Mejía-Cabrera, H. I., Bances-Saavedra, D. E., & Bravo-Ruiz, J. A. (2023). Ransomware Identification Through Sandbox Environment. In *Proceedings of the Future Technologies Conference* (pp. 326-335). Springer.

Perlroth, N., Scott, M., & Frenkel, S. (2017). *Cyberattack hits Ukraine and then spreads internationally.* https://www.nytimes.com/2017/06/27/technology/ransomware-hackers.html

Perper, R. (2019). *Apple will suspend and review a global program that allows contractors to listen to Siri recordings.* https://www.businessinsider.com/apple-suspends-siri-contractors-listen-privacy-system-2019-8

Pew Research Center. (2019). *Social Media Fact Sheet.* https://www.pewresearch.org/internet/fact-sheet/social-media/

Pfleeger, S. L., & Caputo, D. D. (2012). Leveraging behavioral science to mitigate cyber security risk. *Computers & Security, 31*(4), 597–611. doi:10.1016/j.cose.2011.12.010

Pham, M. (2021). *Remote Work Security Survey Results: Is Remote Work Really Secure?* Retrieved on May 4, 2022, from: https://www.wrike.com/blog/remote-work-security-survey/

Pierce, M., Mcmanus, S., Hope, H., Hotopf, M., Ford, T., Hatch, S., John, A., Kontopantelis, E., Webb, R., Wessely, S., & Abel, K. (2021). Mental health responses to the COVID-19 pandemic: A latent class trajectory analysis using longitudinal UK data. *The Lancet. Psychiatry, 8*(7), 610–629. doi:10.1016/S2215-0366(21)00151-6 PMID:33965057

Plimmer, G. (2022, July 14). English water company bosses threatened with jail for sewage pollution. *Financial Times.*

Podsakoff, P. M., MacKenzie, S. B., Lee, J. Y., & Podsakoff, N. P. (2003). Common Method Biases in Behavioral Research: A Critical Review of the Literature and Recommended Remedies. *The Journal of Applied Psychology, 88*(5), 879–903. doi:10.1037/0021-9010.88.5.879 PMID:14516251

Ponta, S., Plate, H., Sabetta, A., Bezzi, M., & Dangremont, C. (2019). A manually-curated dataset of fixes to vulnerabilities of open-source software. In *2019 IEEE/ACM 16th International Conference on Mining Software Repositories (MSR)* (pp. 383-387). IEEE Press. 10.1109/MSR.2019.00064

Potvin, L., Gendron, S., Bilodeau, A., & Chabot, P. (2005). Integrating social theory into public health practice. *American Journal of Public Health, 95*(4), 591–595. doi:10.2105/AJPH.2004.048017 PMID:15798114

PratamaA. R.AlshaikhM.AlharbiT. (2023). Increasing cybersecurity awareness through situated e-learning: A survey experiment. Available at SSRN 4320165. doi:10.2139/ssrn.4320165

Premera, H. H. S. (2020). *Health Insurer Pays $6.85 Million to Settle Data Breach Affecting.* HHS.gov. https://www.hhs.gov/hipaa/for-professionals/compliance-enforcement/agreements/premera/index.html

Przepiorka, A., Blachnio, A., & Cudo, A. (2019). The role of depression, personality, and future time perspective in internet addiction in adolescents and emerging adults. *Psychiatry Research, 272*, 340–348. doi:10.1016/j.psychres.2018.12.086 PMID:30599437

Przepiorka, A., Blachnio, A., & Cudo, A. (2020). Relationships between morningness, Big Five personality traits, and problematic Internet use in young adult university students: Mediating role of depression. *Chronobiology International, 38*(2), 248–259. doi:10.1080/07420528.2020.1851703 PMID:33317359

Public Safety Canada. (2010). *Canada's Cyber Security Strategy.* Public Safety Canada, Government of Canada.

Purwanto, W., Dodge, B., Arcaute, K., Sosonkina, M., & Wu, H. (2023). DeapSECURE Computational Training for Cybersecurity: Progress Toward Widespread Community Adoption. *Journal of Computational Science Education.*

PWC. (2016). *Global Economic Crime Survey 2016: US Results*. PwC. Retrieved from https://www.pwc.com/us/en/forensic-services/economic-crime-survey-us-supplement.html

Rabe, W., & Gippner, O. (2017). Perceptions of China's outward foreign direct investment in European critical infrastructure and strategic industries. *International Politics*, *54*(4), 468–486. doi:10.105741311-017-0044-x

Radu, C., & Smaili, N. (2021). Board Gender Diversity and Corporate Response to Cyber Risk: Evidence from Cybersecurity Related Disclosure. *Journal of Business Ethics*, *177*(2), 351–374. doi:10.100710551-020-04717-9

Ragin, C. (2008). *Redesigning social inquiry: Fuzzy sets and beyond.* University of Chicago. doi:10.7208/chicago/9780226702797.001.0001

Ramírez, M., Rodríguez Ariza, L., Gómez Miranda, M. E., & Vartika. (2022). The Disclosures of Information on Cybersecurity in Listed Companies in Latin America—Proposal for a Cybersecurity Disclosure Index. *Sustainability (Basel)*, *14*(3), 1390. doi:10.3390u14031390

Rawal, B. S., Manogaran, G., & Peter, A. (2023). Cybersecurity for Beginners. In *Cybersecurity and Identity Access Management* (pp. 1–20). Springer. doi:10.1007/978-981-19-2658-7_1

Rawlings, R. (2020). *Password habits in the US and the UK.* Retrieved on May 5, 2022 from: https://nordpass.com/blog/password-habits-statistics/

Redini, N., Machiry, A., Wang, R., Spensky, C., Continella, A., Shoshitaishvili, Y., ... Vigna, G. (2020, May). Karonte: Detecting insecure multi-binary interactions in embedded firmware. In *2020 IEEE Symposium on Security and Privacy (SP)* (pp. 1544-1561). IEEE. 10.1109/SP40000.2020.00036

Redino, C., Nandakumar, D., Schiller, R., Choi, K., Rahman, A., Bowen, E., . . . Nehila, J. *(2022). Zero Day Threat Detection Using Graph and Flow Based Security Telemetry.* arXiv preprint arXiv:2205.02298. doi:10.1109/ICCCIS56430.2022.10037596

Reed, J., Shimizu, A., & Shifflett, J. (2023). *Cost Effectiveness Analysis of the use of Colorless Appropriations in Navy and DoD Software Development Pilot Programs* [PhD Thesis]. Acquisition Research Program.

Reid, A. M., Brown, J. M., Smith, J. M., Cope, A. C., & Jamieson, S. (2018). Ethical dilemmas and reflexivity in qualitative research. *Perspectives on Medical Education*, *7*(2), 69–75. doi:10.1007/S40037-018-0412-2 PMID:29536374

Republic, C. (2015). *National Cyber Security Strategy of the Czech Republic (2015-2020).* Academic Press.

Reuters. (2020). *Italy to launch contact-tracing app to fight coronavirus.* https://www.reuters.com/article/us-health-coronavirus-italy-app-idUSKBN2383EW

Richardson, M. D., Lemoine, P. A., & Waller, R. E. (2020). Planning for cyber security in schools. *The Human Factor*, *27*(2), 23–39.

Rogers, G., & Ashford, T. (2015). Mitigating Higher Ed Cyber Attacks. *Association Supporting Computer Users in Education*, 48. Retrieved from https://liverpool.idm.oclc.org/login?url=https://search.ebscohost.com/login.aspx?direct=true&db=eric&AN=ED571277&site=ed
s-live&scope=site

Romm, T. (2019, August 28). Facebook to require buyers of political ads to provide more information about who paid for them. *The Washington Post.* https://www.washingtonpost.com/technology/2019/08/28/facebook-requirep olitical-campaigns-say-who-paid-their-ads-new-transparency-p ush/

Rothrock, R. A., Kaplan, J., & Van Der Oord, F. (2018). Board role in cybersecurity risks. *MIT Sloan Management Review, 59*(2), 12–15.

Rouse, M. (2017). *Tech target. Cognitive Hacking.* https://watis.techtarget.com/definition/cognitive-hacking

Ryan, F., Coughlan, M., & Cronin, P. (2009). Interviewing in qualitative research: The one-to-one interview. *International Journal of Therapy and Rehabilitation, 16*(6), 309–314. doi:10.12968/ijtr.2009.16.6.42433

Saad, M., Spaulding, J., Njilla, L., Kamhoua, C., Shetty, S., Nyang, D., & Mohaisen, D. (2020). Exploring the attack surface of blockchain: A comprehensive survey. *IEEE Communications Surveys and Tutorials, 22*(3), 1977–2008. doi:10.1109/COMST.2020.2975999

Sadaghiani-Tabrizi, A. (2023). Revisiting Cybersecurity Awareness in the Midst of Disruptions. *International Journal for Business Education, 163*(1), 6.

Sadkhan, S. (2019). *Cognition and the future of information security.* Academic Press.

Saeed, S. A., & Masters, R. M. (2021). Disparities in Health Care and the Digital Divide. *Current Psychiatry Reports, 23*(9), 61. doi:10.100711920-021-01274-4 PMID:34297202

Salemink, K., Strijker, D., & Bosworth, G. (2017). Rural development in the digital age: A systematic literature review on unequal ICT availability, adoption, and use in rural areas. *Journal of Rural Studies, 54*, 360–371. doi:10.1016/j.jrurstud.2015.09.001

Sanchez, G. R., Middlemass, K., & Rodriguez, A. (2022, July 26). *Misinformation is eroding the public's confidence in democracy.* Brookings https://www.brookings.edu/blog/fixgov/2022/07/26/misinformation-is-ero ding-the-publics-confidence-in-democracy/

Santos, J. (2018). *Facebook app impossible to delete from Samsung phones.* https://www.ibtimes.com/facebook-app-impossible-delete-samsu ng-phones-users-complain-2750257

Saunders, M. N. K., Lewis, P., & Thornhill, A. (2019). Research Methods for Business Students. In *Understanding research philosophy and approaches to theory development.* Retrieved from www.pearson.com/uk

Schmeelk, S., & Dragos, D. (2021). *2020 CSJ NICE Special Issue Online.* Academic Press.

Schneier, B. (2013). *Carry On: Sound Advice from Schneier on Security.* John Wiley & Sons, Inc. Retrieved on February 1, 2022, from: https://ebookcentral.proquest.com/lib/bournemouth-ebooks/det ail.action?docID=1568423

Schneier, B. (2015). *Digital Security in a Networked World.* Academic Press.

Schwarz, M., Lackner, F., & Gruss, D. (2019, February). JavaScript Template Attacks: Automatically Inferring Host Information for Targeted Exploits. NDSS.

Schwarz, M., Weiser, S., & Gruss, D. (2019, June). Practical enclave malware with Intel SGX. In *International Conference on Detection of Intrusions and Malware, and Vulnerability Assessment* (pp. 177-196). Springer.

Scroxton, A. (2021). *UK loses £1.3bn to fraud and cyber crime so far this year*. Retrieved on July 4, 2022, from: https://www.computerweekly.com/news/252505825/UK-loses-13bn-to-fraud-and-cyber-crime-so-far-this-year#:~:text=Individual s%20and%20organisations%20in%20the

Seaman, J. (2023). Zero Trust Security Strategies and Guideline. In Digital Transformation in Policing: The Promise, Perils and Solutions (pp. 149–168). Springer. doi:10.1007/978-3-031-09691-4_9

Sears, A., & Jacko, J. A. (2007). *The human-computer interaction handbook: fundamentals, evolving technologies and emerging applications*. CRC Press. doi:10.1201/9781410615862

Seets, C., & Niemann, P. (2022, September 7). *How cyber governance and disclosures are closing the gaps in 2022*. EY - US. Retrieved on December 3, 2022, from: https://www.ey.com/en_us/board-matters/how-cyber-governance-and-disclosures-are-closing-the-gaps-in-2022

Seh, A. H., Zarour, M., Alenezi, M., Sarkar, A. K., Agrawal, A., Kumar, R., & Khan, R. A. (2020). Healthcare Data Breaches: Insights and Implications. *Health Care*, *8*(2), 133. doi:10.3390/healthcare8020133 PMID:32414183

Sekaran Uma, B. R. (2016). *Research Methode for Business: a skill-building approach* (7th ed.). John Wiley & Sons Ltd.

Servidio, R. (2014). Exploring the effects of demographic factors, Internet usage and personality traits on Internet addiction in a sample of Italian university students. *Computers in Human Behavior*, *35*, 85–92. doi:10.1016/j.chb.2014.02.024

Shaikh, F. A., & Siponen, M. (2023). Information security risk assessments following cybersecurity breaches: The mediating role of top management attention to cybersecurity. *Computers & Security*, *124*, 102974. doi:10.1016/j.cose.2022.102974

Shapiro, J., Huo, J., & Benincasa, R. (2020). *In New York Nursing Homes, Death Comes to Facilities with More People of Color*. https://www.npr.org/2020/04/22/841463120/in-new-york-nursing-homes-death-comes-to-facilities-with-more-people-of-color

Shari, A. M. J. (2023). *Knowledge, Attitude, and Practices Towards Internet Safety and Security Among Generation Z in Malaysia: A Conceptual Paper*. Academic Press.

Sharon, T. (2020). Blind-sided by privacy? Digital contact tracing, the Apple/Google API and big tech's newfound role as global health policy makers. *Ethics and Information Technology*, *23*(S1), 1–13. doi:10.100710676-020-09547-x PMID:32837287

Sharpe, W. F. (1970). *Portfolio theory and capital markets*. McGraw-Hill.

Shead, S. (2017). *Google DeepMind's first deal with the NHS was illegal, UK data regulator rules*. https://www.businessinsider.com/ico-deepmind-first-nhs-deal-illegal-2017-6

Shearer, E., & Greico, E. (2019). *Americans Are Wary of the Role Social Media Sites Play in Delivering the News*. Pew Research Center.

Shedden, P., Ahmad, A., Smith, W., Tscherning, H., & Scheepers, R. (2016). Asset identification in information security risk assessment: A business practice approach. *Communications of the Association for Information Systems*, *39*(1), 297–320. doi:10.17705/1CAIS.03915

Showkat, N., & Parveen, H. (2017). *Quadrant-I (e-Text)*. Academic Press.

Shukla, M., Ziya, F., Arun, S., & Singh, S. P. (2023). Cyber Security Techniques Management. In *Holistic Approach to Quantum Cryptography in Cyber Security* (pp. 155–178). CRC Press.

Siegel, D., Bogers, M. L., Jennings, P. D., & Xue, L. (2023). Technology transfer from national/federal labs and public research institutes: Managerial and policy implications. *Research Policy*, *52*(1), 104646. doi:10.1016/j.respol.2022.104646

Simmel, G. (1906). The Sociology of Secrecy and of Secret Societies. *American Journal of Sociology*, *11*(4), 441–498. doi:10.1086/211418

Simmel, G. (1950). The Metropolis and Mental Life. In K. Wolff (Ed.), *The Sociology of Georg Simmel* (pp. 409–424). Free Press.

Simon, J., & Rieder, G. (2021). Trusting the Corona-Warn-App? Contemplations on trust and trustworthiness at the intersection of technology, politics and public debate. *European Journal of Communication*, *36*(4), 334–348. doi:10.1177/02673231211028377

Singer, A., Anderson, W., & Farrow, R. (2013). Rethinking password policies. *Login—. The USENIX Magazine*, *38*, 14–18.

Singh, S. (2022). *Biggest threats to ICS/SCADA systems*. Infosec Resources. Retrieved on February 28, 2022, from: https://resources.infosecinstitute.com/topic/biggest-threats-to-ics-scada-systems/

Singh, U. K., Joshi, C., & Kanellopoulos, D. (2019). A framework for zero-day vulnerabilities detection and prioritization. *Journal of Information Security and Applications*, *46*, 164–172. doi:10.1016/j.jisa.2019.03.011

Smith, S. (2022). *Human-Computer Interaction and Security*. Academic Press.

Smith, N., & Walters, P. (2018). Desire lines and defensive architecture in modern urban environments. *Urban Studies (Edinburgh, Scotland)*, *55*(13), 2980–2995. doi:10.1177/0042098017732690

Snyder, R. (2020). Judge rejects Trump campaign lawsuit seeking to block states election results, says no evidence election was affected by fraud. *The Nevada Independent*. https://tenevadaindependent.com/article/judge-rejects-trump-campaign-lawsuit-seeking-to-block-states-presidential-election-result
s

Solar, C. (2023). *Cybersecurity Governance in Latin America: States, Threats, and Alliances*. State University of New York Press.

Solon, O., & Hern, A. (2017). 'Petya' ransomware attack: what is it and how can it be stopped? *The Guardian*.

Soni, S. (2021, September 27). 2 in 3 Indian SMBs suffered over Rs 3.5 crore business loss in post-pandemic cyber attacks: Survey. *Financial Express*. https://www.financialexpress.com/industry/sme/msme-tech-2-in-3-indian-smbs-suffered-over-rs-3-5-crore-business-loss-in-p
ost-pandemic-cyber-attacks-survey/2338676/

Spadafora, A. (2021). *EA hack reportedly used stolen cookies and Slack to target gaming giant*. TechRadar. Retrieved on September 3, 2022, from: https://www.techradar.com/news/ea-hack-reportedly-used-stolen-cookies-and-slack-to-hack-gaming-giant

Spada, M. M. (2014). An overview of problematic Internet use. *Addictive Behaviors*, *39*(1), 3–6. doi:10.1016/j.addbeh.2013.09.007 PMID:24126206

Spanos, G., & Angelis, L. (2016). The impact of information security events to the stock market: A systematic literature review. *Computers & Security*, *58*, 216–229. doi:10.1016/j.cose.2015.12.006

Srinivasan, J. (2017). Disaster Recovery, an Element of Cyber Security-a Flick Through. *Researchgate.Net*. Retrieved from https://www.researchgate.net/profile/J_Srinivasan/publication/320244744_DISASTER_RECOVERY_AN_ELEMENT_OF_CYBER_SECURITY-A_FLICK_THROUGH/links/59d74e74a6fdcc52acae4816/DISASTER-RECOVERY-AN-ELEMENT-OF-CYBER-SECURITY-A-FLICK-THROUGH.pdf

Stark, L., & Cohen, E. (2020). *All 50 states and D.C. have now certified their presidential election results*. Cable New Network.

Statista. (2021). *Bottled water consumption per capita UK 2013-2026*. Statista. Retrieved on April 11, 2022, from: https://www.statista.com/forecasts/1186840/uk-average-volume-bottled-water-per-capita

Steinberg, L., & Morris, A. (2001). Adolescent development. *Annual Review of Psychology*, *52*(1), 83–110. doi:10.1146/annurev.psych.52.1.83 PMID:11148300

Stemwedel, J. D. (2015). *The philosophy of Star Trek: The Kobayashi Maru, no-win scenarios, and ethical leadership*. Retrieved on November 19, 2021, from: https://www.forbes.com/sites/janetstemwedel/2015/08/23/the-philosophy-of-star-trek-the-kobayashi-maru-no-win-scenarios-and-ethical-leadership/?sh=7a1285be5f48

Stevens, G. (2010). *Federal Information Security and Data Breach Notification Laws*. Library of Congress. Congressional Research Service. https://digital.library.unt.edu/ark:/67531/metadc505501/

Stocking, G., & Sumida, N. (2018). *Social Media Bots Draw Public's Attention and Concern*. Pew Research.

Strahilevitz, L. J. (2012). Toward a positive theory of privacy law. *Harvard Law Review*, *126*, 2010.

Strang, M., & James, W. (2007). *Research Onion*. Academic Press.

Stuart, A. H. (2019). Social Media, Manipulation, and Violence. *South Carolina Journal of International Law and Business*, *15*(2).

Stubley, P. (2021). *China now owns £143bn in UK assets, from nuclear power to pubs and schools*. The Independent. Retrieved on November 3, 2022, from: https://www.independent.co.uk/news/uk/home-news/china-now-owns-ps143bn-in-uk-assets-from-nuclear-power-to-pubs-and-schools-b1841056.html

Suciu, O., Nelson, C., Lyu, Z., Bao, T., & Dumitraş, T. (2022). Expected exploitability: Predicting the development of functional vulnerability exploits. In *31st USENIX Security Symposium (USENIX Security 22)* (pp. 377-394). USENIX.

Sutherland, I., Xynos, K., Jones, A., & Blyth, A. (2012). Protective Emblems in Cyber Warfare. *Australian Information Warfare and Security Conference*. Available from: https://ro.ecu.edu.au/isw/49

Su, W., Han, X., Jin, C., Yan, Y., & Potenza, M. N. (2019). Are males more likely to be addicted to the internet than females? A meta-analysis involving 34 global jurisdictions. *Computers in Human Behavior*, *99*, 86–100. doi:10.1016/j.chb.2019.04.021

Su, W., Han, X., Yu, H., Wu, Y., & Potenza, M. N. (2020). Do men become addicted to internet gaming and women to social media? A meta-analysis examining gender-related differences in specific internet addiction. *Computers in Human Behavior*, *113*, 106480. doi:10.1016/j.chb.2020.106480

Taherdoost, H. (2018). Validity and Reliability of the Research Instrument; How to Test the Validation of a Questionnaire/Survey in a Research. SSRN *Electronic Journal*. doi:10.2139/ssrn.3205040

Taherdoost, H. (2016). Sampling Methods in Research Methodology; How to Choose a Sampling Technique for Research. *International Journal of Academic Research in Management, 5*(2), 18–27.

Taylor, M. L. (2022, March 8). *Combating disinformation and foreign interference in democracies: Lessons from Europe*. Brookings. https://ww.brookings.edu/blog/techtank/2019/07/31/combating-disinformation-and-foreign-interference-in-democracies-lesso ns-from-europe/

Taylor, J., & Turner, R. J. (2002). Perceived Discrimination, Social Stress, and Depression in the Transition to Adulthood: Racial Contrasts. *Social Psychology Quarterly, 65*(3), 213. doi:10.2307/3090120

Taylor, S. B. (2016). Can you keep a secret: Some wish to ban encryption technology for fears of data going dark. *SMU Science and Technology Law Review, 19*(2), 216–248.

Taylor, V., Chappells, H., Medd, W., & Trentmann, F. (2009). Drought is normal: The socio-technical evolution of drought and water demand in England and Wales, 1893–2006. *Journal of Historical Geography, 35*(3), 568–591. doi:10.1016/j.jhg.2008.09.004

TenoveC.BuffieJ.McKayS.MoscropD. (2018). *Digital threats to democratic elections: How foreign actors use digital techniques to undermine democracy*. Center for the Study of Democratic Institutions, The University of British Columbia. doi:10.2139/ssrn.3235819

Teodoro, N., Gonçalves, L., & Serrão, C. (2015). NIST cybersecurity framework compliance: A generic model for dynamic assessment and predictive requirements. *Proceedings - 14th IEEE International Conference on Trust, Security and Privacy in Computing and Communications, TrustCom 2015, 1*, 418–425. 10.1109/Trustcom.2015.402

Thaler, R. H. (2018). From cashews to nudges. *The American Economic Review, 108*(6), 1265–1287. doi:10.1257/aer.108.6.1265

Thales Group. (n.d.). *Beyond GDPR: Data Protection Around the World*. https://www.thalesgroup.com/en/markets/digital-identity-and-security/government/magazine/beyond-gdpr-data-protection-aro und-world

Thatcher, A., & Goolam, S. (2005). Development and psychometric properties of the Problematic Internet Use Questionnaire. *South African Journal of Psychology. Suid-Afrikaanse Tydskrif vir Sielkunde, 35*(4), 793–809. Retrieved May 9, 2022, from https://hdl.handle.net/10520/EJC98345. doi:10.1177/008124630503500410

The United States Senate Republican Policy Committee. (2021, October 5). *Social media and mental health*. Senate Republican Policy Committee. https://ww.rpc.senate.gov/policy-papers/social-media-and-men tal-health

Thomson, I. (2018). *Now that's taking the p... Sewage plant 'hacked' to craft crypto-coins*. Retrieved on February 1, 2022, from: https://www.theregister.com/2018/02/08/scada_hackers_cryptoc urrencies/

Tilly, B. (2014). *Implementing an effective cybersecurity management program*. Retrieved on July 4, 2022, from: https://bakertilly.com/insights/implementing-an-effective-cy bersecuritymanagement-program/

Tirumala, S. S., Valluri, M. R., & Babu, G. (2019). A survey on cybersecurity awareness concerns, practices and conceptual measures. In *2019 International Conference on Computer Communication and Informatics (ICCCI)* (pp. 1-6). 10.1109/ICCCI.2019.8821951

Todic, J., Cook, S. C., Spitzer-Shohat, S., Williams, J. S. Jr, Battle, B. A., Jackson, J., & Chin, M. H. (2022). Critical Theory, Culture Change, and Achieving Health Equity in Health Care Settings. *Academic Medicine*, *97*(7), 977–988. doi:10.1097/ACM.0000000000004680 PMID:35353723

Tongco, M. D. C. (2007). Purposive sampling as a tool for informant selection. *Ethnobotany Research and Applications*, *5*, 147–158. doi:10.17348/era.5.0.147-158

Torroglosa-Garcia, E., Palomares, A., Song, H., Brun, P.-E., Giampaolo, F., Van Landuyt, D., Michiels, S., Podgorelec, B., Xenakis, C., & Bampatsikos, M. (2023). A Holistic Approach for IoT Networks' Identity and Trust Management–The ERATOSTHENES Project. *Internet of Things: 5th The Global IoT Summit, GIoTS 2022, Dublin, Ireland, June 20–23, 2022, Revised Selected Papers, 13533*, 338.

Trinidad, M. G., Platt, J., & Kardia, S. L. R. (2020). The public's comfort with sharing health data with third-party commercial companies. *Humanities & Social Sciences Communications*, *7*(1), 149. doi:10.105741599-020-00641-5 PMID:34337435

Trzebiński, J., Cabański, M., & Czarnecka, J. Z. (2020). Reaction to the COVID-19 Pandemic: The Influence of Meaning in Life, Life Satisfaction, and Assumptions on World Orderliness and Positivity. *Journal of Loss and Trauma*, *25*(6-7), 544–557. doi:10.1080/15325024.2020.1765098

Turner, S. L., Karahalios, A., Forbes, A. B., Taljaard, M., Grimshaw, J. M., Cheng, A. C., Bero, L., & McKenzie, J. E. (2020). Design characteristics and statistical methods used in interrupted time series studies evaluating public health interventions: A review. *Journal of Clinical Epidemiology*, *122*, 1–11. doi:10.1016/j.jclinepi.2020.02.006 PMID:32109503

Turtiainen, H., Costin, A., & Hämäläinen, T. (2023). Defensive Machine Learning Methods and the Cyber Defence Chain. In *Artificial Intelligence and Cybersecurity* (pp. 147–163). Springer. doi:10.1007/978-3-031-15030-2_7

U. S. Department of Energy. (2021). *Colonial Pipeline cyber incident*. Energy.gov. https://www.energy.gov/ceser/colonial-pipeline-cyber-incident

U.S. Government Accountability Office. (2020a). *Clarity on leadership urgently needed to implement the national strategy* fully. https://ww.gao.gov/assets/710/709555.pdf

U.S. Government Accountability Office. (2020b). *Ensuring the security of federal information systems*. https://www.gao.gov/key_issues/ensuring_security_federal_information_systems/issue_summary

U.S. Government Accountability Office. (2020c). *Elections and cyber security*. https://www.gao.gov/key_issues/elections_campaign_finance/issue_summary

U.S. House of Representatives Permanent Select Committee on Intelligence. (2018). *E posing Russia's effort to sow discord online: The Internet Research Agency and advertisements*. https://intelligence.house.gov/social-media-content/

U.S. Senate Select Committee on Intelligence. (2019). *Russian Active Measures Campaigns and Interference in the 2016 U.S. Election Volume 2: Russia's use of social media with additional views*. Author.

Ulven, J. B., & Wangen, G. (2021). A systematic review of cybersecurity risks in higher education. *Future Internet*, *13*(2), 1–40. doi:10.3390/fi13020039

UN News. (2020). *COVID-19 stoking xenophobia, hate and exclusion, minority rights expert warns*. https://news.un.org/en/story/2020/03/1060602

Valentino-DeVries, J., & Singer, N. (2018, Dec 10). *How to stop apps from tracking your location*. https://www.nytimes.com/2018/12/10/technology/prevent-location-data-sharing.html

Valinsky, J. (2019). *Google is collecting health data on millions of Americans*. https://edition.cnn.com/2019/11/12/business/google-project-nightingale-ascension/index.html

Van Hee, L., Van Den Heuvel, R., Verheyden, T., & Baert, D. (2019). *Google employees are eavesdropping, even in your living room, VRT NWS has discovered*. VRT NWS.

Vandewalker, I. (2020). *Digital disinformation and vote suppression*. Brennan Center. https://www.brennancenter.org/our-work/research-reports/digital-disinformation-and-vote-suppression

Vasilogambros, M. (2021, September 21). *Disinformation may be the new normal, election officials fear*. The Pew Charitable Trusts. https://ww.pewtrusts.org/en/research-and-analysis/blogs/stateline/2021/09/21/disinformation-may-be-the-new-normal-electi
on-officials-fear

Veale, M. (2020). *Opinion: Privacy is not the problem with the Apple-Google contact-tracing app*. https://www.ucl.ac.uk/news/2020/jul/opinion-privacy-not-problem-apple-google-contact-tracing-app

Verjans, S. (2005). Bricolage as a way of life - improvisation and irony in information systems. *European Journal of Information Systems*, *14*(5), 504–506. doi:10.1057/palgrave.ejis.3000559

Vetterl, A., & Clayton, R. (2019, November). Honware: A virtual honeypot framework for capturing CPE and IoT zero days. In *2019 APWG Symposium on Electronic Crime Research (eCrime)* (pp. 1-13). IEEE. 10.1109/eCrime47957.2019.9037501

Vishik, C., Matsubara, M., & Plonk, A. (2016). Key Concepts in Cyber Security: Towards a Common Policy and Technology Context for Cyber Security Norms. *International Cyber Norms: Legal, Policy & Industry Perspective*, 221–242.

Vishwakarma, R., & Jain, A. K. (2019, April). A honeypot with machine learning based detection framework for defending IoT based botnet DDoS attacks. In *2019 3rd International Conference on Trends in Electronics and Informatics (ICOEI)* (pp. 1019-1024). IEEE. 10.1109/ICOEI.2019.8862720

VMWare. (2016). *University Challenge : Cyber Attacks in Higher Education A report by VMware exploring the*. Author.

Von Solms, R., & Van Niekerk, J. (2013). From information security to cyber security. *Computers & Security*, *38*, 97–102. doi:10.1016/j.cose.2013.04.004

Wahyuni, D. (2012). The research design maze: Understanding paradigms, cases, methods and methodologies. *Journal of Applied Management Accounting Research*, *10*(1), 69–80.

Walters, R. (2014). *Cyber-attacks on U.S. companies since November 2014*. http://www.heritage.org/cybersecurity/report/cyber-attacks-us-companies-november-2014

Waltzman, R. (2017). *The weaponizing of information*. Senate Armed Services Committee. RAND Corporation. https://www.armedservices.senate.gov/imo/media/doc/Waltzman_04-27-17.pdf

Wang, Y., Jia, X., Liu, Y., Zeng, K., Bao, T., Wu, D., & Su, P. (2020, February). Not All Coverage Measurements Are Equal: Fuzzing by Coverage Accounting for Input Prioritization. NDSS.

Warren, S., & Brandeis, L. (1890). The right to privacy. *Harvard Law Review*, *4*(5), 193–220. doi:10.2307/1321160

Water Innovation 2050. (2021). *UK Water Innovation Strategy 2050*. Water Innovation 2050. Retrieved on April 14, 2022, from: http://waterinnovation2050.org.uk/

Water UK. (2021). *Water meters*. Retrieved on April 13, 2022, from: https://www.water.org.uk/advice-for-customers/water-meters/

Webb, K. (2019). *Amazon just got hit with a lawsuit that claims it's putting children's privacy at risk by recording what they say to Alexa*. Business Insider. https://www.businessinsider.com/amazon-accused-of-violating-child-privacy-laws-alexa-recordings-lawsuit-2019-6

Weber, M. (1987). The Protestant Ethic and the Spirit of Capitalism. Academic Press.

Wedawatta, G., Ingirige, B., & Amaratunga, D. (2011). Case study as a research strategy : Investigating extreme weather resilience of construction SMEs in the. *7th Annual International Conference of International Institute for Infrastructure*, 1–9.

West, D. (2019, August 9). *Foreign campaign intervention may go way beyond Russia to China, Iran, North Korea, and Saudi Arabia*. Brookings. Retrieved from: https://www.brookings.edu/blog/fixgov/2019/08/09/foreign-campaign-intervention-may-go-way-beyond-russia-to-china-iran-north-korea-and-saudi-arabia/

West, R. (2008). *The Psychology of Security | April 2008 | Communications of the ACM*. Retrieved on November 11, 2021, from: https://cacm.acm.org/magazines/2008/4/5436-the-psychology-of-security/fulltext

Westerlund, M., Isabelle, D. A., & Leminen, S. (2021). The Acceptance of Digital Surveillance in an Age of Big Data. *Technology Innovation Management Review*, *11*(3), 32–44. doi:10.22215/timreview/1427

Whitty, M., Doodson, J., Creese, S., & Hodges, D. (2015). Individual Differences in Cyber Security Behaviors: An Examination of Who Is Sharing Passwords. *Cyberpsychology, Behavior, and Social Networking*, *18*(1), 3–7. doi:10.1089/cyber.2014.0179 PMID:25517697

Wiederhold, B. K. (2014). The Role of Psychology in Enhancing Cybersecurity. *Cyberpsychology, Behavior, and Social Networking*, *17*(3), 131–132. doi:10.1089/cyber.2014.1502 PMID:24592869

Williams, C. M., Chaturvedi, R., & Chakravarthy, K. (2020). Cybersecurity Risks in a Pandemic. *Journal of Medical Internet Research*, *22*(9), e23692. doi:10.2196/23692 PMID:32897869

Willis, K., & Sheldon, R. (2022). Research on customers' willingness-to-pay for service changes in UK water company price reviews 1994–2019. *Journal of Environmental Economics and Policy*, *11*(1), 4–20. doi:10.1080/21606544.2021.1927850

Winterrose, M. L., Carter, K. M., Wagner, N., & Streilein, W. W. (2016). Balancing security and performance for agility in dynamic threat environments. In *2016 46th Annual IEEE/IFIP International Conference on Dependable Systems and Networks (DSN)* (pp. 607-617). 10.1109/DSN.2016.61

Wittenberg, M. T., & Reis, H. T. (1986). Loneliness, Social Skills, and Social Perception. *Personality and Social Psychology Bulletin*, *12*(1), 121–130. doi:10.1177/0146167286121012

Witteveen, D. (2020). Sociodemographic inequality in exposure to COVID-19-induced economic hardship in the United Kingdom. *Research in Social Stratification and Mobility*, *69*, 100551. doi:10.1016/j.rssm.2020.100551 PMID:32921869

World Economuc Forum. (2020). *A Preliminary Mapping and Its Implications*. Retrieved on October 14, 2021, from: https://www3.weforum.org/docs/WEF_COVID_19_Risks_Outlook_Special_Edition_Pages.pdf

World Health Organisations Europe. (2010). *Addressing socioeconomic and gender inequities in the WHO European Region Social and gender inequalities in environment and health*. Retrieved on September 22, 2022, from: https://www.euro.who.int/__data/assets/pdf_file/0010/76519/Parma_EH_Conf_pb1.pdf

World Health Organization. (2020). *Coronavirus Disease (COVID-19) - Events as They Happen*. Retrieved on September 14, 2022, from: https://www.who.int/emergencies/diseases/novel-coronavirus-2019/events-as-they-happen

Worldometer. (2022). *Coronavirus toll update: Cases & deaths by country*. Worldometers. Retrieved on September 14, 2022, from: https://www.worldometers.info/coronavirus/

Wu, Y., Edwards, W. K., & Das, S. (2022). SoK: Social cybersecurity. In *2022 IEEE Symposium on Security and Privacy (SP)* (pp. 1863-1879). IEEE. 10.1109/SP46214.2022.9833757

Yang, S., Dong, C., Xiao, Y., Cheng, Y., Shi, Z., Li, Z., & Sun, L. (2023). *Asteria-Pro: Enhancing Deep-Learning Based Binary Code Similarity Detection by Incorporating Domain Knowledge*. arXiv preprint arXiv:2301.00511.

Yasir, S. (2020). *India is Scapegoating Muslims for the Spread of the Coronavirus*. https://foreignpolicy.com/2020/04/22/india-muslims-coronavirus-scapegoat-modi-hindu-nationalism/

Yearwood, K. (2018). *The privatised water Industry in the UK. An ATM for investors*. Public Services International Research Unit (PSIRU) University of Greenwich. Working Paper. Retrieved on April 12, 2022, from: https://gala.gre.ac.uk/id/eprint/21097/

Yen, J.-Y., Ko, C.-H., Yen, C.-F., Wu, H.-Y., & Yang, M.-J. (2007). The Comorbid Psychiatric Symptoms of Internet Addiction: Attention Deficit and Hyperactivity Disorder (ADHD), Depression, Social Phobia, and Hostility. *The Journal of Adolescent Health*, *41*(1), 93–98. doi:10.1016/j.jadohealth.2007.02.002 PMID:17577539

Yin, J., Tang, M., Cao, J., You, M., & Wang, H. (2023). Cybersecurity Applications in Software: Data-Driven Software Vulnerability Assessment and Management. In *Emerging Trends in Cybersecurity Applications* (pp. 371–389). Springer. doi:10.1007/978-3-031-09640-2_17

You, W., Wang, X., Ma, S., Huang, J., Zhang, X., Wang, X., & Liang, B. (2019, May). Profuzzer: On-the-fly input type probing for better zero-day vulnerability discovery. In 2019 IEEE symposium on security and privacy (SP) (pp. 769-786). IEEE.

Young, S. (2008). The neurobiology of human social behaviour: An important but neglected topic. *Journal of Psychiatry & Neuroscience*, *33*(5). PMID:18787656

Zafar, H., Williams, J., & Gupta, S. (2023). *Toward an Effective SETA Program: An Action Research Approach*. Academic Press.

Zhang, P., Zhang, Y., Mu, Z., & Liu, X. (2017). The Development of Conformity Among Chinese Children Aged 9–15 Years in a Public Choice Task. *Evolutionary Psychology*, *15*(4), 147470491774363. doi:10.1177/1474704917743637 PMID:29169263

Zhao, H., Zhang, J., Wu, Q., & Guo, Y. (2019). Inadequate security measures of health surveillance data: A survey of healthcare providers in China. *International Journal of Environmental Research and Public Health*, *16*(12), 2131. PMID:31208146

Zhou, M., & Kan, M.-Y. (2020). *The varying impacts of COVID-19 and its related measures in the UK: A year in review*. Academic Press.

Zhou, S., Yang, Z., Xiang, J., Cao, Y., Yang, M., & Zhang, Y. (2020, August). An ever-evolving game: Evaluation of real-world attacks and defenses in ethereum ecosystem. In *Proceedings of the 29th USENIX Conference on Security Symposium* (pp. 2793-2809). USENIX.

Zhou, Y., Li, D., Li, X., Wang, Y., & Zhao, L. (2017). Big five personality and adolescent Internet addiction: The mediating role of coping style. *Addictive Behaviors*, *64*, 42–48. doi:10.1016/j.addbeh.2016.08.009 PMID:27543833

Ziadia, M., Mejri, M., & Fattahi, J. (2023). Semantics for Security Policy Enforcement on Android Applications with Practical Cases. In *Advances in Computational Intelligence and Communication* (pp. 115–133). Springer. doi:10.1007/978-3-031-19523-5_8

Zscaler. (2020). *30,000 Percent Increase in COVID-19-Themed Attacks*. Zscaler. Retrieved on May 6, 2022, from: https://www.zscaler.com/blogs/security-research/30000-percent-increase-covid-19-themed-attacks

Zuboff, S. (2019). *The Age of Surveillance Capitalism: The Fight for a Human Future at the New Frontier of Power*. Public Affairs.

Zwilling, M., Klien, G., Lesjak, D., Wiechetek, Ł., Cetin, F., & Basim, H. N. (2020). Cyber Security Awareness, Knowledge and Behavior: A Comparative Study. *Journal of Computer Information Systems*, 1–16. doi:10.1080/08874417.2020.1712269

About the Contributors

Festus Fatai Adedoyin is a Fellow of the Higher Education Academy, a Chartered Management and Business Educator, and a lecturer at the Department of Computing and Informatics, Bournemouth University, U.K. Festus leads the Economics of Information Security, Integrated Digital Healthcare Projects, and the Individual Masters Project Units at the department. His current research interest is in the application of Machine and Deep Learning, and Econometrics tools to research stories in Energy and Tourism Economics as well as Finance and Digital Health.

Bryan Christiansen is an Adjunct Professor at Southern New Hampshire University where he teaches undergraduate business courses entirely online. Christiansen is also the Chief Executive Officer of the Utah-based management consultancy, IMPRUVE, LLC. He is fluent in Chinese, Japanese, and Spanish with extensive exposure to Russian and Turkish. Christiansen has given presentations on his field of expertise at numerous universities in Europe, the Middle East, and North America.

* * *

Biodun Awojobi is a Visionary Technology Executive and Professor, Cybersecurity Leader driving innovation at Google, with a passion for building high-performing teams and a commitment to developing talent in Cybersecurity and Data Science

Harsha Baskaran is a software developer and entrepreneur who has been learning and adopting cybersecurity strategies to keep data private for his cloud-based applications built for various clients.

R. Greg Bell is the Associate Dean of Faculty Affairs and Professor of Management at the University of Dallas.

Darrell Norman Burrell is visiting scholar at the Samuel DeWitt Proctor Institute for Leadership, Equity, and Justice at Rutgers University. Dr. Burrell has two doctorate degrees and five graduate degrees. Dr. Burrell received his first doctoral degree in Health Education from A.T. Still University in 2010. In 2021, Dr. Burrell completed his 2nd doctorate, a Doctor of Philosophy (Ph.D.) in Cybersecurity Leadership and Organizational Behavior at Capitol Technology University, Laurel, MD. Dr. Burrell completed a Master of Arts in Interfaith Action at Claremont Lincoln University as a Global Peacemaker Fellow in 2016. He has an EdS (Education Specialist Post Master's Terminal Degree) in Higher Education Administration from The George Washington. He has two graduate degrees, one in Human Resources

Management/Development and another in Organizational Management from National Louis University. Dr. Burrell has a graduate degree in Sales and Marketing Management from Prescott College. He has over 20 years of management, teaching, and training experience in academia, government, and private industry.

Omolara Campbell is a Professor of Development Economics at the Department of Economics and Development Studies, and the Dean of the Faculty of Management and Social Sciences, Lead City University, Ibadan, Nigeria.

Fatma Dogan Akkaya is Assistant Professor and lecturer at the Communication Faculty, Kastamonu University. After receiving her undergraduate education at Marmara University Faculty of Communication in Turkey, she completed her master's degree in Media and Communication at City University of London and her doctorate in Sociology at University of Essex in the UK. Drawing on the disciplines of sociology and communication, she explores the complex social and cultural implications of ever-evolving forms of human and technology interaction. She places significant reliance on the digital ethics perspective as a specialised approach for theoretical analysis, particularly when studying the intricacies of emerging technologies and new media tools.

Stephen G. Fridakis is the Deputy Chief Information Security Officer of Verily, an Alphabet Health Sciences company. He has responsibility for certifications, attestations, security risk and strategic planning. Prior to Verily, he was the CISO of the WW Int'l, HBO, United Nations UNDP, and FAO serving in NY and Italy. His long experience in IT security includes positions at VeriSign, Oracle, Netscape, and DHL. He holds post graduate degrees in Business Administration, and Computer Science, and multiple certifications in IT Security Management and Disaster Recovery. He has served in the USNR and is the holder of multiple patents in IT Security technologies. He is a volunteer EMT and lives in Austin, TX with his family.

Blessing Gavaza is a researcher in the field of information systems, cybersecurity and artificial intelligence. She is a DevOps Engineer at Africa University. Blessing is extremely passionate about innovation and has been a technical consultant for the Africa University innovation hub (i5hub) from its beginnings. She is a businesswoman that has collaborated with a number of startups, including SheCodes, a community of female programmers who coach and inspire young girls interested in coding. Blessing is a co-founder of Kabla Private Limited Company who holds a Master of Commerce in Information Systems Management and a Bachelor of Science in Computer Science.

Madhurima Goswami is aMaster of Commerce student from Christ (Deemed to be University), Bangalore, and a BCom Honours graduate from St. Xavier's College (Autonomous), Kolkata.

Agripah Kandiero (Ph.D.) is the head of the computer science and information systems department at Africa University, a career ICT professional with a passion for positive social change. A problem solver with strong analytics, technical and leadership skills honed in industry, and academia. Worked in the technology industry covering the full lifecycle from project inception through development and testing to post-deployment troubleshooting, stakeholder management, team leadership, and customer support. He holds the following qualifications BSc Computer Science & Statistics double major (University of

Zimbabwe); Honours in Information Systems (University of South Africa), MBA (University of Zimbabwe), MSc Computer Science (WIU, USA), Masters in ICTs (University of Cape Town, RSA), Ph.D. Information Technology (University of the Witwatersrand, RSA).

Vasilis Katos is Professor of Cybersecurity at Bournemouth University (UK) and Head of BU's Computer Emergency Response Team (BU-CERT). He obtained a Diploma in Electrical Engineering from Democritus University of Thrace in Greece, an MBA from Keele University in the UK and a PhD in Computer Science (network security and cryptography) from Aston University. He is a certified Computer Hacking Forensic Investigator (CHFI), who worked in the Industry as Information Security Consultant and served as an expert witness in Information Security in the UK and Greece. Vasilis' research falls in the area of digital forensics and incident response. He has participated in a number of EU and nationally funded research projects and in a number of national and international cyberdefence exercises. He is a member of the editorial board of Computers & Security. In terms of recognition of his research, Vasilis has received keynote speech invitations for international conferences and his research has been addressed by reputable magazines such as the New Scientist.

Chipo Katsande is keen researcher and practitioner with expertise and experience in Database Systems, Software Engineering, Management and Information Systems, Information Security, Systems Development, Administration and Security, Big Data, Analytics and Artificial Intelligence.

Brett J. L. Landry is a cybersecurity practitioner and educator with over thirty years of experience in consulting, teaching, presenting, and researching. He holds multiple esteemed certifications, including Certified Information Systems Security Professional (CISSP), Certified Ethical Hacker (C|EH), Certified Information Systems Auditor (CISA), and Certified in Risk and Information Systems Control (CRISC). As a cybersecurity professor at the University of Dallas, Landry has taught security professionals around the world to address the challenges their organizations face and is frequently asked to present in the U.S., Africa, Asia, Europe, and South America on various topics in cybersecurity. He has been active in the University's Center for Academic Excellence (CAE) in Cyber Defense which is designated by the National Security Agency (NSA) and the Department of Homeland Security (DHS). He has published and presented numerous articles in the areas of Cybersecurity, IT Ethics, IT Management, Network Architecture, and Disaster Recovery to both professional and academic audiences. Before joining academia full-time, Landry developed network and security solutions at Mississippi State University and Hibernia National Bank (now Capital One Bank). As a professor at the University of New Orleans, he led a campus-wide network redesign to address critical outages. While serving as the Dean of UD's Satish & Yasmin Gupta College of Business, Landry's accomplishments were highlighted when he received the Dallas CEO 500 Award recognizing the 500 most influential business leaders in North Texas for 2019, 2020, 2021, and 2022. He attended the University of New Orleans, where he graduated with a B.S. in Management and a concentration in MIS. He received his MS in IT, an MBA, and Ph.D. in Technology Education from Mississippi State University.

Horace C. Mingo, MSc., is a Professional with 20+ years of experience in Information Technology as a Business Analyst, Enterprise Solutions Architect, Software Engineer, and IT Manager. He specializes in cybersecurity, agile projects, software development, IT governance, and project management. Mr. Mingo is a second-year doctoral student at Marymount University. His current research interests are focused on building secure organizational ecosystems for the next generation of industrial controls, supply chains, and infrastructures targeted by malicious entities. He has an AAS in Electromechanical Technology from Excelsior University, a BA in Management & Organizational Development from Spring Arbor University, an MBA in Strategic Management from Davenport University, and a MSc in Information Systems from Lawrence Technological University.

S. Raschid Muller is a Cybersecurity Executive with 20 years of experience working in the federal government. Academically, he serves as a Professor at the University of Maryland Global Campus where he teaches undergraduate courses within the School of Cybersecurity and Information Technology. At the graduate level, he chairs doctoral committees at Capitol Technology University and also teaches doctoral courses within the School of Computer and Information Sciences at the University of the Cumberlands. Dr. Muller previously served as the DISA Information Operation Faculty Chair from 2017-2019 at National Defense University and continues to serve as a guest lecturer. Dr. Muller is a 2020 Brookings Institute - LEGIS Fellow and 2021 U.C. Berkeley ELA Fellow in the Goldman School of Public Policy. In 2020 he served on the House Committee for Homeland Security on Capitol Hill. He has been assigned to the Subcommittee on Cybersecurity, Infrastructure Protection, and Innovation (CIPI) where his portfolio included; Cybersecurity and Infrastructure Security Agency (CISA) oversight, drafting and introducing cyber legislation, election security, and cyber acquisitions.

Renita Murimi is an Associate Professor of Cybersecurity at the Satish and Yasmin Gupta College of Business at the University of Dallas. She received her Ph.D. and M.S. in Electrical Engineering from New Jersey Institute of Technology, and a Bachelor of Engineering in Electronics and Communications from Manipal University. Her research interests focus on cybersecurity, blockchain, and network science.

Calvin Nobles is a Cybersecurity Professional and Human Factors Engineer with more than 25 years of experience. He is a Department Chair and Associate Professor at the Illinois Institute of Technology. He retired from the Navy and worked in the Financial and Services Industry for several years. He authored a book on integrating technologically advanced aircraft into general aviation. He serves on the Cybersecurity Advisory Board at Stillman College and the Intelligence and National Security Alliance Cyber Council. He recently completed a Cybersecurity Fellow at Harvard University.

Godwin Oyedokun is Professor of Accounting & Financial Development at the Department of Management & Accounting, Lead City University, Ibadan, Nigeria.

Wasswa Shafik, IEEE member, P.Eng, received a bachelor of science in Information Technology Engineering with a minor in Mathematics in 2016 from Ndejje University, Kampala, Uganda, a master of engineering in Information Technology Engineering (MIT) in 2020, from the Computer Engineering Department, Yazd University, Islamic Republic of Iran. He is an associate researcher at the Computer Science department, Network interconnectivity Lab at Yazd University, Islamic Republic of Iran, and at Information Sciences, Prince Sultan University, Saudi Arabia. His areas of interest are Computer Vision, Anomaly Detection, Drones (UAVs), Machine/Deep Learning, AI-enabled IoT/IoMTs, IoT/IIoT/OT Security, Cyber Security and Privacy. Shafik is the chair/co-chair/program chair of some Scopus/EI conferences. Also, academic editor/ associate editor for set of indexed journals (Scopus journals' quartile ranking). He is the founder and lead investigator of Digital Connectivity Research Laboratory (DCR-Lab) since 2019, the Managing Executive director of Asmaah Charity Organisation (ACO).

Harmandeep Singh is an academician and researcher with eight years of experience in the field of Accounting and Finance. At present, he is working as an Assistant Professor at Christ (Deemed to be University), Bengaluru. His research area is reporting, online disclosure, social media disclosure, technology acceptance and diffusion. He has nine publications in the journal of repute.

James Taylor has worked in computing for over 25 years. He has an in depth knowledge of the industry and is a frequent speaker at conferences, seminars and exhibitions (such as InfoSec Europe), as well as presenting videos and Webinars. James is currently studying Cyber Security Management at Bournemouth University.

Vidhant Maan Thapa is a student pursuing a B.Tech degree specializing in DevOps at the University of Petroleum and Energy Studies (UPES). He has a keen interest in secure design patterns and testing, and his current research work focuses on handling zero-day vulnerabilities by implementing secure design patterns and extensive fuzzing, with the aim of providing a generic zero-day model. As a dedicated and hardworking student specializing in DevOps, Vidhant Maan Thapa is passionate about acquiring knowledge and skills in the field and aims to contribute to the industry in a meaningful way.

Andreas Vassilakos is a critical infrastructure doctoral candidate at Capitol Technology University. He holds two graduate degrees: a Master of Cyber Forensics and Security and a Master of Business Administration. His research interests are in cyber warfare, supply chain cybersecurity, critical infrastructure, and IT leadership and management. Andreas is an advisory board member for the Center for Cyber Security and Forensics Education (C^2SAFE) at Illinois Tech.

Index

G

H

I

L

M

N

P

Q

R

S

T

U

V

Z

www.ingramcontent.com/pod-product-compliance
Ingram Content Group UK Ltd.
Pitfield, Milton Keynes, MK11 3LW, UK
UKHW051510290926
15471UKWH00008B/1535

9 781668 490198